THE FORMAL COMPLEXITY OF NATURAL LANGUAGE

THE FORMAL COMPLEXITY
OF NATURAL LANGUAGE

Edited by

WALTER J. SAVITCH

*Department of Electrical Engineering
& Computer Sciences, University of California, San Diego, La Jolla, U.S.A.*

EMMON BACH

*Department of Linguistics,
University of Massachusetts, Amherst, U.S.A.*

WILLIAM MARSH

Xerox PARC, Palo Alto, California, U.S.A.

and

GILA SAFRAN-NAVEH

College of Arts & Sciences, University of Cincinnati, Ohio, U.S.A.

D. REIDEL PUBLISHING COMPANY

A MEMBER OF THE KLUWER ACADEMIC PUBLISHERS GROUP

DORDRECHT / BOSTON / LANCASTER / TOKYO

Library of Congress Cataloging in Publication Data

The Formal complexity of natural language / edited by Walter J. Savitch . . . [et al.].
 p. cm. — (Studies in linguistics and philosophy ; v. 33)
 Includes index.
 ISBN 1–55608–046–8.
 1. Grammar, Comparative and general. 2. Generative grammar.
3. Formalization (Linguistics) 4. Mathematical linguistics. I. Savitch, Walter J.,
1943–   . II. Series.
P151.F624 1987
415—dc 19   87–22471
                                                                        CIP

Published by D. Reidel Publishing Company,
P.O. Box 17, 3300 AA Dordrecht, Holland.

Sold and distributed in the U.S.A. and Canada
by Kluwer Academic Publishers,
101 Philip Drive, Assinippi Park, Norwell, MA 02061, U.S.A.

In all other countries, sold and distributed
by Kluwer Academic Publishers Group,
P.O. Box 322, 3300 AH Dordrecht, Holland.

Printed in The Netherlands

CONTENTS

Prologue

I. Early Nontransformational Grammar

II Modern Context-Free-Like Models

III More than Context-Free and Less than Transformational Grammar

Epilogue

INTRODUCTION

Ever since Chomsky laid the framework for a mathematically formal theory of syntax, two classes of formal models have held wide appeal. The finite state model offered simplicity. At the opposite extreme numerous very powerful models, most notable transformational grammar, offered generality. As soon as this mathematical framework was laid, devastating arguments were given by Chomsky and others indicating that the finite state model was woefully inadequate for the syntax of natural language. In response, the completely general transformational grammar model was advanced as a suitable vehicle for capturing the description of natural language syntax. While transformational grammar seems likely to be adequate to the task, many researchers have advanced the argument that it is "too adequate." A now classic result of Peters and Ritchie shows that the model of transformational grammar given in Chomsky's *Aspects* [1] is powerful indeed. So powerful as to allow it to describe any recursively enumerable set. In other words it can describe the syntax of any language that is describable by any algorithmic process whatsoever. This situation led many researchers to reasses the claim that natural languages are included in the class of transformational grammar languages. The conclusion that many reached is that the claim is void of content, since, in their view, it says little more than that natural language syntax is doable algorithmically and, in the framework of modern linguistics, psychology or neuroscience, that is axiomatic. In the view of these researchers, a model of natural language should say something about what is peculiar to language, and any model that is so completely general does not distinguish language from the other abilities to be found in humans, in other organisms, and in machines.

Context-free grammar is a model intermediate between the two extremes of the finite-state and transformational grammars. Moreover, this intermediate model has much to recommend it. It is simple. It includes parse tree structures in a conspicuous way. After being rejected by linguists it was used successful by computer scientists as a model for programming language syntax. Yet most linguists have traditionally assumed it was inadequate to the task of capturing the intricacies of natural language syntax. Recently, vigorous efforts have been mounted to show that it is adequate to that task. The most notable effort in this regard is the work on gpsg (generalized phrase structure grammar) by Gazdar, Pullum, Sag and others of their school. Their work reopened the question of whether or not natural languages are context-free. This anthology traces the responses to this question by presenting representative readings from the recent literature on linguistic theory.

We have grouped the papers into three categories. The first group consists of papers which set the stage for the basic question. They include a proof of the fact that transformational grammars can generate any recursively enumerable set (i.e., mirror any algorithm) as well as a number of the very early papers which address the question of the possible context-freeness of natural language. The second group includes a number of papers about modern versions of context-free grammar for natural language. This group of papers is designed to be a short representative sample and most certainly is not comprehensive. The emphasize is on the gpsg model, but one paper on categorial grammar is also included. The third sections discusses alternatives to the context-free grammar model. That is, models which are more general than the finite state model but less powerful than transformational grammar. Each section is prefaced by a brief introduction and the entire collection is bracket by two papers: a prologue by Peters sets the stage for the mathematical questions addressed in the other papers; an epilogue by Gazdar and Pullum summarizes most of the work to date on the question of whether or not natural language syntax is context-free.

We expect that most readers of this volume will know of the extremely important basic early work on transformational grammar by Noam Chomsky. While some aspects of this work will be reviewed in several of the papers that follow and in this introduction, readers unsure of their background may wish to look at Chomsky's *Syntactic Structures* (1965) or John Lyons' excellent short biography (1977) or the first chapter or two of almost any syntax book. It turns out though that most of the papers in this volume are written in other frameworks and can be read without detailed knowledge of either early or current work on transformational grammar. Indeed some of the papers included can serve as introductions to these alternative grammatical theories.

The story contained in this anthology really starts with Chomsky, but its roots go back to earlier work in mathematical logic. The grammars of Chomsky are in form a type of formal proof system of the kind well know to logicians. The distinction between syntax and semantics, which is absolutely critical to the question under discussion, was a well established distinction in mathematical logic and was imported into linguistics from the writings of Polish logicians working in the 1930's. Another important notion taken from mathematical logic is that of an algorithm a notion that is conspicuously important to computer processing, since it is essentially the notion of a computer program. Its importance to formal linguistics is that we now routinely demand that our grammars are, at least implicitly, algorithms. As historically important as these concepts are, one need not be conversant in the literature of mathematical logic in order to appreciate the papers contained here. These writing presume little or no knowledge of formal logic and only a very basic familiarity with the notion of an algorithm.

While the mathematical questions involved in defining context-free grammars and languages may have deterred some readers from looking closely at the question of whether natural language is context-free, we believe that the mathematical results needed can be covered rather quickly and that the more subtle and interesting questions are those concerned with how the mathematics meshes with natural language as phenomenon and with linguistics as a discipline. We conclude this introduction with a brief review of the basic mathematical concepts involved. Our treatment, though precise, will be rather informal and quite concise. Those desiring more detail can find it in any basic textbook on mathematical linguistics or formal language theory, for example Harrison (1978) or Savitch (1982).

The concept of an *algorithm* is fundamental to virtually all the modern mathematical work in linguistics and related fields. Moreover, if the word "mathematical" is replaced by "formal" so as to include much

which is not blatantly mathematical, then the fundamental importance of
the notion of an algorithm is not diminished. Fortunately, the concept is
so engrained in current thought patterns, that all readers are likely to have
some familiarity with the concept. An *algorithm* is an abstraction of the
idea of a computer program. The reader will not go far astray by thinking
of "algorithm" as a synonym for "computer program". It is however,
important to keep in mind that an algorithm is an idealization of the
notion of a computer program. In particular, pragmatic considerations of
time and storage are not incorporated into the notion of an algorithm. For
example an algorithm to parse English sentences would still be considered
an algorithm, even if it required several centuries to parse simple sentences. In the 1930's and 1940's logicians produced a number of precise
definitions of what constitutes an algorithm. None of them will be
presented here. We simply note that all the definitions were proven
equivalent, and as already alluded to, we note that the notion is provable
equivalent to most any reasonable notion of an abstract computer program. In particular, the famous Turing machine model is one such
abstract notion of a computer program that is equivalent to the notion of
an algorithm.

For purposes of the mathematical analyses discussed here, a language
is identified with the set of all syntactically correct sentences of that
language. Hence a language is just a set of strings made up from symbols
chosen from some finite alphabet. The alphabet for a language is a set of
lexical items out of which the sentences are formed and it is presumed that
this lexicon includes all the words of the language either as individual symbols or as strings of symbols. When we say that an algorithm specifies a
language, we mean that when it is presented with a string of symbols from
the alphabet for that language, the algorithm will determine if the candidate string is in the language, that is, the algorithm will determine if the
candidate string is syntactically well formed. Grammars characterize
languages in a similar way, in that they specify a set of strings over an
alphabet. They also exhibit the syntactic structure of the strings in the
language and that will sometimes be of importance to the issues at hand,
but for our purposes the most important function of a grammar is to

specify a set of strings. Hence, we will be emphasizing what is usually termed *weak generative capacity*.

A computable process is simply one that can be carried out by an algorithm. From the earliest days of the subject there have been, not one, but two generally accepted notions of a computable process: that of *recursive* and that of *recursively enumerable*. For our purposes they are best understood in the context of language recognition. A set of strings (a language) is said to be *recursive* if there is some algorithm which, given any candidate string, will tell whether or not that string is a member of the language in question. Phrased less formally, a language is recursive provide there is some computer program which starting with an input consisting of an arbitrary string (over a suitable alphabet), will output a message correctly stating whether the string *is* in the language (is syntactically well formed) *or is not* in the language. The notion of recursively enumerable is obtained by weakening the demands on the algorithm. A language is said to be *recursively enumerable* (abbreviated *re*) if there is some algorithm which will rule on any candidate string to see if it is in the language, but in this case the algorithm has a less demanding task. For recursively enumerable languages, the algorithm must correctly note those candidate strings which are in the language by outputting a message that says they are in the language. However, if the candidate string is not in the language, then the algorithm may do anything at all so long as it does not lie. If the candidate string is not in the language, the algorithm might say it is not, or it might simply halt without giving any output at all, or it may compute forever without giving any output. To put it less formally, a program for a recursive language must answer *yes or no* to the questions "Is this sentence in the language?" while a program for a recursively enumerable language need only answer *yes* when appropriate but has the option of refusing to respond when the sentence is not in the language.[1]

Notice that every recursive language is, a fortiori, a recursively enumerable language since the algorithm which witnesses its recursiveness also witnesses the fact that it is recursively enumerable. On the other hand, there are recursively enumerable languages which are not recursive language. Hence, the added generality in the definition of a recursively enumerable language is not hollow. The definition of a recursive set (language) is more natural than that of a recursively enumerable set. However, the mathematics often compels us to take the notion of recursively enumerable as the primary notion. The distinction is not critical to most of the arguments in this anthology, and the reader will not be badly misled if he reads "recursive" when he sees "recursively enumerable," although the distinction between the two notions of computable will occasionally be made. Almost all of what is contained in the papers can be comprehended by readers with only a very superficial understanding of these concepts. As one might well expect, the reader needs a somewhat sharper notion of what constitutes a grammar.

For our purposes a *grammar* consists of a finite set of symbols and a finite number of rewrite rules over those symbols. The symbols are divided into two classes called *terminals* and *nonterminals*; one nonterminal is distinguished and called the *start symbol*. A *context-free grammar* is a grammar in which all the rewrite rules are of the form $A \to \alpha$, where A is a nonterminal and α is any (possibly empty) string of symbols (terminals, nonterminals, or a mixture of the two.) For noncontext-free grammars, there may be restrictions placed on when a symbol may be rewritten, but with context-free grammars any nonterminal symbol may be rewritten using any rule that starts with that symbol on the left-hand-side of the arrow. The language *weakly generated* by a grammar is the set of all strings of terminal symbols that can be derived from the start symbol by applying the rewrite rules. When we say that natural language is or is not context-free we are making a statement about languages as sets of strings. A language is said to be a *context-free language* if it is precisely the set of strings that are weakly generated by some context-free grammar.

A simple artificial example may help to illustrate the definition. One context-free grammar consists of the start symbol S which is also the only nonterminal, the two terminal symbols a and b, and the following rewrite rules:

$S \to aSa, S \to bSb,$

$S \to a, S \to aa,$

$S \to b,$ and $S \to bb.$

One string produced by this grammar is *abbba* which is obtained by apply-
ing the rules: $S \rightarrow aSa$ to produce *aSa*, then $S \rightarrow bSb$ to produce *abSba*, and
finally $S \rightarrow b$ to produce *abbba*. The language weakly generated by this
grammar consists of all (nonempty) palindromes over the two symbols *a*
and *b*, that is, all strings that read the same forwards and backwards.

The basic question being addresses in this volume is whether or not
the simple context-free grammar mechanism is capable of weakly generating every possible natural language. One can, as some of the articles do,
take the question in a very strict sense or one can ask, in a less demanding
way, whether the overwhelming bulk of a language's syntax can be so
described. Both versions of the questions merit consideration.

There have traditionally been only two widely used techniques for
answering the strict mathematical question. To show that a language is a
context-free language one normally exhibits a grammar (or something
equivalent such as a pushdown automaton.) To show that a language is
not context-free one normally appeals to the so called *pumping lemma*. To
understand some of the the papers one should be aware of at least the
basic outline of how these arguments are structured.

The technique generally used to show that a language L is not
context-free is as follows:

1.   Find a regular (finite-state automaton checkable) language R such
     that $L \cap R$ is is a language whose structure is easy to to analyze.

2.   Prove that $L \cap R$ is not context-free.

It is provably true that the intersection of a context-free language
(such as L) and a regular language (such as R) is always context-free.
Hence the above two steps immediately imply that L is not a context-free
language. To see this we can start by assume the contrary and deriving a
contradiction: if L where context-free that would imply that that $L \cap R$ is
context-free which directly contradicts our proof that it is not.

There is one refinement to this argument that is frequently used,
often without explicitly noting that it is being used. The language $L \cap R$ is
often simplified by applying a *homomorphism* to the language. A
homomorphism is a mapping that erases some words and rewrites others.

It does not detract from the validity of the argument to apply such a homomorphism to simplify the language $L \cap R$. To complete the argument it suffices to prove that the simplified language is not context-free. In practice this means that the language $L \cap R$ can be simplified by erasing some symbols and by renaming other symbols. The renaming is just a notational convenience. The erasing is a more substantive change and to preserve the validity of the argument the erasing should obey one rule: if a particular symbol is erased, then it cannot be selectively erased; *all* occurrences of that symbol must be erased.

$L \cap R$ is shown to not be context-free by using the pumping lemma. The details of the pumping lemma are not at all inaccessible, but are beyond the scope of this brief introduction. Those readers unfamiliar with it, fortunately do not need to learn it in order to understand the papers in this anthology. Only a few particular cases need to be discussed. For purposes of reading the papers that follow, it will suffice to note that the languages listed below are provably not context-free. And hence, if in the above argument outline $L \cap R$ (possibly simplified by a homomorphism as described above) is any of these, then the argument is valid. The reader who wishes to be spared reading the details can simply take our word on this issue and proceed directly to the papers. The reader who wishes more detail should consult a text book on formal language theory such as Harrison (1978) or Savitch (1982).

Some languages that provably cannot be generated by any context-free grammar:

In all such cases the strings are formed out of symbols from some fixed finite alphabet, such as $\{a, b, c\}$ or the set of all words of English.

(1) The language consisting of all strings (over an alphabet of two or more symbols) of the form xx, that is a string followed by an exact copy of itself.

(2) The language consisting of all strings of the form $a^n b^n c^n$, that is, all a's followed by all b's followed by all c's and with equal numbers of each letter.

(3)   A number of variations on (2). For example, if one merely requires that the number of c's be less than or equal to the number of a's (which equal's the number of b's), then the language is still not context-free. The intuitive idea is that a context-free grammar cannot "count" the a's, b's and c's when they are ordered as follows: first all the a's, then all the b's and then all the c's.

Notes

[1.]Many authors reserve the work "algorithm" for the kind of computation which applies to recursive languages and use the word "procedure" for those which apply to recursively enumerable languages. However, usage is not completely consistent. Our usage reflects conversational usage and is likely to be both the most useful for our purposes and the most comfortable to the greatest number of readers.

References

Chomsky, Noam, *Aspects of the Theory of Syntax*, 1965, The MIT Press, Cambridge, Mass.

Chomsky, Noam, *Syntactic Structures*, 1957, Mouton Publishers, The Hague.

Harrison, Michael A., *Introduction to Formal Language Theory*, 1978, Addison-Wesley, Reading, Mass.

Lyons, John, *Noam Chomsky*, 1977, Penguin Books, New York.

Savitch, Walter J., *Abstract Machines and Grammars*, 1982, Little, Brown and Company.

Acknowledgements

We are grateful to Elisabet Engdahl for a number of helpful comments on the original plan for this volume. We thank Anita Bickford for her help in proofing the papers. We thank Subhana Menis and the Computer Science Laboratory at Xerox Palo Alto Research Center for preparing many of the diagrams. Thanks also go to Florence Holmes, Chiquita Payne, and Virginia Stephens for their assistance in preparing the final typescript and to the Computer Science and Engineering Department at the University of California, San Diego for providing the facilities for preparing the typescript. Most especially, we thank all of the authors for their permission and cooperation in reprinting their articles.

The paper by Janet Dean Fodor originally appeared in J. Lyons (Ed), *New Horizons in Linguistics*, 1970 Penguin Books, New York and is reprinted with the permission of the publisher. The paper by Bach and Marsh originally appeared in NELS8 and is reprinted with the permission of the authors. The paper by Thomas Wasow originally appeared in *Synthese* 39 (1978) 81-104 and is reprinted with the permission of D. Reidel Publishing Co., Dordrecht, Holland. The paper by Gilbert H. Harman originally appeared in *Language* 39 (1963) 597-616 and is reprinted with the permission of the Linguistic Society of America. The paper by P. T. Geach originally appeared in Davidson and Harman (eds.), *Semantics of Natural Language*, 1972, D. Reidel Publishing Co. and is reprinted with the permission of the publisher. The paper by Pullum and Gazdar originally appeared in *Linguistics and Philosophy* 4 (1982) 471-504 and is reprinted with the permission of D. Reidel Publishing Co., Holland. The paper by Gazdar originally appeared in *Linguistic Inquiry* 12 (1981), 155-184 and is reprinted with the permission of The MIT Press. The paper by Uszkoreit and Peters originally appeared in *Linguistics and Philosophy*, 9 (1986), 477-494 and is reprinted with the permission of D. Reidel Publishing Co.. The paper by Emmon Bach originally appeared in F. Landman and F. Veltman (Eds), 1984, *Varieties of Formal Semantics: proceedings of the fourth Amsterdam Colloquium 1982*, Foris Publications, Dordrecht,

Holland and is reprinted with the permission of the publisher. The paper by Bresnan, Kaplan, Peters, and Zaenen originally appeared in *Linguistic Inquiry*, **13** (1982), 613-635 and is reprinted with the permission of The MIT Press. The paper by Stuart M. Shieber originally appeared in *Linguistics and Philosophy* **8** (1985) 333-343 and is reprinted with the permission of D. Reidel Publishing Co. The paper by James Higginbotham originally appeared in *Linguistic Inquiry* **15** (1984), and is reprinted with the permission of The MIT Press. The paper by Christopher Culy originally appeared in *Linguistics and Philosophy* **8** (1985) 345-351. and is reprinted with the permission of D. Reidel Publishing Co. The paper by Marsh and Partee originally appeared in WCCFL 3 and is reprinted with the permission of the authors. The epilogue by Gazdar and . Pullum originally appeared in *New Generation Computing* **3** (1985), 273-306 and is reprinted with the permission of OHMSHA, LTD., Tokyo.

The Editors

PROLOGUE

Stanley Peters

WHAT IS MATHEMATICAL LINGUISTICS?

How, one may reasonably wonder, could mathematics be applied to anything so unquantifiable as language? An analogy with, say, mathematical
physics raises the puzzling question of how one could write equations which
might be solved for the meaning of some French word or the correct case
in German for the object of *glauben*. The source of such confusion is the
common but incorrect idea that all mathematics deals with numbers. Virtually any paper in generative linguistics illustrate how one can make precise statements of a nonquantitative nature about language. Mathematical
linguistics involves studying this sort of statement by applying mathematics. In this chapter we will see how some such applications have yielded
interesting results about language.

A "common sense" approach to the description of language might
suggest that sentences are made up of elementary units — perhaps words
or individual sounds or letters. In speaking, these units are uttered successively one after another and in listening the succession of incoming units is
attended to item by item. Following this line of reasoning we could say
that a grammar of a language is a description of the changes in "state of
mind" of a speaker as he proceeds to utter the units of a sentence or,
equivalently, of the mental changes a hearer undergoes as he receives one
by one the incoming units of a sentence. This "common sense" linguistic
theory was actually proposed, in a slightly restricted form, by the linguist
Charles A. Hockett (1955). Besides according quite well with our first
impressions of how language works, it also conforms to the *Zeitgeist* that
has dominated twentieth century psychology. Associationist theories of
language all seem to support the claim that grammars are of this sort
(Bever, Fodor and Garrett, 1968), though they would have different implications for the size of units (letters, words, phrases, etc.) which the

1

W. J. Savitch et al. (eds.), The Formal Complexity of Natural Language, 1–18.
© *1987 by D. Reidel Publishing Company.*

grammar would deal with. It is therefore of great interest to know whether this very plausible theory is correct. In order to determine this it will be necessary to specify more exactly what the constraints on a grammar are.

At a greater level of detail, a grammar must contain a finite set V of elementary units; we can call V the *vocabulary* of the grammar (although the units it contains do not necessarily correspond to words). Corresponding to the "states of mind" of speaker and hearer, the grammar must contain a set Σ of *state names*. These names are assigned to states arbitrarily, but each member of Σ must name only one "mental state" and in consequence Σ must contain one name for each of the finite number of "states of mind" a speaker-hearer of the language being described may be in as he produces or understands sentences in his language. Certain of those states will be designated *initial states* — in which speaker and hearer begin all linguistic activity — while certain will be designated *completion states* — which they will be in at the end of a complete sentence. If a speaker (hearer) is in a certain "state of mind" and he utters (hears) a vocabulary item, then he will as a result be in another, possibly different, "state of mind" and a grammar must specify which one. Furthermore, since units of the vocabulary are not all equally likely to occur at any given point in a sentence, a grammar should also list the probability of each state-to-state transition as follows: Let σ_1 and σ_2 be state names and let a be a vocabulary item. A grammar must assign each such triple σ_1, a, σ_2 a number between 0 and 1 which is the probability of the speaker's uttering (listener's hearing) the vocabulary item a and entering the state σ_2 if he was immediately before in state σ_1. A grammar of this type will be called a *finite state grammar*.

We shall consider a concrete example. Let the vocabulary V consist of the words *figs, icicles, the, melted,* and *ripened.* Let Σ consist of five state names σ_1, σ_2, σ_3, σ_4, and σ_5; σ_1 being the only initial state and σ_5 the only completion state. The possible state-to-state transitions and their probabilities are shown in (1).

(1)

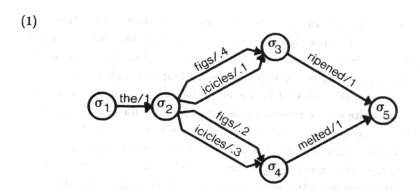

The graph is to be interpreted as follows. Each state is represented by a circle containing its name. From each state except the completion state one or more arrows emanate pointing to the states which can be entered next in the course of uttering or understanding a sentence. Each arrow is labeled with a unit of the vocabulary and the probability of uttering that vocabulary item and entering the state pointed to if the speaker was immediately before in the state at which the arrow originates. Since it is certain that in uttering a grammatical sentence the speaker will leave every state except a completion state, the sum of the probabilities on arrows leaving a noncompletion state must be 1. The grammar described in (1) will specify as grammatical sentences the strings of words listed in (2).

(2) (i)   The figs ripened
     (ii) The figs melted
     (iii) The icicles ripened
     (iv) The icicles melted

It also predicts that not all of these sentences are equally likely to be uttered. The probabilities of being uttered of sentences (2i)-(2iv) are 0.4, 0.2, 0.1 and 0.3 respectively. Our example grammar is, of course inadequate as an account of the English language and any adequate finite state grammar will clearly have to be vastly more complicated.

Having specified more exactly what constitutes a grammar according to our "common sense" linguistic theory, we now wish to test it against the facts. It is not immediately apparent how to write such a grammar for

English or any other language, but this does not demonstrate that the theory is wrong. To show this we would want to prove that no finite state grammar exists which is adequate to describe English (or some other language). We are left in a problematic situation; although the theory is plausible, we cannot show that it is even probably correct since we do not know how to write even a remotely adequate grammar for any language in terms of the theory, but on the other hand we have no proof that the theory is wrong. Furthermore, it is difficult to see how we might arrive at such proof, since the theory seems so attractive in terms of common sense. After all, do people not utter one word after another in speaking and is it not true that the likelihood of a given word's being uttered at a certain time varies depending on what words have preceeded it in the sentence in progress? Direct observation makes our theory seem correct almost by inspection and it is hard to see what facts could prove it wrong.

Nevertheless the theory is wrong and it was work in mathematical linguistics that permitted this to be demonstrated. To see how this was done let us confine our attention to the set of sentences that are allowed by the grammar with nonzero probability, i.e. to the sentences the grammar says are grammatical, ignoring the probabilities assigned to these sentences.

Our arguments against the theory of language outlined above will concern only the way in which finite state grammars structure the set of grammatical sentences and not the probabilities assigned to sentences. Let us note in passing, however, the fact, pointed out by Chomsky (1957b), that although *New York* has greater probability than *Nevada* in the context *I come from* —, this is not a fact about the grammar of English but a fact about the world. Furthermore in the environment *Everyone is taller than* —, both *himself* and *out* have zero frequency of occurrence. But a finite state grammar which assigns *Everyone is taller than himself* and *Everyone is taller than out* zero probability cannot capture the fact, which every English speaker knows, that the former is a grammatical sentence of English while the latter is not. Facts like these make it clear that a grammar should not attempt to account for the relative frequencies with which sentences of a language are uttered since this is possible only at the cost of failing to correctly distinguish grammatical from ungrammatical sentences. Ignoring probabilities, we shall next prove a theorem about finite state grammars.

Let G be any finite state grammar and let $a_1 \ldots a_n$ and $b_1 \ldots b_m$ be arbitrary strings over the vocabulary of G. These strings will be called *completion equivalent* if adding any string $c_1 \ldots c_r$ onto the right of the first two results in strings $a_1 \ldots a_n c_1 \ldots c_r$ and $b_1 \ldots b_m c_1 \ldots c_r$, both of which or else neither of which are complete sentences according to G. Clearly, what strings can be added to a given string $a_1 \ldots a_n$ to yield a complete sentence depends on what states G can be in after emitting $a_1 \ldots a_n$. We shall thus define the *resultant* of a string $a_1 \ldots a_n$ to be the set of states that G can be in after emitting that string if started in any of its initial states. If G cannot emit $a_1 \ldots a_n$ when started in an initial state, then the resultant is the empty set, which contains no states. For example, the resultant of the string *The figs* in the grammar summarized in (1) is the set containing states σ_3 and σ_4. The important thing is that if two strings $a_1 \ldots a_n$ and $b_1 \ldots b_m$ have the same resultant, then they are completion equivalent. For if the result of adding some string $c_1 \ldots c_r$ to the right of $a_1 \ldots a_n$ $(b_1 \ldots b_m)$ is a complete sentence, this means it is possible for G to proceed from some state σ in the resultant of $a_1 \ldots a_n$ $(b_1 \ldots b_m)$ to a completion state while emitting $c_1 \ldots c_r$ and hence G can go from an appropriately chosen initial state to σ while emitting $b_1 \ldots b_m$ $(a_1 \ldots a_n)$ — since $a_1 \ldots a_n$ and $b_1 \ldots b_m$ have the same resultant — and then proceed from there to a completion state, ultimately having emitted the complete sentence $b_1 \ldots b_m c_1 \ldots c_r (a_1 \ldots a_n c_1 \ldots c_r)$. Thus either $a_1 \ldots a_n c_1 \ldots c_r$ and $b_1 \ldots b_m c_1 \ldots c_r$ are both complete sentences or neither is. To illustrate what we have just proved, note that the strings (3i) and (3ii) have the same resultant according to our example grammar.

(3)   (i)   The figs

         (ii)   The icicles

This means that they have to be completion equivalent and thus (4i) and (4ii) are both complete sentences according to the grammar, while neither (5i) or (5ii) is.

(4)   (i)   The figs ripened

         (ii)   The icicles ripened

(5) (i) The figs the

(ii) The icicles the

But observe that there can be only a finite number of different types of completion equivalent strings according to a finite state grammar G; that is one can only collect a finite number of strings such that no two strings in the collection are completion equivalent. For there are only a finite number of different resultants a string can have — a finite set, such as G's set Σ of state names, has only a finite number of subsets — and strings with the same resultant are completion equivalent. What we have just proved forms a part of Nerode's Theorem (see Rabin and Scott, 1959, Theorem 2), the part which we will need for our argument.

Let us now consider how we might apply this theorem to some facts about English. For the sake of simplicity let us first consider an artificial "language" whose vocabulary contains only two items; α and β. Let the grammatical sentences of this language each consist of an arbitrary string of α 's and β 's followed by the reversal of that string; for example, $\alpha\alpha\beta\beta\alpha\alpha$, $\beta\alpha\alpha\beta$, $\alpha\alpha\beta\alpha\alpha\beta\alpha\alpha$ are grammatical sentences while $\alpha\alpha\beta\beta\alpha$ is not. This "mirror image language", is not a finite state language. We will prove that this statement is true by showing that if it were false we could deduce absurdities. For this purpose, suppose that the statement is false — i.e. that the language is finite state — and let G be some finite state grammar of the language. If $\alpha^i\beta$ and $\alpha^j\beta$ were completion equivalent only when i and j are equal (α^i represents i successive occurrences of α), then $\alpha\beta$, $\alpha\alpha\beta$, $\alpha\alpha\alpha\beta$, etc. would constitute an infinite collection of strings no two of which are completion equivalent. Thus there must be two distinct numbers m and n such that $\alpha^m\beta$ and $\alpha^n\beta$ are completion equivalent. Now adding the same string to the right of completion equivalent strings results in strings both of which or neither of which are grammatical sentences. Adding $\beta\alpha^m$ gives $\alpha^m\beta\beta\alpha^m$ — which is a complete sentence according to G — and $\alpha^n\beta\beta\alpha^m$ — which is not, since m and n are not equal. So the assumption that there is a finite state grammar of the mirror image language leads to the contradictory result that $\alpha^n\beta\beta\alpha^m$ both is and is not in the mirror image language and thus this assumption must be false. Therefore, this simple "language" has no finite state grammar. English however, has processes which give it the mirror image property. Hence it has no finite state grammar either.

To see this consider the sentences in (6).

(6) (i)   She is more afraid than you are.
   (ii)   She is less afraid than you are.
   (iii)   She is as afraid as you are.

These sentences contain comparative forming words which go together in certain definite ways. *More* and *less* are paired with *than* and *as* goes only with itself, as the ungrammatical sentences in (7) show.

(7) (i)   She is more afraid as you are.
   (ii)   She is less afraid as you are.
   (iii)   She is as afraid than you are.

We might think of *more, less* and *than* as α-type words and *as* as a β-type word. Now *afraid* in (6) can be replaced by any one of a number of adjectives which may be followed by *that* plus a sentence complement. Consider, for example, (8).

(8) (i)   She is more certain that cats bark than you are.
   (ii)   She is less certain that cats bark than you are.
   (iii)   She is as certain that cats bark as you are.

Other adjectives which could occupy the place of *certain* in (8) are *afraid, astounded, annoyed, overjoyed, relieved, perplexed* and *delighted*. Furthermore, the sentence *Cats bark* in (8i)-(8iii) can be replaced by other sentences, including comparative sentences such as (8), as for example in (9).

(9) She is as certain that she is more dismayed that cats bark than you are as you are.

Thus comparatives can be embedded inside one another and the process can be repeated to obtain embeddings of arbitrary depth. Now the important thing about the resulting set of English sentences is that α-type words must be paired up with α-type and β-type with β-type, so that embedding arranges the comparative forming words *more, less, than* and *as* in the pattern of the α's and β's of the mirror image language. But since no finite state grammar is adequate to specify the sentences of that "language" none is adequate for English either. (Technically, we must intersect the

set of all grammatical English sentences with a finite state language over
the vocabulary *She, is, more, less, than, as, that, you, are, cats, bark, certain, afraid, amazed* and so on, thereby obtaining the subset of English sentences which we are interested in. We then apply a finite transduction to
map that set into the mirror image language and, since the set of finite
state languages is closed under intersection and finite transduction, we
have proved the result.)

Thus, following Chomsky (1956), we have been able to show that the
simple and plausible theory that finite state grammars are the correct
apparatus for specifying the sentences of human languages is wrong. But
is there another lesson we can learn from this result? Perhaps it was a
mistake to think of linguistic description so much in terms of actual
linguistic performance. After all many factors affect language use besides
the nature of language. In addition to the inherent nature of English, factors such as level of attention, memory limitations, set, degree of motivation, etc. determine the actual behavior of us all in speaking, listening,
writing and reading. It was viewing a grammar as a model of linguistic
behavior that made finite state grammars seem almost obviously the
correct sort of apparatus for linguistic description. But we now see that a
model of linguistic performance will not be the same thing as a
specification of the inherent nature of a language. In fact, there is every
reason to think that the former must include the latter as only one of
many components. Thus linguists are now aware that a grammar must
specify the knowledge that a speaker-hearer has of his language, the
knowledge that enables him to speak and understand, technically called his
linguistic competence. Let us next try to see what that competence consists in.

By virtue of knowing English, all of us can see that sentence (10) has
two different meanings which correspond to different groupings of its
words.

(10) Fighting causes wounds.

The first two words can constitute a noun phrase (as in *Fighting causes
wounds people*) or else the last two words can be a verb phrase (giving the
same meaning as *Wounds are caused by fighting*). Every sentence has a

tree structure which indicates the grouping of its elements and the categories each group belongs to. Structurally ambiguous sentences will have more than one tree. For example, sentence (10) has the structures (11i) and (11ii).

(11) (i)   (ii)

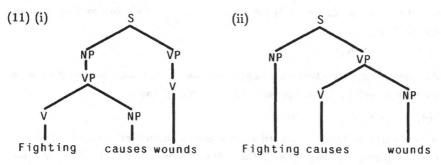

Here S = sentence, NP = noun phrase, VP = verb phrase and V = verb. Our knowledge of English specifies for each English sentence the information contained in its tree(s).

In school, we learned to parse sentences, i.e. to make this information conscious and on its basis to assign to sentences structures similar to trees. Linguists have developed a theory, called *immediate constituent analysis*, which is essentially an elaboration of parsing and which incorporates a type of grammar capable of assigning tree structures such as (11i) and (11ii) to sentences. A grammar of this type, technically called a *phrase structure grammar*, contains two vocabularies, the lexical vocabulary of units out of which sentences are built (e.g. words) and the categorical vocabulary of phrase types appearing in the language the category "sentence" must always be among them. The rules of a grammar specify what internal structure phrases are allowed to have by stating that phrases of a given category (A) may immediately contain a certain sequence ($\alpha_1 ... \alpha_d$) of phrases and words — indicated in tree structures by the node representing the given phrase being above and directly connected to the nodes representing the words and phrases — provided that the phrase in question has a particular sequence ($\beta_1 ... \beta_m$) of words and phrases to its left and a particular sequence ($\gamma_1 ... \gamma_r$) of words and phrases to its right. We can symbolize such a rule in terms of expressions like (12).

(12) $A \rightarrow \alpha_1...\alpha_n \; / \; \beta_1...\beta_m$ _____ $\gamma_1...\gamma_r$

If $m = r = 0$, then any phrase of type A regardless of its context — can satisfy the rule. In this case the rule is called context-free and symbolized by omitting the symbol "/" and everything to its right. Such a rule might say that a verb phrase (VP) may contain a verb (V) followed by a noun phrase (NP).

(13)   VP → V NP

Another phrase structure rule might say that a verb may be analyzed as a transitive verb (V_t) if it appears before a noun phrase.

(14) $V \rightarrow V_t \; /$ _____ NP

A given tree is, thus, in accord with a phrase structure grammar G if the tree's top node is labeled with the category "sentence" and if every node except those at the bottom satisfies some rule of G. We say that a node satisfies rule (12) if it is labeled A, if it is above and directly connected to a sequence of n nodes labeled $\alpha_1, \cdots, \alpha_n$ from left to right and if immediately to its left (right) is a sequence of adjacent nodes labeled $\beta_1, \cdots, \beta_m$ ($\gamma_1, \cdots, \gamma_r$). A grammar G then parses a sequence $a_1...a_r$ of elements of G's lexical vocabulary if one can erect atop the sequence a tree which is in accord with G. (Chomsky and Miller (1963) make use of phrase structure grammars to rewrite strings rather than parse sentences in the above manner and thus they obtain somewhat different theorems about the associated languages (Chomsky, 1963). Our use seems to be more in line with procedures of immediate constituent analysis.)

As an example of a phrase structure grammar let us consider the following. G's lexical vocabulary contains just the units α and β and its categorial vocabulary contains only the category S of sentences. G has the rules (15).

(15) (i) S → α S α (iii) S → α α

     (ii) S → β S β (iv) S → β β

In order to see what the language of G is, let $a_1...a_n$ be any sentence parsed by G. By the definition of "parse", each symbol $a_1, \cdots, a_n$ is an α or a β and one can erect atop $a_1...a_n$ a tree which is in accord with G. But then all nodes except those at the bottom will satisfy one of rules (15i)-

(15iv) and hence will branch to the immediately lower nodes in one of the configurations (16i)-(16iv).

(16)

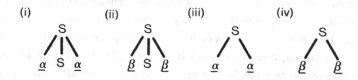

This means that the first symbol a_1 must be the same as the final symbol a_n, the second symbol a_2 the same as the penultimate a_{n-1} etc. But then each sentence parsed by G is a "mirror image" string and all such strings are parsed by G. So the language of G is the mirror image language.

Since phrase structure grammars are capable of parsing the mirror image language, they do not fail for the description of English comparatives (and many similar constructions) as finite state grammars did. Furthermore one can certainly regard a phrase structure grammar as an account of a speaker-hearer's knowledge of his language rather than an account of the operations he performs in speaking and understanding. The theory of immediate constituent analysis appears to meet the objections to finite state grammars we discovered and thus it merits further consideration. At one time it seemed as obvious to linguists that the theory of immediate constituent analysis was correct as it earlier seemed to us that finite state grammar correctly described language. Once again this appearance is misleading since the theory of immediate constituent analysis is factually incorrect.

To see this it will be helpful once again to consider first a simple "language" of α's and β's. This time the grammatical sentences will be all strings which begin with an arbitrary sequence of α's and β's and are completed by a repetition of that sequence. Grammatical sentences include $\alpha\alpha\beta\beta\alpha\alpha\beta\beta$, $\beta\alpha\alpha\beta\alpha\alpha$ and $\alpha\beta\alpha\alpha\beta\alpha$; the strings $\alpha\beta\alpha\alpha$ and $\beta\beta\alpha\beta\alpha\alpha$ are ungrammatical. Chomsky has proved that this reduplicating language does not have a phrase structure grammar in which all rules are context-free. Intuitively the reason for this is quite simple. The only way context-free phrase structure grammars can state constraints between elements of a sentence is by imposing restrictions on what phrases can be immediately contained by phrases of the sentence, as is done by the rules (15). Thus such grammars can capture dependencies between elements of sentences in some language if those dependencies are nested, as in the mirror image language. If the dependencies overlap, however, then context-free rules cannot capture them. But in the reduplicating language the first element of a sentence must be the same as the first one after the midpoint, the second element the same as the second one after the midpoint, etc. Thus dependencies between elements in sentences of the reduplicating language overlap and hence this language has no context-free phrase structure grammar (for a rigorous proof of these remarks see Chomsky (1963, Theorems 15 and 18)). But every language that can be parsed by any phrase structure grammar at all can be parsed by one in which all rules are context-free. This means that the reduplicating language cannot be parsed by any phrase structure grammar. The rather startling result that context-sensitive rules do not expand the set of parsable languages (see Peters and Ritchie, 1969b, Theorem 3.8) does not hold when phrase structure grammars are used as in Chomsky and Miller (1963). As we have noted, however, using them to parse sentences (in our technical sense) is a better reconstruction of immediate constituent analysis.

Many languages exhibit the overlapping constraints of the reduplicating language in certain of their constructions, however an extremely clear example of such constraints can be found in Mohawk, as was pointed out by Postal. Mohawk allows an object noun to be incorporated into the verb. This allows the Mohawk sentence schematically represented as (17i) also to be expressed in the manner represented as (17ii).

(17)

    (i) The-girl finds the-house

    (ii) The-girl house-finds

If a modifier precedes the object noun, then the external object noun phrase may be retained when the noun is incorporated, as in (18).

(18)

    (i) The-girl finds this house

    (ii) The-girl house-finds this house

If the external noun phrase is present in a sentence in which the verb has an incorporated object, then the incorporated noun and the external noun must be the same; so (19) represents an ungrammatical Mohawk sentence.

(19) The-girl house-finds this car.

Now nouns can be derived from verbs in Mohawk, including verbs which have an incorporated noun, so one has sentences such as that represented by (20).

(20) The-girl likes this house-finding

Such derived nouns can be incorporated into the verb, giving sentences such as (21).

(21) The-girl house-finding-likes this house-finding

Since the incorporation of noun into verb and the deriving of noun from verb can be repeated arbitrarily many times, there is an infinite set of Mohawk sentences with the overlapping constraints of the reduplicating language (see Postal, 1964). From this fact, one can demonstrate that Mohawk, like the reduplicating language, has no phrase structure grammar (one intersects with an appropriate finite state language and performs a finite transduction of the resulting set; the closure of phrase structure languages under these operations gives the result.) But if some language cannot be parsed by any phrase structure grammar, then the theory of immediate constituent analysis must be incorrect.

    Once again, the demonstration that an almost obviously correct theory of language is wrong can lead us to ask why we were so misled. As the Mohawk examples illustrate, languages have general rules relating sentences to one another, for instance the Mohawk rule incorporating object nouns into verbs. Phrase structure grammars cannot incorporate such rules and for this reason they are unable to capture such general relationships as those between English active and passive sentences, between declarative and interrogative sentences, etc. Rules relating sentences cannot apply to sentences themselves or to the trees (called surface structures) which we have discussed, since sentences with the same surface structure (except, of course, for the bottom nodes), such as (22i) and (22ii), may be subject to different rules.

(22)

      (i) It is careful to pass fair laws.

      (ii) It is easy to pass fair laws.

For example, the rule forming "pseudo-cleft" sentences applies only in the case of (22i) while the rule of "it-replacement" applies only in the case of (22ii).

Compare (23) and (24).

(23)

      (i) What it is careful of is to pass fair laws.

      (ii) What it is easy (of) is to pass fair laws.

(24)

      (i) Fair laws are careful to pass.

      (ii) Fair laws are easy to pass.

Thus a grammar that can capture these intersentential relations, which form part of speaker-hearers' knowledge of their language, must assign more structure to sentences than just surface structure.

Building on fundamental insights of Zellig Harris, Noam Chomsky invented a theory of grammar which is able to assign this further structure. This theory, known as *transformational grammar*, has been elaborated and refined since by many other workers besides Chomsky. Transformational grammar is treated in many books the reader can refer to for details. Here we must be content with the description of a transformational grammar as containing a base component — which marks off a set of trees (called *deep structures*) much as a phrase structure grammar does, only these trees do not have the associated sentence as their bottom line — and a transformational component — which converts these trees into surface structures. The surface structure of a sentence determines how it is pronounced and the deep structure underlying that surface structure determines the meaning the sentence has. Of course, a sentence may have more than one deep structure (just as (10) has more than one surface structure).

The transformational component consists of a sequence of *grammatical transformations*, which map trees into trees, thereby converting deep structures into surface structures by successive stages. Although transformational grammars are much more complex than finite state or phrase structure grammars, it seems likely that mathematical linguistics will contribute to the development of transformational theory and in fact recently such techniques have been applied.

It has been proved, for example, that the power of transformational grammars to describe languages which are beyond the power of phrase structure grammars, such as the reduplicating language, lies in the possibility of applying grammatical transformations many times in converting a sentence's deep structure(s) into its surface structure(s). It has also been shown that in present versions of transformational theory the possibilities for multiple application of grammatical transformations are too unrestricted, allowing transformational grammars to describe many "languages" which humans could not possibly learn (see Peters and Ritchie 1969c). This is a defect of transformational theory because one fact for which the theory should account is that there is a limited range of languages that humans can learn. The theory should delimit precisely the set of possible languages.

The theory of transformational grammar recaptures the old idea, tracing back at least as far as Lancelot and Arnauld (1660) and possibly to Aristotle, that sentences have an inner structure relating to thought and an outer structure relating to their pronunciation and written representation. According to this tradition, all languages have the same inner structure and differ only in the surface appearance of their sentences. Although transformational grammar developed entirely independently of this tradition, this speculation about universal inner structure is of a great deal of interest even today. Transformational grammars are so complex that it is extremely difficult to see how a child faced with the task of learning the language spoken around him could ever succeed. The only way that he could is to have a great deal of advance knowledge biologically "built in", that is to be genetically preprogrammed to learn a specific sort of grammar. If it should turn out that the grammars of all languages have the same base component, then this fact could be "built in" and the task of learning a language would be enormously simplified for the child. Thus one factual question we would like to have answered is whether there is a universal base component which appears in the grammar of every language. Obviously the answer cannot be determined by any sort of direct observation one might make, since there is no way to observe a sentence's extremely abstract deep structure in its surface appearance. Recall that sentences (22i) and (22ii) were nearly identical on the surface although they differ greatly at the level of deep structure. Evidently we can only determine what the deep structure of a sentence is or what the base component of a language's grammar is by appealing to the theory of transformational grammar to justify whatever hypotheses we might formulate about these matters. We are faced with a problem analogous to that in physics of determining whether or not pulsars are really neutron stars. No conceivable direct observations could settle the question so one must rely upon physical theories to determine this matter of fact. In the case of the possibility that all languages have the same base component, it has been shown (see Peters and Ritchie, 1969c, 1971) that the theory of transformational grammar does not at present permit a determination to be made. Thus linguistic theory will have to be elaborated further before this extremely interesting and important question can be settled.

These are a sample of the results that have been obtained in the mathematical linguistics of transformational grammar. From them and the earlier discussion of finite state and phrase structure grammars the reader may have formed the impression that mathematical linguistics can provide only negative results. This opinion is not entirely correct, although it is common. In fact, other results have been fruitful in suggesting positive modifications in linguistic theory. They have also opened up the prospect of accounting for facts which have eluded explanation until now. To mention only one example, it has been proved that of the languages having context-free phrase structure grammars some have only ambiguous context-free phrase structure grammars. This suggests a possible means of explaining the ubiquitous ambiguity of language. If it can be shown that some future adequate linguistic theory provides a certain set of grammars from which the grammar of every language must be drawn and that all languages must contain certain constructions, then one would hope to prove a theorem stating that if L is a language containing the required constructions and G is a grammar of L chosen from the allowed set, then G is ambiguous. Such a theorem would establish an explanation of the ambiguity of language.

Acknowledgements

This work was supported in part by National Science Foundation Grant GS-2468. The author is indebted to Emmon Bach and Meta Bach for helpful suggestions.

References

Bever, T., Fodor, J., and Garrett, M., (1968) A Formal Limitation of Associationism, In T. Dixon and D. Horton (Eds.) *Verbal Behavior and General Behavior Theory*, Englewood Cliffs, N. J., Prentice-Hall.

Chomsky, N. (1956). Three Models for the Description of Language, *IRE Transactions on Information Theory*, IT-2, 113-124.

_____, (1957b) Review of a Manual of Phonology, *IJAL*, 23, 223-234.

_____, (1963) Formal Properties of Grammars, In R. Luce, R. Bush and E. Galanter (Eds.), *Handbook of Mathematical Psychology*, New York, Wiley.

_____, and Miller, G., (1963) Introduction to the Formal Analysis of Language, In R. Luce, R. Bush and E. Galanter (Eds.), *Handbook of Mathematical Psychology*, New York, Wiley.

Hockett, Charles A. (1955) *A Manual of Phonology*, Bloomington, Ind., Indiana University Press.

Lancelot, C., and Arnauld, A., (1660) *Grammaire Générale et Raisonée*, Reprinted (1967), Menston, England, Scolar Press.

Peters, S., and Ritchie, R., (1969a) A Note on the Universal Base Hypothesis, *JL*, 5, 150-152.

_____, (1969b) Context-Sensitive Immediate Constituent Analysis — Context-free Languages Revisited.

_____, (1969c) On the Generative Power of Transformational Grammars.

_____, (1971) On Restricting the Base Component of Transformational Grammars, *Information and Control* 18, 493-501.

Postal, P., (1964) Limitations of Phrase Structure Grammars, In J. Fodor and J. Katz (Eds.), *The Structure of Language*, Englewood Cliffs, N.J., Prentice-Hall.

Rabin, M., and Scott, D., (1959) Finite Automata and Their Decision Problems, *IBM Journal of Research and Development*, 3, 114-125.

Part I.

Early Nontransformational Grammar

I. EARLY NONTRANSFORMATIONAL GRAMMAR

Introduction

This group of articles sets the stage for the question of the context-freeness of natural language, and more generally, for the study of formal models for syntax.

The first article by Fodor deals with the relationship between linguistics and formal logic. The topic is semantics rather than syntax, but it makes a number of important points about syntax that are important to our study. First it discusses the distinction between syntax and semantics. Secondly it gives a simple example of something that cannot be accomplished by context-free phrase structure rules, namely insuring that there is no redundant quantification in the formulae of first order logic. On this topic, two points on which the paper may be misleading should be clarified. The set of all formulae of first order logic can be generated by a context-free grammar. It is only when one makes constrains on how well behaved the quantification must be that one gets outside the power of a context-free grammar. Also, contrary to the impression given in the paper, an arbitrary phrase structure grammar (one that uses context) is capable of checking for redundant quantifiers and most other reasonable things. However, it is not clear whether or not it can do so naturally. These points about quantification are dealt with in more detail in the paper by Marsh and Partee contained in Part III. The details are important, but the main contribution of the Fodor paper to our study is to give some practice and some feeling for the use of formal systems in the context of linguistics.

The paper by Bach and Marsh presents a proof of the classic result of Peters and Ritchie which states that the transformational grammar model of *Aspects* is capable of generating any recursively enumerable set. The original proof was difficult for all but specialists in the mathematics of formal grammars and computability theory. This version makes the proof as well as the result accessible to a wider audience. The importance of the Peters-Ritchie result cannot be overstated. It dealt a serious, some would

21

W. J. Savitch et al. (eds.), The Formal Complexity of Natural Language, 21–23.

contend fatal, blow to the transformational grammar model. Moreover, it did so on the basis of weak generative capacity alone. Even more surprisingly, it did so on the basis of a purely mathematical proof with no reference to linguistics data. The result showed that the transformational grammar model is capable of generating any recursively enumerable set and so is capable of mirroring any algorithmic process whatsoever. Hence, if the transformational grammar model correctly characterizes human language processing abilities, then there is apparently nothing special about language. Within the transformational grammar framework, language appears to be just one of many manifestations of a general algorithmic ability, with nothing to distinguish it form other mental processes. Yet, if we think that language is a specialized ability, then we would expect it to be restricted in what it can accomplish. In light of the Peters-Ritchie result it makes sense to search for models with a weak generative capacity less than that of the transformational grammar model. One obvious candidate is the context-free grammar model.

The case made in the previous paragraph is a strong one, but not an iron clad one. One can still contend that the transformational grammar model is correct but needs some refining. In later papers Peters and Ritchie (1973a, 1973b) present restricted versions of the transformational grammar model which generate fewer than all the recursively enumerable sets and which can be linguistically motivated. Another possible view is that the transformational grammar model is correct (even the one that generates all recursively enumerable sets) but that it is subjected to certain processing constraints or semantic filtering or some other filtering device and this filtering process restricts the model to the domain we think of as the class of natural languages. All this is possible, but the burden of proof rests on the defenders of the transformational grammar model. The paper by Wasow elaborates a number of these issues regarding various transformational grammar models. It also provides a very good discussion of the true import of weak generative capacity and can serve as another introductory article to this entire collection of papers.

Historically, the paper by Harman precedes the Peters-Ritchie result. Logically, it can be viewed as a complement, and perhaps even a follow-up to that result. It presents one of the first linguistically serious grammars based on modern phrase structure grammar without transformations.

The final paper by Geach presents an early and different view of a context-free type grammar model which laid much of the foundation for current categorial grammar models. This approach is more algebraic in nature than the context-free grammar model employing cancellation rules rather than rewrite rules, but it can be shown that this formalism can be modeled by a context-free grammar, at least with regard to weak generative capacity.

References

S. Peters and R. Ritchie, "On the Generative Power of Transformational Grammars," *Information and Control* **6**, (1973a) 49-83.

S. Peters and R. Ritchie, "Nonfiltering and Local-filtering Transformational Grammars," in J. Hintikka, J. Moravcsik, and P. Suppes (eds.), *Approaches to Natural Language*, (1973b), Reidel, Dordrecht, Holland.

Janet Dean Fodor

FORMAL LINGUISTICS AND FORMAL LOGIC

The recent, and apparently growing, trend among linguists to ransack textbooks of logic might be merely an intellectual fashion, destined like all fashions to fade. But it would be foolish, if not insulting, simply to dismiss it in this way, especially as the interest has not been entirely one-sided. Philosophers, too, are becoming increasingly keen, despite the inaccessibility of some of the material, to acquaint themselves with the results of linguistic research (see, for example, Vendler, 1967). When two disciplines start to become conscious of each other, this awareness may reveal something of interest about the nature of the problems, whether substantive or methodological, which they then find themselves confronting. The boundaries between disciplines are notoriously complex and untidy, and all we can hope to do here is to delineate roughly some of the many interconnexions between logic and linguistics, and then to consider to what extent and in what ways we might expect them to gain by contact with each other. And whether or not the benefits are really all on one side, we may perhaps, as linguists, be forgiven for revealing a selfish preoccupation with what the study of formal logic has to offer us.

It is not difficult to find parallels between a generative grammar of a natural language and a system of formal logic. The syntactic rules of a grammar license the move from one syntactic representation of a sentence to another just as the inference rules of logic (e.g. that 'P' can be inferred from 'P & Q') license the move from one logical formula to another. In both types of system the derivations are quite mechanical, in the sense that whether or not a certain rule applies to a formula can be determined by reference solely to the configuration of symbols in the formula and in the formal statement of the rule. Syntactic derivations therefore formally resemble proofs in logic, and, in line with this, the initial symbol 'S' of the

J. Lyons (Ed), *New Horizons in Linguistics*, 198-214, © 1970 Penguin Books, New York.

W. J. Savitch et al. (eds.), The Formal Complexity of Natural Language, 24–40.

base component of the grammar can be regarded as the analogue of the axioms of the system of logic. The surface structures generated by grammatical rules can be likened to the theorems of a logical system. Despite certain differences (such as the absence in a logical system of the distinction between terminal and non-terminal vocabularies, which is usually made in grammatical systems) both surface structures and theorems are what result when the rules of a system are applied to its axioms.

These parallels could probably be extended, but they are not especially interesting. Any two axiomatic systems will show formal similarities of this kind. In fact even for chess there is an 'axiom' (the initial positioning of pieces on the board) and a set of 'transformational rules' which license moves from one configuration of the pieces to another. More revealing of the relationship between grammars and systems of logic is a comparison of the *functions* of the representations and rules which the two types of system employ. Logical inference rules map formulae into formulae, preserving truth: a false statement must never be derivable from a true one. The mapping which syntactic rules produce might be said to preserve grammatically, although we should have to be quite ingenious in framing our definition of grammaticality for this assertion to have a clear sense. In a grammar of the kind envisaged by Katz & Postal (1964), in which deep syntactic structures contain all that is relevant to the semantic interpretation of sentences, the transformational rules of the syntax preserve meaning, and therefore *a fortiori* preserve truth, but still it is not clear what phrase-structure rules could be said to preserve. In any case, the primary function of syntactic rules is to define the grammatical sentences of a language. The set of well-formed formulae of a system of logic also constitutes a language, an artificial language, explicitly designed, often for some special purpose, and far more restricted in its scope than a natural language such as English or Latin or Vietnamese. It is what are called the formation rules of the logical system that define which of all possible strings of symbols are to count as grammatical in this abstract language, and it is therefore these rules which are the functional counterpart of the syntactical rules of a linguistic system. Although we have called them formation rules, they are usually framed as conditions in the following form:

if so-and-so is a well-formed formula, then such-and-such is also a well-formed formula. There must also, of course, be at least one non-conditional definition of a well-formed formula so that these recursive rules have somewhere to start from. For example one statement of the formation rules of the propositional calculus contains, among others, the rules:

Any propositional variable (i.e. 'P', 'Q', 'R',...) is a well-formed formula (abbreviated to *wff*).
If 'P' is a *wff*, then '~P' is a *wff*.
If 'P' and 'Q' are both *wffs*, then 'P & Q' is a *wff*.

We shall discuss formation rules and compare them with phrase-structure and syntactic-transformation rules in more detail later on. For the moment we should simply note that, as far as their function is concerned, it is the formation rules, and not the inference rules, of a system of logic which are the counterpart of syntactic rules in linguistic descriptions.

   Is there, then, any counterpart in a grammar to the inference rules of logical systems? It might be thought that the answer to this should be 'no', on the grounds that inference rules are concerned with deduction, with the validity of types of argument, and most linguists would agree that the way in which people use the sentences of their language for the purposes of argumentation is not a question which falls strictly within the domain of linguistics, and is certainly not something that we should expect the grammar of a language to characterize. Nevertheless, even though we still know very little about the proper organization of the semantic component of a grammar, it is arguable that something along the lines of inference rules will play a part in a complete description of a natural language. One of the things that a complete description must contain is a specification of the meaning of each grammatical sentence, and, as Strawson says, 'To know the meaning of a ...["statement-making" sentence] is to know under what conditions someone who used it would be making a true statement; to *explain* the meaning is to *say* what these conditions are. One way of giving a partial account of these conditions is to say what some of the entailments of the sentence are' (Strawson, 1952). (Strawson makes it clear that this account must be adapted appropriately to cover sentences which are used to give orders, ask questions, make promises, and so on, as well as those used to make assertions.) It is thus reasonable to suppose that the semantic component must provide representations of sentences which determine the entailments of these sentences. But, since the entailments of a sentence may be infinite, these representations cannot consist of an *enumeration* of the entailments, and the semantic component will have to contain rules corresponding to the inference rules of logic, which will generate the set of entailments from some finite, formulaic representation of a sentence. Beyond this, there is very little to be said at present. Whether or not, for example, there should be a distinct 'logical component' or whether these rules will be an integral part of the semantic component, is a question that we cannot begin to answer until we know a good deal more about other aspects of the semantic component than we do at present.

The meanings which logical symbols have, by virtue of the way they interact with formal inference rules to determine entailments, do not necessarily define one unique interpretation for the formulae of the system. Within the constraints imposed by the nature of inference rules, the system may be susceptible of a number of distinct interpretations, and other rules ('semantical rules') have to be given in order to specify such an interpretation. Putting together all of these observations, then, we can say that linguistic descriptions and logical systems both contain rules which define a set of well-formed strings of the symbols in their respective vocabularies, and both contain rules which provide interpretations for each of these strings. The two types of system might therefore be viewed as doing much the same kind of job, although for different kinds of language. The logician may first devise a system of rules and then study the language which they define, while the linguist constructs his rules so that they define the language which he has decided to study, but both are concerned with a formal statement of the syntax and semantics of a language, whether it be a natural or an artificial one.

Can we, then, say anything revealing about the relationship between the two types of language? We have already seen that systems of formal logic cover a much narrower range of meaning than natural languages. Far fewer semantic distinctions and semantic relationships can be expressed in logical formulae than in the sentences of English, for example. What is gained in return for this restriction of the expressive range of the language studied is determinacy and generality of the relationships within that range. But although the systems of logic which have so far been devised and studied are in fact limited in range, it is not clear that there is in principle any limit to the aspects of meaning which a system of logic *could* represent. Recently, for example, systems which take account of the tense and modality of verbs have been developed (see Prior, 1968; Lewis & Langford, 1959; Hughes & Cresswell, 1968), although previously the effects of these upon the entailments of sentences had to be handled intuitively or not at all. Logicians are generally not interested in the meanings of lexical items, such as *dog, tarnished, wrestle*, but only in some 'grammatical' words like *and, or, if, not, all, the*. The tendency is very naturally to concentrate upon those features which are most general and not limited to discourse on particular topics, such as hi-fi systems or trout fishing, but which keep recurring in discourse on all subjects. Also quite naturally, the logician tends to study those aspects of meaning which are of general philosophical interest. It is not surprising to find that there is a logical system designed to explicate the logical behaviour of the words *necessary* and *possible*, or of *know* and *believe* (Hintikka, 1962), but no system, so far, concerned with the behaviour of the words *finger* and *toe*.

Logicians are anxious not to be confused with lexicographers, but the words *know* and *believe* will, surely, if there is any real distinction to be made between 'lexical' and 'grammatical' words, fall into the former category. In any case, certain aspects of the meanings of other lexical items have long been accepted as legitimate topics for the logician to study; for example, the various properties of relational terms -- transitivity, reflexiveness, symmetry. These properties are important in determining the set of valid arguments into which a relational term can enter. The argument *John is related to Mary, therefore Mary is related to John* is a valid argument, but *John is the father of Mary, therefore Mary is the father of John* is not. To describe the logic of relational words does not, it is true, involve giving a complete analysis of their lexical content, but it does require that some particular aspects or 'components' of their meaning are abstracted out and represented explicitly so that the inference rules can apply to them. It is often said that logic is only interested in the entailments which sentences have by virtue of their form and not of their content, but there are no special syntactic properties of relational words in English from which we could read off such properties as transitivity or reflexiveness. We simply have to consider the meaning of each word and decide into which sub-class it falls. Furthermore these properties are not usually expressed in logic by any interesting configurational property of formulae but simply by means of subscripts on the symbol standing for a relational word. Since it is always possible to represent 'content' as 'form' by some minor notational elaboration such as this, the content-form distinction does not effectively exclude any semantic fact from representation in logical formulae.

If no aspects of the meanings of words are *in principle* excluded from consideration by the logician, but at worst are low on his list of priorities because they are neither very general nor philosophically interesting, then it is no longer so obvious that there is a difference between the types of language which are studied in linguistics and in logic. The logician begins by singling out some small area to which he can approximate with quite simple and general representations and rules, and then slowly extends his compass from there to other areas of the language and to the finer details of those he has already studied. The linguist confronts the whole vast tangle of a natural language head on, extracts certain superficial regularities, and works back from there into the problems that arise in connexion with abstract underlying syntactic and semantic patterning. It is pleasant to dream that on one glorious day they will meet in the middle and between them have solved all the puzzles about the nature of language.

It hardly needs saying that this account of the relationship between the two subjects is an oversimplification. Some logicians would argue that ordinary conversational language is so fuzzy, so vague, imprecise, or downright illogical, that it could never be completely described by a precise system of logical symbols and rules. Even the sentence connectives such as *and* and *or* in English carry implications which are either unsystematic or else difficult to capture in formal rules governing their counterparts in logical notation. (See Strawson, 1952: 78-92, for detailed comparisons.) On the other hand it has also been argued (by Grice, 1967) that these extra implications of the English words are to be explained by reference to the way in which the words are employed in actual conversation, and should not be included in a description of the meanings of the words themselves.

This may be the point at which to correct a misleading impression that may have been given in the preceding discussion. By no means all of formal logic is concerned with characterizing the logic of ordinary language. The development of modern symbolic logic has been intimately bound up with the desire to formalize the foundations of mathematics, and systems of logic were prized mostly for the light they could throw upon mathematical concepts. Logicians are also interested in formal logical systems for their own sake rather than for the sake of their applications. They are interested in determining and comparing general properties of different systems, such as consistency and completeness, in comparing the effect upon the set of theorems of adding or discarding some axiom or rule, and so on. This is exactly like the mathematical linguist who studies the general properties of types of grammar, how the set of sentences generated varies with the type of rule the grammar contains, and so on, with only a glancing interest in how these grammars relate to those of actual languages. Furthermore, even when a logician does set about characterizing some of the logical properties of a natural language, he may well go only a short way with this and devote most of his time and attention to the philosophical implications of the system he has constructed, such as the ontology it presupposes or its bearing upon some well-known paradox or philosophical puzzle. Other logicians (for example, Quine, 1960) see their task not as capturing the complex logic of ordinary language but as constructing some alternative to it, a consistent and precise language with which to supplant ordinary language for the purpose of serious talk on scientific matters. It must be emphasized, therefore, that both in what precedes and in what follows, our discussion of the relationship between linguistics and logic is confined to that corner of logical endeavor which is concerned with explicating the logical relationships exhibited in ordinary language. (For a classic study, see Reichenbach, 1947.)

There is one important way in which the languages studied in logic and linguistics do not coincide, even in principle. The formulae employed in logic are designed to represent the facts about the meaning of a sentence which are relevant to the validity of arguments in which the sentence occurs; it is often said that such a formula represents the 'logical form' of a sentence. Logical formulae cannot be representations of the sentences of a language in the sense of there being one symbol for each word of a surface structure, with configurations of words taken over unchanged as configurations of symbols -- or rather, if they were, then there would be no point at all in translating the sentences into a special logical notation. In actual fact, surface structures almost never express logical form unambiguously and perspicuously, and the systems of notation devised by logicians to make logical form explicit do serve a real purpose. The 'sentences' of the language studied by the logician, that is, the well-formed formulae of his system, are therefore not identical with the surface structures of a natural language. In one sense, logic is not concerned with surface structures at all, for statements about logical properties and relations are supposed to be independent of the facts about particular languages. An account of the logic of the words *believe* and *know*, for example, is not essentially connected with the English language, because for any language which happened to contain words meaning what *believe* and *know* mean in English, the logical behaviour of those words would be described by the systems of rules set up for *believe* and *know*. In this sense it is incidental to the logician exactly how the concepts and propositions he studies are expressed in any particular natural language, and, since surface structures are language-specific, logic is not essentially concerned with surface structures.

On the other hand, one reason given for studying formal logic is that it will enable us to assess the validity of ordinary everyday arguments which are not couched in logical symbols. First we translate the premises and conclusion of the informal argument into formal logical symbols, and then we apply the rules and principles of the logical system to determine whether the formula representing the conclusion is indeed entailed by the conjunction of the formulae representing the premises. But the ultimate usefulness of a system of formal logic in cutting through the uncertainties and unclarities of everyday reasoning will depend crucially upon how precisely the formulae of the logical system can be related to the sentences of the ordinary language. It is little use knowing that an argument expressed in formal notation is valid if we cannot be sure that we have translated correctly between the formulae it contains and the sentences of the informal argument whose validity we wish to assess.

No precise and explicit translation rules relating a natural language and a system of logic have ever been formulated. In logic textbooks the principles of translation are presented informally, and only general hints and rules of thumb are given. Formulae may be loosely associated with characteristic syntactic patterns, but these associations are intended only as a rough and ready guide, and the student must rely upon his own intuitions to supplement and correct them. He must decide for himself when a sentence is ambiguous, what its alternatives senses are, when two sentences are sufficiently similar in relevant respects to warrant representing both by the same propositional variable, how to supply the proper referent of a pronoun, and so on. The fact that generations of students in introductory logic courses have picked up the art of translation without too much difficulty suggests that the task of formulating an explicit set of translation rules is a possible one. It would be rather implausible to maintain that the implicit principles with which someone operates in exercising his skill at translation could never be explicitly characterized.

Nevertheless in carrying out such a translation one draws upon virtually everything one knows about one's language, one's knowledge of the meanings of words and also of how types of syntactic structure determine the way in which the meanings of words combine to define the meanings of phrases and sentences, and so we should not be surprised if it turns out that practically every rule of the grammar of the language must be known before the translation rules can be formally stated. This, of course, is where linguistics has something to contribute to logic, for in writing the grammar of a natural language, we peel away surface variations and ambiguities in sentence structure, and provide formal, explicit, and non-redundant representations of what we might call their 'real' structure. In these underlying structural representations, the grammatical relations which are relevant to meaning are marked, items which are relevant to interpretation but missing from surface structures are supplied, and various bits and pieces of surface structure which are irrelevant to meaning are omitted. A large part of the translation problem is thereby solved, for the logician can now relate his representations of logical form to these underlying structures, which do bear some consistent relationship to the meanings of sentences. He can leave it to the linguist to provide explicit rules which interrelate these structures with the apparently chaotic surface structures of the language.

There are those who are tempted to press this argument further and make a much stronger claim about the interrelationship of underlying linguistic structures and representations of logical form. In its broadest terms the purpose of a grammar is to correlate the meanings of sentences with their sounds. For this purpose we obviously need a representation of the meaning of each sentence and a representation of its pronunciation. The latter is a phonetic representation, and we know quite a lot both about what information it should contain and also about how this information should be expressed. At the other edge of the grammar, few linguists have ventured to specify even what kinds of information should be contained in a semantic representation, let alone in what form it should be expressed. We do know that semantic representations must be mappable, by a set of explicit, and preferably general, rules onto syntactic representations. But now the linguist confronted with the task of specifying these semantic representations and mapping rules seems to be in the same boat as the logician who has to provide translation rules between representations of logical form and syntactic structures - except, of course, that the logician already has his representations. He settled on these by considering certain entailment relationships between sentences and how to capture them in explicit inference rules, for since inference rules are structure-dependent, formulation of the rules will automatically determine how meanings are to be expressed structurally. The strong claim about the relationship between logical formulae and linguistic representations which one might be led to by these observations, is that representations of logical form are identical to the semantic representations of linguistic descriptions, and the translation rules which the logician must state to relate his formulae to sentences of a natural language are identical to the linguistic rules which map semantic representations onto syntactic ones.

The claim is therefore that logic and linguistics will converge not only in what facts about the meanings of sentences they represent, but also in the details of how they represent them. The primary concern of the logician is how these meaning representations interact with inference rules to determine entailment relations between sentences. The primary concern of the linguist is how meaning representations can be mapped onto syntactic and ultimately phonetic representations. The suggestion is that these two considerations will lead to the same conclusions about the form in which meanings should be stated.

Even in its strong form, however, this claim about the relationship between logical and linguistic representation is too vague to be assessed; for even if it is true that the semantic representations provided by a grammar will be identical to the formulae of a system of logic, this says very little until we specify *which* system of logic we have in mind. A number of logical systems have been formulated, and a great many others which no-one has in fact yet described are possible. Even if some could be excluded as obviously inappropriate for the representation of sentences of ordinary language, there will still be a choice to make. For the logician, the existence of more than one type of logical system dealing with the same subject matter is not disturbing (although he may be interested in comparing and contrasting some of their formal properties), but many linguists argue that there must be just one correct grammar for any language, and that, given any two proposals, it should be possible to determine which of them is the more correct, either on the basis of further empirical data, or else by reference to their relative simplicity or conformity to general universal principles concerning linguistic structures. If this is so, the linguist must at the very least *select* from among the various alternative systems which logicians make available, and even then there is no guarantee that the system which is best suited to his purposes has yet been formulated.

To add to this, it is not at all clear when two logical systems differ significantly and when their difference is merely a matter of using one notation rather than another completely equivalent to it. (Is there, for example, a significant difference between Polish notation and the familiar Russell-Whitehead notation for the propositional calculus? Presumably not. Is there a significant difference between a system which employs variables and a system, such as that devised by Quine (1966: 227-35), which uses instead a variety of operators on predicates to represent exactly the same aspects of meaning? Perhaps here there is a difference, but no-one has stated the criteria which are relevant to answering such questions.) The task of selecting the appropriate logical system for purposes of linguistic description is clearly going to be somewhat hampered if we cannot be sure when two logical systems are related in such a way that talk of selecting between them even makes sense. So, quite apart from the obvious fact that logicians have not yet invented formal notations for a vast number of semantic phenomena that would have to be accounted for in a complete linguistic description, the assumption that semantic representations are identical to representations of logical form merely imposes some rather general constraints on the nature of the semantic component, and tells us very little in practice about what semantic representations are like.

Nevertheless since something is always better than nothing and in the area of semantics we are preciously close to having nothing, a system of formal logic can serve as a very useful starting point in thinking about how to represent meaning in linguistic descriptions. By considering the ways in which the logical system both is and is not suitable as a model for linguistic description we may be led to some general conclusions about the kind of semantic representation that is required. How, then, would one set about evaluating a proposed system as a model for linguistic description? Possibly psychological data, if it were obtainable, should be regarded as relevant. It is not easy, though, to imagine what kinds of psychological observation would support even a relatively straightforward hypothesis about semantic structures. In logic, the symbol corresponding to the

English word *or* can be defined in terms of the ones which correspond to *and* and *not*. (Alternatively *and* can be defined in terms of *or* and *not*.) It is conceivable that some linguistic facts might be found which suggested that in the ultimate vocabulary of the semantic component of a linguistic description there is nothing corresponding to the logical symbol for *or*, disjunction being represented instead by the appropriate combination of conjunction and negation. But even if there were differences between *and*-sentences and *or*-sentences according to the various criteria for ease of comprehension or production, there would almost certainly be too many other explanations for such differences for any secure conclusions to be drawn about the psychological validity of a proposed semantic notation.

One criterion which will certainly be relevant to selecting the form in which semantic information is expressed is the simplicity of the rules which interrelate semantic representations and syntactic ones. At this point, however, we can no longer completely ignore, as we have up to now, the formal properties of the rules which effect this mapping, for example the difference between generative theories of semantics and interpretive theories (see above), or between theories which regard only deep structures as relevant to semantic interpretation and those in which surface structures are also interpreted, and so on. For the criterion of simplicity might favour different forms of semantic representation depending on how the mapping is defined in detail and evaluations of the respective merits of alternative proposals will therefore be relative to a particular linguistic theory. The important point, however, is that the form of semantic representations and the nature of the grammatical rules cannot be decided upon independently, any more than semantic representations and inference rules can be chosen independently.

As a simple illustration of this interdependence we may consider the consequences of assuming that the deep structures of a grammar may contain elements formally analogous to the quantifiers and variables of the predicate calculus. The predicate calculus is a well-developed branch of formal logic, and, especially with the extensions to it which are currently being studied, is probably the best candidate available at present as a model for linguistic description. It is therefore of interest to investigate some of the implications of assuming that deep structures resemble the formulae of this system.

It can be demonstrated, for example, that such structures could not be generated by means of a system of phrase-structure rules, at least on the reasonable assumption that one of the conditions these structures must meet is that no variable may be bound by more than one quantifier. The set of structures to be generated will thus contain those analogous to the formulae

> (x) Fx
> ($\exists$ x) (Fx & Gx)
> (x) ($\exists$ y) Rxy

etc., but none like

> (x) & ($\exists$ y) z
> F ($\exists$ x) y
> (x) ($\exists$ x) Fx
> ($\exists$ x) (Fx & (x) Gx).

If it is assumed that the base (or 'deep') structures of a natural language contain analogues to the quantifiers and variables of the predicate calculus, with scope defined as it is in the predicate calculus, then it follows that the rules of the base component must somehow impose this constraint. Any rule which has the effect of introducing a quantifier into a structure must be restricted in such a way that it does not do so when the variable that the quantifier would bind is already bound by some quantifier present in the string. This constraint cannot, however be stated within the format of phrase-structure rules.

Phrase-structure rules are of the form: **XAY** → **XZY** where **X**, **Y** and **Z** are variables ranging over strings of grammatical symbols, and A is a variable ranging over single grammatical symbols (see above, and cf. Postal, 1964a, Chapter 3, for some further constraints on phrase-structure rules). The point of the X and Y here is to specify the context in which the symbol A may be 'rewritten as' the string Z. (If X and Y are both

null, the rule is called a 'context-free phrase-structure rule': if either X or
Y is not null, the rule is called 'context-sensitive'.) The form of a phrase-
structure rule thus allows *positive* contextual restrictions - if such-and-such
a symbol (or symbols) is present in a given string, then the rule may apply
to that string. We cannot, however, with a rule of this form, require that
some symbol or other be *absent from* a string as a condition of the applicability of the rule. The only way in which a negative condition of this kind
could be stated is indirectly, by listing as positive contextual conditions
upon the applicability of the rule all contexts *other than* the one that has
to be excluded. Another way of putting this is to say that it is not possible
to indicate in a phrase-structure rule that it is debarred from applying in
some context; we can only state the contexts in which the rule does apply.

The condition mentioned above that is to be imposed upon rules
introducing quantifiers into base structures is a negative condition. A rule
may introduce a quantifier only if there is not already present in the structure some quantifier binding the variable it would bind. There is no way
of stating this condition if only positive contextual constraints can be
imposed. This can be demonstrated informally in the following way. To
state the condition using *positive* contextual specifications only would
require finding some symbol or set of symbols, say W, such that if W is
present in a string, then a rule which introduces a quantifier to bind some
variable v is applicable to that string. But there can be no such set of
symbols W. For the presence of W in a string must guarantee that the
position into which the quantifier is to be inserted is not within the scope
of a quantifier binding v. Otherwise the introduction of the quantifier
would be illegitimate, and W would not be doing the work required of it.
The rule may apply to any well-formed structure U containing W. But if
U is well-formed, so is, for example, the string (v)(U&Fv), or its analogue
in linguistic notation. This string also contains W since it contains U, but
it violates the constraint on the legitimate introduction of a quantifier over
the variable v, for the whole formula is within the scope of a quantifier
binding v. Therefore the presence of W is not, after all, a sufficient condition for the applicability of the rule. This argument holds however we
select W; therefore the constraint on quantifier introduction cannot be

stated using positive contextual conditions only, and therefore it cannot be stated in a phrase-structure rule.

To demonstrate that deep structures formally analogous to the formulae of the predicate calculus cannot be generated by a phrase structure system is not, of course, to demonstrate that such structures cannot be part of a linguistic description. What has been shown is simply that any grammar which does employ structures like these must also contain some more powerful type or rule which imposes the necessary constraints on variables and quantifiers. Within the framework of transformational grammar, there are in fact a number of ways in which this might be done. Quantifiers and variables might, for example, be treated as lexical items, to be introduced into structures by the lexical insertion transformation. If this transformation, as defined by Chomsky (1965), were extended somewhat in power, then it could be used to impose the necessary constraints on quantificational structures. Alternatively, deep structures containing redundant quantifiers might be generated by the phrase structure rules, but 'filtered out' at some point during the transformational derivation. Each of these approaches involves using a rule with transformational power to impose the constraints, and they are therefore not subject to the argument about phrase structure rules given above.

It is worth bearing in mind, however, the other alternative of giving up the hypothesis that quantifiers and their scope should be represented in the grammar of a natural language as they are in the predicate calculus. This is certainly an elegant system for representing scope relationships but it is not the only possible one, and some other might suit the needs of the linguist better. What we ultimately have to maximize is the simplicity and generality of the grammar as a whole, and we cannot automatically assume that any given system of logic, however simple and elegant it is in itself, will necessarily contribute to this.

References

Chomsky, N., *Aspects of the Theory of Syntax*, M.I.T. Press, Cambridge, Mass., 1965.

Grice, H. P., "Logic and Conversation", Unpublished MS. of the William James Lectures, Harvard University, 1967. (Partially printed as Grice (1975) and Grice (1978).)

Grice, H. P., "Logic and Conversation", In Cole, P. and J.L. Morgan (Eds.), *Syntax and Semantics 3: Speech Acts*, New York: Academic Press, 1975, 41-58.

Grice, H. P., "Further Notes on Logic and Conversation", In Cole, P. (Ed), *Syntax and Semantics 9: Pragmatics*, New York: Academic Press, 1978, 113-28.

Hintikka, J., *Knowledge and Belief.* New York: Cornell University Press, 1962.

Hughes, G.E. and J.J. Cresswell, *An Introduction to Modal Logic.* London: Methuen, 1968.

Katz, J. and Postal, P., *An Integrated Theory of Linguistic Descriptions.* (Research Monographs, 26). Cambridge, Mass.: M.I.T. Press, 1964.

Lewis, C.I. and C.H. Langford, *Symbolic Logic*, 2nd ed. New York: Dover Publications, 1959.

Prior, A.N., *Time and Modality*, 2nd Edition, Oxford: Clarendon Press, 1968.

Quine, W.V., *Words and Object*, Cambridge, Mass.: M.I.T. Press, 1960.

Quine, W.V., *Selected Logic Papers*, New York: Random House, 1966.

Reichenbach, H., *Elements of Symbolic Logic*, New York: Macmillan Co., 1947.

Strawson, P.F., *Introduction to Logical Theory*, London: Methuen, 1952.

Vendler, Z., *Linguistics in Philosophy*, New York: Cornell University Press, 1967.

Emmon Bach and William Marsh

AN ELEMENTARY PROOF OF
THE PETERS-RITCHIE THEOREM

0. Introduction

The mathematical results about various classes of transformational grammars continue to play a role in linguistic discussions. Peters and Ritchie
(1973a) proved that transformational grammars of the "standard" sort
with a context-sensitive base were equivalent to unrestricted rewriting systems (equivalently, Turing machines) in their weak generative capacity,
that is, that there was such a grammar for every recursively enumerable
language. The proof can be presented informally and is easy to grasp (see
Bach, 1974, for an informal presentation of the proof).

A further and stronger result was proved in Peters and Ritchie
(1971): Limiting the base to a context-free, finite state or even to a fixed
base makes no difference. A transformational grammar still has the unrestricted power of the most powerful systems studied in recursive function
theory (e.g. again Turing machines). This result is even more interesting
for linguistic theory than the previous one. In the first place, if you think
that the excessive power of transformational grammars is something to
worry about, then this result pinpoints just where the trouble lies. It is in
the transformational component of a standard grammar, since restricting
the base does not decrease the power of the system. Second, the result is
relevant to the idea that there is a universal set of base rules. This idea
was advanced by a number of linguists in the sixties and is still assumed in
some of the mathematical and empirical studies of learnability (Hamburger and Wexler, Culicover and Wexler). The result shows that it follows from the formal properties of the theory that there is such a base (in
fact, infinitely many) and that the hypothesis thus has no empirical content within a formalization of the standard theory.

In contrast to the proof of the first theorem, the proof of the fixed-
base theorem (as we may call it) is exceedingly complex and it is likely

41

W. J. Savitch et al. (eds.), The Formal Complexity of Natural Language, 41–55.

that many linguists simply have to take it on faith. The proof proceeds by constructing a complex transformation which, given an input containing all the elements of the basic vocabulary (plus some other junk), will imitate computations of a given Turing machine. The purpose of this paper is to present an alternative proof for the same result, but one which we feel is somewhat easier to grasp. The central idea of the proof is to set up a base component which generates deep structures that represent all possible computations by a Turing machine with a given vocabulary and then use transformations which are constructed to match the instructions of a given machine to cull out just those final strings which would be computed by the machine.

The theorem in question states that for any alphabet A there is a regular base B such that for any recursively enumerable set R in A* there is a transformational grammar which weakly generates R from B. For concreteness we will fix $A = \{0,1,\#\}$. We hope that our proof is easily accessible to anyone who knows what a transformation and a Turing machine are. Since we expect that most of our readers are linguists, we will provide some background on Turing machines, though for reasons of clarity and economy of presentation we will present this more as a review than an introduction to the material.

In Section 1 we recall, or rather, avoid, some standard definitions concerning Turing machines and give an example which will be carried through the paper. In Section 2 we present a grammar for our fixed regular base B. In Section 3 we define the transformational grammar which mimics our example Turing machine and in Section 4 prove the Peters-Ritchie theorem. We close with a few comments in Section 5.

1. Turing Machines

One of several provably equivalent definitions of the notion of algorithm was given by A. M. Turing in terms of very simple idealized computers, several years before the actual building of the first electronic computers. These "Turing machines" are myopic and methodical creatures which operate in a series of steps on a "tape" of "squares," each one of which contains one symbol from an alphabet or terminal vocabulary A; a single step is either a rewriting of a single symbol or a move to an adjacent square. Our machines can look at only one square at a time, and the step taken by the machine depends only on the symbol on that square and the "state" the machine is in; at the end of each step the machine moves into a (possibly) new state. Figure (1) illustrates a typical moment in the life of a Turing machine.

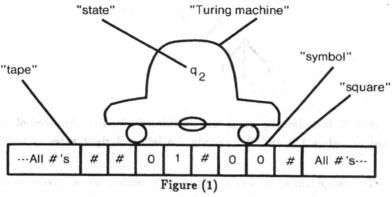

Figure (1)

Note that we include a # as a "blank" symbol, and picture the tape as being infinite in each direction, but all blanks after a certain point.

It is convenient to insert the state into the string being operated on just to the left of the symbol being considered and to describe the whole situation by the "configuration" (which we treat as a sentence);

$$\# \, 0 \, q_2 \, 1 \, \# \, 0 \, 0 \, \#.$$

We will modify this unspeakable sentence slightly and parse it

Note that q_3, for example, would be encoded by

and that C includes the state the machine is in and the symbol being looked at, while LT and RT encode the left and right sides of the tape respectively.

To recapitulate, a Turing machine's action at a given moment depends only on the state it's in and the symbol on the one square it can see; actions are limited to exactly one of

(1)   rewriting the symbol it sees,
(2)   moving one square to the left
(3)   moving one square to the right,

and (4)   stopping forever.

Thus we can describe a Turing machine as a set of quadruples, and we hereby introduce Charlie, our example Turing machine, and label each quadruple for future reference.

"Charlie" (a typical Turing machine)

(1)	q_0	#	0	q_1	(3)	q_0	1	R	q_0
(2)	q_0	0	L	q_0	(4)	q_1	0	R	q_1
					(5)	q_1	1	#	q_2

The first symbol is the state the machine is in before the action, the second the symbol it is looking at, the third encodes the action taken, and the fourth, the state the machine goes into. We will illustrate by giving three typical biographies or "computations" performed by Charlie, which vary depending on the world (i.e., tape) that he is thrust into.

Our three example worlds are #1#, #10#, and #010#. A Turing machine always starts life in state q_0 on the left-most non-# on a tape.

The first biography goes

$$\#1\# \rightarrow \#q_01\# \rightarrow \#1q_0\#\# \rightarrow \#1q_10\# \rightarrow 10q_1\#\# \#10\#$$

The second arrow shows an application of quadruple (3) (another # is added to the right end of the tape for convenience). The third arrow shows an application of (1) and the fourth, of (4). Since no quadruple begins with $q_1\#$, Charlie stops, and the last string shows how he has left the world.

While the life just portrayed is quite conservative, our next biography is of a typical liberal: Charlie lives forever, moving back and forth from left to right, but never accomplishes anything

$$\#10\# \rightarrow \#q_010\# \rightarrow \#1q_00\# \rightarrow \#q_010\# \rightarrow \ldots.$$

Our third biography turns out as a tragedy:

$$\#010\# \rightarrow \#q_0010\# \rightarrow \#q_0\#010\# \rightarrow \#q_10010\# \rightarrow$$
$$\#0q_1010\# \rightarrow \#00q_110\# \rightarrow \#00q_2\#0\# \rightarrow \#00\#0\#$$

The sadness lies in the fact that although Charlie stops, we have a convention that if a Turing machine leaves on "internal" blank on the tape, the string is "filtered."

We thus say that Charlie (1) = 10, read "Charlie of 1 is 0," but that Charlie (10) and Charlie (010) are undefined. We hope that the notions illustrated above are clear; we refer readers wanting formal definitions to Davis (1968).

Finally a set R of strings over A is called "recursively enumerable" if there is a Turing machine M such that R is the set of (unfiltered) outputs of computations by M beginning on strings of A* which aren't totally blank.

2. A Grammar for B

In this section we give a grammar for our fixed base language B, which the reader can check is the regular set

$$0\#1 \ (\#A^*0\#1(\#)^*A^*\#)^*$$

where the Kleene X* indicates the set of all strings - even the empty one - formed from the strings or symbols in X. The base structures encode all possible sequences of Turing machine configurations, among which are included all computations done by any Turing machine on any legal starting tape. The transformational grammar for a given machine M among other actions selects out from B only the computations M performs, making sure everything else in B ends up getting filtered. Our grammar, which uses the non-terminals S, LT, C, RT, Q, and BEG, contains the following sixteen rules:

$$
\begin{array}{lll}
S \rightarrow S \ LT \ C \ RT & LT \rightarrow \# & Q \rightarrow Q \# \\
S \rightarrow BEG \ LT \ C \ RT & RT \rightarrow \# & Q \rightarrow Q \# 1 \\
BEG \rightarrow 0 \# 1 & &
\end{array}
$$

$$
\left. \begin{array}{l}
LT \rightarrow LT \ a \\
RT \rightarrow a \ RT \\
C \rightarrow Q \ a
\end{array} \right\} \quad \left\{ \begin{array}{l}
\text{for all} \\
a \in V_T
\end{array} \right.
$$

3. Transformations

The transformational grammar which mimics a given Turing machine will have transformations of four classes: Beginning, Rewriting, Movement, and Ending, which appear in this order in the cycle. Beginning and Ending transformations apply only to sentences containing no embedded sentences, while the others apply only to sentences containing exactly one embedded sentence.

Proposition 1. It follows that if any cycle ends with an embedded sentence, no transformations will apply at higher cycles.

Before defining our transformations let us agree to use Q_i to denote

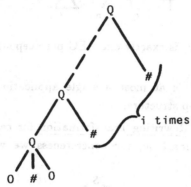

Our two <u>Beginning Transformations</u> will delete a BEG from deep structures that encode computations that start in q_0 at the leftmost non-blank symbol:

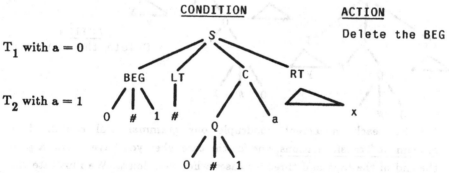

Since none of the other transformations to be introduced will apply to any sentence containing a BEG, it will follow that

Proposition 2. Deep structures whose deepest S do not encode proper Turing machine beginnings are filtered and in the others, the deepest S is left in the form

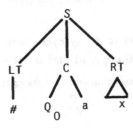

Note also that since there is exactly one BEG per deep structure, it follows that

Proposition 3. There is at most a single application of a Beginning Transformation to a deep structure.

There will be one <u>Rewriting Transformation</u> for each rewriting quadruple in the Turing machine; for concreteness we will give that for $q_0\#0q_1$.

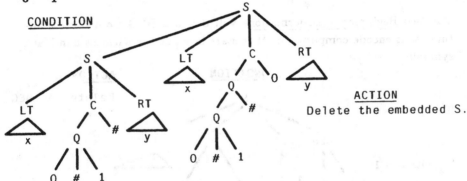

For each movement quadruple our grammar will contain four <u>Movement Transformations,</u> one for the case when you have to add a # to the end of the tape and three for cases when you don't. We illustrate the condition of these transformations for the quadruple $q_0 0Lq_0$; the actions are always deleting the embedded S.

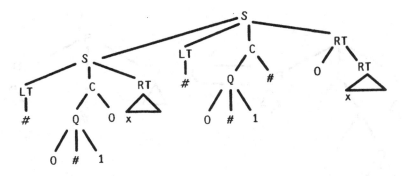

And for each a ∈ A,

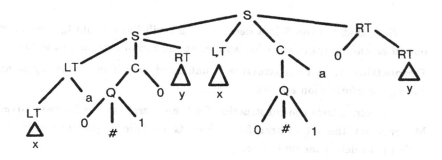

We wish to note the obvious

Proposition 4. (i) Rewriting and Movement Transformations apply only to sentences with exactly one embedded S; (ii) At most one of them can apply to any such sentence; (iii) If one does apply, it encodes exactly the correct action of the Turing machine being mimicked and leaves a sentence which encodes the result of that action (and contains, therefore, no embedded S).

Finally, there will be one <u>Ending Transformation</u> for each pair $q_i a$ where $a \in A$ and Q_i occurs in a quadruple in our machine but the machine contains no quadruple beginning with $q_i a$. For Charlie, $q_1 \#$ is a case in point and we put in the transformation

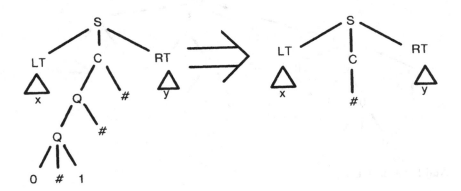

Note that the top S in a deep structure will have all its Q's removed only if an ending transformation applies at the end of its cycle, so we have

Proposition 5. A deep structure is unfiltered only if in its last cycle an ending transformation applies.

We summarize the construction for the general case as follows: Given M construct the set of transformations G as follows (in each case the action is to delete the underlined part).

I. For each $a \in V_T - \{\#\}$:

$$\underline{BEG\#}$$

II. For each quadruple $q_i abq_j$ in M:

$$\underline{LT \; Q_i \; a \; RT} \; LT \; Q_j \; b \; RT$$

III. For each quadruple $q_i aLq_j$ in M:
for each $b \in V_T$ (including #)

$$[Xb] \; Q_i \; a \; Y \; [X] \; Q_j \; b \; [a \; Y]$$
$$\underline{LT \qquad\;\; LT \quad\;\; RT}$$

IV. For each quadruple $q_i a R q_j$ in M:

    for each $b \in V_T$

    [X] Q_i a [bY] [Xa] Q_j b [Y]
    <u>LT   RT</u> LT   RT

V. For each quadruple $q_i a$ such that $q_i \in$ the set of states for M, $a \in V_T$, but there is no quadruple beginning $q_i a$ in M:

    LT $\underline{Q_i}$ a RT

4. Proof by Example

Consider the deep structure

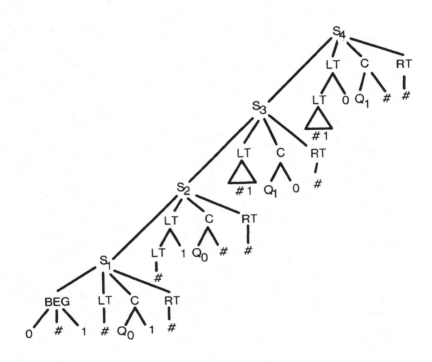

where we subscript S's for easy reference. Observe that T_2 and no other transformation applies to S_1; that the movement transformation that goes with $q_0 1 R q_0$ applies at S_2, deleting what was left of S_1; that the rewrite transformation we illustrated applies to S_3; and that a movement and then an ending transformation applies to S_4, leaving

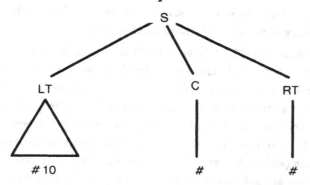

The extra "external" # doesn't hurt anything and the sentence is the output 10 = Charlie (1). Thus the transformational grammar exactly mimics the first example computation in Section 1.

To "see" that the G constructed for a machine M correctly models M, consider an arbitrary computation C by M on a string $\underline{x}$;

$$\# \underline{x} \# = \alpha_0 \to \alpha_1 \to \alpha_2 \to \dots. \to \alpha_n = \underline{y}.$$

Clearly there is a deep structure D which encodes C just as that beginning section 4 encoded our first example computation. Just as clearly, the appropriate transformations will apply one at a time to leave just y with possible extra #'s at each end of the cycle on the top-most S. On the other hand, by Propositions 2 and 5, only deep structures that begin and end correctly will be unfiltered by G; by Proposition 4 only Rewrite and Movement transformations that correctly encode M every apply; and by Proposition 1 if on any cycle no transformation applies the resulting sentence is filtered.

5. Comments

We close with a few comments on properties of the grammars that result from our construction and on the relation between the grammars and various constraints that have been suggested in the literature.

The grammar obeys the property of subjacency which has figured both in Chomsky's discussions of conditions on rules (e.g., 1973) and in the work of Wexler, Culicover, and Hamburger on learnability. Indeed, using a grammar which does obey this property simplifies the construction considerably. The result shows that subjacency has no effect on the weak generative capacity of the class of transformational grammars.

Peters and Ritchie (1973b) have investigated a class of grammars that they call "local-filtering" transformational grammars. Such grammars meet the restriction that all internal blocking symbols (##) must be removed from a structure at the end of the cycle on that structure. They show that this condition has an effect on the generative power of the system since the grammars will not now represent every recursively enumerable language (although they will represent some non-recursive languages). Our grammars are not local-filtering, obviously, but since they obey subadjacency are "local 1" filtering. This shows that relaxing local filtering to filtering with some fixed bound on the depth of the filtering gives you all the power of non-local-filtering grammars.

References

Bach, Emmon (1974). *Syntactic Theory*. New York.

Chomsky, Noam (1973). 'Conditions on Transformations.' In Stephen R. Anderson and Paul Kiparsky, eds., *A Festschrift for Moris Halls*.

Cullicover, Peter and Kenneth Wexler (1977). 'Some Syntactic Implications of a Theory of Language Learnability.' In P. W. Culicover, T. Wasow, and A. Akmajian: eds., *Formal Syntax*. New York.

Davis, Martin (1968). *Computability and Unsolvability.*. New York.

Hamburger, Henry and Kenneth N. Wexler (1973). 'Identifiability of a Class of Transformational Grammars.' In K. J. J. Hintikka, J. M. E. Moravcsik, and P. Suppes, eds., *Approaches to Natural Language*. Dordrecht.

Peters, P. S., Jr. and R. W. Ritchie (1971). 'On Restructing the Base Component of Transformational Grammars.' *Information and Control*, 18: 483-501.

Peters, Stanley and R. W. Ritchie (1973a). 'On the Generative Power of Transformational Grammars.' *Information Science*, 6: 49-83.

Peters, P. Stanley, Jr., and R. W. Ritchie (1973b). 'Nonfiltering and Local-filtering Transformational Grammars.' In K. J. Hintikka, J. M. E. Moravcsik, and P. Suppes, eds., *Approaches to Natural Language*. Dordrecht.

Thomas Wasow

ON CONSTRAINING THE CLASS OF
TRANSFORMATIONAL LANGUAGES*

1. Two Views of Constraints

The need to add constraints to the theory of transformational grammar
has been one (perhaps the) central goal of research by generative grammarians over the last decade. A number of important proposals have
resulted from this research, most notably those due to Bresnan (1976),
Chomsky (1973), Culicover and Wexler (1977), Emonds (1976), and Ross
(1967). The first section of this paper is devoted to distinguishing between
and considering the relative merits of two different views of the purpose of
such constraints. The second and third sections attempt to add substance
to my position by showing how progress towards the goals defended in the
first section can be achieved.

The key distinction I want to discuss in this paper is the difference
between restricting the class of grammars made available by a theory of
grammar and restricting the class of languages which can be generated by
the grammars the theory makes available. These are not equivalent. For
example, the literature provides two different characterizations of the
notion of a context sensitive grammar: one definition (e.g. Wall, 1972, p.
212) requires that each rewrite rule be of the form $xAy \rightarrow xwy$, where A is a
non-terminal symbol, x, y, and w are strings of terminal and/or nonterminal symbols, and w is non-null; the other definition (e.g., Hopcroft
and Ullman, 1969, p. 13) requires only that the right side of each rewrite
rule be no shorter than the left side. Clearly, the class of grammars permitted by the first definition is a proper subset of that permitted by the
second definition; but it is not difficult to prove that the two classes of
grammars generate the same class of languages (see Kuroda, 1964).[1] Or, to

Synthese 39 (1978) 81-104. All Rights Reserved.
Copyright © 1978 by D. Reidel Publishing Company, Dordrecht, Holland.

W. J. Savitch et al. (eds.), The Formal Complexity of Natural Language, 56–86.

pick a linguistically more interesting example, the class of transformational grammars, but not the class of languages generated, would be restricted by a constraint to the effect that no terminal symbol could be immediately dominated by a branching node; for if G is a grammar not satisfying the constraint, we can design a grammar G' which satisfies the constraint and generates the same language. This can be done as follows: for each terminal symbol, a, of G, (i) add a new non-terminal symbol A and a new base rule $A \rightarrow a$; and (ii) substitute 'A' for all occurrences of 'a' in the rules of G, except where a is deleted by a specified deletion. It is evident that G and G' will generate the same language, at least in any version of transformational grammar which has been proposed to date.

Although the class of grammars may be restricted without changing the class of languages, the converse is, of course, not true; that is, it is not possible to limit the class of languages without limiting the class of grammars. Thus, the goal of constraining the class of transformational languages is an inherently more ambitious one than that of constraining only the class of transformational grammars. We can now ask whether there is any reason to aspire to this more ambitious goal. Before responding affirmatively, I want to argue that the question posed is less esoteric than it appears, and that the answer that one gives to it will reflect one's fundamental conception of what generative grammar is about.

Why seek to constrain transformational theory at all? The answer lies in what Chomsky (1972b, p. 67) calls "the fundamental problem of linguistic theory", namely, that of accounting for the possibility of language acquisition. On the basis of exposure to a relatively small sample of a language, any normal child is able to attain mastery over the infinite set of sentences which constitute that language. Thus, the child "will know a great deal about phenomena to which he has never been exposed" (Chomsky, 1972a, p. 159). Furthermore, these phenomena "are not 'similar' or 'analogous' in any [as yet] well-defined sense to those to which he has been exposed. . .This disparity between knowledge and experience is perhaps the most striking fact about human language. To account for it is the central problem of linguistic theory" (Chomsky, 1972a, pp. 159-160). The problem, then, is basically the problem of induction: how do children choose among the infinitely many logically possible generalizations from the finite corpora of data to which they have been exposed at a given time? In the case of language learning, the problem is compounded by the striking contrast between the immense complexity of natural language, on the one hand, and the speed and ease with which language acquisition actually occurs, on the other.

Chomsky pointed out that this problem can be solved, if we attribute to children a powerful innate language-learning capacity. In Chomsky's words (1968, p. 60):

> A scientist who approaches phenomena of this sort without prejudice or dogma would conclude that the acquired knowledge must be determined in a rather specific way by intrinsic properties of mental organization. He would then set himself the task of discovering the innate ideas and principles that make such acquisition of knowledge possible.

Linguists working on the problem of constraining transformational theory have tended, I think, to view themselves as just such scientists.

Insofar as the acquisition of language is facilitated by innate mechanisms, these mechanisms will manifest themselves in what is acquired. Careful and detailed investigations into the structure of particular languages ought therefore to reveal the influence of the innate factors, in the form of universal principles governing the organization of grammars. This is what constraints are supposed to be, and it is the psychological claims connected with them that provide them with their significance.

In the above discussion, I have tried to remain neutral on the question of whether or not constraints ought to limit the class of languages which can be generated. Let us now consider how the different answers to this question bear on the psychological issues.

Consider first the position that it is sufficient to find limitations on the class of grammars, regardless of whether the limitations restrict the class of languages generated; I will call this 'the G-view'.[2] Grammars are descriptions of languages; constraints on grammars which do not constrain the set of languages generable limit only the sorts of description allowable.

Hence, if one wants to draw psychological conclusions from such constraints, one must assume that the linguists' grammars stand in a very close correspondence with portions of the speaker's mental representation of the language.

A brief digression on this latter notion is in order here. I am assuming (along with most current research on these questions) that use and understanding of a language can profitably be described at one level (see Osherson and Wasow, 1976) in computational terms, that is, as a series of decisions or information exchanges. If we wish to claim (as I think most psycholinguists do) that the language user actually performs those computations (unconsciously, for the most part), then each step must take some time. Hence, a crucial test of adequacy for such a model is its ability to make correct real-time predictions (though the diversity of factors which can influence real-time linguistic processing makes it quite hard to control tests of such predictions adequately). I further assume that it is possible to specify a set of algorithms, strategies, and/or heuristics which determines the course of these computations. Such a set is analogous to a computer program, in that it governs the computations which underlie the output; a mental program of this sort is what I mean by the phrases 'the speaker's mental representation of the language' and 'real-time process model'. Let us measure the 'psychological reality' of a grammar[3] by the degree of correspondence between it and the speaker's mental representation of the language.[4]

Various types of evidence can be adduced for evaluating the psychological reality of grammars. A minimal condition for the attribution of psychological reality to a grammar is that its assignments of grammaticality conform with the judgments of native speakers. There seems to be little disagreement on this point, so I need not dwell on it here. Stronger evidence for the psychological reality of a grammar could consist of demonstrations that some measure of complexity definable in terms of the grammar correlates well with observable psychological complexity. For example, if the grammar indicates that construction A is more complex that the construction B (say, because it involved additional rule applications), and it turned out that children consistently acquired construction A first, then this would lend support to claims of psychological reality (see C. Chomsky, 1969). Or, if a number of expressions in a child's language changed simultaneously, this could be taken as evidence for the psychological reality of a grammar that treated them as the same at some level. Evidence from problems in linguistic performance can be an indication of psychological complexity and hence of psychological reality of grammars. Thus, aphasia (e.g. Jakobson, 1941) and slips of the tongue (Fromkin, 1973) can lend support to claims of psychological reality. Finally, as indicated above, real-time tests provide the most versatile and potentially the most finely calibrated measure of complexity; hence, they also constitute the acid test for claims of psychological reality for grammars (provided, of course, that extragrammatical factors in psychological complexity can be controlled for). There are, then, various degrees of psychological reality which can be attributed to grammars, and various types of evidence bearing on such attributions.

Constraints on the form of linguists' grammars can tell us something about speakers' mental representations of languages only insofar as they are psychologically real, in the sense discussed above. Since it is surely some sort of real-time process model which the child develops in language acquisition, proponents of the G-view can claim that their constraints contribute to the solution of the problem of language acquisition only to the extent to which they assume that their grammars are psychologically real.

Consider now the alternative position, which I call 'the L-view'. The L-view advocates seeking constraints on grammars which will have the effect of limiting the class of transformational languages. Such constraints narrow the notion 'possible human language', thereby making claims about the limits of language acquisition, regardless of whether the grammars themselves have any psychological reality. A restriction on the class of languages constitutes a partial solution to the problem of language acquisition, irrespective of questions of psychological reality. Limitations on the class of languages provide boundary conditions on real-time process models, for the exclusion of certain languages necessarily excludes certain grammars. Hence, constraints which limit the class of languages generable must restrict the class of hypotheses available to the language learner.

Even more importantly, in my opinion, constraints which limit the class of languages make claims about the very fundamental question of human linguistic capacities (though without necessarily saying anything about how these capacities are implemented). A metaphor might be instructive here: one can describe the class of functions computable by means of a given computer without saying or knowing anything about its hardware or program.[5] In the case of the machine, such a description may be an essential part of characterizing what sort of device it is; similarly, I believe, a precise characterization of the class of 'possible human languages' would tell us something important about human nature. I emphasize that I view the formulation of such a characterization as a central goal for psycholinguists, quite independent of how useful it might turn out to be in the development of better real-time process models.

Given that the two conceptions of constraints are coupled with very different views of the relationship between linguistics and psychology, it is natural to ask which of these views holds more promise. It is my contention that the strong claims regarding psychological reality which the G-view requires are quite implausible; hence, I adopt the L-view.

One initial cause of skepticism towards claims for the psychological reality of grammars is the lack of convincing psycholinguistic evidence in support of such claims. The last 15 years have seen investigators employ numerous experimental paradigms to test the match between the linguist's grammars and the mental operations involved in language use. The results of such work should not encourage proponents of the G-view (see Fodor et al., 1974 for a summary of these results). Of course, the G-view advocate could argue that the experiments were poorly constructed, or that the grammars on which they were based were inadequate, even on purely linguistic grounds. Be that as it may, the relevant psycholinguistic literature cannot be said to provide support for the G-view.

Even on a priori grounds, however, it is unreasonable to expect the sort of grammars that linguists construct to be psychologically real, in the sense in which I have been using that phrase. Linguists formulate grammars on the basis of judgments of grammaticality[6] - in other words, on the basis of facts about the language. The grammar, as I stated above, is a means of describing the language, and it is always possible to describe any language in many different ways, i.e., there are many different grammars for the same language, some of them more psychologically real than others. I claim that there is no way of inferring what descriptions speakers in fact employ in their use of language, other than from evidence about actual use, viz., the types of psycholinguistic evidence discussed above. Again, the computer metaphor can be instructive. Suppose we feed positive integers into our hypothetical computer, and it responds by printing out, for each input, the number which is the sum of all the positive integers less than or equal to the input number. We can easily write many different 'grammars' for the 'language' generated by the machine. In the absence of additional evidence about the machine's behavior, there is no way of knowing what sort of procedure it is actually using in its computations. It might, for example, simply add up all the numbers in question; alternatively, it might multiply the input number by its successor and divide by two. Additional evidence might help us eliminate one of these hypotheses: for example, suppose we find that the speed with which computers of this type complete computations is proportional to the number of elementary operations (of addition and multiplication) involved; if we discover further that the time it takes our computer to respond is not appreciably larger on large inputs than on small ones, then we can reasonably exclude the hypothesis that our machine actually adds all the integers together. Notice, however, that this real-time evidence required for eliminating one hypothesis about the 'psychologically real' algorithm is precisely analogous to the sort of psycholinguistic evidence which has *not* figured into the construction of existing fragments of generative grammars. I contend that there is no reason to think that the inference from purely linguistic evidence to the internal representation would be any more feasible in the case of humans than in the case of computers.[7]

Thus, it appears that the proponent of the G-view must be committed to the proposition that the sort of evidence which transformational grammarians rely on in practice is inadequate in principle for the achievement of their goals. Not wishing to allow such a serious disparity between the goals and the methods of generative grammar, I conclude that the *G*-view is to be rejected in favor of the *L*-view.

2. The Need for Limits on the Class of Languages

Having adopted the *L*-view, I have now committed myself to the position that constraints on grammars are likely to contribute to the solution of the 'fundamental problem' only if they restrict the class of languages which can be generated. I will therefore attempt to demonstrate that it is possible to discover plausible and linguistically interesting constraints which have the effect of limiting the class of transformational languages.[8]

The need for such a demonstration is accentuated by the fact that it is widely - but mistakenly - believed that the work of Peters and Ritchie (1971, 1973a) shows the theory of transformational grammar to be inherently universal in power, i.e., that it is impossible to restrict the class of transformational languages. Because of the widespread misunderstandings of the Peters and Ritchie results, it might be useful to insert a few remarks here about what this important work does and does not show, before turning to some suggestions regarding plausible grammatical constraints that will restrict the class of languages generable.

The most famous of the Peters and Ritchie results is a proof that a formalized version of the theory of grammar outlined in *Aspects of the Theory of Syntax* can provide a grammar for any recursively enumerable set. The heart of the proof (Peters and Ritchie, 1971, pp. 487-493) is the formulation of a transformation that will mimic the behavior of an arbitrary Turing machine. A subsequent lemma shows that this result holds even if the base component is a fixed regular grammar. Taken by themselves, these results suggest that transformational theory in its first ten years had made no progress towards specifying the class of possible human languages. It is less widely known, however, that Peters and Ritchie have explored at some length the question of what kinds of modifications of their formalized version of the *Aspects* theory would suffice to restrict the class of generable languages (see especially Peters and Ritchie (1973a, § 6) and 1973b)). For example, Peters and Ritchie (1973b) observe that the use made of the "filtering function of transformations" (see Chomsky,

1965, p. 139) is crucial to the correct operation of the transformation formulated by Peters and Ritchie (1971) which simulates Turing machines. Further, the way in which the filtering function is employed in that proof is essentially more powerful than any proposed use of it for describing natural languages; and, as Peters and Ritchie observe, there is no known motivation for permitting the more powerful type of filtering used in their 1971 proof. More specifically, Peters and Ritchie (1973b, pp. 186-193) prove that there are recursively enumerable sets for which no (context-free based) transformational grammar can be constructed, if the *Aspects* theory is modified in such a way as to require that filtering is performed cyclically, rather than at surface structure. Indeed, Peters and Ritchie (1973b) show that such a version of transformational grammar excludes certain context sensitive languages (though it allows other languages which are not context sensitive, or even recursive).

I find this result very encouraging, for it shows that limitations on the generative capacity of transformational grammars can be attained without sacrificing any formal devices required for the description of actual languages. I am further encouraged by the fact that the class of languages allowed by this modified *Aspects* theory "does not fit into well-known hierarchies of languages" (Peters and Ritchie, 1973b, p. 186); neither is the class of possible human language likely to fit into these hierarchies, since any class of languages high enough on the hierarchies to include all the human languages will also include many languages which are not plausible candidates for human languages, e.g., finite languages, or Peters and Ritchie's (1973b, p. 184) language $L_{e_2} = \{a^n | \; n = 2^{2^m}, \; m \geqslant 0\}$ (which, though context sensitive, is not generable by a 'local filtering' transformational grammar). Thus, the version of transformational grammar investigated by Peters and Ritchie (1973b) seems to constitute a step in the right direction.

Still, further restrictions on the class of transformational languages are necessary before the theory of transformational grammar can be taken seriously as a characterization of 'possible human language'. There are two ways in which the theory is insufficiently restrictive: it provides grammars for languages which are (intuitively speaking) too complex to be human languages, and it provides grammars for languages which are not complex enough to be human languages.

Taking the latter point first, I contend that languages must exceed some lower limit of complexity in order to qualify as 'possible human languages'. I believe, for example, that linguistic theory should exclude finite sets from the class of languages it can provide grammars for. Similarly, while mirror-image languages are context-free (and hence quite low on existing hierarchies), they are probably not possible human languages. Since the class of languages generated by local-filtering transformational grammars includes all context-free languages (and, hence, all finite sets), I believe it is in need of further constraints. The present paper contains no specific proposals for setting such a lower limit on complexity for possible human languages.

Turning now to the other sort of case, it would seem that non-recursive sets are not possible human languages[9] for reasons first noted by Putnam (1961). Chief among these reasons is what Putnam calls "the self-containedness of language", that is, the ability of all normal humans to arrive at judgments regarding the grammaticality of strings of words from their native language "without reliance on extralinguistic contexts" (Putnam, 1961, p. 99). Taken together with the computational model of mental processes which has come to dominate cognitive psychology (and which I equate with what Putnam refers to as his "over-all mechanistic view of the brain"), the ability of humans to classify sentences into grammatical and ungrammatical without requiring any additional data implies that natural languages are recursive sets.

Notice, incidentally, that the ability of speakers to make finer judgments than simple 'grammatical' or 'ungrammatical', i.e., the existence of degrees of grammaticality (or "squishiness", as Ross would term it), does not undermine this argument, so long as speakers have definite judgments. What would constitute a counterexample is a string of words regarding whose grammaticality speakers simply had no opinion, except when extralinguistic input was provided. I think Putnam is correct in supposing that such strings do not exist (ignoring such irrelevant extralinguistic factors as memory limitations).

This kind of consideration suggests that the theory of transformational grammar should include constraints which insure that only recursive sets will be generated. I emphasize, however, that the arguments given in Section I of this paper provide sufficient motivation for adopting any tenable restriction on the set of transformational languages. Putnam's observations only lend special emphasis to the desirability of finding constraints which will guarantee recursiveness. The rest of this paper will be devoted to considering how this might be achieved.

3. Ways of Restricting the Class of Transformational Languages

The groundwork for discovering the required constraints was laid by Peters and Ritchie (1973a, §6). After proving the excess power of the *Aspects* theory, Peters and Ritchie considered informally how a proof of recursiveness for some version of transformational grammar might proceed. It is easy to see how the sentences of any transformational language can be recursively enumerated: simply generate the possible base structures and run each of them through all possible transformational derivations, listing any sentences which result. This procedure will not serve as a decision procedure because, at any given time, we have no way of knowing whether a string which has not yet appeared on our list will eventually show up; thus only the language, and not its complement, will in general be enumerable in this manner. If, however, we had some effective way of associating with each string x that we want to test a natural number n_x, representing the maximum number of derivations we need to try before listing x as a non-sentence, then we would have a decision procedure. More specifically, consider the following notions, adapted from Peters and Ritchie's work.[10]

(1)   The c-depth of a given tree is the maximal number of cyclic nodes[11] on any branch of that tree (where a branch of a tree is a connected path through the tree between the root and a terminal node).

(2)   Measuring the size of a tree in terms of c-depth, the *cycling function*, f_G, of a transformational grammar, G, is defined as follows:

$$f_G(x) = \begin{cases} 0 \text{ if } x \text{ is not in } L(G), \text{ the language generated by } G \\ \text{the c-depth of the smallest base tree from which } x \text{ can} \\ \quad \text{be derived, if } x \text{ is in } L(G). \end{cases}$$

Peters (1973, p. 383) shows that, given $f_G(x)$, it is possible to compute a bound on the number of cyclic nodes in the smallest base tree from which x could be derived. Peters and Ritchie (1973a, Lemma 6.3) show that from this bound it is possible to compute a bound on the number of terminal nodes in the smallest base tree from which x could be derived. Hence, we can decide whether x is in $L(G)$ simply by running through all of the derivations on base structures with no more terminal nodes than the computed bound. Since there can be only finitely many such base structures (given Peters and Ritchie's, 1973a definition of "reduced well-formed labeled bracketing"), this procedure will be effective. Thus, $L(G)$ is recursive if f_G is bounded by a recursive function.[12] The problem, then is to find linguistically plausible grammatical constraints which will have the effect of insuring that f_G is so bounded for any choice of G. Since f_G relates the string to the size of its deep structure, it is clear that the crucial class of transformations needing constraints must be deletions.[13] This is of some interest in itself: it shows that some empirically motivated constraints will not help us to achieve recursiveness, since they do not restrict deletions. A notable instance is Emond's (1976) Structure Preserving Constraint.[14]

Another step towards finding grammatical constraints which would insure recursiveness was provided by some very interesting observations of Peters (1973). Peters noticed that, if the number of terminal nodes deleted on any cycle is less than the number of terminal nodes in the matrix of that cycle (that is, nodes in that cycle but no earlier one), then the c-depth of the smallest deep structure for a generable string must be less than the length of that string. To be a bit more precise, let us say (following Peters, 1973, p. 382) that a grammar has the *Survivor Property* if it meets the following condition: "if ϕ is the input domain of any cycle. . . and ψ is the output of that cycle, then ψ contains more terminal nodes than any subpart of ϕ on which the transformational cycle operated earlier in the derivation;" it is evident that, in a grammar, G, possessing the Survivor Property, $f_G(x) \leqslant l(x)$ for every string x (where $l(x)$ is the length of x). Hence, grammars possessing the Survivor Property generate only recursive languages (since $l(x)$ is recursive). Peters (1973) claims that all existing transformational grammars do possess the Survivor Property (with a few minor exceptions which do not affect the proof of recursiveness); this suggests that we should seek constraints on grammars which will entail the Survivor Property.

It seems, however, that the Survivor Property does not hold in the grammar of English. Assuming that S and NP are cyclic nodes (see note 11), the standard derivations of the following examples will counter-exemplify the Survivor Property.

(3) $[_S [_{NP}$Students who need to _____] take remedial courses].

(4) $[_{NP}$Armenians $[_S$ I know _____]] love lamojens.

In (3), the output of the S cycle has seven terminal nodes, the same number as the output of the bracketed NP cycle; similarly, in (4), each bracketed cycle contains three terminals at its output.[15] Thus, it seems that constraints which entail the Survivor Property might be too restrictive.

Fortunately, a slightly weaker property than the Survivor Property will suffice for a proof of recursiveness. Adhering to the spirit of Peter's terminology, let us say that a grammar has the *Subsistence Property* if it satisfies (5):

(5)   If ϕ is the input domain of any cycle and ψ is the output of that cycle, then ψ contains no fewer terminal nodes than any subpart of ϕ on which the transformational cycle operated earlier in the derivation.

The Subsistence Property, then, is simply the Survivor Property with strict inequality changed to inequality or equality. It has been proved by Myhill (1976) that any grammar possessing the Subsistence Property will generate a recursive language. Hence, if we can find plausible constraints on the form of grammars which have the Subsistence Property as a consequence, we will have succeeded in excluding nonrecursive sets from the class of transformational languages.[16]

Let us now consider some candidates for constraints on grammars which will have the effect of limiting the class of languages which can be generated to recursive languages. An obvious proposal is simply to disallow deletion transformations.[17] In fact, Jackendoff (1969, p. 30) once put forward such a proposal on purely linguistic grounds. However, Jackendoff's alternative to deletion requires the addition of a rather rich set of filters (vis., his "rules of semantic interpretation"), which might very well affect generative capacity. Furthermore, I do not believe that this constraint is tenable. Convincing arguments for the existence of syntactic deletions have been put forward by Bresnan (1975, 1977), and by Sag (1976). Hence, rather than investigate the mathematics of Jackendoff's 'cut-free' system, I will turn to less radical constraints on deletions.

Transformational grammars permit two sorts of deletions: deletions under identity and deletions of specified terminal symbols (see, e.g., Peters and Ritchie, 1973a, p. 62). I will consider how various combinations of these two types of deletions might lead to violations of the Subsistence Property.

There is only one way in which a single application of a deletion under identity could lead to a violation of the Subsistence Property. It is best explained through an example. Consider (6), in which the C's are cyclic nodes and the t's are terminal nodes.

(6)

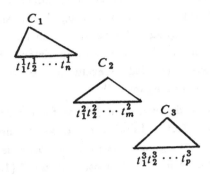

If, on the cycle determined by C_1, a transformation deletes $t^3_k \ldots t^3_{k+r}$ under identity with $t^2_j \ldots t^2_{j+r}$, where $r > n$, then the derivation will violate the Subsistence Property, for the number of terminals in the output of the C_1 cycle will be (at most) $n + m + p - r$, which is less than $m + p$, the number of terminals in C_2 at the input to the C_1 cycle. Of course, such a situation can arise only if the relevant deletion rule failed to apply on the C_2 cycle, in spite of the fact that all of the structure relevant to its operation is within the domain of the C_2 cycle. There is, however, an independently motivated constraint on grammars which rules out such derivations, namely, Chomsky's (1973, p. 243) Strict Cycle Condition, given here as (7).

(7)   No rule can apply to a domain dominated by a cyclic node A in such a way as to affect solely a subdomain of A dominated by a node B which is also a cyclic node.

Two words used in (7) are vague enough to require some further elaboration. First of all, it will not do for our purposes to take the word 'rule' as meaning 'transformation'. It would be possible to formulate a transformation which, say, permuted t^1_1 and t^1_2, while deleting $t^3_k \ldots t^3_{k+r}$ under identity with $t^2_j \ldots t^2_{j+r}$; by virtue of the permutation in C_1, this transformation would seem to obey (7) while still producing a violation of the Subsistence Property. Such cases can be ruled out if we interpret 'rule' in (7) as referring to elementary transformations (see Peters and Ritchie, 1973a, p. 59). The other vague term is 'affect'. As a working definition of this word, let us say that the elements affected are just those analyzed by one of its target predicates, in the sense of Bresnan (1976, p. 11). That is, the elements affected are, roughly speaking, those 'mentioned' by a deletion elementary transformation (including, under this formulation, both the pre-movement and post-movement position of moved items--see note 17). Thus, in particular, when something is deleted under identity, both the deleted material and the material 'controlling' the deletion are affected, in this sense. Rephrasing (7), then, we get (8).

(8) Let B be a cyclic node contained within another cyclic node A, and let T be an elementary transformation. T may not apply on the cycle determined by A in a manner such that the target predicates of T analyze only elements of B.

Notice, incidentally, that (8) does not require that any affected elements be strictly within the matrix cycle, i.e., in the current cycle but no earlier one. Condition (8) only rules out cases in which one earlier cycle contains all affected elements. Hence, cases like (9) are consistent with this interpretation of strict cyclicity, even though neither the deleted *VP* nor its antecedent is in the main clause on the earliest cycle where *VP* Deletion could occur.[18]

(9) [students [who can do the homework] help students [who can't do the homework]] $\Rightarrow$
Students who can do the homework help students who can't.

Notice, also, that such cases could never violate the Subsistence Property.

In short, a single application of a deletion under identity consistent with the Strict Cycle Condition (as reformulated in (8)) cannot violate the Subsistence Property.

The Subsistence Property could still be violated, however, by multiple deletions under identity on a single cycle.[19] Using figure (6) again suppose that both $t_i^2 \ldots t_{i+j}^2$ and $t_k^2 \ldots t_{k+j}^2$ are deleted under identity with $t_h^l \ldots t_{h+j}^l$ (on the C_1 cycle, of course), where $2j > n$. Then, at the end of the C_1 cycle, the number of terminals is $p+m+n-2j$, which is less than $p+m$, the number of terminals in C_2 prior to the C_1 cycle. Such violations of the Subsistence Property can be ruled out by a constraint like (10).[20]

(10) On any cycle, no more than one occurrence of a symbol may be deleted under identity with any given occurrence of that symbol.

(10) receives some independent empirical support from examples like (11).

(11) a. John is too intelligent to debate.
  b. John is ready to photograph.
  c. John is too nice to ask them to kill.
  d. John is weird enough to expect her to study.

Each of these sentences is ambiguous, in that *John* may be interpreted as coreferential with either the subject or the object of the infinitive. In many versions of transformational grammar, this ambiguity would be accounted for by postulating two derivations for each sentence. One derivation would involve deleting the complement subject under identity with the matrix subject (see, e.g., Rosenbaum, 1965), and the other would involve deleting the complement object under identity with the matrix subject (see Lasnik and Fiengo, 1974). In each sentence, then, the matrix subject can control deletion of either the complement subject or the complement object. What is important for present purposes is that none of the sentences in (11) has an interpretation under which *John* is coreferential with both the complement subject and the complement object. For example (11b) cannot mean that John is ready to photograph himself, and (11c) cannot mean that John would not ask them to kill him (John). In other words, while *John* can control deletion of either the complement subject or the complement object, it cannot control deletion of both in a single derivation. This is precisely what (10) requires. Hence, the lack of a third reading for the examples in (11) provides empirical support for (10).[21]

In a transformational grammar whose only deletions were deletions under identity, (8) and (10) would suffice to guarantee that the Subsistence Property held, and hence that the language generated was recursive. Let us now consider specified deletions, that is, deletions of specific lexical material mentioned in the structural conditions of the transformations.

There is only one way for specified deletions by themselves to violate the Subsistence Property, namely, by deleting more terminal symbols on a given cycle than are contained in the matrix of that cycle. For example, if $t_q^1 \ldots t_n^1$ and $t_1^2 \ldots t_r^2$ in (6) were deleted by specified deletions in the C_1 cycle, where $r > q$, then the Subsistence Property would be violated. This would be possible only if a specified deletion could delete material that was within the domain of an earlier cycle. The Strict Cycle Condition prevents this from happening, except where some of the deleted material is in the matrix cycle. Hence, specified deletions alone can violate the Subsistence Property only if some specified deletion applies to material on both sides of a cycle boundary. This possibility can be excluded by means of either (12) or the stronger (13).

(12) No string containing the boundary of a cyclic node may be affected by a specified deletion.

(13) No specified deletion may affect more than one terminal node.

The only potential counterexample to (12) in the literature is Performative Deletion (see Ross, 1970), which might be formulated so as to delete all of the matrix clause, plus the complementizer of the next clause down. Since I find the case for the existence of this rule singularly unpersuasive, I am quite willing to postulate a constraint which would rule it out in principle Further, Ross (1970) claims that Performative Deletion applies only once per derivation. As Peters (1973) observes, rules which can apply only once (i.e., 'root' transformations, in the sense of Emonds, 1976) will never lead to undecidability. Given a surface string and a finite list of root transformations (each one subject to the usual recoverability condition), it is clearly possible to compute a maximum size for the structure prior to the application of any of these rules. Hence, all of the constraints proposed can be weakened so as to apply only to cyclic (non-root) transformations without leading to non-recursiveness.

Given this observation, I believe that it is possible to strengthen (12) to (13). Aside from Performative Deletion, the only proposed counterexample to (13) I know of are *To Be* Deletion, 'Whiz Deletion', and Imperative Deletion. I have voiced my doubts about the existence of *To Be* Deletion elsewhere (Wasow, 1977), so I will say no more about it here; I am also skeptical about the existence of Whiz Deletion, for reasons given by Williams (1975). Imperative Deletion (see Akmajian and Heny, 1975) is a root transformation, and hence presents no problem.[22]

I have now exhibited constraints which will prevent the Subsistence Property from being violated either by deletions under identity or by specified deletions (except in the benign case of root transformations). What remains to be shown is how to prevent interactions of the two types of deletions from violating the Subsistence Property. This can occur if a specified deletion deletes material which has served as a controller for a deletion under identity. This can be illustrated using diagram (6) again: suppose $t_1^2 \ldots t_n^2$ are deleted under identity with $t_1^1 \ldots t_n^1$ (assuming $m \geqslant n$, of course), and then t_1^1 is deleted by a specified deletion. Then the number of terminal nodes remaining after the C_1 cycle will be $p + m - 1$, which is less than $p + m$, the number of terminal nodes in C_2 at the beginning of the C_1 cycle. In order to guarantee recursiveness of transformational languages, then, we will want to impose some constraint or constraints which will prevent this sort of interaction between the two kinds of deletions.

Because specified deletions play a relatively minor role in transformational analyses of actual languages, it is not difficult to formulate constraints that will have the effect of preventing the unwanted interactions. (14) is a candidate which strikes me as very natural.

(14) a.   Specified deletions may delete only grammatical formatives
(or 'function words'); and

   b.   Grammatical formatives may not be controllers for deletions under identity.

I think it is fair to say that something like (14) is widely
assumed by transformationalists. The only proposals I know of which
would involve the specified deletion of something which could control
a deletion under identity are, once again, Performative Deletion, Whiz
Deletion, and Imperative Deletion. As noted above, the first and last
of these can be accommodated by limiting the applicability of the constraints proposed here to cyclic transformations. I also noted that two
of these potential counterexamples are extremely questionable rules.

Although the notion 'grammatical formative' has never been
made precise, it does not matter for our purposes how it is ultimately
defined: conditions (8), (10), (12), and (14) will jointly guarantee
recursiveness on any definition of 'grammatical formative'.

My purpose in this section has been to argue that the goal of the
theory of generative grammar, on the L-view, is attainable. In other
words, I claim that it is possible to restrict substantially the class of
languages which transformational grammars can generate by means of
the sort of constraints on grammars which might be (and, in some
cases, have been) proposed for purely linguistic reasons. I offer the
results of Peters and Ritchie (1973b) concerning local-filtering grammars, together with the relative ease with which recursiveness of
transformational languages can be guaranteed, as evidence for my
claim (see Lapointe, 1977 for another set of constraints which will
suffice). It is of some interest that at least one of the new constraints
(viz., (10)) which has emerged from this attempt to restrict the class
of transformational languages serves to account for an otherwise unexplained set of facts about English. Thus, an unexpected dividend of
adopting the L-view may be the discovery of new constraints useful to

the working grammarian. I conclude, then, that the *L*-view of the goals of grammatical theory is preferable to the *G*-view, and that those goals are not unrealistically ambitious -- that is, that the program so conceived has realistic chances for success.

Footnotes

*A great many people have given me extremely valuable suggestions which affected the final form of this paper. I wish to especially thank Noam Chomsky and Dan Osherson both for getting me thinking about the issues in this paper in the way that I do, and for giving me very detailed and helpful comments on an earlier version of the paper. I am also indebted to the following people for useful comments: Emmon Bach, Eve Clark, Herb Clark, David Evans, Vicki Fromkin, Ron Kaplan, Steve Lapointe, Julius Moravcsik, Dick Oehrle, Barbara Partee, Bill Paxton, Stan Peters, Tom Roeper, Justine Stillings, and Steve Weisler. Any shortcomings are of course my responsibility.

1 Clearly, I am here concerned with 'weak generative capacity' (cf. Chomsky, 1965, p. 60), and this might be criticized as a linguistically uninteresting concern. Note, however, that two theories might differ in the grammars they allow and still be equivalent in strong generative capacity. For instance, the next example in the text seems to be such that the grammars allowed by the two theories provide each sentence with phrase markers which are identical in all linguistically interesting respects. More importantly, notice that any two theories allowing grammars for all recursively enumerable sets are identical in both strong and weak generative capacity.

2 I think that this view is the more common one among generativists who have thought about the issue. Chomsky has at times explicitly endorsed the *G*-view, but some of his work seems more equivocal on the subject:

It might conceivably turn out that this theory is extremely powerful (perhaps even universal, that is, equivalent in

generative capacity to the theory of Turing machines) [foot-
note omitted] along the dimension of weak generative capacity. It will not necessarily follow that it is very powerful
(and hence to be discounted) in the dimension which is ultimately of real empirical significance.
(Chomsky, 1965, p. 62)

The innate organizing principles severely limit the class of
possible languages.
(Chomsky, 1968, p. 50)

The child cannot know at birth which he is going to learn.
But he must 'know' that its grammar must be of a
predetermined form that excludes many imaginable
languages.
(Chomsky, 1968, p. 60).

there are innumerable 'imaginable' languages...that
are...not possible human languages in a psychologically
important sense, even though they are quite able, in principle, to express the entire content of any 'possible human
language'.
(Chomsky, 1970b, pp. viii-ix)

linguistic theory must...specify the notion 'human language'
in a narrow and restrictive fashion.
(Chomsky, 1972b, p. 67)

Reduction of the class of available grammars is the major
goal of linguistic theory...Note that reduction of the class of
grammars is not in itself an essential goal, nor is restriction
of the class of generable languages; it is the class of 'available' grammars that is important. We might in principle
achieve a very high degree of explanatory adequacy and a
far-reaching psychological theory of language growth even

with a theory that permitted a grammar for every recursively enumerable language.
(Chomsky, 1977, p. 125)

[3]Chomsky has often used the term 'grammar' ambiguously to mean
either the linguist's description of the language or the speaker's internal-
ized representation of it. He has, however, been careful to point out this
ambiguity (e.g., Chomsky, 1968, p. 58). I will limit my use of 'grammar'
to the linguist's description.

[4]I believe that this is a fair explication of the standard usage of the
term 'psychological reality' in current linguistic and psycholinguistic discussions, though I agree with Chomsky (1976b) that there are grounds for
questioning the appropriateness of the terminology. I realize, too, that the
notion 'degree of correspondence' is not fully clear. What I have in mind is
very roughly this: if a grammar constitutes an identifiable part of a real-
time process model, then it is psychologically real; if some elements of a
process model can be identified with portions of the grammar (e.g., if we
can identify separate syntactic, semantic, and phonological components in
both), then we can attribute some psychological reality to the grammar;
and if none of the structure of the grammar can be identified in a real-time
process model, then the grammar is psychologically unreal.

[5]Much the same point is made by Kac (1974) and Osherson and
Wasow (1976).

[6]Certain more or less precise notions about 'simplicity', 'evaluation',
'capturing linguistically significant generalizations', etc. also play a role, of
course. In general, these have also not been based on psycholinguistic evidence, so my remarks below apply even if we take these factors into
account.

[7]It is clear that many generativists would dispute this contention.
A particularly forceful statement of the opposing position is the following
quote from Katz (1964, p. 133):

The linguistic description and the procedures of sentence
production and recognition must correspond to independent
mechanisms in the brain. Componential distinctions

between the syntatctic, phonological, and semantic components must rest on relevant differences between three neural submechanisms of the mechanism which stores the linguistic description. The rules of each component must have their psychological reality in the input-output operations of the computing machinery of this mechanism.

[8]The skeptical reader might well ask what grounds there are for believing that the class of possible human languages is, in fact, restricted; for, as Ron Kaplan and Bill Paxton have pointed out to me, the facts of language acquisition do not suffice as an argument for the existence of restrictions on the class of languages. It seems to me that studies of language universals such as those of Greenberg (1963) and the Stanford Language Universals Project provide prima facie evidence for limitations on humanly possible languages. Other sorts of arguments will be cited below.

[9]Hintikka (1975) has argued that English is not recursively enumerable, much less recursive. Hintikka's claim, if correct, would render ill-conceived not only my claim in this paragraph, but the entire enterprise of generative grammar. I personally remain unconvinced by Hintikka's 'any thesis', which is an essential part of his argument; but discussion of that thesis in this paper would clearly take me too far afield. See Guttman and Stillings (in preparation) for another challenge to the claim that English is recursive.

[10]The definition of c-depth is derived from Peter's notion of S-depth (1973, p. 383); the definition of cycling function I give here differs in one or two respects from that given by Peters and Ritchie (1973a), but it conforms to that used in some of Peters and Ritchie's more recent work (except as noted in the next footnote).

[11]I use the notion of *cyclic node* throughout where Peters and Ritchie use S, in order to accommodate versions of the Extended Standard Theory incorporating cycles on non-sentential constituents (see Chomsky, 1970a, Akmajian, 1975).

[12]In fact, Peters and Ritchie (1973a) prove a good deal more about the relationship between $L(G)$ and f_G.

[13]The importance of constraining deletions was first noticed by Putnam (1961).

[14]Kravif (1974) made the same observation, and attempted to prove that a grammar obeying Emond's constraint could be constructed for any recursively enumerable set. Her proof makes use of some transformations which cannot be stated within the formalism of Peters and Ritchie (1973a), as well as some which violate the principle of recoverability of deletions (Peters and Ritchie, 1973a, p. 62), but I believe that her result is true, even when the formalism and principles of Peters and Ritchie (1973a) are strictly adhered to.

[15]In fairness to Peters (who did not allow for an NP cycle), it should be noted, first, that cases like (3) and (4) do not occur if S is the only cyclic node (due to the mysterious impossibility of derivations like (i)), and, second, that they do not seem to be able to 'cascade' to produce long sequences of cycles with no change in the number of terminals.

(i)   [$_S$[$_S$John's trying to make me mad] makes me mad] $\Longrightarrow\!\!\!\!\!/\Longrightarrow$
             John's trying to makes me mad.

Thus, it may well be possible to show that c-depth in natural languages is never more than double the length. Note, incidentally, that apparent counterexamples to the Survivor Property like (ii) can be eliminated if we assume that VP Deletion occurs on the S_2 cycle.

(ii)   [$_{S_1}$ The man who lost his wallet wanted [$_{S_2}$ the man who lost his wallet to lose his wallet]] <u>Equi</u> $\longrightarrow$
             [The man who lost his wallet wanted [to lose his wallet]]
             <u>VP Deletion</u> The man who lost his wallet wanted to.

[16]I will not consider here the possibility that the Subsistence Property should simply be added to the theory of transformational grammar as a universal constraint on derivations. My reason for ignoring such a proposal is that it is linguistically uninteresting - that is, there is no set of data which it would help us to account for. Rather, the sole purpose of such a constraint would be to limit the class of generable languages; as such, it would be of no more interest to the linguist than a constraint stipulating that only grammars of recursive languages are allowable. See

Lapointe (1977, section 2.1) for a more thorough discussion of this point.

[17]Putnam (1961) makes this suggestion. Note that it would require a modification of Peters and Ritchie's (1973a, p. 62) definition of transformations, since they treat movement transformations as copying followed by deletion.

[18]Chomsky (1973, p. 247) gives a second formulation of the Strict Cycle Condition which would rule out derivations like (9). Apparently, Chomsky took the two formulations to be equivalent, but (9) shows that they are not.

[19]I am grateful to Emmon Bach and Barbara Partee for pointing this out to me. An earlier draft of this paper had overlooked this fact.

[20]Notice that (10) does not prevent a single item from being moved twice in one cycle, since the copying component of each movement rule creates a new controller for the deletion component. It does, however, rule out using a moved item for the controller of a subsequent deletion. If such sequences are in fact possible, (10) could be restricted to 'true' deletions by the simple expedient of introducing a new movement elementary transformation.

[21]I know of one class of clear counterexamples to (10), namely so-called across-the-board deletions, e.g. (i).

(i) This is the book that Roy wrote_____, Ed edited_____, and Rob reviewed_____.

Interestingly, across-the-board deletions are problematical for another reason as well: a crucial step in the argument from the bounding of the cycling function to recursiveness (viz., the argument that no application of a deletion under identity can reduce length by more than half - cf. Peters and Ritchie (1973a, p. 80)) fails to go through if we allow across-the-board deletions. (I am indebted to Emmon Bach for pointing this out to me.) It will not be completely clear whether these problems can be overcome until an adequate formalization of such rules has been devised. I am optimistic, however, that they can be. My optimism is based on the following very informal considerations. Across-the-board deletions seem to apply only in islands, that is, in structures, which are impervious to virtually all other kinds of transformations (see Ross, 1967); hence, there is reason to believe that at least a fragment of each cyclic node must appear on the surface. But if the surface must contain both one copy of the deleted material and a piece of each cyclic node from which material was deleted, then a bound on the size of the pre-deletion structure is effectively computable, given the size of the surface string. Incidentally, it should be evident from the text that I assume (with standard accounts of transformational grammar) that each transformation applies at most once per cycle.

[22]Note also that there is some evidence for breaking Imperative Deletion into two parts, one deleting *you* and the other deleting *will*, thus bringing it into conformity with (13). The evidence consists of imperatives like (i) in which it appears that *will* but not *you* has been deleted.

(i)   You be careful (,won't you?).

References

Akmajian, A. 'More Evidence for the NP Cycle,' *Linguistic Inquiry* **6**, 115-129, 1975.

Akmajian, A. and Heny, F., *An Introduction to the Principles of Transformational Syntax*, MIT Press, Cambridge, Mass., 1975.

Bresnan, J., 'Comparative Deletion and Constraints on Transformations,' *Linguistic Analysis* 1, 25-74, 1975.

Bresnan, J., 'On the Form and Functioning of Transformations,' *Linguistic Inquiry* **7**, 3-40, 1976.

Bresnan, J., 'Variables in the Theory of Transformations,' in Culicover, Wasow, and Akmajian (1977).

Chomsky, C., *The Acquisition of Syntax in Children from Five to Ten*, MIT Press, Cambridge, Mass., 1969.

Chomsky, N., *Aspects of the Theory of Syntax*, MIT Press, Cambridge, Mass, 1965.

Chomsky, N., 'Language and the Mind', *Psychology Today*, 48-68, 1968.

Chomsky, N., 'Remarks on Nominalization', R. Jacobs and P. Rosenbaum, *Readings in English Transformational Grammar*, Ginn and Co., Waltham, Mass., 1970a.

Chomsky, N., Preface to *Introduction to Formal Grammars*, M. Gross and A. Lentin, Springer-Verlag, New York, 1970b.

Chomsky, N., *Language and Mind*, Harcourt, Brace, Jovanovich, New York, 1972a.

Chomsky, N., 'Some Empirical Issues in the Theory of Transformational Grammar', S. Peters, *The Goals of Linguistic Theory*, Prentice-Hall, Englewood Cliffs, NJ., 1972b.

Chomsky, N., 'Conditions on Transformations', S. Anderson and P. Kiparsky, *Festschrift for Morris Halle*, Holt, Rinehart, and Winston, New York, 1973.

Chomsky, N., 'On the Biological Basis of Language Capacities', ms., 1976.

Chomsky, N., 'On Wh-Movement', Culicover, Wasow, and Akmajian, 1977.

Culicover, P., T. Wasow, A. Akmajian, *Formal Syntax*, Academic Press, New York, 1977.

Culicover, P., K. Wexler, 'Some Syntactic Implications of a Theory of Language Learnability', Culicover, Wasow, and Akmajian (eds.), 1977.

Emonds, E., *A Transformational Approach to English Syntax*, Academic Press, New York, 1976.

Fodor, J., T. Bever, and M. Garrett, *The Psychology of Language*, McGraw-Hill, New York, 1974.

Fromkin, V., 'Slips of the Tongue', *Scientific American*, **229**, 110-117, 1973.

Greenberg, J., *Universals of Language*, MIT Press, Cambridge, Mass., 1963.

Guttman, S., J. Stillings, 'Some Formal Properties of Core Grammars with the Hypothesis of Indeterminacy', Dept. of Linguistics, U of Mass., Amherst, Mass., In preparation.

Hintikka, J., 'On the Limitations of Generative Grammar', *Proceedings of the Scandinavian Seminar on Philosophy of Language* 1, 1-92,Filosofiska forening & Filosofiska Institutionen vid Uppsala Universitet, Upsala, vol. 1, 1975.

Hopcroft, J., J. Ullman, *Formal Languages and their Relation to Automata*, Addison-Wesley, Reading, Mass., 1969.

Jackendoff, R., *Some Rules of Semantic Interpretation for English*, MIT dissertation, Cambridge, Mass., 1969.

Jakobson, R., *Child Language, Aphasia, and Phonological Universals*, Mouton, The Hague, 1941.

Kac, M., 'Autonomous Linguistics and Psycholinguistics', Linguistic Society of America summer meeting, 1974.

Katz, J. 'Mentalism in Linguistics', *Language* 40, 124-137, 1964.

Kravif, D., 'The Structure Preserving Constraint and the Universal Base Hypothesis', *Linguistics* 116, 21-48, 1974.

Kuroda, S.Y., 'Classes of Languages and Linear Bounded Automata', *Information and Control* 7, 207-223, 1964.

Lapointe, S., 'Recursiveness and Deletion', *Linguistic Analysis* 3, 227-266, 1977.

Lasnik, H., R. Fiengo, 'Complement Object Deletion', *Linguistic Inquiry* 5, 535-572, 1974.

Myhill, J., 'Transformational Grammars with Restricted Deletions', ms., 1976.

Osherson, D., T. Wasow, 'Task-Specificity and Species-Specificity in the Study of Language: A Methodological Note', *Cognition* 4, 202-214, 1976.

Peters, S., 'On Restricting Deletion Transformations', M. Gross, M. Halle, and M-P. Schützenberger, eds., *The Formal Analysis of Natural Language*, Mouton, The Hague, 1973.

Peters, S., R. Ritchie, 'On Restricting the Base Component of Transformational Grammars', *Information and Control* 18, 493-501, 1971.

Peters, S., R. Ritchie, 'On the Generative Power of Transformational Grammars', *Information Sciences* 6, 49-83, 1973a.

Peters, S., R. Ritchie, 'Nonfiltering and Local-filtering Transformational Grammars', J. Hintikka, J. Moravcsik and P. Suppes, eds., *Approaches to Natural Language*, Reidel, Dordrecht, Holland, 1973b.

Putnam, H., 'Some Issues in the Theory of Grammar', G. Harman, *On Noam Chomsky* (1974), Anchor Books, Garden City, New York, 1961.

Rosenbaum, P., *The Grammar of English Predicate Complement Constructions*, MIT Press, Cambridge, Mass., 1965.

Ross, J., *Constraints on Variables in Syntax*, MIT dissertation, Cambridge, Mass., 1967.

Ross, J., 'On Declarative Sentences', R. Jacobs and P. Rosenbaum, eds., *Readings in English Transformational Grammar*, Ginn and Co., Waltham, Mass., 1970.

Sag, I., 'Deletion and Logical Form', MIT dissertation, Cambridge, Mass., 1976.

Wall, R., *Introduction to Mathematical Linguistics*, Prentice-Hall, Englewood Cliffs, New Jersey, 1972.

Wasow, T., *Transformations and the Lexicon*, P. Culicover, T. Wasow, and A. Akmajian, eds., 1977.

Williams, E., 'Small Clauses in English', J. Kimball, ed., *Syntax and Semantics* 4, Academic Press, New York, 1975.

Gilbert H. Harman

GENERATIVE GRAMMARS WITHOUT TRANSFORMATION RULES

A Defense of Phrase Structure

1. Introduction and Summary.[1]

A phrase-structure grammar has been written which generates exactly the set of sentences generated by a fairly large transformational grammar written by Noam Chomsky.[2] The phrase structure version of Chomsky's grammar is included in the appendix. It is written in an abbreviated notation which is explained below.

Chomsky and others[3] have argued that a theory of language which supposes that the grammar of a natural language may be completely described by means of a phrase-structure grammar must be inadequate. They have also argued that no phrase-structure grammar will be adequate for giving a full grammatical description of sentences in English. Their arguments, however, have been based on a very particular definition of phrase-structure grammar which greatly restricts the amount of information supplied by such a grammar. In this paper, it is argued that there is no reason to place these restrictions on the notion of phrase-structure grammar and that, if Chomsky's conception is modified slightly to permit grammars of the type described in this paper, objections against the theory of such a grammar can be met. If this point can be shown, there is no need to introduce transformational rules into generative grammars of natural languages.

Chomsky's notion of 'levels of success' for grammatical description provides a convenient background for his critique of phrase structure. It

Language 39 (1963) 597-616. All Rights Reserved.
Copyright © 1963 by Linguistic Society of America.

W. J. Savitch et al. (eds.), *The Formal Complexity of Natural Language, 87–116.*

will be argued that the critique of phrase structure depends upon too narrow an interpretation; some natural modifications of Chomsky's strict interpretation will be defended. A small sample phrase-structure grammar, equivalent to part of Chomsky's in *Syntactic structure*, is given in the text. I conclude that the transformational grammar has no advantage over the phrase-structure grammar.

2. Levels of Success for Grammatical Description.

The background for the critique of phrase structure is based on Chomsky's *Syntactic structures* and a recent article.[4]

A grammar must be distinguished from a general theory of language. A grammar 'can be viewed as a device of some sort for producing the sentences of the language under analysis'.[5] That is, a grammar specifies the set of well-formed ('grammatical') sentences and indicates how each sentence is to be analyzed grammatically.

> More generally, linguists must be concerned with the problem of determining the fundamental underlying properties of successful grammars. The ultimate outcome of these investigations should be a theory of linguistic structure in which the descriptive devices utilized in particular grammars are presented and studied abstractly, with no specific reference to particular languages. One function of this theory is to provide a general method for selecting a grammar for each language given a corpus of sentences of this language.[6]

Having distinguished a grammar from the theory (in accordance with which the grammar was presumably constructed), we may turn to Chomsky's distinction between three levels of grammatical description.

> Within the framework outlined above, we can sketch various levels of success that might be attained by a grammatical description associated with a particular linguistic theory. The lowest level of success is achieved if the grammar presents the

observed, primary data correctly. A second and higher level of success is achieved when the grammar gives a correct account of the linguistic intuition of the native speaker, and specifies the observed data (in particular) in terms of significant generalizations that express underlying regularities in the language. A third and still higher level of success is achieved when the associated linguistic theory provides a general basis for selecting a grammar that achieves the second level of success over other grammars consistent with the relevant observed data that do not achieve this level of success. In this case, we can say that the linguistic theory in question suggests an explanation for the linguistic intuition of the native speaker. It can be interpreted as asserting that data of the observed kind will enable a speaker whose intrinsic capabilities are as represented in this general theory to construct for himself a grammar that characterizes exactly his linguistic intuition.

For later reference, let us refer to these roughly delimited levels of success as the levels of *Observational Adequacy, Descriptive Adequacy,* and *Explanatory Adequacy,* respectively.[7]

To claim that a certain type of grammar cannot achieve descriptive adequacy is to claim that there are certain real grammatical properties and relations which cannot be described in grammars of that type. If a theory of grammar lacks explanatory adequacy, then even if the grammar allows correct description, the theory provides no motivation[8] for the grammar to give the correct description rather than some incorrect description.

In considering the critique of phrase structure below, I will not discuss arguments purporting to show that phrase structure ultimately lacks observational adequacy. I will, instead, consider arguments that it must lack descriptive and explanatory adequacy, since these are the arguments that its opponents have depended on.

3. Critique of Phrase Structure.

Chomsky's argument against the theory of phrase structure involves two steps. The first depends upon an explicit formal definition of the sort of grammar which is to count as a phrase-structure grammar. This step properly includes a defense of the definition as a reasonable explication of a certain conception of grammar; otherwise the second step of the argument might turn out to be irrelevant. This second step consists in a proof that phrase-structure grammar, so defined, is defective on both the descriptive and the explanatory levels. Both steps are important, although in practice attention has been focused mainly on the second.

The first step, then, consists in finding a formal model for a certain type of linguistic description. 'Customarily, linguistic description on the syntactic level is formulated in terms of constituent analysis (parsing). We now ask what form of grammar is presupposed by description of this sort.'[9] In other words, the first step makes explicit 'the form of grammar associated with the theory of linguistic structure based upon constituent analysis'.[10]

Chomsky defines his model for this type of grammar in the following passage:[11]

A particularly simple assumption about the form of grammars...would be that each rule be an instruction of the form 'rewrite ϕ as ψ (symbolically, $\phi \to \psi$), where ϕ and ψ are strings of symbols. Given such a grammar, we say that σ' follows from σ if $\sigma = ... \phi ...$ and $\sigma' = ... \psi ...$, (that is, if σ' results from substitution of ψ for a certain occurrence of ϕ in σ), where $\phi \to \psi$ is a rule of grammar. We say that a sequence of strings $\sigma_1,...,\sigma_n$ is a ϕ-DERIVATION if $\phi = \sigma_1 = \sigma_1$ and for each i, σ_{i+1} follows from σ_i. A ϕ-derivation is TERMINATED if its final line contains no substring χ such that $\chi \to \omega$ is a rule. In particular, we will be interested in terminated #S#-derivations; that is, terminated derivations that begin with the string #S#.

Suppose that each syntactic rule $\phi \rightarrow \psi$ meets the additional condition that there is a single symbol A and a non-null string ω such that $\phi = \chi 1 A \chi 2$ and $\psi = \chi 1 \omega \chi 2$. This rule thus asserts that A can be rewritten ω (i.e., ω is of type A) when in the context $\chi_1 - \chi_2$, where χ_1 or χ_2 may of course, be null. A set of rules meeting this condition I will call a CONSTITUENT STRUCTURE GRAMMAR. If in each rule $\phi \rightarrow \psi$, ϕ is a single symbol, the grammar (and each rule) will be called CONTEXT-FREE; otherwise, CONTEXT-RESTRICTED.

Associated with every derivation in a constituent structure grammar will be a 'labelled tree diagram'.[12] A tree diagram of the derivation of a sentence graphically represents a grammatical analysis of the sentence into labelled phrases. As Chomsky has defined 'constituent structure', the grammar provides no more grammatical information about a sentence than is provided by the set of distinct labelled tree diagrams associated with the various possible derivations for that sentence. That is, the grammar can tell us about certain types of grammatical ambiguity (when the set of distinct tree diagrams has more than one element), and can also tell us the grammatical category of words and phrases, but cannot tell us more.

As Chomsky sees it, the theory of phrase structure is that constituent-structure grammars, as he has defined these, suffice for giving all the grammatical information about sentences in a language. He criticizes this theory on two counts, claiming that constituent-structure grammars of English must lack both descriptive and explanatory adequacy.

There are two ways in which it is supposed that constituent-structure grammars, as defined must fail to reach the level of descriptive adequacy. First, there are supposed to be cases in which these grammars impose 'more structure' than really exists. A purported example is the coordination involved in simple conjunction, where a phrase B, B, B, *and* B (with any number of B's) is of category A. Chomsky assumes that the correct representation of phrase structure for such phrases must be of the sort in Figure 1. But if this assumption is accepted, and if it is also true that the length of such conjunction is unbounded, then a constituent-structure grammar would require an infinite number of rules (A→B; A→B *and* B; A→B, B, *and* B; A→B, B, B, *and* B; etc.). But since a constituent-structure grammar is defined to have a finite number of rules, it cannot correctly represent the structure and must impose extra structure.[13]

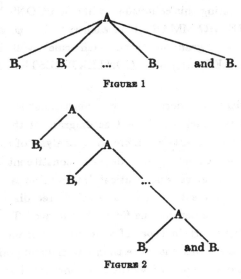

FIGURE 1

FIGURE 2

This first argument is not complete until the assumption mentioned above is proved. Without such proof, the argument remains incomplete, since it may turn out to be grammatically correct to assign extra structure to elements coordinated in conjunction. If in some way it were possible to prove the assumption, it would follow that this kind of grammar must impose extra structure, as in Figure 2, which by hypothesis is incorrect.

The second argument against constituent-structure grammar is more straightforward. It relies on the fact that there are kinds of grammatical properties and relations which a complete grammar of English should reveal but which cannot be mentioned in a constituent-structure grammar in Chomsky's sense. In other words, there are more grammatical properties and relations than are involved in classifying a word or phrase as of a certain grammatical category.

This is particularly clear for grammatical relations. A statement about grammatical category says that a given word or phrase belongs to a certain category, a relational statement says that one word or phrase bears some grammatical relation to another. it is logically true that there are relational statements which cannot be reduced to statements of category. F or example, to say that two sentences are related as active and passive is not to say that one is of the category of the other. The fact cannot be expressed in a constituent-structure grammar as Chomsky has defined it, since there is no way to represent this relation by means of a statement of the form: X is of grammatical category Y.[14]

Now consider a noun phrase like *the shooting of the hunters*. This phrase is ambiguous in a way which cannot be described in a constituent-structure grammar, since the ambiguity depends upon whether *hunters* is taken as subject or as object of *shoot*, and since there is no way to represent these possibilities as mere differences in grammatical category.[15]

On the other hand, it is possible to represent the ambiguity by allowing two different methods of generation for this phrase. Furthermore, the grammar might 'reveal' (without 'expressing') the difference between the two interpretations by means of appropriately named categories, e.g. Subject-Present-Participle and Object-Present-Participle. But, even though such revelation might be possible, the actual statement (that two sentences are related as active and passive) has no place in this type of grammar as Chomsky has defined it.

Hence, even though the first argument is incomplete, the second is enough to establish the conclusion that constituent-structure grammar, as Chomsky defines it, must fail to attain the level of descriptive adequacy.

Now, if a grammar must fail to give correct grammatical descriptions, it follows that the corresponding theory of grammar cannot motivate correct description. Since, however, questions of descriptive adequacy are sometimes confused with questions of explanatory adequacy, it will be worthwhile to examine a particular argument which shows that Chomsky's constituent structure lacks explanatory adequacy in at least one area where it attains descriptive adequacy.

Consider again the phrase *the shooting of the hunters.* It is possible to represent the fact that this phrase is ambiguous by providing for it two different methods of generation (two nonequivalent derivations). Even though this ambiguity may be expressed in a constituent-structure grammar, the theory of such a grammar, as Chomsky understands it, provides no motivation for allowing the grammar to express the ambiguity. Grammars which achieve some descriptive adequacy still fail to attain explanatory adequacy.

The theory of constituent structure (in Chomsky's sense) tells us to prefer a simpler grammar to a more complex one, and a grammar which reveals the ambiguity will be more complex because it contains more rules.[16] Since a constituent-structure grammarian cannot make use of various grammatical regularities in order to simplify his grammar, there is no motivation for revealing these regularities in the way that the grammar is written. This holds for instance for the active-passive relation and the handling of the auxiliary verb.[17] From the failure of phrase structure, thought to be shown in this way, it is inferred that transformation rules must be included in any adequate grammar.[18]

4. Rejection of the Critique.

In this section I will show the extent to which the critique of phrase structure depends upon placing unmotivated restrictions on the constituent-structure-grammar. I will suggest and defend some ways of relaxing these restrictions. In the next section I will discuss the theory which results from making these modifications.

Chomsky has placed unnecessary restrictions on his formal account of phrase-structure theory in at least four ways. First, the amount of grammatical information made available by a grammar has been restricted to information about the grammatical category of words and phrases. Hence any grammar which expresses more information, no matter how much it looks like a phrase-structure grammar in other respects, will not count as phrase structure. If we write the grammar in a notation which make it obvious that there is an active-passive relation between sentences, we still cannot allow this to be stated in the grammar; as soon as we allow this, it ceases to deal with constituent structure in Chomsky's sense.

Second, the rules in Chomsky's constituent-structure grammar permit only 'continuous phrases'. Such a grammar will be unable to show that some phrases are discontinuous, like *call...up* in *I called him up*.

Third, Chomsky puts two requirements on the grammar which together lead to unnecessary restrictions. These are that it must be possible to rewrite any symbol at any time that a rule applies (so that in general there will be a choice as to which symbol one wishes to rewrite next) and that the labeled tree must be recoverable from the 'derivation' as that has been defined.[19] From these two requirements Chomsky tries to argue that a constituent structure grammar must contain no deletes, i.e. rules of the form A → Ø, where X + Ø + Y is always the same as X + Y. The argument is, roughly, that given the string X + A + A + Y and the rule A → Ø to get the string X + A + Y, the tree is not uniquely recoverable, since the rule could have been applied to delete either of the A's, and since not enough information has been given to determine which of the A's actually was deleted. Of course this argument should only rule out deletes in special circumstances; but Chomsky takes it to be sufficient to rule out all deletion.

Fourth, it is assumed that the evaluation measure m for phrase-structure grammar will select the 'simplest' (i.e the shortest) constituent-structure grammar which generates all the sentences of some particular corpus or some particular language. Hence any theory not based upon this measure will not count for Chomsky as a theory of phrase structure. This last restriction is most severe, since the arguments concerning the level of explanatory adequacy all depend on the particular choice of an evaluation measure and since there is an unlimited number of possible measures which one might choose.

Once it is seen how the critique of phrase structure depends upon making very severe assumptions about the theory, it is possible to accept the critique as applying to what we may call the theory of restricted constituent-structure grammar, without questioning other more realistic theories of phrase-structure grammar. It does not matter that the theory of restricted constituent-structure is not adequate if some similar theory (with slightly different formal properties) is adequate.

I propose to show how Chomsky's conception of phrase structure may be modified in order to avoid the difficulties discussed.

First, it is irrational to restrict the amount of information expressed by the grammar to statements about grammatical category. The irrationality is dimly realized when phrase-structure grammars are allowed to express the fact that certain sentences are grammatically ambiguous by showing at least two distinct labelled tress for each.[20] Ambiguity is not a category in the way that *noun* is a category. But if phrase-structure grammars may express ambiguity, there is no reason why they should not be allowed to express other grammatical facts if there is some easy to make this possible.

I think that Chomsky would be willing to agree that there is no a-priori reason to limit the information made available by a phrase-structure grammar. The restriction must be based on a belief that there is no natural way in which certain grammatical information can be revealed by this kind of grammar. In his discussion of co-occurrence in 'The logical basis of linguistic theory'[21] he seems willing to accept a way of 'extending the definition of "grammatical relation" within the framework of phrase-structure theory if it could be shown that co-occurrence relations provide a workable method for such extension. To be sure, Chomsky rejects this particular proposal on the grounds that it is unworkable; but that he was willing to consider it suggests that he would be unwilling to place an a-priori limit on the information made available within the framework of phrase structure. To admit this is to give up any hope of finding a conclusive argument that phrase structure cannot reach the level of descriptive adequacy. The critique must rest on the claim that the theory cannot attain the level of explanatory adequacy.

We must also permit rules which generate discontinuous phrases. We must allow this, first, because it is clear that such phrases occur in natural languages. Second, Yngve has provided a neat formal apparatus for handling discontinuous elements within the framework of generative grammar.[22] And third, most recent conceptions of grammatical structure involve some notion of phrase structure with discontinuous elements; this point is demonstrated in considerable detail in a forthcoming work by Paul Postal.[23] A rejection of phrase structure which ignores discontinuities is thus pointless. Again I think that Chomsky implicitly acknowledges the point. In a footnote in *Syntactic structures* he suggests that 'extending' phrase structure to account for discontinuities would not affect the critique of phrase structure.[24]

Further, there is no reason to restrict the grammar by allowing no deletions. If we want them included in the grammar, there are several ways in which we can modify earlier restrictions so as to permit them. We can change the requirement that it must always be possible to explain any symbol in the string to which a rewriting rule applies. Instead, we may require that (say) the leftmost symbol which it is possible to explain must always be expanded first.[25] Or we can change the definition of 'derivation' so as to make it clear from the derivation what symbol has been expanded. (Or we can define a 'derivation' as a sequence of labeled trees.) In a word, all arguments that phrase structure grammars will not attain the level of descriptive adequacy can be met.

It may seem that if this is true in theory it is still untrue in practice, because of the great number of phrase-structure generation rules needed to generate all the sentences of a natural language. In *Syntactic structures*, Chapter 5, Chomsky has presented many examples of the rapid increase in the number of phrase-structure rules as more and more of English is accounted for. This is, as we have seen, the main basis for the claim that phrase-structure grammar cannot attain the level of explanatory adequacy. Even if we forget that argument for the moment, we must realize that each multiplication of the rules results in a multiplication of the practical difficulty of writing the rules down.

The proper answer to this practical problem is that it is only a technical difficulty. Being only technically a difficulty, it can be overcome by changing techniques. We require some technique which will enable us to write and grasp millions of rules at once; that is, we require a useful way of abbreviating large sets of rules.

I have already mentioned how a careful choice of notation helps enlarge the descriptive power of the grammar. For example, we may describe a category by means of a basic category notation 'NounPhrase' with several subscripts: 'NounPhrase/Subject, Present Participle', where the prior part of the label indicates the basic category and the rest indicates that the noun phrase is the subject of a nearby present participle. This use of subscripts in the basic notation leads to easy abbreviation. For example, X→Y + Z may abbreviate the set of rules with X (followed by any subscripts whatever) on the left side, indicating that it is to be rewritten as Y followed by Z, where Y and Z each are to retain the subscripts that occur with X. If a grammar allows such abbreviation and contains N possible subscripts, one abbreviated rule can stand for 2^N unabbreviated rules. This could easily cut down the number of rules to manageable size. (That this is in fact the case may been by comparing grammars below with their transformational counterparts).

To refute the charge that phrase-structure grammar must fail to attain the level of explanatory adequacy it is enough to point out, as I already have, how it depends upon a particular conception of the evaluation function m, namely shortness of the set of unabbreviated rules. It is true that the phrase structure grammarian limited to unabbreviated rules cannot capitalize on regularities in the language in order to shorten his set of rules; but if he uses some other method for selecting his grammar, this criticism cannot be used against him. In particular, regularities in the language will enable him to write a shorter set of rules if he uses the type of abbreviation just discussed. If he decides that the function m should select the grammar that is most easily abbreviated, he will have provided motivation for allowing the grammar to express certain regularities of the language and will be able to explain them.

5. Discontinuous-Constituent Phrase-Structure Grammar with Subscripts and Deletes.

This section describes the basic structure grammar and an abbreviated notation for the phrase-structure rules. An account is given of the information which the grammar makes available and the evaluation function m is defined. This is followed by a phrase-structure version of part of the grammar contained in the appendix to *Syntactic structures*, and the two versions of the grammar are compared.

The basic grammar uses generation rules adapted from rules suggested by Victor Yngve.[26] These rules are of two types:

(1) A = Z, where A is a single constituent and Z is a string of zero or more constituents separated by plus signs, e.g. A + B + C.

(2) A = X + ... +Y, where A is a single constituent and X and Y are strings of constituents separated by plus signs.

A generation rule is an instruction for rewriting a single constituent as a string of constituents. Initially this string consists of one constituent (the initial constituent). At each stage in the expansion of the string one must find the leftmost constituent to which at least one rewriting rule applies.[27]

Rules of type 1 instruct us to rewrite the constituent A by the string Z. Rules of type 2 instruct us to rewrite the constituent A by the string X and to insert the string Y after that constituent which follows A before the application of this rule to the string. If no constituent thus follows A, then the effect of a type-2 rule reduces to that of a rule of type 1.

Phrase-structure generation rules may also be written in a convenient abbreviated form. In the abbreviated set of generation rules, each constituent consists of a basic constituent followed after a slash (/) by an unordered sequence of zero or more (up to N for some finite N) subscripts. If the basic constituents are A, B, and C, and the possible subscripts are J, K, and L, there are 24 possible constituents: A/ (which we may represent as A alone); A/J; A/K; A/L; A/J,K (which is the same as A/K,J);...;B;B/J;...;C;...;C/J,K,L.

Generation rules:

$$S = A + B$$
$$A = A + D$$
$$A = E + \ldots + F$$
$$B = G + H$$
$$G = H + \ldots + I$$

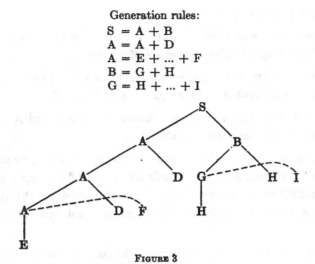

FIGURE 3

In an abbreviated phrase-structure generation rule A→Z or A→X + ... +Y, the symbol A represents any constituent with or without subscripts; X, Y, and Z are strings of 'elements' separated by plus signs. Each element is a basic constituent optionally followed after a slash by an unordered sequence of subscripts; a subscript in an element may be preceded by a minus sign; and the slash after an element may be followed by ERASE OTHERS.

The subscripts on A (at the left side of the rule) indicate where the rule is to apply; namely, to any constituent C such that A and C have the same basic constituent and such that C has at least every subscript on A.

C will be expanded into a possibly discontinuous sequence of constituents whose basic constituents correspond to the basic constituents of elements in the appropriate expansion rule. If an element does not contain the symbol ERASE OTHERS, we are to write the basic constituent of the element with all subscripts which occur on C, excepting only subscripts occurring on the element which are preceded by a minus sign. If the element contains a subscript G which is preceded by a minus sign, we are to delete G from the subscripts on the constituent if it occurs among these subscripts. If the element contains a subscript G not preceded by a minus sign, we are to add G to the subscript of the constituent we are writing. If the element contains the symbol ERASE OTHERS we are to write the subscripts only if they are contained in the element and are not preceded by a minus sign. A sample abbreviated grammar is given in Figure 4.

ABBREVIATED RULES

A	$\rightarrow$	B/ERASE OTHERS + B + C/ERASE OTHERS
A/J,K	$\rightarrow$	B +...+ B/ERASE OTHERS
B/L	$\rightarrow$	A/-L
B/K	$\rightarrow$	C/ERASE OTHERS + C

CORRESPONDING UNABBREVIATED RULES

$$A = B + B + C$$
$$A/J = B + B/J + C$$
$$A/J,K = B + B/J,K + C$$
...
$$A/J,K = B/J,K + ... + B$$
$$A/J,K,L = B/J,K,L + ... + B$$
$$B/L = A$$
$$B/J,L = A/J$$
$$B/K,L = A/K$$
...
$$B/K = C + C/K$$
$$B/K,L = C + C/K,L$$
$$B/J,K = C + C/J,K$$
$$B/J,K,L = C + C/J,K,L^{28}$$

Figure 4

The grammar will always be written in its abbreviated form.[29] Generally, it will turn out that we can separate those rules which are used to select subscripts (put restrictions on a phrase) from those which expand a constituent into several constituents on the basis of restrictions recorded in the subscripts. We can easily give grammatical meaning to the subscripts so used to select restrictions.

For instance,[30] if we distinguish a set of 'choice of restriction rules' from a set of 'choice of expansion rules' on the basis of the last paragraph, we can say that the same choice of restrictions has been made in the derivation of two different sentences if the derivations of both sentences include the same rules from the set of choice of restriction rules. The same choice of expansions is made if the derivations of both sentences include the same rules from the set of expansion rules.

Sentences will count as grammatically similar to the extent that the same choice of expansions has been made in their derivations. Sentences are 'transformationally related' to the extent that the same choice of restrictions is made in their derivations and if the same lexical choices are made where possible. Grammatical similarity of phrases and transformational relations among phrases are defined in the same way.

Finally, I tentatively adopt the following partial evaluation function: it selects (from among grammars which all generate the language and nothing else) that grammar whose abbreviation is shortest, choosing among equally short abbreviated grammars on the basis of 'depth' considerations, where 'depth' is understood in the sense of Yngve.[31]

To compare on a small scale the type of grammar envisioned here with transformational analysis, I have written a grammar which partially corresponds to the transformational grammar in *Syntactic structures* 111-3. The phrase-structure grammar generates the same sentences as Chomsky's rules 1-12, 15-21. (Notice that a misprint has resulted in two rules numbered 21.)

The initial constituent in the phrase structure grammar is S.

1.   S→ S1/NUMBER-SG
       S→ S1/NUMBER-PL

2.   S1→ S2/MODE-ACT
       S1→ S2/MODE-PASS

3.   S2→ NP/CASE-NOM,NOT-WH + VP/TYPE-DECL,NOT-WH
         S2→ VP/TYPE-QUES,NOT-WH + NP/CASE-NOM,NOT-WH
         S2→ WH-WORD + VP/TYPE-DECL,NOT-WH
         S2→ WH-WORD + VP/TYPE-QUES,WH + NP/CASE-NOM,NOT-WH

4.   NP/WH→ Ø
         NP/NOT-WH→DETERMINER + NOUN

5.   VP→VP1/NOT-NEGATIVE
         VP→VP1/NEGATIVE

6.   VP1→VP2/AUX-MODAL
         VP1→VP2/AUX-HAVE
         VP1→VP2/AUX-BE
         VP1/TYPE-DECL,NOT-NEGATIVE→VP2/AUX-NONE
         VP1/MODE-PASS→VP2/AUX-NONE
         VP1/MODE-ACT→VP2/AUX-DO

7.   VP2/TYPE-DECL→FINITE-VERB + VP3
         VP2/TYPE-QUES→FINITE-VERB + ... + VP3

8.   VP3/AUX-MODAL→INFINITIVE/AUX-HAVE,-AUX-MODAL + VP3/AUX-
         HAVE,-AUX-MODAL
         VP3/AUX-MODAL→INFINITIVE/AUX-BE,-AUX-MODAL + VP3/AUX-BE,
         -AUX-MODAL
         VP3/AUX-MODAL→INFINITIVE/AUX-NONE,-AUX-MODAL + VP3/AUX-
         NONE,-AUX-MODAL
         VP3/AUX-HAVE→PAST-PART/AUX-BE,-AUX-HAVE + VP3/AUX-BE,-AUX-
         HAVE
         VP3/AUX-HAVE→PAST-PART/AUX-NONE,-AUX-HAVE + VP3/AUX-NONE,
         -AUX-HAVE
         VP3/AUX-BE→PRES-PART/AUX-NONE,-AUX-BE + VP3/AUX-NONE,-AUX-
         BE
         VP3/AUX-DO→INFINITIVE/AUX-NONE,-AUX-DO + VP3/AUX-NONE,
         -AUX-DO
         VP3/AUX-NONE,MODE-PASS→PAST-PART/MODE-ACT,-MODE-PASS +
         BNP
         VP3/AUX-NONE,MODE-ACT→NP/CASE-ACC

9.   BNP→by + NP/CASE-ACC

LEXICON

Strings generated by the preceding syntactical rules are converted into English sentences by using appropriate lexical rules. These are not considered part of the syntactical rules. The following rules are intended only as an example.

```
WH-WORD→ what
FINITE-VERB/AUX-MODAL,NEGATIVE→can't,won't,mustn't
FINITE-VERB/AUX-MODAL,NOT-NEGATIVE→can,will,must
FINITE-VERB/AUX-HAVE,NEGATIVE,NUMBER-SG→hasn't
FINITE-VERB/AUX-HAVE,NEGATIVE,NUMBER-PL→haven't
FINITE-VERB/AUX-HAVE,NOT-NEGATIVE NUMBER-SG→has
FINITE-VERB/AUX-HAVE,NOT-NEGATIVE,NUMBER-PL→have
FINITE-VERB/AUX-BE,NEGATIVE NUMBER-SG→isn't
FINITE-VERB/AUX-BE,NEGATIVE,NUMBER-PL→aren't
FINITE-VERB/AUX-BE,NOT-NEGATIVE,NUMBER-SG→is
FINITE-VERB/AUX-BE,NOT-NEGATIVE,NUMBER-PL→are
FINITE-VERB/AUX-DO,NEGATIVE,NUMBER-SG→doesn't
FINITE-VERB/AUX-DO,NEGATIVE,NUMBER-PL→don't
FINITE-VERB/AUX-DO,NOT-NEGATIVE,NUMBER-SG→does
FINITE-VERB/AUX-DO,NOT-NEGATIVE,NUMBER-PL→do
FINITE-VERB/AUX-NONE,MODE-PASS→FINITE-VERB/AUX-BEᵣ-AUX-
      NONE,MODE-ACTᵣ-MODE-PASS
FINITE-VERB/AUX-NONE,MODE-ACT,NUMBER-SG→hits,takes,walks,reads
FINITE-VERB/AUX-NONE,MODE-ACT,NUMBER-PL→hit,take,walk,read
INFINITIVE/AUX-HAVE→have
INFINITIVE/AUX-BE→be
INFINITIVE/AUX-NONE,MODE-ACT→hit,take,walk,read
INFINITIVE/AUX-NONE,MODE-PASS→be
PAST-PART/AUX-BE→been
PAST-PART/AUX-NONE,MODE-ACT→hit,taken,walked,read
PAST-PART/AUX-NONE,MODE-PASS→been
PRES-PART/AUX-NONE,MODE-ACT→hitting,taking,walking,reading
PRES-PART/AUX-NONE,MODE-PASS→being
DETERMINER→the
NOUN/CASE-NOM,NUMBER-SG→man,ball
NOUN/CASE-NOM,NUMBER-PL→men,balls
NOUN/CASE-ACC→man,men,ball,balls
```

It will be observed that the phrase-structure grammar plus the lexicon as given will generate sequences of words rather than of representations of phonemes. In comparing the phrase-structure and transformational versions, we are interested only in the syntactic parts of the grammars.

In length the grammars are about the same. They provide the same grammatical information. The phrase-structure grammar is at least as well motivated as the transformational.[32]

6. Conclusion.

The critique of phrase structure consists in the construction of a formal model of phrase-structure theory and the demonstration that this is inadequate as a complete theory of grammar. The defense of phrase structure consists in repudiating the formal model. There are good reasons for repudiating the model of constituent structure, as Chomsky defines it, and for replacing it with a model which obviates the original criticisms.

Appendix

I give here a phrase-structure syntax equivalent to the syntactical part of the transformational grammar which Chomsky describes in his paper 'A transformational approach to syntax'. The phrase-structure grammar here described and the smaller grammar in the text have also been written in the form of COMIT computer programs which randomly produce sentences in accordance with the phrase-structure rules. Since the phrase-structure and transformational grammars are equivalent, these sentences are also produced in accordance with the rules of the transformational grammar. By examining the sentences thus produced we are able to see how the grammar may be improved. But since I wish to present phrase-structure grammar equivalent to a particular transformational grammar, I have left the phrase-structure grammar in its original state. Hence not all the sentences constructed in accordance with this grammar are well-formed.

1.   Determination of sentence type.

S→S1/CLAUSE.TYPE:SENTENCE,A,B,C,D,E,X,Y

S1→S2/SUBJ.NUM.SING.

→S2/SUBJ.NUM.:PLUR.

S2→S3/PRONOUN.SUBJ.

→S3/NOUN.SUB.

S3→S4/SUBJ.CATEGORY:HUMAN

→S5/SUBJ.CATEGORY:CONCRETE,SUBJ.PERSON:3

S3/SUBJ.NUM:SING.→S5/SUBJ.CATEGORY:ABSTRACT,SUBJ.PERSON:3

S4/PRONOUN.SUBJ→S5/SUBJ.PERSON:1

S4/PRONOUN.SUBJ→S5/SUBJ.PERSON:2

S4→S5/SUBJ.PERSON:3

S5/A→S13/VP:BE,BE
S5/B→S6/VP:VT,NON.BE
S5/C→S13/VP:VS,NON.BE
S5/D→S13/VP:VP:VI,NON.BE
S5/E→S13/VP;BECOME,NON.BE
S6→S7/OBJ.NUM.:SING.
 →S7/OBJ.NUM.:PLUR.
S7→S8/PRONOUN.OBJ.
 →S8/NOUN.OBJ.
S8 →S9/OBJ.CATEGORY:HUMAN
 →S10/OBJ.CATEGORY:CONCRETE,OBJ.PERSON:3
S8/OBJ.NUM.:SING→S10/OBJ.CATEGORY:ABSTRACT,OBJ.PERSON:3
S9/PRONOUN.OBJ.→S10/OBJ.PERSON:1
S9/PRONOUN.OBJ.→S10/OBJ.PERSON:2
S9→S10/OBJ.PERSON:3
S10/SUBJ.CATEGORY:HUMAN→S13/VERB.TYPE:VT1
S10/OBJ.CATEGORY:HUMAN→S13/VERB.TYPE:VT2
S10/SUBJ.CATEGORY:HUMAN,OBJ.CATEGORY:CONCRETE→S13/VERB/.TYPE:VT31
S10/SUBJ.CATEGORY:HUMAN,OBJ.CATEGORY:CONCRETE→S13/VERB/.TYPE:VT32
S10→S11/VERB.TYPE:VT4
S11/SUBJ.CATEGORY:HUMAN→S12/COMP.
S11→S13/VT4-TYPE:VTX,PRT
S12→S13/VT4.TYPE:VTA

 →S13/VT4.TYPE:VTB
 →S13/VT4.TYPE:VTC
 →S13/VT4.TYPE:VTD
 →S13/VT4.TYPE:VTE
 →S13/VT4.TYPE:VTEE
 →S13/VT4.TYPE:VTF
 →S13/VT4.TYPE:VTFF
 →S13/VT4.TYPE:VTG
 →S13/VT4.TYPE:VTGG

S13/Z→VP/CLAUSE.TYPE:INFINITIVE
S13/Y→S14/MODE:ACTIVE
S13/X,Y,VP:VT→S14/MODE:PASSIVE,BE,-NON.BE
S14/CLAUSE.TYPE:SENTENCE→S15/QUESTION
S14→S15/NO.QUESTION
S15/CLAUSE.TYPE:SENTENCE,QUESTION→so+S16/LENGTH:SHORT
S15/CLAUSE.TYPE:SENTENCE,NO.QUESTION→S16/LENGTH:SHORT.
S15→S16/LENGTH:LONG

2. Basic sentence expansion
    S16/LENGTH:LONG→S17+ADV.

S16→S17

S17/CLAUSE.TYPE:SENTENCE→S18

S17/SUBJ.IN.GENITIVE→S18

S17/CLAUSE.TYPE:INFINITIVE→VP

S17/CLAUSE.TYPE:INTRASITIVE.PARTICIPIAL→LEX/INFLECTION:
PRES.PART.,AUX:NONE+of+NP/ROLE:SUBJ.,CASE:ACC.

S17/CLAUSE.TYPE:TRANSITIVE.PARTICIPIAL→LEX/INFLECTION:PRES.
PART.,AUX:NONE+of+NP/ROLE:OBJ.,CASE:ACC.

S18/QUESTION,LENGTH:LONG→WH.NOM. + S19/WH.NOM,-QUESTION,
NO.QUESTION

S18/QUESTION,LENGTH:LONG,VP:VT→WH.ACC+S19/WH.ACC

S19→S20/WH.NONE

S19/MODE:ACTIVE→NP/ROLE:SUBJ.,CASE:NOM.+VP

S19/MODE:PASSIVE→NP/ROLE:OBJ,CASE:NOM.+VP

S20/MODE:ACTIVE→VP+NP/ROLE:SUBJ.,CASE:NOM.

S20/MODE:PASSIVE→VP+NP/ROLE:OBJ.,CASE:NOM.

3.   The noun phrase

3a.   Obligatory deletes

NP/ROLE:PRED→NP1/CASE:NOM.

NP/WH:NOM,CASE:NOM.→∅

NP/WH:NOM,CASE:ACC.

NP/WH:ACC.,CASE:NOM→NP1

NP/WH:ACC.,CASE:ACC.→∅

NP/WH:NONE→NP1

3b.   Optional deletes

NP1→NP2

NP1/ROLE:OBJ.,VERB.TYPE:VT1,MODE:ACT.→∅

NP1/ROLE:OBJ.,VT4:VTG→∅

NP1/ROLE:OBJ.,VT4:VTGG→∅

NP1/ROLE:OBJ.,VT4:VTF→∅

NP1/ROLE:OBJ.,VT4:VTFF→∅

3c.   'Self' on pronouns set.

NP2/CASE:ACC.,PRONOUN.SUBJ.,PRONOUN.OBJ.,ROLE:OBJ→NP3/SELF

NP2→NP3/NOT.SELF

3d.   Noun phrase number.

NP3/ROLE:SUBJ.→NP3A

NP3/ROLE:OBJ.→NP3B

NP3/ROLE:PRED.→NP3A

NP3A/SUBJ.NUM.:SING.→NP4/NMR:SG.
NP3A/SUBJ.NUM.:PLUR.→NP4/NMR.PL.
NP3B/OBJ.NUM.:SING.→NP5/NMR:SG.
NP3B/OBJ>NUM.:PLUR.→NP5/NMR:PL.

3e.   Genitives.
NP4/CLAUSE.TYPE:SENTENCE→NP5
NP4/SUBJ.IN.GEN,ROLE:SUBJ.→NP5/CASE:GEN.,-CASE:NOM.

3f.   Type of noun phrase chosen.
NP5/ROLE:SUBJ.→NP5A
NP5/ROLE:OBJ.→NP5B
NP5/ROLE:PRED.→NP5A
NP5A/PRONOUN.SUBJ.→NP6
NP5A/NOUN.SUBJ.→ T + N
NP5B/PRONOUN.OBJ.→ PP
NP5B/NOUN.OBJ.→T + N

3g.   Special nominalization.
NP6/SUBJECT.CATEGORY:CONCRETE→NP7
NP6/SUBJECT.CATEGORY:ABSTRACT→NP7
NP7/CASE:GEN.→NP8 + 's
NP7/CASE:NOM.→NP8
NP7/CASE:ACC.→ NP8
NP8→S1/CLAUSE.TYPE:PARTICIPLE,SUBJ.IN.GENERATIVE,B,C,D,E,X,Y,
   ERASE.OTHERS
      →S1/CLAUSE.TYPE:INFINITIVE,SUBJ.IN.GENITIVE,B,C,D,E,X,Y,
   ERASE.OTHERS
      →S1/CLAUSE.TYPE:NOMINALIZATION,SUBJ.IN.GENITIVE,B,C,D,E,X,Y,
   ERASE.OTHERS   →T + S1/CLAUSE.TYPE:INTRASITIVE.PARTICIPIAL,D,Y,ERASE.
   OTHERS   →T + S1/CLAUSE.TYPE:TRANSITIVE.PARTICIPIAL,B,Y,ERASE.
   OTHERS   →S1/CLAUSE.TYPE:ADJ.NOM.,SUBJ.IN.GENITIVE,A,Y,ERASE.OTHERS

3h.   Noun modification.
N→N1
N→A + N1

BNP→BY + NP/ROLE:SUBJ,CASE:A

3i   Modifier.
A   →   A + A1
   →   A1
   →   LEX/VP:VI,NOT.BE,AUX:NONE,INFLECTION:PRES.PART,ERASE.
         OTHERS

A1 → ADJ.

A1/ROLE:PRED → LEX/VP:VT,VERB.TYPE:VT32,NOT.BE,AUX:NONE,IN-
FLECTION:PRES.PART.,ERASE.OTHERS

A1/CASE:ACC. → LEX/VP:VT,VERB.TYPE:VT32,NOT.BE,AUX:NONE,IN-
FLECTION:PRES.PART.,ERASE.OTHERS

4. Verb phrase.

4a. Optional passive to active.

VP/VERB.TYPE:FIVE,MODE:PASS.,LENGTH:LONG → VP1/MODE:ACT,
-MODE:PASS.,XX,-X

VP/VP → VP1/X

4b. Variations on normal verb phrase.

VP1/CLAUSE.TYPE:SENTENCE → VP2

VP1/CLAUSE.TYPE:PARTICIPLE → LEX/INFLECTION:PRES.PART.,AUX:
NONE

VP1/CLAUSE.TYPE:INFINITIVE → to + VP2

VP1/CLAUSE.TYPE:NOMINALIZATION → LEX/INFLECTION:NOMINALIZA-
TION,AUX:NONE

4c. Verb phrase proper.

VP2→   VP3/PAST.TENSE

→   VP3/PRES.TENSE

VP3→   VP4/NEGATIVE

→   VP4/NOT.NEGATIVE

VP4/NOT.NEGATIVE,NO.QUESTION → VP5/AUX:NONE

VP4/BE → VP5/AUX:NONE

VP4/QUESTION,NON.BE → VP5/AUX:DO

VP4/NEGATIVE,NON.BE → VP5/AUX:DO

VP4→   VP5/AUX:MODAL

→   VP5/AUX:HAVE

→   VP5/AUX:BE

VP5/MODE:ACT → VP5A

VP5/MODE:PASS → VP5B

VP5A/SUBJ.NUM:SING. → VP6/SING.VERB.

VP5A/SUBJ.NUM:PLUR → VP6/PLUR.VERB

VP5B/OBJ.NUM.SING. → VP6/SING.VERB

VP5B/OBJ.NUM:SING. → VP6/PLUR.VERB

VP6/LENGTH:SHORT → LEX/INFLECTION:FINITE

VP6/LENGTH:LONG,QUESTION → LEX/INFLECTION:FINITE + ... + VP7

VP6/LENGTH:LONG,NO.QUESTION → LEX/INFLECTION:FINITE + VP7

VP7/AUX:MODAL → LEX/INFLECTION:INFINITE,AUX:HAVE,-AUX:
MODAL + VP7/AUX:HAVE,-AUX:MODAL

VP7/AUX:MODAL → LEX/INFLECTION:INFINITE,AUX:BE,-AUX:MODAL +
VP7/AUX:BE,-AUX:MODAL

VP7/MODAL → LEX/INFLECTION:INFINITE,AUX:NONE,-AUX:MODAL +
VP7/AUX:NONE,-AUX:MODAL

VP7/AUX:HAVE → LEX/INFLECTION:PAST.PART.,AUX:BE,-AUX:HAVE +

VP7/AUX:BE,-AUX:HAVE
VP7/AUX:HAVE → LEX/INFLECTION:PAST.PART.,AUX:NONE,-AUX:HAVE
    + VP7/AUX:NONE,-AUX:HAVE
VP7/AUX:BE → LEX/INFLECTION:PRES.PART.,AUX:NONE,-AUX:BE +
    VP7/AUX:NONE,-AUX:BE
VP7/AUX:DO → LEX/INFLECTION:PAST.PART.,AUX:NONE,-AUX:DO +
    VP7/AUX:NONE,-AUX:DO
VP7/AUX:NONE → VP8

4d. Remaining part of verb phrase.
    VP8/VP:BE → VP8A
    VP8/VP:VT → VP8B
    VP8/VP:VS → ADJ
    VP8/VP:VI → Ø
    VP8/VP:BECOME → VP8C
    VP8A → NP/CASE:NOM,ROLE:PRED
         → ADJ
         → ADV1
    VP8B/XX → easily
    VP8B/X,MODE:ACT. → NP/CASE:ACC,ROLE:OBJ.
    VP8B/X,MODE:PASS. → LEX/NON:BE,INFLECTION:PAST.PART.BNP
    VP8C/WH.ACC → Ø
    VP8C/WH.NOM → VP9
    VP8C/WH:NONE → VP9
    VP9→ ADJ
         → NP/CASE:ACC.

4e. Passive by clause.
    BNP → by + NP/ROLE:SUBJ,CASE:ALL

4f.   Complement and particle placement.
    LEX/AUX:NONE,BE→LEX/AUX:BE,-AUX:NONE
    LEX/AUX:NONE,NON.BE→LEX1
    LEX/AUX:HAVE→VOCAB
    LEX//AUX:BE→VOCAB
    LEX/AUX:DO→VOCAB
    LEX1/COMP→LEX2
    LEX1/PRT→LEX3
    LEX1→VOCAB
    LEX2/MODE:ACT→VOCAB+...+COMP.
    LEX2/MODE:PASS.→VOCAB + COMP.
    LEX3/MODE:ACT.VOCAB + PRT
        →VOCAB +...+PRT
    LEX3/MODE:PASS.→VOCAB+PRT

4g.   Form of verb complement
        COMP/VT4.TYPE:VTA→COMP1
        COMP/VT4.TYPE:VTB→ to + be + AORN
        COMP/VT4.TYPE:VTC→ NP/CASE:ACC,ROLE:OBJ.
        COMP/VT4.TYPE:VTD→ADV1
        COMP/VT4:VTD→ADV1
        COMP/VT4:VTE/COMP2
        COMP/VT4.TYPE:VTEE→COMP3
        COMP/VT4.TYPE:VTF→COMP2
        COMP/VT4.TYPE:VTFF→COMP3
        COMP/VT4.TYPE:VTG
        COMP/VT4.TYPE:VTGG
        COMP1→ADJ
           →NP/CASE:ACC,ROLE:OBJ
        COMP2→COMP4/INFLECTION;PRES.PART.ERASE.OTHERS
        COMP3→toCOMP4/INFLECTION:INFINITIVE,ERASE.OTHERS
        COMP4→S5/Y,B,C,D,E

5.   Lexicon. Strings generated by the preceding syntactical rules are converted into English sentences by using appropriate lexical rules. Since the lexical rules are not considered part of the syntactical rules, they take various forms. To save space I do not give a complete set of lexical rules for this grammar, but sample rules to show that all necessary information is contained in subscripts.

PRT→out,in,up,away
ADJ→very+ADJ→

   →old, sad
ADJNOM→oldness,sadness
ADV→at three o'clock,
   yesterday, in the morning,
   every morning
   →ADV1
ADV1→there,away,home,in the
 house, at the theatre
WH.NOM/MODE:ACT→WH.NOM1
PER1SG/NOT.SELF→PER1SGA
PER1SGA/CASE:NOM→I
etc.
N1/CASE:NOM→N1A
N1A/ROLE:SUBJ→N2
N2/SUBJ.CATEGORY:HUMAN→
   NOHUM
NOHUM→MAN,BOY
NOHUM→MAN,BOY

WH.NOM/MODE;PASS→WH.NOM2
WH.NOM1/SUBJ/CATEGORY:
   HUMAN
   →who
etc.
PP/ROLE:SUBJ.→PP1
   PP1/SUBJ.CATEGORY:
   HUMAN→
   PP1A
PP1A/SUBJ.PERSON:1→PP.PER1
PP.PER1/NMR.SG.→PER1SG
PER1SG/SELF→myself
VERB/VP:VT→VT
etc.
VT/VERB.TYPE:VT1→VT1
VT4/VT4.TYPE:VTA→VTA
etc.
VS→FEEL,SEEM

VI→ARRIVE,DISAPPEAR
VT1→ADMIRE,FIND

NOCON→TABLE,BOOK
NOAB→sincerity,justice
MAN/NMR.SG→man
etc.

VOCAB/MODE:ACTIVE→VOCAB1
VOCAB1/SUBJ.PERSON:1→VOCAB2/
  VERB.PERSON:1
etc.
VOCAB2/AUX:MODAL→MODAL
MODAL→CAN,WILL,MAY,SHALL,
  MUST
etc.
VERB/VP:BE→BE

VT2→TERRIFY,ASTONISH
VT31→FIND,COMPLETE
VT32→EAT,SMOKE
VTA→CONSIDER,BELIEVE
VTB→KNOW,RECOGNIZE
VTC→ELECT,CHOOSE
VTD→KEEP,PUT
VTE→FIND,CATCH
VTEE:PERSUADE,FORCE
VTF→IMAGINE,PREFER
VTFF→WANT,EXPECT
VTG→AVOID,BEGIN
VTGG→TRY,REFUTE
VTX→TAKE,BRING

Footnotes

[1]This article was written while I was a member of the Mechanical Translation Group, Research Laboratory of Electronics, Massachusetts Institute of Technology. The work was supported in part by the National Science Foundation, and in part by the U.S. Army Signal Corps, the Air Force Office of Scientific Research, and the Office of Naval Research. I am indebted to Victor Yngve for suggestions which greatly improved the argument presented here.

[2]The phrase-structure grammar allows for 'discontinuous constituents'. The type of grammar is like that described in Yngve, 'A model and an hypothesis for language structure', *Proceedings of the American Philosophical Society* 104, 444-66 (1960). The grammar is described in detail in §5 of this paper. The transformational grammar is to be found in Noam Chomsky, 'A transformational approach to syntax', *Third Texas conference on problems of linguistic analysis in English* 138-44 (1958; published 1962).

[3]Chomsky, op.cit. 124-58; *Syntactic structures* (The Hague, 1962), especially Chapter 5; 'Explanatory models in linguistics', *Proceedings of the 1960 International Congress on Logic, Methodology, and Philosophy of Science,* ed. Suppes, Nagel, and Tarski (Stanford, 1962); 'The logical basis of linguistic theory', *Preprints of papers for the Ninth International Congress of Linguists* 509-74 (Cambridge, Mass., 1962); R. B. Lees, review of *Syntactic structures* in *Lg.* 33.375-407 (1957); *The grammar of English nominalizations* (Bloomington, 1960).

[4]'The logical basis of linguistic theory'.

[5]*Syntactic structures* 11.

[6]Ibid. Cf. Chomsky, 'On the notion rule of grammar', *Structure of language and its mathematical aspects,* ed. Jakobson, *Proceedings of symposia in applied mathematics* 12.6 (Providence, 1961): 'By a "grammar of the language L" I will mean a device of some sort (that is, a set of rules) that provides, at least, a complete specification of an infinite set of grammatical sentences of L and their structural descriptions. In addition to making precise the notion "structural description", the theory of grammar should meet requirements of the following kind. It should make available:
(1) (a) a class of possible grammars $G_1, G_2,...,$
     (b) a class of possible sentences $S_1, S_2,...,$
     (c) a function f such that $f(i,j)$ is the set of structural descriptions of the sentence S_i that are provided by the grammar G_j.
     (d) a function $m(i)$ which evaluates G_i,
     (e) a function g such that $g(i,n)$ is the description of a finite

automaton that takes sentences of (b) as input and gives structural descriptions assigned to these sentences by G_1 (i.e. various, perhaps all, members of $f(i,j)$) as output, where n is a parameter determining the capacity of the automaton.'

[7]'The logical basis of linguistic theory' 514.

[8]Formally, this motivation will ideally be provided by the function m(i) mentioned in footnote 6. The use of the evaluation function m(i) is explained further in 'On the notion rule of grammar' 7: 'That is, m may be a measure of complexity that leads to choice among alternative proposed grammars that are compatible with given data.' (This is also discussed in almost all the references in footnote 3.) A choice of one grammar over another which accounts for the same data (generates the same sentences) will be motivated if and only if the selected grammar has a higher value (according to the function m) than the other grammar. Note that in practice it will probably be impossible to give an exact specification of m. For example, Lees has noted that 'no natural science can claim...a true evaluation procedure' (review of Chomsky 380). This is an important point, as will appear in what follows.

[9]*Syntactic structures* 26. Various names have been given to the theory of grammar for which a formal model is sought: Formal structural linguistics, IC analysis, traditional notion of parsing (Chomsky, 'A transformational approach to syntax' 124); taxonomic model applied to syntax (Chomsky, 'Logical basis of linguistic theory' 510); constituent structure, immediate-constituent analysis (Chomsky, 'On the notion rule of grammar' 9, 15); phrase structure, bracketing, immediate-constituent analysis (lees, review of Chomsky, 385).

[10]*Syntactic structures* 29.

[11]'On the notion rule of grammar' 8-9. See also Chomsky, 'On certain formal properties of grammars', *Information and Control*, No. 2 (1959).

[12]These diagrams are explained in *Syntactic structures*, Chapter 4.

[13]'The extreme example of this difficulty is the case of true coordination, e.g. "the man was old, tired, tall,..., but friendly." The only correct P-Marker (i.e. 'phrase marker') would assign no internal structure at all within the sequence of coordinated items. But a constituent structure grammar can accommodate this possibility only with an infinite number of rules; that is, it must necessarily impose further structure in quite an arbitrary way." - Chomsky, 'On the notion rule of grammar' 15.

[14]I am not sure that this criticism of phrase structure has ever been explicitly made, though it is as valid as the preceeding. The more usual criticism is that a description which reveals the active-passive relationship cannot be motivated, which appears to be the criticism that constituent structure fails to reach the level of explanatory adequacy. However, one reason why such a description cannot be motivated is that the description cannot occur in a constituent structure grammar as Chomsky has defined it, e.g. *Syntactic structures* 88-91.

[15]Chomsky, op.cit.88

[16]Loc.cit.

[17]More details in Chomsky, *Syntactic Structures*, Chapters 5-8, especially Chapter 8, 'The explanatory value of linguistic theory'. Cf. 'The logical basis of linguistic theory' 517-24.

[18]'The motivation for adding transformational rules to the grammar is quite clear...'---'On the notion rule of grammar'17.

[19]See the passage quoted above, at footnote 11.

[20]A standard example is *They are (flying planes)* as compared with *They (are flying) planes.*

[21]529-30.

[22]Yngve, 'A model and an hypothesis for language structure'.

[23]Paul M. Postal, *Constituent structure: A study of contemporary models of syntactic description* (to appear).

[24]41-2, footnote 6.

[25]This is Yngve's rule, which I also accept in the grammars given below.

[26]'A model and an hypothesis for language structure'.

[27]More formally: In the string $X + C + Y$ (where X and Y are strings of constituents) 'expand' constituent C if and only if (a) there is a rule with C on the left side and (b) there is not a constituent B included in the string X so that there is a rule with B on the left side.

[28]The subscript notation suggested here is based on that in the computer language COMIT, which is particularly suited for use in writing generative

grammars. See V.H. Yngve, *Introduction to COMIT programming* and *COMIT programmers' Reference Manual* (Cambridge, Mass., 1962).

[29]We could even forget that the abbreviated form abbreviates anything and take it to be basic.

[30]These are of course only rough suggestions. There is no reason why exact specification of such description must be given before a fairly large grammar has been written. A detailed treatment of these issues appears in David Allen Dinneen, *A left-to-right generative grammar of French* (Cambridge, Mass., 1962). Dinneen's distinction between the 'grammar of specifiers' and the 'grammar of sentences' is a much more sophisticated distinction than mine between 'restriction rules' and 'expansion rules'.

[31]'A model and an hypothesis for language structure'.

[32]Other grammars of this form have ben written at MIT and elsewhere for English, German, French, Finnish, and Arabic. Many of these grammars are in the form of computer programs for generating actual sentences. An example is Arnold C. Satterthwait, *Parallel sentence-construction grammars of Arabic and English* (Cambridge, Mass., 1962).

P. T. Geach

A PROGRAM FOR SYNTAX

The program for syntax which I describe here is not one I can claim as specially my own. The two basic ideas are due to Frege: analysis of an expression into a main functor and its argument(s), and distinction among categories of functors according to the categories of arguments and values. The development of a handy notation for categories, and of an algorithm to test whether a string of expressions will combine into a complex expression that belongs to a definite category, is due to the Polish logicians, particularly Ajdukiewicz. My own contribution has been confined to working out details. So my program is not original, but I think it is right in essentials; and I am making propaganda for it by working it out in some particular instructive examples. I think this is all the more called for because some recent work in syntax seems to have ignored the insights I am trying to convey.

I shall begin with some thoughts from Aristotle's pioneering treatise on syntax, the *De Interpretatione*. Aristotle holds that the very simplest sort of sentence is a two-word sentence consisting of two heterogeneous parts - a name, and a predicative element (rhēma). For example, 'petetai Sōkratēs', 'Socrates is flying'. This gives us an extremely simple example for application of our category theory:

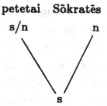

petetai   Sōkratēs
s/n   n
s

Davidson and Harman (eds.), *Semantics of Natural Language*, 483-497. All rights reserved
Copyright © 1972 by D. Reidel Publishing Company, Dordrecht-Holland.

117

W. J. Savitch et al. (eds.), The Formal Complexity of Natural Language, 117–131.

The two-word Greek expression as a whole belongs to the category s of sentences; 'petetai' is a functor that takes a single name (of category n) 'Sōkratēs' as argument and yields as a result an expression of category s. Ajdukiewicz represented functorial categories by a fractional notation; α/β would be the category of a function that operates upon a single argument of category β to yield an expression of category α, so that we have a "multiplying out" of category indices. This notation becomes awkward to print when indices become complex; so following a suggestion of my Leeds colleague Dr. T. C. Potts I shall henceforth rather write ':$\alpha\beta$' for such a functorial category. (This device makes bracketing theoretically superfluous, but in practice I shall insert parentheses sometimes to facilitate reading.) Our first rule then is the multiplying-out rule:

$$:\alpha\ \beta\ \beta \to \alpha$$

For instance,   :sn n → s.

Aristotle observed that one may get a sentence from a rhēma like 'petetai' not only by combining it with a name but also by combining it with a quantified phrase like 'pās anthrōpos', 'every man'. He further observed that these two types of sentence behave quite differently under negation; the negation of 'petetai Sōkratēs' is 'ou petetai Sōkratēs', when the negation 'ou' attaches to the rhēma 'petetai'; the negation of 'pās anthrōpos petetai' is 'ou pās anthrōpos petetai', where the negative attaches to the quantified phrase 'pās anthrōpos'. This is a profound insight, ignored by those who would lump together proper names and phrases like 'every man' as Noun Phrases; we have two different syntactical categories. It is easy to find in the Ajdukiewicz scheme another category that will yield the category s when combined with the category :sn; for we shall have, by the general rule, ::s:sn :sn → s. But this is not enough to exhaust the Aristotelian insight. We should wish to make 'ou petetai' 'does not fly' a syntactically coherent sub-string of 'ou petetai Sōkratēs', and on the other hand to make 'ou pās anthrōpos' 'not every man' a syntactically coherent sub-string of 'ou pās anthrōpos petetai'. But by the Ajdukiewicz criteria for a string's being syntactically coherent (SC), neither string will come out as SC. To negation 'ou', we must assign the category :ss of a sentence-forming operator upon sentences; and neither the category-indices ':ss :sn' of 'ou petetai' nor the indices ':ss :s:sn' of 'ou pās anthrōpos' multiply out by Ajdukiewicz' rule to a single index of the whole expression. These are two particular cases of a general fact, noticed by medieval logicians: that a sentence may contain a *formale*, formal element - Ajdukiewicz' main functor - negation of which *is* negation of the whole proposition.

Intuitions about the SC nature of sub-strings are fallible, but are *pro tanto* evidential; we need to check our general theories of syntax against such intuitions, and also to correct our intuitions against wider insights. By the two-way process we may hope to get steadily closer to truth. In this case, we can satisfy the demands of intuition if we supplement the Ajdukiewicz multiplying-out rule with a recursive rule:

$$\text{If } \alpha \ \beta \to \gamma, \ \alpha :\beta\delta \to :\gamma\delta.$$

This already covers the Aristotelian and medieval cases. For suppose the main functor of a sentence is of category :sβ, so that we have a sentence by adding a β expression. We then have by our recursive rule:

$$\text{Since } :\text{ss s} \to \text{s}, \ :\text{ss} :\text{s}\beta \to :\text{s}\beta.$$

And this covers all cases in which negation, of category :ss, operates upon a sentence of structure :sβ β. The string of expressions categorized as:

$$:\text{ss} :\text{s}\beta \ \beta,$$

may be split up in two ways into SC sub-strings; namely, we may regard negation (:ss) as operating on the whole sentence categorized as :sβ β; or, we may regard it as combining with the :sβ expression to form a complex :sβ expression, which then combines with the β expression to form a sentence. The two Aristotelian examples are covered by this account if we take β=:sn and β=:s:sn.

Such possibilities of multiple analysis do not mean that we have a syntactically ambiguous string. We have a single "proper series of indices", as Ajdukiewicz calls it, for a given sentence; the different ways of multiplying out the indices reveal two different but equally legitimate ways of dissecting out an SC sub-string from a larger SC string.

The Ajdukiewicz scheme allows for functors that take more than one argument. In the present discussion it will be enough to consider functors that take two arguments of the same category: if this category is β and α

is the category of the functor plus its two arguments, I give the functor the category $:\alpha(2\beta)$. We get in Ajdukiewicz the rule for multiplying out with such category indices:

$$:\alpha(2\beta)\ \beta\ \beta \to \alpha.$$

Once again I add a recursive rule:

If $\alpha\ \beta\ \beta \to \gamma$, then $\alpha:\beta\delta:\beta\delta \to :\gamma\delta$.

A medieval example may serve to illustrate the newly introduced categories. 'John or James came' need not be transformed into 'John came or James came' before we investigate its SC character; we can show it to be SC as it stands. But we cannot treat it as having the same simple subject-predicate structure as 'John came', only having a complex subject 'John or James' instead of the single name 'John'. For whereas the negation of 'John came' attaches to the predicate 'came', 'John or James came' has to be negated by negating 'or' - '*neither* John *nor* James came'. So my medieval writer justly took 'or' to be here the *formale* or main functor. 'John or James' may be regarded as a restricted existential quantification - 'for some x in the university {John, James}, x...'; so we assign to it, just as we do to 'pās anthrōpos' or 'every man', the category :s:sn. The functor 'or' will then be assigned the category :(:s:sn)(2n), which combines with two names of category n to yield an :s:sn expression; and this in turn combines with the predicate 'came' of category :sn to yield a sentence. Negation, of category :ss, will combine with a functor of category :(:s:sn)(2n) to yield a functor of the same category; we see this by twice applying our recursive rule:

:ss s → s

ergo, :ss :s:sn → :s:sn

ergo, :ss :(:s:sn)(2n) → :(:s:sn)(2n).

I shall now briefly sketch how the traditional apparatus of Parts of Speech get reshaped in an Ajdukiewicz grammar. I shall consider only some of the traditional list.

I. Verbs

Intransitive verbs like 'come' or 'petetai' may be categorized as :sn. A transitive verb along with its noun-object, a phrase like 'loves Socrates', will likewise be of category :sn; 'loves' itself is thus most conveniently categorized as ::snn. 'Every Greek loves Socrates' then admits of a double dissection into SC sub-strings; we need this, because we need to recognize both 'loves Socrates' and 'every Greek loves' as SC expressions that may recur in other contexts e.g. in the relative clauses 'who loves Socrates' and 'that every Greek loves'. (When symbolizing a piece of argument stated in the vernacular, we might find it convenient to represent either recurrent phrase by the same one-place predicate letter each time it occurred.) In fact, 'loves Socrates' gets categorized as ::snn n, which multiplies out to :sn by the Ajdukiewicz rule; and then 'Every Greek loves Socrates' will be categorized as :s:sn :sn, which multiples out to s. On the other hand, 'every Greek loves' gets categorized as :s:sn ::snn; this multiplies out to :sn by our recursive rule:

Since :s:sn :sn → s, :s:sn ::snn → :sn.

So 'Every Greek loves Socrates' comes out as :sn n, and thus again as s. Once again, we have two equally legitimate analyses, not a syntactic ambiguity.

II. Conjunctions

The term 'connective' is preferable, since 'conjunction' is indispensable as a name for one of the truth-functions. Traditional grammar distinguishes subordinating and coordinating connectives; in one case, e.g. with 'if', the connective is felt to go with the clause that follows it; in the other case, e.g. 'and', 'or', the connective is felt to be joining two clauses, not going with one rather than the other. No such distinction is needed for the binary sentence-connectives in a formal system, which may very well be taken to be all of one category; but for analysis of the vernacular it seems better to recognize a syntactical distinction between the two sorts of connectives. A subordinating connective would be of category ::sss; so such a connective together with the clause following it would be of category ::sss s, i.e. :ss, which is the category of a sentence-forming operator upon a sentence. A coordinating connective, on the other hand, would be of category :s(2s). A string categorizable as :s(2s) s s has as a whole the category s; but just as the category indices ':s(2s) s' do not multiply out to a single index, so we need not take either 'John ran and' or 'and Jane rode' to be an SC substring of 'John ran and Jane rode'.

Grammarians have often taken sentences in which a coordinating connective joins expressions other than sentences to be derived from sentences in which the same connective joins sentences. I regard this view as whole erroneous. Our theory of categories does not restrict the possible arguments of an :s(2s) connective to a pair of sentences; on the contrary, by our recursive rule we have that a pair of the category :sβ may also be so connected to form a third:

Since :s(2s) s s → s, :s(2s) :sβ :sβ → :sβ, whatever category β may be.

And so we obtain a correct analysis of a sentence like:

All the girls admired, but most boys detested, one of the saxophonists.

This is not equivalent, as a moment's thought shows, to:

All the girls admired one of the saxophonists, but most boys detested one of the saxophonists,

and cannot sensibly be regarded as a transformation of it. The expressions 'all the girls admired' and 'most boys detested' are in fact each assignable to the category :sn, as we saw before regarding 'every Greek loved'; so the coordinating connective 'but' can combine them to form a single string of category :sn. Since 'one of the saxophonists' is plainly a quantifying expression like 'every man', it is of category :s:sn; this is the main functor, operating upon 'All the girls admired, but most boys detested', of category :sn, to yield a sentence. The change of intonation pattern marked by the second comma, as contrasted with the smooth run in the sentence:

All the girls were thrilled, but most boys detested one of the saxophonists,

is easily explained: 'most boys detested one of the saxophonists' is an SC substring (in fact a sentence) in the latter example but not in the former, and the change of intonation shows our feeling for this. (Just as 'Plato was bald' has a different intonation pattern when it stands by itself and when it comes as part of 'The man whose most famous pupil was Plato was bald'; in the latter context it is patently not an SC string.)

Similarly, a subordinating connective along with the clause following it will come out, as I said, in the category :ss, that of a sentence-forming operator upon sentences; but it does not follow that such a unit can be read only as attached to an entire main clause; on the contrary, we must sometimes so regard it as attached to an expression of another category. A good medieval example of syntactical ambiguity brings out this point:

Every man dies when just one man dies

This could be true (and was once, in this sense, a presumption of English law) as denying the possibility of quite simultaneous deaths; in the other possible sense, it could be true only if there were just one man, so that his death was the death of every man. The first sense requires us to take the subordinating connective plus its clause, 'when just one man dies', as going not with 'Every man dies' but just with 'dies', as we may see from the paraphrase:

It holds of every man that he dies when just one man dies (namely he himself and nobody else).

The second sense affirms that the universal death of mankind happens along with the death of one and only on man; here, the whole sentence 'Every man dies' is operated on by the sentence-forming operator 'when just one man dies'.

III. Adverbs

Some adverbs, as the name suggests, are verb-forming operators upon verbs, and are thus of category :(:sn)(:sn). Thus 'passionately protested' comes out as of the same category with 'protested' (I am taking this as an intransitive verb of category :sn) but also 'passionately loved' comes out as of the same category with 'loved', namely ::snn, for we have:

Since :(:sn)(:sn) :sn → :sn, :(:sn)(:sn) ::snn → ::snn.

And as in the other example we have a double possibility of analysis that corresponds to no syntactical ambiguity: 'passionately/loved Mary' and 'passionately loved/Mary' alike work out as SC, and here once more we are just picking out subordinate SC strings in alternative ways from an SC string.

Two adverbs can be joined by a coordinating connective -- 'passionately and sincerely', 'improbably but presumably'. On the other hand a combination like 'passionately and presumably' sounds like nonsense. It is nonsense; it involves a confusion of syntactical categories. For an adverb like 'improbably' or 'presumably' is to be taken, in at least some cases, not as modifying the verb, but as modifying the whole sentence -- its category must thus be :ss. Two adverbs of category :ss can be joined with the connective 'but' of category :s(2s); for by our recursive rule:

Since :s(2s) s s → s, :s(2s) :ss :ss → :ss.

So 'improbably but presumably' comes out as a complex adverb of category :ss. Again, but our recursive rule:

Since :s(2s) s s → s, :s(2s) :sn :sn → :sn

Since :s(2s) :sn :sn → :sn, :s(2s) :(:sn)(:sn) :(:sn)(:sn)

→ :(:sn)(:sn).

So 'passionately and sincerely' comes out as of category :(:sn)(:sn), like its component adverbs. But an operator of category :s(2s) can take only two arguments of like category; so if we attempt to join with 'and' the adverbs 'passionately', of category :(:sn)(:sn), and 'presumably', of category :ss, we get syntactical nonsense.

IV. Prepositions

A prepositional phrase may be an adverb of category :(:sn)(:sn), like 'in London' in 'Raleigh smoked in London'; if so the preposition in the phrase is of category ::(:sn)(:sn)n. On the other hand, in the sentence 'Nobody except Raleigh smoked', 'nobody except Raleigh', like plain 'nobody', is a quantifying expression, of category :s:sn. So 'except Raleigh' is a functor turning one quantifying expression into another -- thus, of category :(:s:sn)(:s:sn); and 'except' itself is of category ::(:s:sn) (:s:sn) n. As before, expressions of the same category can be joined with coordinating connectives but not expressions unlike in category; for example, we may assume that 'before' and 'after' are both of category ::(:sn)(:sn)n, so 'before or after' is well-formed, as we may see:

Since :s(2s) s s → s,   :s(2s) :sn :sn → :sn

ergo,   :s(2s) :(:sn)(:sn) :(:sn)(:sn)

→:(:sn)(:sn)

ergo,   :s(2s)::(:sn)(:sn)n ::(:sn)(:sn)n

→::(:sn)(:sn)n.

But though 'Nobody smoked before or after Raleigh' is well-formed, 'Nobody smoked before or except Raleigh' is syntactical nonsense, because 'before' and 'except' differ in category.

The preposition 'by' is of different category, again, in the use it has with the passive construction; 'was hit by' must be regarded as formed by a logical operation upon 'hit', and the functor is of category :(::snn)(::snn), since ::snn is the category of 'hit'. The word "governed" by 'by' is thus not syntactically connected with it, since ':(::snn)(::snn)' and 'n' do not multiply out to give a single index. Why anyone should call a 'by' phrase an Adverbial of Manner I can only dimly imagine, calling to mind half-remembered school exercises in parsing. (How, in what manner, was Caesar killed? By Brutus. Very well then, 'by Brutus' is an Adverbial of Manner, just like 'brutally'!)

The categorizing of prepositions, however, raises very serious difficulties for our whole theory of categories - difficulties which I think can be overcome only by introducing a further powerful, recursive, procedure for establishing that an expression is SC. For example, 'some city' like 'every man' is of category :s:sn; but if we assign 'in' to category ::(:sn)(:sn)n, not only is the functor incapable of taking 'some city' as an argument as it can take 'London', but also the whole sentence 'Raleigh smoked in some city' cannot be made out to be SC by any way of multiplying out the category indices of 'Raleigh' (n), 'smoked' (:sn), 'in', and 'some city'. The only arrangement of the indices that multiplies out to 's' is this:

:s:sn	::(:sn) (:sn) n	n	:sn
(some city)	(in)	(Raleigh)	(smoked)

but this gives rather the syntactical analysis of 'Some city smoked in Raleigh'.

Our recursive·procedure is supplied by the well-known logical device - well expounded e.g. in Quine's *Methods of Logic* - of introducing a predicate as an interpretation of a schematic letter in a schema. If 'F' is of category :sn, the schema 'F(London)' will be SC and of category s. Now if 'F(London)' is SC, so will '(Some city)F' be - since ':s:sn :sn' gives 's'. We now reason thus: We have seen how to assign categories to the expressions in 'Raleigh smoked in London' so as to show it is SC and of category s. We may accordingly assign 'Raleigh smoked in $\frac{1}{-}$' as the interpretation of the one-place predicate letter 'F' in the SC schema 'F(London)'. But then also the corresponding interpretation of the SC schema '(Some city)F' will be SC; and this interpretation is the sentence 'Raleigh smoked in some city'; so this sentence is also SC.

Some quite short sentences require a number of steps like this to show they are SC. I shall give an example presently; but I must first explain how to categorize the reflexive pronouns in '-self'. Such a pronoun can be attached to a transitive verb of category ::snn to yield a one-place predicate of category :sn. We have already seen two ways of so attaching an expression to a transitive verb; both ':s:sn ::snn' and '::snn n' multiply out to ':sn'. But a reflexive pronoun plainly is not either a name, or a quantifying expression like 'every man'. Nor is it a mere proxy or substitute for an expression of one of these categories; we might take ; 'himself' in 'Judas hanged himself' to go proxy for 'Judas', but there is nothing 'himself' would be taken as proxy for in 'The Apostle who hanged himself went to Hell', and plainly 'hanged himself' is not syntactically different in the two sentences. The only category that gives the right result is ::sn::snn, since ::sn::snn ::snn → :sn. We may now consider our example, recalling ones of medieval vintage:

Every number or its successor is even.

We begin with the clearly well-formed sentence: '8 or 3 is even'. If we give the numerals the category n of proper names (shades of Frege!) then 'is even' will be of category :sn and this entence will be of the same syntax in essentials as our previous example 'John or James came'.

Since '8 or 3 is even' is SC, we may take '8 or $\frac{1}{-}$ is even' as the interpretation of the one-place predicate letter 'F' (category :sn) in the SC schema 'F(3)'. Now if 'F(3)' is SC, then if we assign to '5's successor' the quantifier category :s:sn (there are arguments for doing this, but I omit them for simplicity of exposition), the schema '(5's successor) F' will be SC. But the corresponding interpretation of *this* schema will be the sentence:

> 8 or 5's successor is even.

So this sentence is SC.

We now treat ' $\frac{1}{}$ or $\frac{2}{}$'s successor is even' as the interpretation of the two-place predicate letter 'R' in the schema 'R(8,5)'. If 'R' is of category ::snn, and each of '8', '5' is of category n, this schema is SC. But then also the result of operating on 'R' with a reflexive pronoun, 'R($\frac{1}{}$, itself)', will be an SC *one*-place schematic predicate; since we just saw that is how the reflexive pronoun works, to turn a two-place predicate into a one-place predicate. And the corresponding interpretation of 'R($\frac{1}{}$, itself)' will be:

> $\frac{1}{}$ or itself's successor is even.

So this counts as an SC one-place predicate. English accidence of course demands that one rewrite 'itself's' as 'its'.

Finally, since we may treat ' $\frac{1}{}$ or its successor is even' as an interpretation of the one-place predicate letter G, and since with the quantifying expression 'Every number' prefixed we get an SC schema '(Every number)G', we get as the relevant interpretation of this schema:

> Every number or its successor is even.

So *this* is an SC sentence; which was to be proved.

Grammarians may find my interpretation of this sentence extremely farfetched. They should consider, however, that it does correspond to the obviously correct paraphrase:

> It holds of every number that it or its(own) successor is even.

Moreover, other analyses, more comfortable to the ideas that come naturally to grammarians, lead us into a bog of absurdity. We cannot construe our sentence on the model of:

> Every man or every woman will be shot.

For this is equivalent to 'Every man will be shot or every woman will be shot'; but no such equivalence holds in our case - the irrelevant falsehood

'Every number is even' has nothing to do with the syntax of our example. (Nor need 'Every man or every woman will be shot' itself be construed as *short for* a disjunction of sentences, though it is *equivalent* to one; for it is easily shown by our rules that the two quantifying expressions 'every man' and 'every woman', of category :s:sn, can in their own right be joined by 'or', category :ss, to form an expression of that same category.) As for taking 'number or its successor' as a complex term, that lets us in at once, as my medieval predecessors noticed, for an absurd "syllogism":

Every number is a (number or its successor).

Every (number or its successor) is even.

ergo: Every number is even!

V. Relative Pronouns

Quine and I have both repeatedly argued that the use of relative pronouns may fruitfully be compared to that of bound variables. The question is, though, which kind of expressions throws light on the syntax of the other kind; the syntax of bound variables is very complicated and unperspicuous, as we may see e.g. from the need for rules in logic books to guard against unintended "captures" of variables in formulas introduced by substitution. Ajdukiewicz attempted to modify his scheme of categories so as to assign categories to quantifiers that bind variables; but his theory is manifestly inadequate - it takes no account of the fact that a variable is bound to a quantifier containing an *equiform* variable: for Ajdukiewicz '$(x)(Fxy)$' would not differ syntactically from '$(z)(Fxy)$', so far as I can see.

It occurred to me that some light might be thrown on the matter by constructing a simple combinatory logic, on the lines of Quine's paper 'Variables explained away'. I cannot claim any algorithmic facility in working with combinators, but I have reached results encouraging enough to be worth reporting.

To translate into a combinatory notation the English sentence:

Anybody who hurts anybody who hurts him hurts himself.

I began with an obvious translation of this into quantifier notation (variables restricted to persons; 'H $\underline{1}\,\underline{2}$' = '$\underline{2}$ hurst $\underline{1}$'):

$$(x)((y)(Hxy \rightarrow Hyx) \rightarrow Hxx)$$

and then devised the following set of combinators:

'Univ': when a predicate followed by a string of variables has prefixed to it a universal quantifier binding just the last variable of the string, we may instead delete the last variable and prefix 'Univ'; e.g. '$(x)(Fx)$' becomes 'Univ F' and '$(x)(Ryx)$' becomes 'Univ Ry'.

'Imp': if the antecedent of a conditional consists of a predicate followed by a string of variables, and the consequent consists of a predicate followed by just the same string, then we may instead write 'Imp' followed by the two predicates followed by the string of variables. E.g. '$Rxy \rightarrow Sxy$' becomes 'Imp R S xy'; '$Fz \rightarrow Gz$' becomes 'Imp F G z'.

'Ref': if a predicate is followed by a string of variable ending with repetition of a variable, we may instead delete the repetition and prefix 'Ref' to the predicate. E.g. 'Rxx' becomes 'Ref Rx', and '$Syxx$' becomes 'Ref Syx'.

'Cnv': the result of prefixing 'Cnv' to a predicate followed by a string of two or more variables is tantamount to the result of switching the last two variables of the string. E.g. 'Ryx' may be rewritten as 'Cnv R xy', and '$Rxyx$' as 'Cnv R xxy'.'

We now eliminate, step by step, the variables in the above formula. '$Hxy \rightarrow Hyx$' may be rewritten as '$Hxy \rightarrow$ Cnv H xy', and then as 'Imp H Cnv H xy'.

So '$(y)(Hxy \rightarrow Hyx)$' may be rewritten as '(y)(Imp H Cnv H xy)' and thus as 'Univ Imp H Cnv H x'.

'Hxx' may be rewritten as 'Ref H x'; so since '$(y)(Hxy \rightarrow Hyx)$' may be rewritten as 'Univ Imp H Cnv Hx', '$((y)(Hxy \rightarrow Hyx) \rightarrow Hxx)$' may be rewritten as:

Imp Univ Imp H Cnv H Ref H x.

Finally, to get an equivalent of the whole formula, we get the effect of the prenex '(x)' by deleting the final 'x' and prefixing 'Univ':

Univ Imp Univ Imp H Cnv H Ref H.

It is fairly easy to see how the symbols of this string should be assigned to categories. 'Univ F', when 'F' is one-place, is a sentence of the same form as 'Everyone smokes'; 'Univ', like 'everyone', is of category

:s:sn. 'H', like the transitive verb 'hurts' that it represents, is of category ::snn. 'Imp' is a connective that combines two predicates to form a predicate with the same number of places; it is thus of category ::sn(2:sn). 'Ref', like a reflexive pronoun, reduces a predicate of $n+1$ places to a predicate of n places; it is thus of category ::sn(::snn). And 'Cnv' turns a many-place predicate into one of the same number of places; it is thus of category :(::snn)(::snn). (It might seem as if these assignments of categories were too restrictive of the arguments these functors would be allowed to operate on. But in view of our recursive rules this is not so. For example, 'Imp' could combine two predicates of category ::snn to form a third:

$$::sn(2:sn) \ :sn \ :sn \rightarrow :sn$$
$$ergo, \quad ::sn(2:sn) \ ::snn \ ::snn \rightarrow ::snn.)$$

We may now check that the above string is, as Ajdukiewicz would say, well-formed throughout and of category s. 'Cnv H' is of category ::snn, since we have

$$:(::snn)(::snn) \ ::snn \rightarrow ::snn.$$

So 'Imp H Cnv H' is of category ::snn, since we have:

$$::sn(2:sn) \ :sn \ :sn \rightarrow :sn.$$

Hence, by the recursive rule:

$$::sn(2:sn) \ ::snn \ ::snn \rightarrow ::snn.$$

So 'Univ Imp H Cnv H' is of category :sn, since we have:

$$:s:sn \ :sn \rightarrow s$$
$$ergo, \quad :s:sn \ ::snn \rightarrow :sn.$$

Now also 'Ref H' is of category :sn, since we have:

$$::sn(::snn) \ ::snn \rightarrow :sn.$$

Hence 'Imp Univ Imp H Cnv H Ref H' is of category sn

$$::sn(2:sn) \ :sn \ :sn \rightarrow :sn.$$

Finally, since 'Univ' is of category :s:sn, the category of the whole works out as s.

Now this string of predicates and combinators can at once be translated, word for word, into pidgin English:

Univ   Imp Univ   Imp H   Cnv H   Ref H

anybody who anybody who hurt get hurt by hurt self.

(Some small changes of word order were made to improve this mock-up of English: 'Cnv' was rendered by 'get' before the argument of the functor and 'by' after it, and 'Ref' by 'self' after rather than before the argument of this functor.) I suggest, therefore, on the strength of this example (and of others I have not space for here) that we may hope to get a good mock-up of the use of relative pronouns in the vernacular by exercise in combinatory logic.

An interesting confirmation of this conjecture comes to us when we observe that in the above sentence 'Univ Imp' is an SC sub-string:

Univ   Imp

:s:sn :(:sn)(2:sn) → :s(2:sn),

by our recursive rule since :s:sn :sn → s.

Accordingly, we could definitionally introduce a new combinator of category :s(2:sn), say 'Unimp', and rewrite our string as 'Unimp Unimp H Cnv H Ref H'. The new string may also be translated straight into pidgin English:

Unimp Unimp H   Cnv H   Ref H

Whoever whoever hurt get hurt by hurt self.

And this seems to give a correct account of the logical syntax of the relative pronoun 'whoever'. Of course these results are most unnatural from the point of view of school grammar; in 'anybody who hurts...' the major division would be taken to come not after 'who' but after 'anybody', and 'who hurst...' would be taken as an SC sub-string somehow "modifying" 'anybody'. But if we are to get a scientific insight into syntax we mustn't be afraid to break Priscian's head. As Descartes said, *manum ferulae subduximus* - we no longer need hold out our hand to be caned by pedants.

Such are some specimens of the work I have done to carry out this Polish program. Much more remains to be done; it is like fitting together a huge jig-saw puzzle. But I hope I may have persuaded some readers that further following of this path is worth while.

Part II.

Modern
Context-Free-Like Models

II. MODERN CONTEXT-FREE-LIKE MODELS

Introduction

The first paper in this section is by Pullum and Gazdar. It contends that up to the time of that paper's publication nobody had presented a sound proof that any natural language is not a context-free language, when viewed as a string set. In particular, it attacks the classic argument that the *respectively* construct forces English to be a noncontext-free language. The origins of the argument for the *respectively* construct are in a paper by Bar-Hillel and Shamir (1964). That paper is concerned primarily with finite-state rather than context-free language issues. The *respectively* argument is not actually present in the paper but is alluded to and can be reconstructed from that paper using standard techniques. Since the Pullum and Gazdar paper reconstructs the argument in more detail than the original paper, we have not included the Bar-Hillel and Shamir paper at all. The Pullum and Gazdar paper makes a strong attack on the data used to show that *respectively* is not a context-free construct. However, it does not deal with the mathematical argument directly and does not dispose of the possibility of a *respectively* type structure at least potentially existing in some language. For example, it may exist in the semi-natural language of mathematical English. one point that Pullum and Gazdar fail to make in their review of the case against context-freeness is that all of the purportedly noncontext-free constructions in natural language are rare and usually quite peripheral. This is perhaps the most telling point. If all but a very small and marginal fraction of natural language is context-free, then the context-free grammar model has succeeded as well as we normally expect scientific theory to succeeded in modeling data. In our opinion, the Pullum and Gazdar paper may not be as ironclad as they would lead you to believe, but they make a very compelling argument nonetheless.

The following article, by Gazdar, presents a linguistically serious context-free grammar for a fragment of English. It presents one of the earlier versions of gpsg (generalized phrase structure grammar). Gpsg was designed to be a notational extension of context-free grammar which is

W. J. Savitch et al. (eds.), *The Formal Complexity of Natural Language*, 135–137.

weakly equivalent to context-free grammar, and under many views of the meaning of strong equivalence, it is even designed to be strongly equivalent to it. The Gpsg model has undergone numerous changes and refinements since this pioneering work. We chose this paper, rather than one of the later more complicated and more adequate models, because it shows the basic ideas underlying gpsg in a clean uncluttered setting that cannot be found in the later papers.

As the gpsg model has evolved it has been attacked on several fronts. One such attack questions whether the gpsg model is in fact weakly equivalent to context-free grammar. Gpsg uses meta-rules to accomplish many of the things that are handled by transformations in a transformational grammar framework. Meta-rules are a scheme for generating new context-free phrase structure rules form old ones. In gpsg a grammar is defined by giving a finite set of context-free phrase structure rules and a finite set of meta-rules which allow you to extend the list of phrase structure rules by application of the meta-rules. Gazdar, Pullum, Sag, and the gpsg school claim that this is a highly useful notational device, but after all is said and done, it is just a way of describing a finite number of context-free phrase structure rules and so gpsg is weakly equivalent to context-free grammar. The paper by Uszkoreit and Peters shows that for at least one definition of meta-rule, a grammar with meta-rules is capable of generating any recursively enumerable set and hence is equivalent to the most general of the transformational grammar models. The result by Uszkoreit and Peters is mathematically sound. The current version of gpsg is indeed weakly equivalent to context-free grammar. The apparent contradiction has to do with the definition of "meta-rule". The original and very natural definition of meta-rule was some what vague, and as made precise by Uszkoreit and Peters, was seen to allow the production of infinitely many phrase structure rules. In current versions of gpsg, some constraint is always imposed to insure that only finitely many phrase structure rules are produced by the combination of base rules and meta-rules. That would seem to make the Uszkoreit and Peters result now irrelevant. However, the result still points out that a natural yet suitably restricted definition of meta-rule may still be missing from gpsg.

The final paper by Bach presents a version of categorial grammar, a model which has been receiving increased attention in recent years, partly because of the renewed interest in nontransformational theories. The classical models of categorial grammar, which allowed specification of directionality between functor and argument and used only functional application, were shown early on to be weakly equivalent to context-free grammars. The paper by Geach in the first section of this book contains proposals for extending the categorial grammar model. In recent work, the importance of functional composition and type-lifting operations of the sort proposed by Geach has been recognized. The Bach paper points out that these extensions do turn out to have crucial consequences for weak generative capacity.

Reference

Y. Bar-Hillel and E. Shamir, "Finite State Languages: Formal Representations and Adequacy Problems," reprinted in Y. Bar-Hillel (ed), 1964, *Language and Information*, Addison-Wesley, Reading Mass., 87-98.

Geoffrey K. Pullum and Gerald Gazdar

NATURAL LANGUAGES AND
CONTEXT-FREE LANGUAGES

0. Introduction

In his 1956 paper 'Three Models for the Description of Language' Noam Chomsky posed an interesting open question: when we consider the human languages purely as sets of strings of words (henceforth *stringsets*), do they always fall within the class called *context-free languages* (CFL's)? Chomsky declared that he did not know the answer to this question, and turned to a very different set of questions concerning relative elegance and economy of different types of description. Since 1956 various authors (Chomsky included) have attempted to provide answers in the negative, and the negative answer is now the standardly accepted one. We take up the question again in this paper, and show that it is still open, as all the arguments for the negative answer that have been provided in the literature are either empirically or formally incorrect.

The question of where the natural languages (as stringsets) are located on the 'Chomsky hierarchy' (Type 0 or recursively enumerable languages, Type 1 or context-sensitive languages, Type 2 or CFL's Type 3 or finite state languages (FSL's)) is an intrinsically interesting one. As Kimball (1973, 26) remarks:

The [Chomsky hierarchy] represents the fact that regular languages [i.e. FSL's - GKP/GJMG] are the simplest or least complex, the CF languages are next, and the CS are the most complex of the phrase sructure languages. In a certain sense, the problem faced in the construction a theory of universal grammar is to determine exactly how 'complex' natural language is.

In the past fifteen years or so, concern with questions of 'generative capacity' has declined somewhat, but, clearly, the mathematical properties of the object of study are of intrinsic interest regardless of whether or not

Linguistics and Philosophy 4 (1982) 471–504.
Copyright © 1982 by D. Reidel Publishing Co., Dordrecht, Holland.

W. J. Savitch et al. (eds.), The Formal Complexity of Natural Language, 138–182.

it is currently fashionable to stress such properties. Moreover, there are certain very important applications of work on this question. One area of application is the study of recognition algorithms and a second is the study of language identification algorithms (cf. Gazdar (1982) for discussion). The question we are concerned with is of interest in connection with machine processing of natural language. Compiler design for CFL's is a fairly well explored problem (see Aho and Ullman 1972, 1973), but designing compilers for non-CFL's can be grossly more difficult. Nor is this a concern that can be relegated to the field of computer programming; for those who take seriously the thesis of Fodor (1975), language acquisition for a human learner is nothing more or less than the construction of a program to compile the natural language into the human machine code (or whatever intermediate code is used for thinking).

Prescinding away from application, however, the work of assessing the validity of claims about the alleged non-context free character of human languages is inherently rewarding in that in some cases it leads to the consideration of complex and descriptively interesting data (cf. especially the facts from Dutch and Mohawk discussed below). It also has the potential of being highly relevant to theoretical linguistics in a way that has not hitherto been noted. Suppose some piece of mathematical work were able to show of some theory -- say, the arc pair grammar of Johnson and Postal (1980) or the 'government-binding' theory of Chomsky (1981) -- that it necessarily only defined grammars for CFL's.[1] If it were generally believed that the natural languages had already been shown not be a subset of the CFL's, the theory would immediately be charged with inadequacy, on the grounds that for some natural languages it would not provide for even a weakly adequate grammar (i.e. one that generated the right set of strings). But if the general belief about natural languages were incorrect, the theory (in principle, perhaps a correct theory) would have been unwarrantedly dismissed. As an insurance against such easily conceivable situations arising, we need to be sure that questions of weak generative capacity have not been incorrectly answered and prematurely closed.

We shall discuss first, in Section 1, the general background to the issue, and some of the prevailing misconceptions embodied in the linguistic literature. We then consider the only five published arguments for the non-context-freeness of natural languages: one involves comparative clauses in English (Section 2); one applies the pumping lemma directly to English (Section 3); one hinges on constructions with *respectively* (Section 4); one is based on facts of Dutch 'verb raising' sentences (Section 5); and one depends on aspects of noun incorporation in Mohawk (Section 6). In Section 7 we offer our conclusions.

1. Folklore

Introductory textbooks on generative grammar often mention the alleged 'inadequacy' of context-free phrase structure grammar (CF-PSG) for the description of natural language. But even the best of them offer only non sequiturs as backing for such denigration. A typical example from what is widely acknowledged to be one of the best textbooks of its type is the following piece of reasoning from Akamajian and Heny (1975, p. 86), which follows their introduction of a phrase structure rule for 'AUX' which fails to allow for a phrase structure description of auxiliary-initial interrogatives in a non-redundant way:

Since there seems to be no way of using such PS rules to represent an obviously significant generalization about one language, namely, English, we can be sure that phrase structure grammars cannot possibly represent *all* the significant aspects of language structure. We must introduce a new kind of rule that will permit us to do so.

There are several non sequiturs here, the central one being that the fact that "there seems to be no way of using such PS rules" for some task does not license the inference that no successful phrase structure (CF-PSG) account could possibly be devised.[2]

Culicover (1976, 50) argues very similarly, also on the basis of the English auxiliary system, claiming that it is "impossible to capture the observed generalizations in purely phrase structure terms". And, as pointed out by Hurford (1980, pp. 135ff) in a perceptive review of the two texts just cited, Culicover makes other such claims elsewhere in his book. After a discussion of *wh*-movement constructions he concludes that "the phrase structure analysis will not be sufficient to generate English" (p. 28), and three pages later he diagrams an abstract configuration (somewhat reminiscent of subject-verb concord) that he claims "cannot be described by phrase structure rules alone" (p. 31). Culicover is quite wrong in his claims about phrase structure grammar; simple CF-PSG's can be constructed (and are constructed by Hurford) to describe the phenomena cited.

The belief that CF-PSG is inadequate to cope with long-distance dependencies, syntactic concord, and so on, is well entrenched. Grinder and Elgin (1973, p. 57) go so far as to claim that even verb agreement in simple sentences "demonstrates clearly the inadequacy of... the CF-PSG". They exhibit some simple examples, and then assert that

> any set of CF-PSG rules that generate (correctly) the sequences [*The girl kisses the boy*] and [*The girls kiss the boy*] will also generate (incorrectly) the sequences [**The girl kiss the boy*] and [**The girls kisses the boy*]. The grammatical phenomenon of Subject-Predicate Agreement is sufficient to guarantee the accuracy of [the statement that] English is a not a CF-PSG language (p. 59).

The phenomenon guarantees no such thing, of course.[3]

Nor is the character of the problem changed when agreement-rule effects are exhibited across unbounded distances in strings. Yet Bach (1974, p. 77) states that

> to describe the facts of English number agreement is literally impossible using a simple agreement rule of the type given in a PSG, since we cannot guarantee that the noun phrase that determines the agreement will precede (or even be immediately adjacent to) the present-tense verb.

And Bresnan (1978, p. 38) makes the following claim:

> In contrast to the local type of number agreement..., the distant type of agreement... cannot be adequately described even by context-sensitive phrase structure rules, for the possible context is not correctly describable as a finite string of phrases.

Bresnan is referring to the interaction of *wh*-extraction and number agreement in examples like *Which problems did your professor say she thought were unsolvable?* It is perhaps worth demonstrating that far from being beyond the capacities of even context-sensitive phrase structure grammar, the phenomenon Bach and Bresnan are referring to can be described by a *finite state* grammar. Here is a simple finite state grammar with only three nonterminal symbols which generates an infinite subset of English including the example just cited.[4]

> S → *Which problem did your professor say* T
>
> S → *Which problems did your professor say* U
>
> T → *she thought* T | *you thought* T | *was unsolvable?*
>
> U → *she thought* U | *you thought* U | *were unsolvable?*

This is not a proposed fragment of the grammar of English, of course; it is presented merely as a simple proof that an infinite language with long-distance dependencies and syntactic concord over unbounded domains can be an FSL.[5]

The views we have been discussing seem to have become a kind of folklore within generative grammar, frequently repeated for the benefit of the young though not provided with any scientific backing. We find the familiar claims about the 'inadequacy' of CF-PSG reiterated or simply assumed in linguistic works of all kinds. We find introductory texts, beside the ones already cited, saying things like, "Phrase-structure rules are not sufficient to account for all syntactic knowledge" (Fromkin and Rodman, 1979, pp. 234-235) and "We must assume that any phrase-structure grammar of a natural language will need to make extensive use of context-sensitive rules" (Allerton, 1980, p. 82). We find technical papers in syntax making similar claims, as when Selkirk (1977, p. 285) takes it to be "the single most important contribution to the development of linguistic theory in this century" that "the inadequacy of phrase structure grammars as a model of linguistic structure" has been demonstrated.[6] In discussions of parsing we find Winograd (1972, p. 42) asserting that "context-free parsers...cannot handle the full complexity of natural language", and Langendoen (1975, p. 536n) claiming that "the generative capacity...of CFPS grammars is too small to be of linguistic interest". And in Pinker's review of the formal literature on learnability we find the assumption that "natural languages are not context-free" being accepted without remark as if it were quite uncontroversial (Pinker, 1979, p. 223).

The introductory texts and similar expository works in the field of generative grammar offer nothing that could be taken as a serious argument for the claim that natural languages are not CFL's, and yet the general assumption in the literature is nevertheless that this claim is true. It is reasonable, therefore, to assume that everyone is tacitly relying on more technical arguments available elsewhere, which are presumably thought too complex for pedagogical works but nonetheless trustworthy. What form would a trustworthy argument take? A natural language (and indeed, any language) will have an infinite number of grammars that generate it, and one clearly cannot search through an infinite set of grammars to see if one of them is a CF-PSG. Hence a demonstration by enumeration of candidate grammars in order to show that they fail (the standard expository technique) is out of the question. We must utilize the various theorems about CFL's that have been proved in purely mathematical work on properties of stringsets.

One theorem about CFL's is the so-called 'pumping lemma'. Only once to our knowledge has anyone attempted to apply the pumping lemma directly to a natural language, and we discuss the (unsuccessful) result below in Section 3.

More useful than the pumping lemma are two closure properties of the CFL's: they are closed under intersection with FSL's, and closed under homomorphisms. The former property means that if one can define an FSL F such that $L \cap F = L'$ and L' is not a CFL, then neither is L. The latter property implies that if one can construct a homomorphism (a sequence-preserving symbol-by-symbol mapping) that converts L to L' and L' is not a CFL, then neither is L.

To use these properties to prove theorems about natural languages it is necessary to ensure that L' is in each case transparently non-context-free, ideally a language that can directly be shown not to be a CFL by application of the pumping lemma. Most published arguments have depended on setting some natural language as L and (implicitly in some cases) letting L' be an instance of what we shall call an *xx language*. The canonical instances of *xx* languages are

$\{xx \mid x \in L((a+b)^*)\}$ and $\{xx \mid x \in L((a+b)^+)\}$. We shall call a language an xx language just in case it can be mapped into one or other of these under the operations of homomorphism and intersection with FSL's. All xx languages in this sense are non-context-free. The proof that the canonical xx languages are not CFL's is straightforward (see. e.g., Aho and Ullmann (1972, p. 198)), and the non-context-freeness of xx languages in general immediately follows from the closure properties of CLF's mentioned above. Therefore, if a natural language can be shown to be an xx language, that natural language will not be a CFL. Sections 4, 5, and 6 analyze all the published attempts to obtain such a result that we are aware of. First, however, we must dispose of two unsuccessful arguments that do not have this form, in sections 2 and 3.

2. Comparatives

Chomsky (1963, pp. 378-9) based an argument on what we shall refer to as an xy language, i.e. one whose grammar requires *nonidentity* between substrings x and y in its sentences.

It should be observed that a language is also beyond the weak generative capacity of context-free grammars...if it contains an infinite set of phrases $z_1, x_2...$, sentences of the form $\alpha x_i \beta x_j \gamma$ if and only if i is *distinct* from j ... . Thus in the comparative construction we can have such sentences as *That one is wider than this one is DEEP* (with heavy stress on *deep*), but not **That one is wider than this one is WIDE* — the latter is replaced obligatorily by *That one is wider than this one is*. Thus in these constructions, characteristically, a repeated element is deleted and a nonrepeated element receives heavy stress. We find an unbounded system of this sort when noun phrases are involved, as in the case of such comparatives as *John is more successful as a painter than Bill is as a SCULPTOR*, but not **John is more successful as a painter than Bill is as a PAINTER...*, these constructions show that natural languages are beyond the range of the theory of context-free grammars of PDS automata, irrespective of any consideration involving strong generative capacity.

Chomsky is claiming two things. First, that English contains a set of sentences of the form $\alpha x \beta y \gamma$ where β is arbitrary central material (such as (-er) *than this one is*) and the phrases x and y have to meet the condition that they are *not* identical.[7] And second, that a set of strings meeting these conditions (an '*xy* language') cannot be enumerated by a CFG, so English cannot either.

We consider the empirical premise first. Chomsky, as pointed out by Bresnan (1976, pp. 373-4), no longer regards sentences such as (1) below as ungrammatical.

(1)   That one is wider than this one is WIDE.

In fact, in the course of arguing against Bresnan's analysis of comparative clauses, he cites the example in (2):

(2)   What is more, this desk is higher than that one is HIGH.
      (Chomsky, 1977, p. 122)

We are entirely persuaded by Chomsky's argument that this sentence is grammatical. We presume that the same should be said of (1), and that Chomsky's original judgement on it (1963, p. 378) was wrong.

There is a second problem with the factual basis of the argument. Green (1971, p. 560) observes that sentences like (3) seem very peculiar (ungrammatical, in her view).

(3)   John is as fat as Bill is obese.

This is an equative; but the same kind of oddness is felt in (4).

(4)   John is fatter than Bill is obese.

The linguistic strangeness of these sentences seems to be due to the fact that the two adjectives employed are synonymous, so that in virtually any context it would have been a good deal simpler and less puzzling to have used the elliptical variants (5), (6).

(5)   John is as fat as Bill is.

(6) John is fatter than Bill is.

But exactly the same can be said regarding (1) for this has an elliptical variant as well, as Chomsky stresses:

(1)   That one is wider than this one is WIDE.
(7)   That one is wider than this one is.

The only circumstance in which (1) would not share the oddness of examples like (3) and (4) would be one in which (7) did not sufficiently emphasize that the adjective in the *than*-clause was *wide* as opposed to some alternative with which the speaker wanted to contrast it. In other contexts, whatever semantic or pragmatic explanation covers (3) and (4) -- and there must be one -- will also cover (1). Thus whatever residual linguistic oddness inheres in Chomsky's crucial examples has an independent explanation unrelated to questions of superficial nonidentity of adjectives. The syntactic nonidentity condition is not only unnecessary (given that (1) is grammatical), it would also have been insufficient in failing to eliminate (3) and (4).

We now turn to the formal side of the argument, which is so flawed that any remaining uncertainty about the data discussed above is an irrelevance.

Chomsky does not actually give a demonstration that a homomorphism or an intersection with a finite state language could connect English in the appropriate way to an xy language. We can ignore this because there is a far more serious formal flaw in his argument. Although Chomsky's crucial premise is that xy languages are inherently non-context-free, he neither supplies nor alludes to a proof of this. Nor could he, in fact, for it is false. There are infinitely many context-free xy languages. To illustrate, we shall take an example based on the specifications given by Chomsky above. We assume a terminal vocabulary $\{a, b, \alpha, \beta, \gamma\}$, and consider the language denoted by (8).

(8) $\{\alpha x \beta y \epsilon \gamma \mid x, y \in L((a+b)^*) \land x \neq y\}$

This is a CFL. Rather than use the pumping lemma to prove it, we shall simply exhibit a CF-PSG that generates the language.[8]

(9)   (a) S → α S′ γ | α S″γ

       (b) S′ → CS′C | Dβ | β D

       (c) S″→ AB′ | BA′

       (d) A → CAC | a(D)β

       (e) B → CBC | b(D)β

       (f) A′ → a(D)

       (g) B′ → b(D)

       (h) C → a | b

       (i) D → C(D)

Since it is rather hard to see that the language described in (8) is a CFL even when (9) is provided, a few words of explanation are in order. The grammar in (9) develops terminal strings in three main ways. Rule (9a) starts things off by placing α at the beginning and γ at the end of the string. Recursion through S′ using the first alternative in (9b) yields an S′ flanked by equal numbers of a's and/or b's. To stop the recursion, use the second alternative in (9b), which places a D and the center marker β in that order. D can dominate any number greater than one of a's and/or b's. Thus there will be at least one more charcter before the β than after it, so the x string (between α and β) will differ in length from the y string (between β and γ). The third alternative in (9b) handles the converse case (more characters in y than in x) analogously. This leaves the problem of generating the strings where x is the same length as y but x and y are different. For x to differ from y other than in length, there must be some j such that at the jth character, x has an a and y has a b or conversely. To ensure the former, use the second alternative of (9a), and then expand S″ by means of the first half of (9c) to derive AB′. Recursion i times on (9d) leads to an A with i instances of a or b characters on each side. To stop this recursion, use the second alternative in (9d) to introduce an a followed by an optional further sequence of a or b characters (dominated by D) and a β. Expand B′ via (9g), as b followed by an optional string of a's and/or b's. The specified a introduced by (9d) will be preceded by exactly i characters from the set $\{a,b\}$, and exactly i characters from this set will separate β from the specified b that (9g) supplies. Thus x will differ from y at the $i{+}1$th symbol: x will have an a where y has a b. The converse is also provided for in an obvious way via recursion on B (using rules (9e) and (9f)). These hints should suffice to enable the reader to check with paper and pencil that the grammar in (9) guarantees dissimilarity between the $\alpha...\beta$ and $\beta...\gamma$ strings and thus generates the language described in (8).

This proves that the formal premises for Chomsky's argument are as invalid as the empirical ones, and the entire argument is unsalvageable.[9]

3. Pi

In a recent book concerned with applying logical theory to the social sciences, Elster (1978) touches on the question we are considering in this paper, and offers an original argument purporting to show that English is not a CFL. The argument involves applying the pumping lemma directly to a set of English sentences about the decimal expansion of pi. Since the argument is fairly concise, we reproduce it in full below**.

Bar-Hillel *et al.* have proved the following theorem:

Let A be a context-free grammar and $L(A)$ the set of sentences generated by A. Then there exists a number p such that for any z in $L(A)$ longer than p, there exist z, u, w, v, y such that

(*i*) $x = zuwvy;$

(*ii*) $zu^m wv^m y \in L(A)$ for all m;

(*iii*) *u and v are not both empty.*

More briefly the theorem states that in a language generated by a context-free grammar any sufficiently long sentence can be extended by indefinite repetition of *two* subparts without violation of grammaticality, just as we know that in languages generated by a finite state grammar any sufficiently long sentence can be extended by indefinite repetition of one subpart. In order to prove the inadequacy of context-free grammars for natural languages, we must come up with a counterexample of a grammatical sentence that cannot be extended in this way. The counter-examples of the form 'If^k it blows, (then it rains)^k' will not do for this purpose, for these sentences *can* be indefinitely extended by repetition of the two exponential blocks. Now let us look at the following sentences:

B_1: The first two million numbers in the decimal expansion of π are $a_1 a_2 \cdots a_{2000000}$.

B_2: The first two million numbers in the decimal expansion of π are $a_1 a_2 \cdots a_{2000000000000}$.

$\vdots$

B_k: The first two(million)^k numbers in the decimal expansion of π are $a_1 a_2 \cdots a_{2 \cdot 10^{6k}}$.

$\vdots$

Given a context-free grammar and the number p of the above theorem, it is easy to find a k such that B_k *is longer than p. Such a B_k must then permit a double extension as stated in the theorem. It is not difficult to see that these extensions must occur within the blocks* 'million^k' *and* '$a_1 \cdots a_{2 \cdot 10^{6k}}$' *if the result is not to be obviously ungrammatical. Suppose, then, that u in the theorem has the form* 'million^q' *and v the form* '$a_r \cdots a_t$'. *Choosing m=2 in the theorem, it then states that the following* sentence must be a grammatical one if we assume that the context-free grammar in question is adequate for English.

C: The two million^{k+q} *first numbers in the decimal expansion of π are* $a_1 \cdots a_t a_r \cdots a_t \cdots a_{2 \cdot 10^{6k}}$

I shall show that C is not a grammatical sentence in English. If C is grammatical, then the number 'two million^{k+q}' *must be the same as the number* '$2 \cdot 10^{6k} + t - r + 1$' , *i.e. the same as the number of numbers in the decimal expansion. Note that this is a requirement not of mathematics, but of linguistics, just as the lack of grammaticality of the sentence,*

D: the two largest animals in the zoo are a mouse,

is a matter of linguistics, and not of mathematics (or of zoology). But as $q \geqslant 1$ and $t - r + 1 \leqslant 2 \cdot 10^{6k}$ *we have*

$$2 \cdot 10^{6k} + t - r + 1 \leqslant 4 \cdot 10^{6k} < 2 \cdot 10^{6k+1} < 2 \cdot 10^{6(k+q)}.$$

whereas the grammaticality of C would require $2 \cdot 10^{6k} + t - r + 1 = 2 \cdot 10^{6(k+q)}$.

The flaw in this argument is not hard to detect. Elster is assuming that the following principle is a rule of English grammar:

(10) In the construction 'The W_1 are W_2' , the number of entities listed in W_2 must correspond to the number named in W_1 .

His only evidence for this principle is the ungrammaticality of (11a).

(11) (a)* The two largest animals in the zoo are a mouse.

(b) The two largest animals in the zoo are a mouse and a gerbil.

But the ungrammaticality of (11a) does not require his principle as an explanation, since it already follows from one of the most familiar, and least controversial, rules of English grammar, namely the rule that requires predicates to agree with their subjects in number. This rule accounts for the contrast between (11a) and (11b), as well as for the patterns of grammaticality shown in (12) and (13):

(12) (a) Mickey is a mouse.

(b)* Mickey are mice.

(c)* Mickey and Minnie is a mouse.

(d) Mickey and Minnie are mice.

(13) (a) The largest animal in the zoo $\left\{ \begin{array}{c} \text{is} \\ *\text{are} \end{array} \right\}$ Mickey.

(b) *The largest animal in the zoo $\left\{ \begin{array}{c} \text{is} \\ \text{are} \end{array} \right\}$ Mickey and Minnie.

(c)* The two largest animals in the zoo $\left\{ \begin{array}{c} \text{is} \\ \text{are} \end{array} \right\}$ Mickey.

(d) The two largest animals in the zoo $\left\{ \begin{array}{c} *\text{is} \\ \text{are} \end{array} \right\}$ Mickey and Minnie.

However, crucially, the following strings *are* grammatical sentences of English:

(14) (a) The two largest animals in the zoo are Mickey, Minnie and Donald.

(b) The three largest animals in the zoo are Mickey and Minnie.

Such sentences are necessarily false (or, perhaps, necessarily truth-valueless), and consequently infelicitous qua utterances. Elster's mistake is to confuse grammaticality with felicity. His argument based on pi has no bearing on English or any other natural language. There would be a few more cases to deal with grammatically in a language with morphological distinctions between singular, dual, and trial, but larger numbers govern plural concord in such languages, and our point could be made in exactly the same way. Elster's assumption that the sentences in (14) are ungrammatical is wrong in the same way that it would be wrong to try to achieve a syntactic account of what is peculiar about the examples in (15).

   (15) (a)   Here are six random integers: 3, 17, 8, 9, 41.

           (b)   Our three main weapons are fear, surprise, ruthless efficiency, and a fanatical devotion to the Pope.

           (c)   There'll be Bob, Carol, Ted, Alice, Bruce, Martha, Mike, and that's eight including the two of us.

In short, Elster's argument depends on a confusion between grammar and arithmetic.

4. Respectively

Bar-Hillel and Shamir (1960, p. 96) present the earliest argument that English is an xx language and thus not a CFL. They suggest that a string of the form

John, Mary, David, ...are a widower, a widow, a widower, ---, respectively

is a grammatical sentence if and only if the three dots are replaced by a string of any length of proper names, with repetitions and commas between the names, and the three dashes by a string of equally many phrases of one of the forms 'a widower' or 'a widow' and such [that] whenever the nth proper name is male (or female), the nth phrase is 'a widower' (or 'a widow').

They then say that they regard this as "almost conclusive" proof that English is not a finite state language, and that it "shows also the inadequacy of the simple phrase structure grammars".

Daly (1974, pp. 57-60) gives a detailed critique of their argument as it stands, pointing out that what it asserts about English is quite untrue, and that formally its authors have not even begun to make a case that English is not CF. But we shall not review Daly's discussion, for what is important is not the failure of Bar-Hillel and Shamir to make an argument but the possibility that a valid argument might be based on *respectively*-constructions.

Langendoen (1977, pp. 4-5) has attempted to reconstruct the *respectively* argument with different examples and a secure formal basis. He first defines the language that we exhibit as the regular expression in (16);

(16) **(the woman + the men)$^+$ and (the woman + the men)
(smokes + drink)$^+$ and (smokes + drink) respectively.**

The expression **(a+b)$^+$** denotes the set of all non-null strings consisting of *a*'s and *b*'s, so (16) contains an infinite set of strings like *the woman the men the men and the men drink drink smokes smokes and smokes respectively*, where no matching up between the singular and plural noun phrases and verbs need be present. This simply defined language is a FSL. Langendoen then considers the intersection of (16) with English. This, he claims, will be the language defined in (17):

(17) {xx' *respectively* | $x \in L$ ((**the woman + the men)$^+$ and (the woman + the men))** and x' is the corresponding string that has *smokes* in place of *the woman* and *drink* in place of *the men*}

Langendoen notes, correctly, that (17) is not a CFL; but since the intersection of a CFL and an FSL is always a CFL, and since (17) is (putatively) the intersection of (16) and English, English cannot be a CFL.

This would be a sound argument if its premises were all true, but we dispute one of the premises, namely the characterization of English that is assumed. The argument crucially turns on the grammatical status of the following sentences, which we do not mark with our own judgements but leave to the reader to assess or test out with informants before continuing.

(18) (a) The woman and the men smokes and drinks respectively.

(b) The woman and the men smokes and drink respectively.

(c) The woman and the men smoke and drinks respectively.

(d) The woman and the men smoke and drink respectively.

Our judgements are as follows. All of (18a-c) we find ungrammatical. While (18d) is of uncertain status, it is the only one we could conceivably accept (assuming that the meaning intended for each of these strings is 'The woman smokes and the men drink'). But what the *respectively* argument uses as a premise is a characterization of English under which (18b) alone is grammatical, the others all being ungrammatical. This does not seem correct to us (and nor does it seem correct to Geoffrey Sampson, who makes the same point we are making here, on the basis of a different example, in Sampson (1975, pp. 205-206)).

Even more tellingly, consider the data in (19).

(19) (a) The man and the woman smokes and drinks respectively.

(b) The man and the woman smoke and drink respectively.

We find we can tolerate (19b), but we reject (19a) completely. This is the exact converse of the grammaticality assignments assumed in Langendoen's characterization of English *respectively* constructions on subject-verb pairs.

We also find, more generally, that it is not true, as every version of the *respectively* argument seems to assume, that there is some numerical matching between syntactic elements in every grammatical sentence containing *respectively*.[10] Simple expositions of the *respectively* construction generally point to strings like (20) and call them ungrammatical.

(20) Ira, Walt, and Louise have been dating Frank, Edith, Cedric, and Bruce, respectively.

Such sentences (of which more below) are indeed odd; but that is not because of some one-to-one mapping requirement on syntactic constituents. Suppose that someone has just been attempting to pick out, on a mass photo of the LSA membership, all those who reside in New York, and the last two faces they point to are those of Jerry Sadock and Arnold Zwicky. One might utter (21):

(21) The people you have indicated are all New York residents except for the last two. They live in Chicago and Columbus respectively.

In this case, the nonlinguistic context picks out a unique ordered set of people with whom Chicago and Columbus can be appropriately associated; but the sentence that contains *respectively* has an odd number of noun phrases in it, so pairing of constituents certainly cannot be part of the correct characterization of *respectively* sentences.[11]

If the oddity of (21) does not arise from the odd number of noun phrases it contains, then what causes it? De Cornulier (1973) provides what we think is the right answer (see also, Hinton 1978). The way

Langendoen's or any other version of the *respectively* argument treats the item *respectively* implies that it is without inherent meaning. While all other adverbs in the language will be lexical items with their own semantic contribution to make to the meaning of sentences in which they occur, *respectively* will be a syncategorematic item, introduced as a property of the syntactic construction in which it occurs (the way the past participle-forming morpheme-*en* is often treated in transformational analyses of the passive construction.) De Cornulier suggests that it has a straightforward meaning, albeit a metalinguistic one. It can be roughly paraphrased as 'each in the order in which I cite them'. (One might revise this to 'each in the order indicated or implied', given cases like (21).) He points out that (22a) and (22b) -- which he gives in French, though nothing changes under our translation into English -- seem odd to the same degree and intuitively for the same reason:

(22) (a) Paul, Mary and Jack are respectively (male) cousin, uncle, and aunt to Robert.

   (b) Paul, Mary and Jack are, in the order in which I cite them, (male) cousin, uncle, and aunt to Robert.

But it would be absurd to attempt a syntactic account of why (22b) is odd. And as soon as an appropriate semantic or pragmatic account is set up, it will generalize to (22a), provided that *respectively* is assigned a meaning similar to the one de Cornulier suggests for it.[12]

Since *respectively* constructions have figured in arguments that phrase structure grammar must be abandoned in favour of transformational grammar, it is worth observing that no observationally adequate syntactic description of these constructions was ever provided in the transformational literature. This is presumably a rather surprising and disturbing fact if the construction in question really was one of the main reasons for the complete abandonment of phrase structure grammar in favour of the less constrained transformational model of syntactic theory.

Summarizing, we find that in the case of the *respectively* argument, the crucial data purporting to show English not to be CF are firstly mistaken at the level of observational adequacy, and secondly, illustrative only of semantic or pragmatic points insofar as they illustrate anything. We consider the *respectively* argument, therefore, to be completely without force.

5. Dutch

An ingenious attempt to show that Dutch is not context-free has been made by Huybregts (1976). This article was only published in working-paper form and may not represent the author's current views, so rather than address ourselves closely to the text of Huybregts' paper, we shall address the facts, and show that no argument of the sort Huybregts advances can in fact succeed.

Although the verb is final in the verb phrase of a simple subordinate clause in Dutch, when transitive infinitival VP's are nested the verbs do not appear in the order that would be predicted simply by nesting one VP inside another as in (23).

(23)

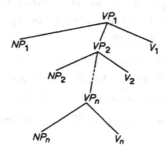

Instead, the string will generally look like this:

(24) $NP_1 \, NP_2 \cdots NP_n \, V_1 \, V_2 \cdots V_n$.

Here $V_1 \cdots V_{n-1}$ are taken to be verbs that select a direct object NP and a complement VP (cf. *make*, *let*, or *help* in English), and V_n is some transitive verb. For all i (where $1 \leqslant i \leqslant n$), NP_i is the direct object of V_i, and is present because V_i is subcategorized to require it. Thus we have the beginnings of an argument of the same sort as the *respectively* argument, it might be claimed: Dutch has an infinite subset with an unbounded cross-serial dependency of the type $a_1 a_2 ... a_n b_1 b_2 ... b_n$, which can be mapped by a homomorphism into an xx language, and thus is not context-free. However, the actual situation is rather different, as we shall show, and ultimately no such argument can be made.

Consider some concrete examples. Example (25) is a grammatical subordinate clause in Dutch.

(25) dat Jan [Marie Pieter Arabish laat zien schrijven]
　　　 that Jan Marie Pieter Arabic let　see　write
　　　 'that Jan let Marie see Pieter write Arabic'

The bracketed portion contains three verbs (the first finite, the others infinitival) and three NP's. The first NP is, in some sense, the direct object of the first V and the subject of the second; the second NP is, in the same sense, the object of the second V and the subject of the third; and the third NP is the object of the third V.

Not all verbs are transitive, of course. When selected verbs in the above example are replaced by verbs of other valencies, the number of NP's required changes. If *schrijven* 'write' is replaced by *liegen* 'lie', (25) becomes the ungrammatical (26):

(26) *dat Jan [Marie Pieter Arabisch laat zien liegen]
　　　 that Jan Marie Pieter Arabic　　let　see　lie
　　　 '*that Jan let Marie see Pieter lie Arabic'

Similarly, ungrammaticality results if the number of NP's is altered, say by adding *Hans*:

(27) *dat Jan [Marie Pieter Arabisch Hans laat zien schrijven]
　　　 that Jan Marie Pieter Arabic　 Hans let　see　write
　　　 '*that Jan let Marie see Pieter write Arabic Hans'

However, additional verbs can be inserted if they are *intransitive* VP-complement-taking verbs:

(28) dat Jan [Marie Pieter Arabisch wil laten zien schrijven]
　　　 that Jan Marie Pieter Arabic　will let　 see write
　　　 'that Jan will let Marie see Pieter write Arabic'

Thus the number of NP's that can be permitted in such strings is a function of the number of V's and the valencies of those V's.

However, this does not mean that the stringset of Dutch is non-context-free. Even when we keep in mind that the first verb in each example is finite and all the others are in their infinitive forms, and that the final verb has to be one that does *not* take a VP complement, it is trivially easy to write a CF-PSG to assign the right number of NP's to go with the number of V's selected.

Take first the case where only ordinary NP's are involved (i.e. excluding verbs that take PP complements, verbs like *regenen* that demand a particular NP (*het* 'it') as subject, and so on). What we have to do is to ensure that each of the relevant class of VP's contains some number n of NP's, a finite VP-complement-taking verb, a string x of nonfinite VP-complement-taking verbs, and a final transivite or intransitive verb, such that x contains $n-2$ transitive verbs if the finite verb and the last verb are both transitive, $n-1$ if only one of the finite verb and the last verb is transitive, and n transitive verbs otherwise. This will guarantee that each transitive verb has an NP to be its direct object, and that no intransitive verbs will get objects. The following grammar does it. (We use an arbitrary initial symbol A. Note that the grammar generates subordinate clause verb phrases, not sentences, and that for simplicity all NP's are taken to be simple names.)

(29) (a) Syntactic rules

    A → BCD | CE

    C → BCF | CG | BH | I

  (b) Lexicon

    B: *Marie, Pieter*, other personal names

    D: *schrijven*, other transitive infinitives

    E: *liegen*, other intransitive verbs

    F: *laten*, other transitive VP-complement-taking infinitives

    G: *willen*, other intransitive VP-complement-taking infinitives

    H: *laat*, other finite transitive VP-complement-taking verbs

    I: *wil*, other finite transitive VP-complement-taking verbs

The tree this grammar assigns to the VP of example (28) is shown in (30).

(30)

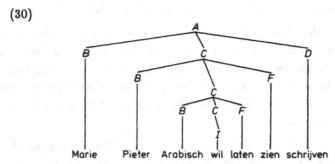

The grammar provides for intransitive verbs to occur interspersed with the transitive ones (*laten, zien*) shown in this example. Using *willen* yields for the most part very peculiar results for semantic reasons. Category I should be assumed to be augmented with such verbs as *scheen te* 'seemed to' (with *te* treated, to avoid complications, as part of the verb), and category G should likewise be assumed to contain *schijnen te* 'to seem to' etc. These details do not affect the point under discussion here. For a summary of the behavior of various verbs in this construction, see Zaenen (1979).

What this grammar does not guarantee, quite deliberately, is that all the sentences it provides for will mean something sensible. For example, sentences like the following will be generated:

(31) (dat Jan) Marie Arabisch Pieter wil laten zien schrijven
     (that Jan) Marie Arabic Pieter will let   see   write
     '(that Jan) will let Marie see Arabic write Pieter'

This is, of course, a 'selection restriction' violation. The non-syntactic status of selection restrictions is surely quite uncontroversial by now. It is not for the syntax to rule out examples of this sort, for the above example is perfect under the assumption that there is a language or writing system called 'Pieter' and a person named 'Arabisch' has learned to write.

When we turn to examples involving verbs that take complements other than NP (like *schrijven*) or nothing (like *liegen*), things are only slightly more difficult. Suppose there are n classes of verbs in Dutch, V_1 thru V_n, each taking different combinations of NP's, PP's, or whatever as their subcategorized complements. Let us use the notation X_i for whatever string of phrases V_i is subcategorized to take. All we need is a set of n categories C_1 through C_n and for each verb class V_i we can provide a set of rules as shown in (32), the lexicon apart from the entry for V_i being shown in (29b).

(32) $A \rightarrow C_i V_i$

    $C_i \rightarrow BC_i F \mid C_i G \mid BX_i J \mid X_i I$

    $J \rightarrow H(E) \mid I(E)F$

    $E \rightarrow G(E)$

An example of how this grammar would generate a ditransitive case with *geven* 'give' is provided in (33). We assume that *geven* belongs to a class called V_3, so the rule schema '$C_i \rightarrow BX_i J$' in (32) is instantiated here by a rule '$C_3 \rightarrow BBBJ$', allowing the appearance of *geven* to correlate with the appearance of a pair of extra NP's:

(33) (a)   (dat Jan) Marie Pieter Hans Fido moet laten zien geven

           that Jan Marie Pieter Hans Fido must let   see   give

          '(that Jan) must let Marie see Pieter give Hans Fido'

    (b)

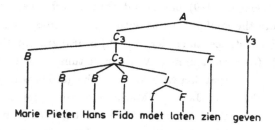

Allowing for a subject that is (let us assume) syntactically selected, like the *het* 'it' that goes with *regenen* 'rain', is also very easy. The above grammar makes X_i the final part of the preverbal half of the VP and V_i the final verb. By using the same mechanism we could make X_j be *het* where V_j is *regenen.* But this would give a word order that happens not to occur. It seems that *het* always assumes a special clitic position at the beginning of the VP. This is even easier to generate. Adding the rule 'A → *het* C *regenen*' to the grammar in (29a) is all that is necessary.

We must stress at this point that the foregoing examples of grammars and trees are not proposals concerning the grammar of Dutch or its constituent structure. The reader will note, for example, that the trees we have drawn are quite unsuitable for compositional semantic interpretation: semantic rules for assigning correct interpretations to Dutch sentences, constituent by constituent from the bottom up, cannot (as far as we can see) be provided on a rule-by-rule basis for the grammars given above. We do not intend to imply that they could. Although we have hypotheses in mind concerning the correct way to describe Dutch, this is not the place to develop them.[13] Our grammars are simply aids to showing, rather informally, that the facts we find in Dutch subordinate verb phrases are not incompatible with Dutch being a CFL.

Even syntactically, many details of Dutch are being glossed over, and many complications in the real situation are being ignored. However, the syntactic aspects of the Dutch situation that are suppressed here so far do not lend themselves to supporting any kind of stringset argument. In some cases, they make a valid stringset argument even harder to achieve. For example, Zaenen (1979) points out that a verb like *wil* does not always occur before the nonfinite verbs with which it co-occurs. Beside the order in (34a), for instance, the order in (34b) is also grammatical.

(34) (a)   dat Jan met Marie in de tuin   wil spelen
           that Jan with Marie in the garden will play

     (b)   dat Jan met Marie in de tuin   spelen wil
           that Jan with Marie in the garden plan will
           'that Jan will play with Marie in the garden'

This additional variation makes it much harder to begin setting up an argument involving a formal cross-serial dependency structure of the type $a_1 a_2 \cdots a_n b_1 b_2 \cdots b_n$, which is what Huybregts (1976) purports to do (but does not do). The task of setting up such an argument is similarly made harder by the fact that many transitive verbs can be used intransitively, so that it will not necessarily cause ungrammaticality if an NP is removed from a well-formed example. The reader can verify this by experiment. It is in fact quite difficult to construct examples that convincingly change their grammaticality when random NP's or verbs are inserted or removed, since so many strings turn out to be grammatical by accident under an unintended interpretation, or ungrammatical by virtue of extraneous factors that do not relate to the alleged dependency between NP's and verbs.

It is difficult to tell at this stage whether some CFL-inducing theory of grammar might be capable of providing for an adequate grammar for Dutch and a semantic interpretation system to go with it. However, that is not the claim at issue. We are concerned here with the thesis that Dutch, as a stringset, is not a CFL. We have said enough to show that there is no reason at all to believe that claim.

6. Mohawk

The best known and most influential argument for the non-context-freeness of a natural language is due to Postal (1964). Postal argues that the interaction of the processes of nominalization and incorporation in Mohawk (a Northern Iroquoian language of Quebec and upper New York state) yields a property that places Mohawk outside the CFL's. In brief, a verb in Mohawk can incorporate a noun-stem, i.e. it can have the internal structure [$_\mathrm{V}$ Prefixes Noun-stem Verb-stem Suffixes]. It incorporates the noun-stem of its subject if it is intrasitive, or the noun-stem of its direct object if it is transitive. Thus we have sentences consisting of single words with morpheme glosses like 'it-tree-stands' or 'he-meat-eats' and meanings like 'The tree stands', 'He eats meat'. But a verb like 'meat-eat' can be nominalized to make a noun meaning 'meat-eating', and this noun could itself be incorporated into a verb, which could be nominalized, and so on. Hence Mohawk has an infinite set of noun-stems. But sometimes a verb with an incorporated subject (object) noun-stem occurs with an overt subject (object) NP. In such cases the noun-stem in the verb must exactly match the noun-stem in the external NP. This is string-copying over an infinite set of strings (the set of noun-stems), hence Mohawk is an xx language and not a CFL.

Postal's paper has been criticized in the subsequent literature, but the critiques have had little impact. The best known critique is Reich (1969). Of this paper, Levelt (1974, 21n) says: "The large number of essential errors in this article...gives rise to some doubt as to the carefulness of the editors of *Language*". Fittingly, Reich's paper (which includes, among other things, an assertion without proof that the FSL's are not a subset of the CFL's) has been generally ignored by linguists.

There are certainly mathematical flaws in Postal's argument the way he originally gave it. The major one is that Postal relies on the following as his chief mathematical premise:

(35) It has been proven by Chomsky that the language consisting of all and only the strings [XX] is not a context-free language, where X varies over an infinite set of strings in an alphabet of two or more symbols. (1964, p.146)

The theorem Postal alludes to was never proven by Chomsky, and could not be, because it is not a theorem at all. There are languages of the type specified that are CFL's, as noted by Daly (1974, p. 68) and Elster (1978, p. 47).[14] An additional flaw is that Postal assumes:

(36) It can be demonstrated that Mohawk lies outside the bounds of context-free description by showing that it contains, as a subpart, an infinite set of sentences with formal properties of the language [XX]. (1964, p. 147)

This is not correct, as can be readily seen by noting that the non-CFL $\{xx \mid x \in L((a+b)^+)$ is an infinite proper subpart of the context-free (and finite state) language denoted by the expression $(a+b)^+$. This formal inadequacy is commented on by Daly (1974) and also by Fidelholtz (1975, p. 496, fn. 2).

However, these mathematical slips are unimportant, because they have been remedied by Langendoen (1977) who characterized precisely the conditions under which languages of the sort alluded to in (35) are non-context-free, and shows how to give a formally valid proof that Mohawk is non-context-free by intersecting it with a FSL to obtain a provably non-context-free by intersecting it with a FSL to obtain a provably non-context-free xx language. He does this as follows. First he sets up the following abbreviations:

(37) a = the translation into Mohawk of 'the man'

b = the translation into Mohawk of 'admired'

c = the translation into Mohawk of 'liking (of)'

d = the translation into Mohawk of 'praising (of)'

e = the translation into Mohawk of 'house'

Then he defines the finite state language $F = a(c+d)^*eb(c+d)^*e$. F contains all possible strings having the form *the man x-house-admired y-house* where x and y are arbitrary strings with meanings such as 'praising-of-liking-of-liking-of-praising-of-praising-of-liking-of' and so on. Postal's claim about Mohawk is that sentences from F will only be grammatical Mohawk sentences if the first string from $(c+d)^*$ is identical to the second (i.e. if x is the same as y), so Langendoen intersects F with Mohawk and obtains the language $L^m = \{a\,x\,e\,b\,x\,e \mid x \in L((c+d)^*)\}$. *This is an xx* language and thus not a CFL. Hence Mohawk is not a CFL.

Langendoen's version of the argument ignores one point that Postal mentions: there is a requirement "that a Modifier constituent precede the noun whose stem is to be doubled" (1964, p. 147, fn. 29). This is not a trivial point, because if the modifier (demonstrative, possessive, or whatever) is essential, as Postal claims, then F does not intersect with the set of stem-doubling sentences in Mohawk at all. Assume, then, that we take account of this point by adding a Mohawk modifier such as *thik*ʌ 'that' after b in the specification of F. There are then no flaws in the argument at all. We only need the crucial empirical premises about what is grammatical in Mohawk (and thus what is in L^m) *to be sound*.

Reich (1969, p. 833) correctly summarizes the three empirical premises as follows:

The first is that the acceptable [read 'grammatical' - GKP/GJMG] sentences of Mohawk include...sentences where the incorporated object co-occurs with an identical direct object which has been preceded by a modifier. The second...is that there are no Mohawk sentences of this type in which the object of the verb and the incorporated object are not identical; that is, there are no Mohawk sentences of this type which are in the form $XY[X \neq Y$ - GKP/GJMG]. The third...is that the nouns which are used as objects (both incorporated and free-standing) can be arbitrarily long, because of a process of making a noun out of a verb containing an incorporated noun.

The first premise should not be in doubt. Postal discusses the object-doubling construction in his dissertation (Postal (1962); see pp. 290ff) and gives elicited examples like (38).[15]

> (38) i?i knuhsnuhwe?s thikʌ kanuhsa
> I   house-like   that   house
> 'I like that house'

Those anxious to be assured that this construction occurs in spontaneous text need look no further than Michelson (1980, 29, line 21), where the stem -ri(h)w- 'matter' occurs incorporated in a verb with the stem -yʌ - 'put' and also in its object NP.

Reich's main attack is based on rebutting the third premise. He cites Floyd Lounsbury as claiming that "you never get more than one incorporation at the creative (syntactic) level", i.e. if an incorporated noun-stem itself contains an incorporated noun-stem, the latter is a frozen part of "a common idiom, a lexeme in the language" (1969, p. 834). Thus, Lounsbury is claiming, there is no productive feeding of incorporation by nominalization and conversely; the closest approach to this comes when incorporation happens to involve a noun stem which contains the lexically frozen remains of an incorporation which is not synchronically the result of the syntactic incorporation rule. This may be so,[16] but we are not inclined to take up this line of argument. As already noted (see Note 13), we do not necessarily accept that the lexicon of a natural language has to be a finite list, so a version of Langendoen's argument might be constructible even if Lounsbury were right. Moreover, we certainly do not follow Reich in his view that if the longest incorporated noun-stem ever observed in a text had, say only three layers of repeated incorporation, the correct grammar should set a three-layer limit. We accept the standard idealization, with its corollary that the set of attested and likely-to-be-attested sentences does not exhaust the set of grammatical sentences.

We believe that the Achilles' heel of the Mohawk argument lies in the second premise mentioned in the quote above; but no one has previously shown this. Reich mentions that Lounsbury has 'reservations' about the second premise, and gives translations of, but does not exhibit, three sentences which Lounsbury claims violate the identity requirement. He does not go into any detail. Postal acknowledges in his paper that there are other incorporation constructions than the one he is talking about;

There are certain other cases where a verb contains an incorporated noun stem which does not match the following external noun stem. These are due to minor rules and do not affect the present discussion. (1964, p. 148, fn. 30)

What has to be shown if Postal's argument is to be impugned is that the other cases referred to *do* affect the present discussion, and affect the soundness of Langendoen's reformulation of the argument.

One example of the sort of construction Postal was referring to is the construction generally known as *classificatory incorporation* in the literature on Iroquoian (see, e.g., Woodbury, 1975). These are mentioned in footnote 19 on pp. 405-406 of Postal (1962). Postal's analysis of incorporation makes reference to a morpheme called 'inc' which is replaced by a noun-stem when the incorporation transformation ('T-incorporation') applies, or is spelled out in one of various forms as an empty morph (cf. Lounsbury, 1953, p. 75) if incorporation does not apply. In the footnote cited he states that in addition to what T-incorporation does:

there appear to be a few special rules which replace the inc marker by certain noun stems before T-incorporation applies. One such rule inserts the stem *naskw* 'animal' when the object noun of the sentence is a member of Noun $Stem_{mammal}$. Thus we would get such sentences as

sawatis hranaskwhinu? ne yaoahkwari 'John will buy a bear'

And there are other cases where a stem with a more general meaning is inserted. I have found cases where the stem for 'berry' *hy* is used with fruits, where the stem for 'water' *hnek* is used with drinkable liquids, etc.

Marianne Mithun (personal communication) supplies a typical example of this sort:

(39) wa?k*hnek*ahnĩnu? ne otŝi?tsa?
I-*liquid*-bought   flower/wine
'I bought the wine.'

Here the meaning of the incorporated stem resolves the ambiguity of the external stem -*tsi?ts*-, which means both 'flower' and Other examples are supplied by Bonvillain (1974, pp. 21-22); e.g. (40).

(40) wake*selehta*hni:nu?se? ne? 'bike'
I her-*vehicle*-bought   bike
'I bought her a bike.'

These and similar cases certainly show that there are instances of incorporated noun-stems in transitive verbs that fail to match the noun-stems of their direct object NP's so that Postal's argument as originally set out is invalidated empirically as well as formally. But when we examine the form of the Langendoen version of Postal's case (henceforth the LP argument), we find that provided classificatory incorporation is limited to a finite list of simple stems (as Postal strongly implies it is), the construction has no implications for the LP argument at all. It is far too simplistic to assume that *any* discovery of stem-matching failure will entail irreparable failure of the whole argument.

Consider another kind of case, alluded to in Reich's discussion: null head nouns in subject or object NP's with modifiers. Postal (1962, p. 395) cites the following pair of sentences as synonymous:

(41) (a)   ka*nuhsrak*ʌ   thikʌ ka*nunhsa*
it-*house*-white   that   *house*
'That house is white.'

(b)   ka*nuhsrak*ʌ   thikʌ
it-*house*-white   that
'That house is white.'

Here an intransitive subject is seen with and without its head noun. The same possibility is present for a direct object, as shown by this example from Bonvillain and Francis (1980, p. 80, line 27; morpheme segmentation on p. 88):

(42) k*eli*?wañu:we?s ki?

    I it-*idea*-like   this

    'I agree to this'.

Again we appear to have a counterexample to the claim that incorporated stems match external stems. But if the LP argument as summarized above is examined closely, it will be found that the argument is only concerned with those sentences that are in Mohawk and have glosses of the form '(the) man *x*-house-admired that *y*-house' (correcting for the presence of the modifier as mentioned above), where *x* and *y* are noun-stems formed by using incorporations and nominalization to combine 'praise' and 'like'. Strings that do not end with the form meaning 'house' are not relevant at all. Thus the LP argument is fully robust enough to stand up to Reich's criticism, insofar as the evidence he offers is concerned.

However, there is a construction in Mohawk that has much more serious implications for the LP argument. Essentially all the relevant facts are to be found in Postal (1962), though we shall cite one or two other sources as well. We shall call the construction at issue the *possessed incorporation* construction. Briefly, when the subject or direct object NP of a verb contains a possessive NP modifier, it is possible to incorporate the noun-stem denoting the possessed entity, keeping the external NP; but it is also possible to drop the possessed noun from the external NP so that the possessor noun constitutes the whole of the subject or direct object NP. In the latter case the verb agrees with the possessor. These facts are illustrated in (43).

(43) (a)   i?i k-nuhwe?s ne ka-*nuhs*-a?

             I   like   *house*

             'I like the house.' (Postal 1962, p. 283, E147; morpheme gloss added.)

     (b)   i?i k-nuhwe?s ne sawatis hra-o-*nuhs*-a?

             I   like   John('s)   *house*

             'I like John's house.' (Postal 1962, p. 321, E243; morpheme gloss added.)

(c)   iʔi k-*nuhs*-nuhweʔs ne sawatis hrao-*nuhs*-a?
        I   *house- like*   John('s)   *house*
        'I like John's house.' (Postal, 1962, p. 291 E168;
        morpheme gloss added.)

(d)   iʔi hrai-*nuhs*-nuhweʔs ne sawatis
        I   *house*-like   John
        'I like John's house.' (Postal, 1962, p. 320, E239;
        morpheme gloss added.)

(e)   *iʔi hrai-nuhweʔs ne sawatis hrao-*nuhs*-a?
        I   like   John('s)   *house*
        (Postal, 1962, p. 321, E244; morpheme gloss added.)

In (40a) we see a simple example with subject, verb, and object. (The subject pronoun *iʔi* 'I' would normally be dropped.) A similar sentence with a possessive NP in the object phrase is shown in (40b). In (40c) the noun-stem denoting the possessed item, i.e. the head of the object NP, has been incorporated, but is also present in the object NP. In (40d) the head noun has been dropped from the object NP, leaving the incorporated noun-stem as the only realization of the notion 'house', and now the verb shows a different agreement pattern: as (40c) illustrates, the prefix *hrai-* is not correct for sentences with object NP's like 'John's house'. It is the appropriate prefix for sentences like 'I like John' (see, e.g., Postal's sentence E159 (1962, p. 285) for a similar case), and this is the prefix taken by the verb in (40d).

An example like (40d) clearly shows an incorporated noun-stem that fails to match the noun-stem of the direct object of its host verb, which crucially must not occur if Postal's overall argument is to be sound.[17] It seems clear that in constructing the argument he assumed that additional considerations of detail like the agreement pattern seen in (40d) would suffice to isolate the possessed incorporation construction (his 'possessor agreement' construction: 1962, p. 319) so that it could be set aside as irrelevant. But he has not provided a demonstration that this can be done. It seems to us that the LP argument does not survive once possessed incorporation sentences are brought into consideration. What is crucial for the LP argument is that sentences of Mohawk with glosses like 'The man praising-of-liking-of-house-admired that liking-of-praising-of-house' should be ungrammatical. But it is clear from the above discussion that such sentences will not be ungrammatical at all; they will merely have absurd meanings as their only possible readings -- in the case just cited, the meaning will be 'The man admired that liking-of-praising-of-house's praising-of-liking-of-house'. Verb agreement facts do not affect this conclusion in any way, for the abstract head nouns meaning 'liking-of-praising-of-house' and 'praising-of-liking-of-house' will determine the same agreement prefixes. The contrast between (40c) and (40d) only arises because of the contrast in agreement class memberships between the masculine human noun *sawatis* 'John' and the nonhuman noun *-nuhs-* 'house'. In the type of sentence that figures in the LP argument, the noun stems we are concerned with are always, and crucially, abstract nouns built up by iteration of the operations of incorporation and nominalization.

Thus the construction we call possessed incorporation demonstrates that the intersection of Langendoen's language F with Mohawk will in fact not be of the form ...x...x... where $x \in L\ ((c+d)^*)$, but rather of the form ...x...y..., where x and y are drawn from $L((c+d)^*)$ but are not necessarily identical. This is just another way of saying that Mohawk has F, a FSL, as an infinite subset. Nothing whatever follows about the context-freeness of Mohawk, and thus the LP argument against Mohawk being a CFL fails like all the previous arguments.

7. Conclusions

Notice that this paper has not claimed that all natural languages are CFL's. What it has shown is that every published argument purporting to demonstrate the non-context-freeness of some natural language is invalid, either formally or empirically or both.[18] Whether non-context-free characteristics can be found in the stringset of some natural language remains an open question, just as it was a quarter century ago.

Whether the question is ultimately answered in the negative or the affirmative, there will be interesting further questions to ask. If it turns out that natural languages are indeed always CFL's, it will be reasonable to ask whether this helps to explain why speakers apparently recognize so quickly whether a presented utterance corresponds to a grammatical sentence or not, and associate structural and semantic details with it. It might also be reasonable to speculate about the explanation for the universally context-free character of the languages used by humans, and to wonder whether evolutionary biological factors are implicated in some way (Sampson (1979) could be read in this light). And naturally, it will be reasonable to pursue the program put forward by Gazdar (1981, 1982) to see to what extent CFL-inducing grammatical devices can be exploited to yield insightful descriptions of natural languages that capture generalizations in revealing ways.

If a human language that is not a CFL is proved to exist, on the other hand, a different question will be raised: given the non-context-free character of human languages in general, why has this property been so hard to demonstrate that it has taken over twenty-five years to bring it to light since the issue was first explicitly posed? If human languages do not have to be CFL's, why do so many (most?) of them come so close to having the property of context-freeness? And, since the CFL's certainly constitute a very broad class of mathematically natural and computationally tractable languages, what property of human beings or their communicative or cognitive needs is it that has caused some linguistic communities to reach beyond the boundaries of this class in the course of evolving a linguistic system?

Either way, we shall be interested to see our intial question resolved, and further questions raised. One cautionary word should be said, however, about the implications (or lack of them) that the answer will have for grammatical studies. Chomsky has repeatedly stated that he does not see weak generative capacity as a theme of central importance in the theory of grammar, and we agree. It is very far from being the case that the recent resurgence of interest in exploring the potential of CF-PSG or equivalent systems will, or should, be halted dead in its tracks by the discovery (if it is ever forthcoming) that some natural language is not a CFL. In the area of parsing, for instance, it seems possible that natural languages are not only parsed on the basis of constituent structure such as a CF-PSG would assign, but are parsed as if they were finite state languages (see

Langendoen (1975) and Church (1980) for discussion along these lines). That is, precisely those construction-types that figure in the various proofs that English is not an FSL appear to cause massive difficulty in the human processing system; the sentences crucial to the proofs are for the most part unprocessable unless they are extremely short (yet the arguments for English not being an FSL only go through if length is not an issue). This means that in practice properties of the finite state grammars are still of great potential importance to linguistic theory despite the fact that they do not provide the framework for defining the total class of grammatical sentences. The same would almost certainly be true of CF-PSG's if they were shown to be inadequate in a similar sense. It is highly unlikely that the advances made so far in phrase structure description could be nullified by a discovery about weak generative capacity. Moreover, there are known to be numerous ways in which the power of CF-PSG's can be marginally enhanced to permit, for example, xx languages to be generated without allowing anything like the full class of recursively enumerable or even context-sensitive languages (see Hopcroft and Ullmann (1979, Chapter 14) for an introduction to this topic, noting especially Figure 14.7 on p. 393). The obvious thing to do if natural languages were ever shown not to be CFL's in the general case would be to start exploring such minimal enhancements of expressive power to determine exactly what natural languages call for in this regard and how it could be effectively but parsimoniously provided in a way that closely modelled human linguistic capacities.

In the meantime, it seems reasonable to assume that the natural languages are a proper subset of the infinite-cardinality CFL's, until such time as they are validly shown not to be.

Footnotes

*A brief, preliminary statement of the view developed in this paper appeared in an unpublished paper by Gazdar, 'English As a Context-free Language', in April 1979. The authors jointly presented an early version of the present paper at the University of York in January 1980, and a more recent version was presented by Pullum at the University of California, San Diego, in May 1981. We thank Paul Postal, Mark Steedman, Thomas Wasow, David Watt, and our anonymous referees for their detailed comments on the whole paper, some of which improved it enormously. Wallace Chafe, David Dowty, Elisabet Engdahl, Aravind Joshi, D. Terence Langendoen, Alexis Manaster-Ramer, Marianne Mithun, Stanley Peters, Robert Ritchie, Jerrold Sadock; Ivan Sag, Geoffrey Sampson, Paul Schachter and Annie Zaenen also helped us with correspondence or suggestions. Some of the people mentioned take strong exception to our views, so their willingness to help must be seen as courtesy rather than concurrence. Our work was partially funded by grants from the National Science Foundation (grant No. BNS-8102406) and the Sloan Foundation to Stanford University, where the hospitality of the Department of Linguistics gave us the conditions under which we could finish the paper, and also by a grant from the Social Science Research Council, U.K. (grant No. HR-5767) to the University of Sessex. Offprint requests should be directed to Pullum at Cowell College, University of California (UCSC), Santa Cruz, California 95064.

[1]Note that although a language is by definition a CFL if there is a context-free phrase structure grammar (CF-PSG) that generates it, it does not follow that if a grammar G generates a CFL, G is a CF-PSG (though it does follow that a weakly equivalent CF-PSG must exist). A grammar of any arbitrary type might happen to generate a CFL. And for all we know, it might be that arc pair grammars of 'government-binding' grammars *always* do.

[2]Another is that if PS rules are unsuccessful on their own, then a new type of rule must be introduced. See Gazdar *et al.* (1981) for a CF-PSG that captures the generalization Akmajian and Heny are concerned with by means of a device for collapsing rules rather than a new rule type.

[3]See Gazdar (1982) for a brief discussion of how subject-verb agreement facts can be elegantly described by collapsing sets of CF-PSG rules.

[4]From this point on, any unexplained notation for representing grammars, expressions, or languages will be taken from Hopcroft and Ullmann (1979), see especially pp. 28-29 and 79-80. Note in particular that we write regular expressions (for representing FSL's) in boldface; A^* means the set of all strings of members of A; A^+ *means all the nonempty members of A^*; $L(\phi)$* means the language denoted by ϕ; and we use the notation 'A $\to$ B | C' to mean 'A rewrites as either B or C'. We also use the standard abbreviation 'A $\to$ B(C)D' to mean 'A rewrites as either BCD or BD'.

[5]An equivalent demonstration is to show that the fragment of English involved is representable by a regular expression:

((Which problem did your professor say ((she+you) thought)* was unsolvable)+(Which problems did your professor say ((she+you) thought)* were unsolvable))

[6]Selkirk does not specifically say that she means inadequacy as regards weak generative capacity, of course. She might mean that it has been demonstrated that CF-PSG's cannot assign appropriate structural descriptions to sentences. But in fact this claim has not been demonstrated either, and it is much harder to investigate rigorously. While matters of weak generative capacity (ability to generate stringsets) are relatively well understood in mathematical terms, notions like 'strong generative capacity' (never formally explicated in the literature, but having something to do with generating the 'right' tree-set for a given stringset) are far less amenable to formal work, because issues about what trees to assign to what strings depend on much more subtle and indirect arguments and evidence. If generally current transformationalist views on what surface structures are like are assumed, then for a well-studied language like English, CF-PSG does rather well (see e.g. Gazdar (1981)).

[7]What would count as identity here is rather hard to define precisely, because the identity relation must ignore the presence of the inflectional comparative suffix -er, and also has to ignore morphologically determined suppletion, as seen in (i), which must, presumably, be counted ungrammatical in the same way as (1) despite its superficially nonidentical adjective stems.

(i)   This one is better than that one is GOOD.

[8]We would not have succeeded in constructing this grammar without the help of Aravind Joshi, Stanley Peters, and Robert Ritchie, who told us it was possible and gave us hints on how to start looking for the grammar in (9).

Note that the complement of (8) in $\alpha(a+b)^*\beta(a+b)^*\gamma$ is not a CFL but an xx language. However, the CFL's are not closed under complementation (Hopcroft and ULlmann, 1979, pp. 134-135), so this is not a perplexing fact.

[9]English comparative clauses can in fact be described fairly elegantly with a CF-PSG; see Gazdar (1980).

[10]This assumption is, of course, crucial to Corstius's $a^n b^n c^n$ *version of the respectively* argument (see Levelt (1974, pp. 31-32)). If, as we maintain, the assumption is false, then his argument does not go through.

[11]McCawley (1968, pp. 164, 168) cites examples which illustrate this point.

[12]Wachtel (1981) argues that language-particular gender/number assignments give rise to a language-imposed classification of referents in cases of pragmatically controlled anaphora. His position, taken together with de Cornulier's metalinguistic analysis of sentences like (22a) and (22b), would lead us to expect sentences of the form shown in (i) and (ii) in a language with gender indications -a, -b, and -c.

(i)   In my view, oranges-a, lemons-b, and bananas-c are, respectively, delicious-a, bitter-b, and fattening -c.

(ii)   In my view, oranges-a, lemons-b, and bananas-c are, in the order in which I cite them, delicious-a, bitter-b, and fattening-c.

So, even in such a language, it would be neither necessary nor desirable to impose a purely syntactic matching condition on sentences like (i).

[13]One line we think worth exploring would be based on the notion of the lexicon as an infinite set of forms generated by a recursive procedure. It is not really in doubt that something along these lines will in due course have to be developed. As explicitly noted by Langendoen (1981), there are infinite sets of related words in English - for example, number names, and recursively constructed ancestor terms like *great-great-grandfather.* (Interestingly, Langendoen observes that no non-context-free or even non-finite-state sets of words can be found in currently known languages, though such sets can readily be invented. The lexicon of a human language may be infinite, but will apparently always be an FSL.) What needs to be examined is whether Dutch could be said to have an indefinitely extensible set of verbs with meanings like 'see write', 'let see write', 'help let see write', etc. It is a moot point whether a system could be set up to provide for an infinite set of internally complex members of the category V, and associate the members syntactically and semantically with the appropriate number of NP arguments, and still be CFL-inducing. (If it were not CFL-inducing, it would be an excessively powerful system along the relevant parameter, because it seems clear that all we are trying to do is to assign appropriate structural descriptions to a context-free set of sentences.)

[14]Daly's example is $\{ab^n ab^n | n \geqslant 0.\}$ A CF-PSG with the rules $S \to aZ,\ Z \to bZb\,|\,a$ generates it.

[15]The following points are relevant to any careful study of the Mohawk examples. We shall be quoting Mohawk examples both in Postal's fairly abstract phonological representation, as in (38), and in the phonemic notations used by other Iroquoianists. Agreement on spelling of morephemes should not therefore be expected (though the spelling of the mid-central nasal vowel has been silently normalized to $\wedge$ throughout). Mohawk has a rich morphophonemics, so stems and other formatives will appear in varying shapes even within one example in one transcription system. Incorporated noun-stems and their glosses will be italicized for the reader's convenience, but morpheme segmentation and glossing is in

general kept to a minimum. Unexplained prefixes, infixes, and suffixes are usually agreement inflections, epenthetic vowels, and markers of aspect respectively. The particle *ne* which appears in later examples and is ignored in glossing is commonly translated as 'the' in the literature. It occurs with proper names as well as common nouns. The proper name *sawatis* is always glossed as 'John'; it is the Mohawk transliteration of the French *Jean-Baptiste* 'John the Baptist'.

[16]There are a mass of lexical restrictions on incorporation: verbs stems that do not allow any incorporation, noun-stems that cannot be incorporated, verb-stems that are required to have an incorporated noun-stem, and perhaps some noun-stems that only occur incorporated (see Postal, 1962, p. 286). Postal mentions that the verbs that permit no incorporation may be in a majority. Such lexical idiosyncrasy tends to increase the plausibility of the claim that Reich attributes to Lounsbury.

[17]It is worth remarking that examples like (40d) are not marginal or peculiar in Mohawk. With an inalienably possessed item as the incorporated element they are extremely common; in Bonvillain and Francis (1980) there are a number of examples like these:

> kwiskwis ya?tho?*nyukwaɪhshta?*
>
> pig   he it-*snout*-grabbed
>
> 'he grabbed the pig's nose' (line 60, p. 84; morpheme segmentation on p. 92)
>
> saho*hna?ts*li?khú:ne? ne kwiskwis
>
> while-he it-*ass*-bite the pig
>
> saho*hna*?tsli?khú:ne? ne kwiskwis
>
> while-he it-*ass*-bite the pig
>
> 'while he kept biting the pig's ass' (line 68, p. 85; morpheme segmentation on p. 93).

But alienably possessed stems occur in this construction too, as seen in (43d) in the text. Postal confirms this point, and has checked it with another Mohawk specialist (Karin Michelson).

[18]After this paper was completed, Arnold Zwicky reminded us of the existence of his (1963) paper on this topic, which we had overlooked. The most convincing example discussed there involves the names for very large

numbers in English. Assume that the largest number that has a one-word name is named *zillion*. Then the square of this number has to be called (*one*) *zillion zillion*. An even larger number is *one zillion zillion, one zillion, and one*. But **one zillion, one zillion zillion, and one* is not a legal name for this number, or for any number. In general, the powers of zillion must be given in such a way that *zillion^n* *follows* *zillion^{n+1}* *for all n*. But a language of the general form

$$\{pz^{n_1}pz^{n_2}...p^{n_i} \mid (\forall_j, 1 \leqslant j \leqslant i)(n_j > n_{j+1})\}$$

is not context-free, as Zwicky shows. It follows that there is an infinite set of number names in English that is not context-free (and it is extractable by means of intersection with a regular set). The interest of this argument in the context of the study of natural languages is, however, greatly lessened by the fact that it deals with the internal structure of elements of a representational system for mathematics. We would maintain that knowledge of how to construct such number names (which, of course, has to be explicitly taught to children who speak English perfectly well) is knowledge of mathematics rather than of language.

References

Aho, A. V. and J. D. Ullmann: 1972, *The Theory of Parsing, Translation and Compiling*, Volume I: *Parsing* (Prentice-Hall, Englewood Cliffs, New Jersey).

Aho, A. V. and J. D. Ullmann: 1973, *The Theory of Parsing, Translation and Compiling*, Volume II: *Translation and Compiling* (Prentice-Hall, Englewood Cliffs, New Jersey).

Akmajian, A. and F. Heny: 1975, *An Introduction to the Principles of Transformational Syntax* (MIT Press, Cambridge, Mass.).

Allerton, D. J.: 1980, *Essentials of Grammatical Theory* (Routledge and Kegan Paul, London).

Bach, E.: 1974, *Syntactic Theory* (Holt Rinehard and Winston, New York).

Bar-Hillel, Y. and E. Shamir: 1960, 'Finite State Languages: Formal Representations and Adequacy Problems', reprinted in Y. Bar-Hillel (1964), *Language and Information* (Addison-Wesley, Reading, Mass.), pp.87-98.

Bonvillain, N.: 1974, 'Noun Incorporation in Mohawk', in M. K. Foster (ed.), *Papers from the 1972 Conference on Iroquoian Research* (National Museum of Man, Ottawa, Canada), pp. 18-26.

Bonvillain, N. and B. Francis: 1980, 'The Bear and the Fox, in Akwesasne Mohawk', in Mithun and Woodbury (eds.), pp. 77-95.

Bresnan, J. W.: 1976, 'Evidence for a Theory of Unbounded Transformations', *Linguistic Analysis* 2, 353-393.

Bresnan, J. W.: 1978, 'A Realistic Transformational Grammar', in M. Halle, J. W. Bresnan, and G. A. Miller (eds.), *Linguistic Theory and Psychological Reality* (MIT Press, Cambridge, Mass.).

Chomsky, N.: 1956, 'Three Models for the Description of Language', *I. R. E. Transactions on Information Theory*, Volume IT-2, Procedings of the Symposium on Information Theory, September, pp. 113-123.

Chomsky, N.: 1963, 'Formal Properties of Grammars', in R. D. Luce, R. R. Bush, an dE. Galanter (eds.), *Handbook of Mathematical Psychology*, Volume II (John Wiley, New York).

Chomsky, N.: 1977, 'On *Wh*-Movement', in P. Culicover, T. Wasow, and A. Akmajian (eds.), *Formal Syntax* (MIT Press, Cambridge, Mass.).

Chomsky, N.: 1981, *Lectures on Government and Binding* (Foris, Dordrecht).

Church, K. W.: 1980, *On Memory Limitations in Natural Language Processing*, MSc Dissertation, MIT, Cambridge, Mass.

Cornulier, B.de: 1973, 'But If "Respectively" Meant Something?', *Papers in Linguistics* 6, 131-134.

Culicover, P. W.: 1976, *Syntax* (Academic Press, New York).

Daly, R. T.: 1974, *Applications of the Mathematical Theory of Linguistics* (Mouton, The Hague).

Elster, J.: 1978, *Logic and Society: Contradictions and Possible Worlds* (John Wiley, New York).

Fidelholtz, J.: 1975, Review of J. Kimball, *The Formal Theory of Grammar*, *Language* 51, 493-499.

Fodor, J. A.: 1975, *The Language of Thought* (Thomas Crowell, New York).

Fromkin, V. and R. Rodman: 1978, *An Introduction to Language*, Second Edition (Holt Rinehart and Winston, New York).

Gazdar, G.: 1980, 'A Phrase Structure Syntax for Comparative Clauses', in T. Hoekstra, H. van der Hulst and M. Moortgat (eds), *Lexical Grammar* (Foris Publications, Dordrecht), pp. 165-179.

Gazdar, G.: 1981, 'Unbounded Dependencies and Coordinate Structure', *Linguistic Inquiry* 12, 155-184.

Gazdar, G.: 1982, 'Phrase Structure Grammar', in P. Jacobson and G. K. Pullum (eds.), *The Nature of Syntactic Representation* (D. Reidel, Dordrecht, Holland), 131-186.

Gazdar, G., G. K. Pullum, and I. A. Sag: 1981, *Auxiliaries and Related Phenomena in a Restrictive Theory of Grammar* (Indiana University Linguistics Club, Bloomington, Ind.).

Green, G. M.: 1971, 'Unspeakable Sentences, Book I', *Linguistic Inquiry* 2, 560.

Grinder, J. T. and S. H. Elgin: 1973, *Guide to Transformational Grammar* (Holt Rinehart and Winston, New York).

Hinton, G.: 1978, 'Respectively Reconsidered', *Pragmatics Microfiche* 3.3, 912-914.

Hopcroft, J. and J. D. Ullmann: 1979, *Introduction to Automata Theory, Languages and Computation* (Addison-Wesley, Reading, Mass.).

Hurford, J. R.: 1980, 'Generative Growing Pains', *Lingua* 50, 117-153.

Huybregts, M. A. C.: 1976, 'Overlapping Dependencies in Dutch', *Utrecht Working Papers in Linguistics* I, 24-65.

Johnson, D. E. and P. M. Postal: 1980, *Arc Pair Grammar* (Princeton University Press, Princeton, N. J.).

Kimball, J.: 1973, *The Formal Theory of Grammar* (Prentice-Hall, Englewood Cliffs, New Jersey).

Langendoen, D. T.: 1975, 'Finite State Parsing of Phrase-Structure Languages and the Status of Readjustment Rules in the Grammar', *Linguistic Inquiry* 6, 553-554.

Langendoen, D. T.: 1977, 'On the Inadequacy of Type-3 Grammars for Human Languages', in P. J. Hopper (ed.), *Studies in Descriptive and Historical Linguistics: Festschrift for Winfred P. Lehmann* (John Benjamin, Amsterdam, Holland), pp. 159-171.

Langendoen, D. T.: 1981, 'The Generative Capacity of Word-formation Components', *Linguistic Inquiry* 12, 320-322.

Levelt, W. J. M.: 1974, *Formal Grammars in Linguistics and Psycholinguistics*, Volume II: *Applications in Linguistic Theory* (Mouton, The Hague, Holland).

Lounsbury, F.: 1953, *Oneida Verb Morphology* (Yale University Publications in Anthropology, No. 48, Yale University, New Haven, Conn.).

McCawley, J. D.: 1968, 'The Role of Semantics in a Grammar', in E. Bach and R. T. Harms (eds.), *Universals in Linguistic Theory* (Holt Rinehart and Winston, New York).

Michelson, K.: 1980, 'Mohawk Text: The Edge of the Forest Revisited', in Mithun and Woodbury (eds.), pp. 26-40.

Mithun, M. and H. Woodbury (eds.): 1980, *Northern Iroquoian Texts* (IJAL Native American Texts Series, No. 4) (University of Chicago Press, Chicago/University Microfilms International, Ann Arbor, Mich.).

Pinker, S.: 1979, 'Formal Models of Language Learning', *Cognition* 7, 217-283.

Postal, P. M.: 1962, *Some Syntactic Rules in Mohawk*, Doctoral Dissertation (Yale University, New Haven, Conn.; published by Garland, New York, 1979).

Postal, P. M.: 1964, 'Limitations of Phrase Structure Grammars', in J. A. Fodor and J. J. Katz (eds.), *The Structure of Language: Readings in the Philosophy of Language* (Prentice-Hall, Englewood Cliffs, N.J.), pp. 137-151.

Reich, P. A.: 1969, 'The Finiteness of Natural Language', *Language* 45, 831-843.

Sampson, G.: 1975, *The Form of Language* (Weidenfeld and Nicolson, London).

Sampson, G.: 1979, 'A Non-Nativist Account of Language Universals', *Linguistics and Philosophy* 3, 99-104.

Selkirk, E. O.: 1977, 'Some Remarks on Noun Phrase Structure', in P. W. Culicover, T. Wasow and A. Akmajian (eds.), *Formal Syntax* (Academic Press, New York), pp. 285-316.

Wachtel, T.: 1981, 'Sex and the Single Pronoun', unpublished paper (University of Warsaw).

Winograd, T.: 1972, *Understanding Natural Language* (Academic Press, New York). Also *Cognitive Psychology* 3, No. 1 (1972).

Woodbury, H.: 1975, 'Onondaga Noun Incorporation: Notes on the Interdependence of Syntax and Semantics', *International Journal of American Linguistics* 41, 10-20.

Zaenen, A.: 1979, 'Infinitival Complements in Dutch', *Papers from the Fifteenth Regional Meeting* (Chicago Linguistic Society, Chicago, Ill.), pp. 378-389.

Zwicky, A. M.: 1963, 'Some Languages That Are Not Context-free', Quarterly Progress Report of the Research Laboratory of Electronics, MIT, 70, 290-293.

Gerald Gazdar

UNBOUNDED DEPENDENCIES AND
COORDINATE STRUCTURE

Consider eliminating the transformational component of a generative grammar. In particular, consider the elimination of all movement rules, whether bounded or unbounded, and all rules making reference to identity of indices. Suppose, in fact, that the permitted class of generative grammars constituted a subset of those phrase structure grammars capable only of generating context-free languages. Such a move would have two important metatheoretical consequences, one having to do with learnability, the other with processability. In the first place, we would be imposing a rather dramatic restriction on the class of grammars that the language acquisition device needs to consider as candidates for the language being learned. And in the second place, we would have the beginnings of an explanation for the obvious, but largely ignored, fact that humans process the utterances they hear very rapidly.[1] Sentences of a context-free language are provably parsable in a time which is proportional to the cube of the length of the sentence or less (Younger (1967), Earley (1970)). But no such restrictive result holds for the recursive or recursively enumerable sets potentially generable by grammars which include a transformational component.

My strategy in this article will be to assume, rather than argue, that there are no transformations, and then to show that purely phrase structure (PS) treatments of coordination and unbounded dependencies can offer explanations for facts which are unexplained, or inadequately explained, within the transformational paradigm.

In section 1, I shall briefly outline a phrase structure treatment of coordination that eliminates the need for a rule of Coordination Reduction (CR). This proposal is but a minor variant of a schema that has become

Linguistic Inquiry Volume 12, Number 2, Spring 1981, 155-184.

W. J. Savitch et al. (eds.), The Formal Complexity of Natural Language, 183–226.

standard in recent years. Section 2 shows how the syntax and semantics of unbounded dependencies can be handled in a PS grammar which employs complex symbols. English relative clauses and constituent questions are used to exemplify the apparatus. Section 3 then demonstrates that Ross's Coordinate Structure Constraint (CSC) and the "across-the-board" (ATB) violations of it follow as theorems from the grammar fragments given in the previous two sections. Detailed consideration is given to the data and to an alternative analysis, given in Williams (1977; 1978). Finally, section 4 argues that the apparent boundedness of rightward dependencies is a consequence of independently motivated constraints on parsing and that the syntax can thus treat such dependencies as unbounded. A general schema is given for rightward dependencies, and it is shown that this interacts with the coordination schema to generate all those sentences produced by the transformation known as Right Node Raising (RNR), together with some that such a rule ought to produce but cannot.

I shall follow McCawley (1968) and interpret phrase structure rules as node admissibility conditions rather than as string-to-string mapping rules. Accordingly, I shall not use the familiar rewrite arrow notation for PS rules, but shall instead use a notation which reflects more directly the relation such rules bear to the (sub)trees that they admit. Instead of (1), then,

(1) S → NP VP

I shall write (2),

(2) [s NP VP]

and analogously for all other rules.

I shall assume that each syntactic rule in the grammar should be associated with a semantic rule which gives the meaning of the constituent created by the syntactic rule as a function of the meaning of the latter's parts.[2] I assume further that the semantic rules should take the form of rules of translation into intensional logic.

I take a rule of grammar to be a triple of which the first member is an arbitrary integer (the number of the rule), the second is a PS rule, and the third is a semantic rule showing how the intensional logic representation of the expression created by the PS rule is built up from the intensional logic representations of its immediate constituents. I shall use a Montague-like prime convention in the semantic rules: *NP′* stands for the (complex) expression of intensional logic which is the translation of the subtree dominated by NP, *run′* is the constant of intensional logic which translates the word *run* in English, etc.

Within this framework, the first rule of a grammar might be this:

(3) $\langle 1,\ [_s\ NP\ VP],\ VP'(\char94 NP')\rangle$

I shall use *rule* to refer both to the triple and to its second and third members (sometimes qualifying the latter with *syntactic* and *semantic*, respectively), but this should not lead to any confusion.

1. Coordination

Consider (4):

(4) $\alpha \rightarrow \alpha_1 \ldots \begin{Bmatrix} or \\ and \end{Bmatrix} \alpha_n$

where α is any syntactic category

Phrase structure rule schemata more or less like (4) are nothing new. They date back at least as far as Dougherty (1970) and can be found in many more recent works (e.g. Jackendoff (1977, 51)). But they have never amounted to a sufficient theory of constituent coordination in transformational grammar, for two reasons. First, as long as one retains a rule like Passive as an operation which maps into sentences rather than into verb phrases, it is impossible, as Schachter (1976, 236-237) points out, to use the schema to generate the conjoined VPs in a sentence like (5):

(5)   The Dodgers beat the Red Sox and were beaten by the Giants.

To handle such sentences, one has to postulate a rule of Coordination Reduction (CR) which applies to coordinate sentences, deletes material under identity, and regroups the remainder. Second, no transformational grammarian has ever indicated what the semantics for the rule schema might be. This point should not be taken lightly: one advantage of the CR theory was that it treated (almost) all coordination as underlyingly sentential, and a fully explicit semantics for sentential coordination was to be found in propositional logic. The CR theory consequently made strong explicit predictions about what reduced coordinate sentences meant. But in the absence of any semantics, the schema in (4) makes no semantic predictions. For example, it does not even predict that (5) is synonymous with (6):

(6)   The Dodgers beat the Red Sox and the Dodgers were beaten by the Giants.

However, if (as we are assuming) there are no transformations, then there is no Passive transformation and the syntactic problem does not arise. And the semantic problem is solved by Cooper (forthcoming), Gazdar (1980a), and Keenan and Faltz (1978), who have independently provided a model-theoretic semantics for crosscategorial coordination (without invoking an interpretive rule of CR-in-Reverse).

In the classical analysis of a sentence like (5), we begin with a sentence like (7):

(7)   The Dodgers beat the Red Sox and the Giants beat the Dodgers.

Passive applies in the second conjunct to give us (6), and then CR applies to give us (5). This analysis is hopeless for a sentence like (8) (cf. Jackendoff (1977, 193-194)):

(8)   Different teams beat the Red Sox and were beaten by the Giants.

The classical analysis can handle the syntax, of course, but only at the cost of making nonsense of the semantics.

There is one remaining problem with schema (4): it assigns coordinate expressions the wrong surface structure. Ross (1967, 90-91) shows that there are phonological and syntactic reasons for believing that the coordinating word forms a constituent with the immediately following node and is not simply a sister of all the conjuncts. Suppose then that we allow the names of coordinating morphemes to appear as features on categories, and eliminate the feature by means of a rule schema which expands such categories as the named coordinating morpheme, followed by the category (as in (10), below). This will in turn allow us to revise (4) in such a way as to capture Ross's observations regarding surface constituent structure:

(9) $\langle 2, [\,_\alpha \alpha_1, ..., \alpha_n], \beta'(\alpha_1\,', ..., \alpha_n\,') \rangle$
 $\underset{[\beta]}{}$

where $\beta \in$ {and, or} and α is any syntactic category

(10)[3] $\langle 3, [\,_\alpha\, \beta\, \alpha], \alpha' \rangle$
 $\underset{[\beta]}{}$

where $\beta \in$ {and, or, . . .} and α is any syntactic category.

Schemata (9) and (10) then combine to give us subtrees like these:

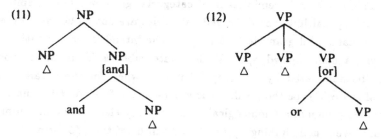

Note that (9) is only intended to handle constituent coordination and thus make the CR transformation otiose. There is no claim that, on its own, it will do the work associated with such transformations as Right Node Raising (see section 4 below) or Gapping (see Stump (1978) for a nontransformational treatment). In particular, we must assume that whatever mechanism is responsible for "gapped" VPs (i.e. VPs lacking the head verb and possibly contiguous constituents) is responsible for Williams's (1978, 38) example (13), rather than CR, as Williams assumes.

(13) John gave the books to Mary and the records to Sue.

The problem here, as Williams notes, is that the direct and indirect objects of *give* do not form a constituent and cannot therefore be conjoined in virtue of the schema in (9).

2. Unbounded Dependencies

Phrase structure grammars can handle unbounded dependencies in an elegant and general way, provided that we exploit the resources offered by a complex symbol system and by the possibility of making statements about the set of rules that the grammar may employ.[4] The paragraphs that follow will, unavoidably, be somewhat technical.

Let V_N be the set of *basic* category symbols (i.e. the set of all nonterminal symbols standardly used). Then we define a set $D(V_N)$ of *derived* categories as follows:

(14) $D(V_N) = \{\alpha/\beta\colon \alpha, \beta \in V_N\}$

Suppose, counterfactually, that S and NP were the only basic categories; then the set of derived categories would consist of S/S, S/NP, NP/NP, and NP/S. This notation is reminiscent of categorial grammar but, despite a tenuous conceptual link, these derived categories are not to be interpreted in the way categorial grammar prescribes. The intended interpretation is as follows: a node labeled α/β will dominate subtrees identical to those that can be dominated by α, except that somewhere in every canonical subtree of the α/β type there will occur a node of the form β/β dominating a resumptive pronoun, a phonologically null dummy element, or the empty string, and every node linking α/β and β/β will be of the σ/β form. Intuitively, then, α/β labels a node of type α which dominates material containing a hole of type β (i.e. an extraction site on a movement analysis). So, for example, S/NP is a sentence which has an NP missing somewhere.

Of course, defining a new set of syntactic categories is not of itself sufficient to ensure that the trees in which they figure have the property just described: we need, in addition, a set of rules to employ them.

What we have to do is define a set of rules each of which expands a derived category just as the corresponding basic rule would have done for the basic category, except that exactly one of the dominated categories is now paired with the same hole-indicating category as is the dominating category. The set of such rules will consequently allow the hole information to be "carried down" the tree.[5]

Let G be the set of *basic* rules (i.e. the set of rules that a grammar not handling unbounded dependencies would require). For any syntactic category β, there will be some subset of the set of the nonterminal symbols V_N, each of which can dominate β according to the rules in G. Let us call this set V_β ($V_\beta \subseteq V_N$). Now, for any category $\beta(\beta \in V_N)$ we can define a (finite) set of *derived* rules $D(\beta, G)$ as follows:

(15) $D(\beta,G)=\{[_{\alpha/\beta} \sigma_1....\sigma_i/\beta....\sigma_n]:[_{\alpha} \sigma_1....\sigma_i....\sigma_n]\in G \& 1 \leqslant i \leqslant n \& \alpha, \sigma_i \in V_\beta\}$

An example of the application of (15) should make this clearer. Suppose that the set G of basic rules looks like this:

(16) a. $\{[_s \text{ NP VP}],$
    b. $[_{VP} \text{ V } \overline{VP}],$
    c. $[_{VP} \text{ V NP}],$
    d. $[_{PP} \text{ P NP}],$
    e. $[_{\overline{S}} \text{ that S}],$
    f. $[_{VP} \text{ V } \overline{S}],$
    g. $[_{\overline{VP}} \text{ to VP}],$
    h. $[_{VP} \text{ V NP PP}],$
    i. $[_{NP} \text{ NP PP}]\},$

Then the set D(NP,G) will look like this:

(17) a. $\{[_{S/NP} \text{ NP/NP VP}],$ $[_{S/NP} \text{ NP VP/NP}],$
    b. $[_{VP/NP} \text{ V } \overline{VP}/\text{NP}],$
    c. $[_{VP/NP} \text{ V NP/NP}],$
    d. $[_{PP/NP} \text{ P NP/NP}],$
    e. $[_{\overline{S}/NP} \text{ that S/NP}],$
    f. $[_{VP/NP} \text{ V } \overline{S}/\text{NP}],$
    g. $[_{\overline{VP}/NP} \text{ to VP/NP}],$
    h. $[_{VP/NP} \text{ V NP/NP PP}],$ $[_{VP/NP} \text{ V NP PP/NP}],$
    i. $[_{NP/NP} \text{ NP/NP PP}],$ $[_{NP/NP} \text{ NP PP/NP}]\}$

The set D(PP,G) will look like this:

(18) a. $\{[_{S/PP} \text{ NP/PP VP}],$ $[_{S/PP} \text{ NP VP/PP}],$
    b. $[_{VP/PP} \text{ V } \overline{VP}/\text{PP}],$
    c. $[_{VP/PP} \text{ V NP/PP}],$
    d. $[_{PP/PP} \text{ P NP/PP}],$
    e. $[_{\overline{S}/PP} \text{ that S/PP}],$
    f. $[_{VP/PP} \text{ V } \overline{S}/\text{PP}],$

g. $[_{\overline{VP}/PP}$ *to* VP/PP],

h. $[_{VP/PP}$ V NP/PP PP], $[_{VP/PP}$ V NP PP/PP],

i. $[_{NP/PP}$ NP/PP PP], $[_{NP/PP}$ NP PP/PP]}

Derived rules have no special lexical or semantic properties. Thus, all derived rules will have the same rule numbers, the same subcategorization properties, and the same semantic translations as the basic rules from which they derive. Consequently, they do not need to be separately listed or separately specified; everything about them can be predicted from (15), taken together with the basic rules.[6]

We can formalize certain island constraints, if we wish, simply by stipulating that certain types of derived rule are not employed by a language (or by any language, if the constraint suggested is intended as a universal).[7] Suppose we wanted to impose the A-over-A Constraint. Then we could add a condition to (15) that $\alpha \neq \beta$. This would have the effect of preventing the creation of any derived rules of the form shown in (19):

(19) $[_{\alpha/\alpha}\cdots]$

Adding a condition that $\alpha \neq$ NP to (15) would have the effect of imposing Horn's (1974) NP Constraint. And language-particular constraints, such as one against stranding prepositions, can also be imposed by prohibiting certain classes of derived rule (all rules of the form $[_{PP/NP}\cdots]$ in the case of impermissible preposition stranding).

Thus, constraints once thought of as constraints on permissible movement can be reconstructed as constraints on permissible rules.[8]

The only island constraint I want to consider here is Ross's Left Branch Condition (1967, 114):

(20) *The Left Branch Condition*

No NP which is the leftmost constituent of a larger NP can be reordered out of this NP by a transformational rule.

This could be approximately reconstructed in terms of derived rules as (21):

(21) *$[_{NP/NP}$ NP/NP...]

I propose to adopt a generalized version of (21) in the discussion that follows. The Generalized Left Branch Condition (GLBC) will block NP dependencies into left branches of any constituent defined by (15):

(22) *Generalized Left Branch Condition*
$$*[\,_{\alpha/\beta}\ \sigma/\beta\ \cdots\,]$$
where α and σ are any node labels, and $\beta = \text{NP}$

GLBC could be incorporated in (15), if one wished, by stipulating that $\neg\,(i = 1\ \wedge\ \beta = \text{NP})$. I will consider the motivation for this implausible-looking island constraint later in the article.[9]

In addition to derived rules, we need *linking* rules (these will be a subset of the basic rules) to introduce and eliminate derived categories. For the majority dialect of English (British or American), we need only the following rule schema to eliminate derived categories:

(23) $\langle 4, [\,_{\alpha/\alpha}\ t], \text{h}_{\alpha} \rangle$
where $\alpha \in V_N$

Here h_{α} (mnemonic for *hole*) is a distinguished variable ranging over denotations of type α (i.e. NP denotations if $\alpha = \text{NP}$, PP denotations if $\alpha = \text{PP}$, etc.). t is a dummy element postulated solely for phonological reasons (that is, it will serve to block contraction). It serves no semantic function (h_{α} is the variable, not t), and for other dialects or languages we could replace t with the empty string e (which would have no phonological effects) or with a proform. It will become apparent in what follows that t is placed precisely in those complement subject positions where contraction-inhibiting phonological effects have been noted, and consequently the analysis faces none of the difficulties besetting the analyses criticized in Postal and Pullum (1978).

The apparatus developed above can be used to handle all constructions involving an unbounded dependency.[10] However, since exactly the same principle is involved in every case, it will suffice here to illustrate its application by reference to just two constructions, namely English restrictive relative clauses and constituent questions.

I will assume that relative clauses are dominated by a sentential category R: if one is in the business of generating surface structures directly by means of context-free PS rules, then one cannot identify R with $\overline{S}$ for obvious reasons. We will distinguish sentential categories by means of the following features: $\pm$C(omplement), $\pm$R(elative), and $\pm$Q (interrogative). In this system, S is [-C, -R, -Q], R is [+C, +R, -Q], root interrogatives ("Q") are [-C, -R, +Q], and embedded interrogatives ("$\overline{Q}$") are [+C, -R, +Q].[11] If we assume that [+C, -R, -Q] can expand only as *that-S* (i.e. the *that* is not optional), then we can use $\overline{S}$ as an abbreviation for [$\pm$ C, -R, -Q] (thus regaining the optionality of *that* in most environments). Some verbs and adjectives subcategorize for [+C, -R, -Q] rather than $\overline{S}$; consequently, the *that* is obligatory in these contexts (see Shir (1977, 62-63) for relevant data). Likewise, sentential subjects and topicalized extraposed clauses must be [+C].

The rule which introduces R is simply this:[12]

(24) $\langle 5, [_{NP} \text{ NP R}], \lambda R[\text{NP}'](\text{R}') \rangle$

The semantics I am assuming is essentially the NP-S semantics introduced by Cooper (1975) and Bach and Cooper (1978), and developed by McCloskey (1978; 1979), from which further details should be sought. All NPs are assumed to contain a free set variable R. Rule (24) abstracts on this variable and applies the resulting function to the set denoted by the relative clause. The relative clause meaning is thus quantified into the NP meaning. The following two rules expand R,

(25) $\langle 6, [_{R} \underset{\substack{\pm WH \\ +PRO}}{(NP)} S/NP], \lambda n[\lambda h_{NP}[(S/NP)'](NP') \wedge R(n)] \rangle$

(26) $\langle 7, [_{R} \underset{\substack{+WH \\ +PRO}}{PP} S/PP], \lambda n[\lambda h_{PP}[(S/PP)'](PP') \wedge R(n)] \rangle$

where[13]

(27) NP[$\pm$R, +WH, +PRO] $\rightarrow$ *who*, where *who'* $= \lambda PP(n)$

(28) NP[+R, -WH, +PRO] $\rightarrow$ *that*, where *that'* $= \lambda PP(n)$

These rules induce trees such as (29), (30):

(29)

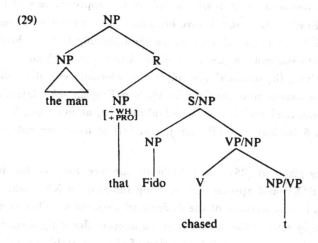

(30)

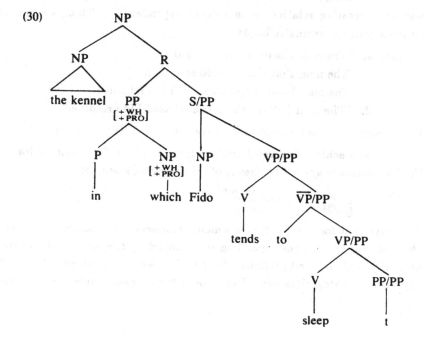

The syntax here is fairly straightforward. Relative clauses consist of a pronominal NP or PP followed by an S with a hole of the appropriate sort in it. In Chaucerian English, this would have been an $\overline{\text{S}}$ rather than an S (see Bresnan (1976, 357)). The rules given capture the following facts without any need for separate statements (i.e. conditions, filters, etc.): (i) no piedpiping in *that*-relatives, (ii) optional pied-piping in *wh*-relatives, (iii) obligatory absence of a *that*-complementizer in Modern English *wh*-relatives, (iv) obligatory c-command position of the *wh*-phrase, (v) at most one hole in the complement S (except in ATB cases), and (vi) at least one hole in the complement S.

The semantics given in (25) and (26) binds the free variable h_{XP} in the translation of S/XP and applies the resulting function to XP′, which will itself contain a free occurrence of the designated variable n. This variable is then bound by abstraction to form an expression denoting a set.[14] An additional complication is the reintroduction of the R variable in order to allow stacked relatives and contextual binding (see Mc Closkey (1979, 217-221) on the need for the latter).

Notice that, given our adoption of the GLBC, we at present have no way of generating relatives with subject dependencies. Thus, we cannot derive any of the examples in (31):

(31) a. *The man chased Fido returned.
　　 b. The man that chased Fido returned.
　　 c. The man (who) I think chased Fido returned.
　　 d. *The man (who) I think that chased Fido returned.

I shall return to this issue when we have considered iterrogatives.

We can achieve Subject-Auxiliary Inversion in a PS grammar for the English auxiliary system by means of the following metarule:[15]

$$(32) \qquad [_{\substack{VP \\ [+FIN \\ +AUX]}} V \ X] \Rightarrow [_{Q} \ \substack{V \\ [+FIN \\ +AUX]} NP \ X]$$

This says that for every VP rule which introduces a tensed auxiliary verb, there is also to be a corresponding rule expanding the sentential category Q as the auxiliary verb, followed by NP, followed by whatever the auxiliary verb subcategorizes for. Thus, the VP rule responsible for a subtree like (33) will be mapped by the metarule into a Q rule which in turn will induce subtrees like (34):

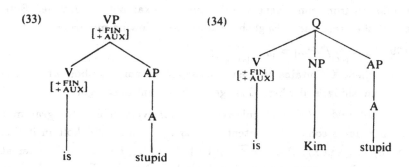

Given (32), the rule for root constituent questions follows straightforwardly:

(35) $\langle 8, [\,_{Q\ _{[+WH]}^{\alpha}}\ Q/\alpha], \lambda p\ \exists\ n[\lambda h_\alpha[[(Q/\alpha)\,'][(\alpha\,')](p)]]\rangle$

where $\alpha \in \{NP, PP, AP, AdvP\}$

The semantics assumed in (35) is due, essentially, to Karttunen (1977). This rule then allows us to generate such sentences as (36a-d):

(36) a. Who did you think Mary saw?

  b. In which car was the man seen?

  c. How slowly would you say he was driving?

  d. How suspicious was Mary?

But, as it stands, (35) will not allow us to generate the following, perfectly grammatical, sentences of English:

(37) a. Who saw the man?

  b. Which man drove the car?

There is no auxiliary verb in either (37a) or (37b), but since Q necessarily dominates an auxiliary verb, these examples are inevitably excluded from the scope of (35). Clearly, what we need is a rule like (38):

(38) $[_Q \underset{[+WH]}{NP} \quad \underset{[+FIN]}{VP}]$

Now we could simply add (38) to the rules of the grammar and leave it at
that. But it would be more interesting if we could show that the form of
(38) followed from some general principle, for example a metarule. Suppose that the grammar of English includes the following metarule:

(39) $[_\alpha X \underset{[-C]}{\Sigma} /NP...] \Rightarrow [_\alpha X \underset{[+FIN]}{VP} ...]$

where X contains at least one major category symbol, where α is
anything, and where Σ ranges over sentential categories.

Consider what this metarule requires: for every rule in the grammar
which introduces some [-C] sentential category with an NP hole in it (i.e.
Q/NP, S/NP, and $\overline{S}$/NP--since $\overline{S}$ can be [-C]) which has as a left sister at
least one major category symbol (i.e. N, NP, V, VP, A, AP, P, etc.), there
is to be a corresponding rule which is identical except that the Σ/NP is
replaced by a tensed VP.[16] The GLBC blocks all subject dependencies;
but, if subject dependencies were permitted, then the residues (i.e. the sentences with t as subject) would be indistinguishable from tensed VPs.
Metarule (39) claims that these constituents, which look just like tensed
VPs, are exactly that.[17] This should become clearer if we give some examples of rules which meet the input conditions of (39) and then show what
the rules created from them by (39) look like. The grammar will contain
the following rules, all of which are input to (39):

(40) a. $[_Q \underset{[+WH]}{NP} Q/NP]$ (root constituent questions, (35)
above)

b. $[_{\overline{Q}} \underset{[+WH]}{NP} S/NP]$ (embedded constituent questions)

c. $[_R \underset{\substack{\pm WH \\ +PRO}}{NP} S/NP]$ (relative clauses, (25) above)

d. $[_S NP S/NP]$ (NP topicalization)

e. $[_{VP/NP} V \overline{S}/NP]$

f. $[_{VP/NP} V NP \overline{S}/NP]$ (derived rules)

g. $[_{VP/NP} V PP \overline{S}/NP]$

Metarule (39) applies to (40a-g) to give us (41a-g), respectively:

(41) a. $\left[_{Q} \underset{[+WH]}{NP} \underset{[+FIN]}{VP} \right]$ (= 38))

b. $\left[_{\overline{Q}} \underset{[+WH]}{NP} \underset{[+FIN]}{VP} \right]$

c. $\left[_{R} \underset{\left[\substack{\pm WH \\ +PRO} \right]}{NP} \underset{[+FIN]}{VP} \right]$

d.[18] $\left[_{S} NP \underset{[+FIN]}{VP} \right]$

e. $\left[_{VP/NP} V \underset{[+FIN]}{VP} \right]$

f. $\left[_{VP/NP} V NP \underset{[+FIN]}{VP} \right]$

g. $\left[_{VP/NP} V NP \underset{[+FIN]}{VP} \right]$

The output root constituent question rule (41a) now allows us to generate the auxiliaryless questions in (37):

(42) a.

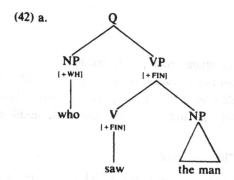

b.

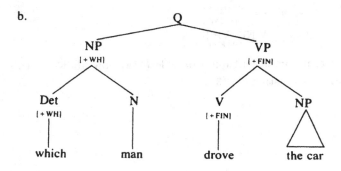

Notice that in the output relative clause rule (41c), the head NP is not optional, as it was in (25), because the metarule requires the X variable to be nonempty in order to be applicable. This means that a relative clause cannot be realized as a bare tensed VP, and we are therefore still unable to generate (31a), repeated here:

(31) a.   *The man chased Fido returned.

But we can now generate examples (31b) and (31c), which the GLBC earlier prevented us from generating:

(43) a. (= (31b))

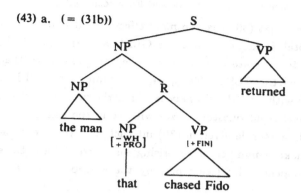

b. (= (31c))

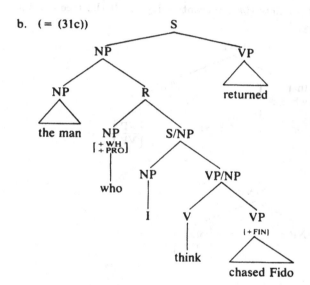

The metarule will not apply to the rule which expands $\overline{S}$, since the X variable must contain a major category symbol.[19] Therefore, we will not have a rule of the form shown in (44):

(44) *[$\overline{S}$/NP *that* VP]
$\phantom{(44) \quad *[\overline{S}/NP \ that \ }$[+FIN]

Consequently, our grammar still cannot generate (31d), as we would wish:

(31) d.   *The man (who) I think that chased Fido returned.

So far we have seen that (39) has two main effects: (i) it allows us to generate all the acceptable examples that the GLBC appeared to block, while not allowing us to generate any of the unacceptable examples that are rightfully blocked by the GLBC. Thus, we can maintain the GLBC. And (ii) it provides us with an NP VP analysis of matrix subject relatives and matrix subject constituent questions. We will see in the next section that the GLBC and the metarule given in (39) interact with the coordination schema (9) to make a number of surprising but correct predictions about possible ATB dependencies (see especially the examples in (60)-(61), below).

The GLBC predicts the unacceptability of all the tree configurations shown in (45)-(48):

(45)[20] *

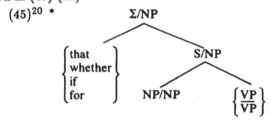

(46)   *

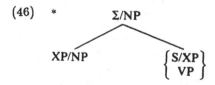

(47)   *

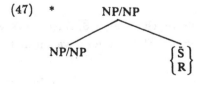

$(48)^{21}$ * NP/NP

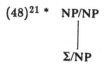

Σ/NP

Thus, the grammar will be unable to generate any of the strings shown in (49):

(49)

a. *Who did you believe that *t* came?   (structure(45))
b. *Who did you wonder whether *t* came?   (structure(45))
c. *Who did you wonder if *t* came?   (structure(45))
d. *Who did you arrange for *t* to come?   (structure(45))
e. *Which table did you wonder on *t* Kim put the book?   (structure(46))
f. *Which did you buy the table on *t* Kim put the book?   (structure(46))
g. *Who did you wonder *t* saw Kim?   (structure (46))
h. *Which did you buy the table *t* supported the book?   (structure (46))
i. *The fact, I put it down to *t* that Kim came.   (structure (47))
j. *The table, I put Kim on *t* which supported the book.   (structure (47))
k. *The table, that I put Kim on *t* surprised Kim.   (structure (48))
l. *The exam, whether Kim passes *t* matters to Sandy.   (structure (48))

Notice that if *it*-clefts on NP are introduced by a rule like (50),

(50) [vp V NP R]

then the GLBC will not block "extraction" of the NP introduced by the rule, since it is not on a left branch. Predictably, then, the following example (which I owe to Stan Peters) is acceptable:

(51) Who is it that Mary likes?

The proposals made here, which have so far been motivated on purely syntactic grounds, commit us to the claim that relatives and interrogatives with a dependency into the matrix subject argument have a rather different structure from all other relatives and interrogatives. This is illustrated in (52) and (53). Under our analysis, matrix subject relatives will have the structure shown in (52a), whereas other relatives will have the one shown in (52b):[22]

(52) a.

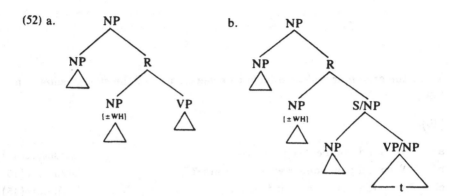

b.

Likewise, matrix subject questions will have the structure (53a), whereas other constituent questions will have structure (53b):

(53) a.

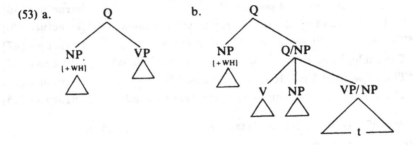

b.

A derived category has to contain twice as much syntactic information as a basic category. This suggests that structures which involve derived categories will impose a heavier processing load than those that do not. If this is so, then our analysis predicts that matrix subject relatives and questions will be significantly easier to process than all other relatives and questions (excluding polar interrogatives). This prediction is borne out, both developmentally and for adult speakers, by a substantial body of recent psycholinguistic work.[23] Furthermore, that (52a) is a possible structure for matrix subject relatives makes it much less surprising that all languages allow the construction of such relatives (Keenan and Comrie (1977)), even those which have no mechanism inducing unbounded dependencies.

3. Constraints on Coordinate Structure

A consequence of the analysis of unbounded phenomena that we have put forward is that subtrees that contain an externally controlled hole are of a different syntactic category from those that do not. An $\overline{S}$ which has an NP missing somewhere will be of category $\overline{S}$/NP, not $\overline{S}$ and a VP which contains a missing PP will be of category VP/PP. Now, according to the coordination schema in (9), only items of the *same* syntactic category can be conjoined.[24] It follows that, while we can conjoin a VP with a VP, for example, we cannot conjoin a VP with a VP/NP or a VP/PP any more than we can conjoin it with an $\overline{S}$. But we can conjoin an $\overline{S}$/NP with an $\overline{S}$/NP, or a VP/PP with a VP/PP. Thus, the effect of (9) in place of a rule of CR is to entirely eliminate the need for Ross's (1967) Coordinate Structure Constraint (CSC) or Williams's (1977; 1978) Across-the-Board (ATB) Convention. Given (9), we simply cannot generate strings like (54) and (55):

(54) *John is easy to please and to love Mary.

$$(= \overline{VP}/NP \ \& \ \overline{VP})$$

(55) *The man who Mary loves and Sally hates George computed my tax.

$$(= S/NP \ \& \ S)$$

Permissibility of coordination has traditionally been taken as evidence for sameness of syntactic category, but no one has previously drawn the relevant inference from Ross's CSC facts, assuming instead a quite different explanation for the impossibility of coordination in these cases.[25]

The ATB exceptions to the CSC are predicted by (9):

(56) John is easy to please and to love.

$$(= \overline{VP}/NP \ \& \ \overline{VP}/NP)$$

(57) The man who Mary loves and Sally hates computed my tax.

$$(= S/NP \ \& \ S/NP)$$

But we will not get ATB dependencies when the holes are of different categories:

(58) a. The kennel which Mary made and Fido sleeps in has been
     stolen.   (=S/NP & S/NP)
    b. The kennel in which Mary keeps drugs and Fido sleeps has
       been stolen.   (=S/PP & S/PP)
    c. *The kennel (in) which Mary made and Fido sleeps has been
     stolen.   (=S/NP & S/PP)

The same is true in the following comparative examples from Williams (1977, 421):

(59) a. John saw more horses than Bill saw or Pete talked to.
                           (=S/NP & S/NP)
    b. John saw more horses than Bill saw cows or Pete talked to
     cats.   (=S/QP & S/QP)
    c. *John saw more horses than Bill saw cows or Pete talked to.
                           (=S/QP & S/NP)

As Williams points out (1977, 421), a theory employing a rule of CR and the CSC "will be hard pressed to avoid generating [59c]". In fact, Williams's own (1978) rule of CR avoids generating (59c) only because of an otherwise unmotivated constraint which prevents CR from "eating into Ss" (1978, 38).

    Williams (1978) draws attention to a curious fact about the coordination of relative clauses: a relative with a matrix subject NP dependency cannot be conjoined with any other kind of relative, whereas a relative with an embedded subject NP dependency behaves quite normally with respect to ATB coordination. The relevant data are as follows ((60c) = (16) from Williams (1978, 34), and I owe (60d) to Paul Hirschbühler):[26]

(60) a. I know a man who Bill saw and Mary liked.
                        (= S/NP & S/NP)
    b. I know a man who saw Bill and liked Mary.
                        (= VP & VP)

c. *I know a man who Bill saw and liked Mary.

$$(= \left\{ \begin{array}{l} \text{S/NP\&VP} \\ \text{VP/NP\&VP} \end{array} \right\})$$

d. I know a man who Mary likes and hopes will win.

$$(= \text{VP/NP \& VP/NP})$$

This acceptability pattern is exactly as predicted by the VP analysis of subjectless relatives proposed in the last section. Notice that just the same pattern obtains for indirect questions, as our Σ/NP-to-VP metarule would lead us to expect:

(61) a. I wonder who Bill saw and Mary liked.

$$(= \text{S/NP \& S/NP})$$

b. I wonder who saw Bill and liked Mary.

$$(= \text{VP \& VP})$$

c. *I wonder who Bill saw and liked Mary.

$$(= \text{S/NP \& VP})$$

d. I wonder who Mary likes and hopes will win.

$$(= \text{VP/NP \& VP/NP})$$

The grammaticality distribution in (60) and (61) cannot be explained by a theory which requires all the holes in an ATB construction to have the same case: such a theory incorrectly predicts that (60d) and (61d) will be ungrammatical.[27]

It is worth pointing out that the treatment of the interaction of unbounded dependencies and coordination detailed in this article makes exactly the right predictions about what Grimshaw (1978) refers to as "complementizer conjoined *wh* phrases". Consider her examples:

(62) *John asked who and where Bill had seen.

[= Grimshaw's (4b)]

(63) *John asked who and what bought.

[= (6)]

(64) Which book and which pencil did John buy?

[= (8a)]

(65) *Where and when did Bill put the book?

$$[= (9a)]$$

(66) On which table and under which flower pot did John put the keys? $[=(11)]$

(67) a. To which city and to which conference did Bill go?

$$[=(12)]$$

     b. To which city and which conference did Bill go?

$$[=(15a)]$$

     c. Which city and which conference did Bill go to?

$$[=(15b)]$$

     d. * Which city and which conference did Bill go to _____ to _____? $[=(14a)]$

     e. *Which city and to which conference did Bill go to?

$$[=(14b)]$$

     f. *To which city and which conference did Bill go to?

$$[=(14c)]$$

In every case Grimshaw's explanation for the (un)grammaticality of an example carries over to the present analysis. Examples (62) and (67e) are ruled out because they involve coordination of unlike categories; (63) because *who and what* cannot be both subject and object of *bought* and yet there are both subject and object holes in the sentence; (65) because *put* subcategorizes for a locative adverbial (hence, the *wh*-phrase must also be locative, but *where and when* is not); (67d) because on (coordinate) *wh*-NP cannot bear a dependency relation to two (noncoordinate) holes; and (67f) because a *wh*-PP cannot bear a dependency relation to an NP hole. Thus, no extra apparatus is needed to handle conjoined *wh*-phrases: the pattern of acceptability exhibited in (62)-(67) simply follows from the coordination and dependency schemata given as (9) and (15) taken together with uncontroversial assumptions about subcategorization.

However, the approach advocated here cannot, at present, explain the contrast between (68a) and (68b) noted by Williams (1978, 35), since both will be generated:

(68) a.   *John, who and whose friends you saw, is a fool.

(= NP & NP)

   b.   John, to who and to whose friends that letter was
         addressed, is a fool.   (= PP & PP)

William's own explanation for this contrast depends crucially on what he refers to as a "quite particular" asymmetric redefinition of *factor* (1978, 32) and an equally particular assumption about the structural description for the rule of *Wh* Movement (1978, 35). There are two problems with his account, one theoretical and the other empirical. The theoretical problem is this: if the rule of *Wh* Movement looks like (69), then William's "quite particular" redefinition of *factor* will not do any work:

(69)   SD: W   COMP   Y $\overline{\text{X}}$ Z
                                  [+WH]
              1   2   3   4   5
        SC: 1   4   3 ϕ 5

So, instead of the rather simple and elegant (69), Williams must state *Wh* Movement in a way which makes essential reference to tree structure in the structural description, contrary to the definition of a transformation as an operation on an unbracketed string of category symbols as in classical transformational grammar.

   The empirical problem is that William's redefinition of *factor* predicts that the following English sentences will be ungrammatical:[28]

(70) a. I wonder when and how often she went that day.

   b. I wonder who and whose friends he handed over to the FBI.

Since both sentences are entirely grammatical, Williams would be forced to modify his definition of *factor* to accommodate them. But any such modification will inevitably allow (68a) to be generated: thus, in the end Williams's analysis is also unable to explain the contrast between (68a) and (68b). These examples are therefore irrelevant to choosing between his proposals and those made.[29]

4. Rightward Dependencies

As is well known, rightward displacement of constituents is subject to a constraint having to do with "heaviness": roughly speaking, the heavier the displaced constituent, the better the sentence sounds. This fact is hard to capture in the formalism of a generative grammar (whether phrase structure or transformational) and it seems reasonable, and probably not controversial, to suppose that it may be a fact that ought to be captured not in that formalism, but rather in one's model of language perception and/or production.[30]

Another familiar fact about rightward displacements is their apparent clause-boundedness. This was first noted by Ross (1967, 166), and the stipulation he made against unbounded rightward movement has come to be known as the "Right Roof Constraint" (RRC, hereafter). Subsequent work has shown that the RRC is neither universal nor absolute. Languages as diverse as Circassian, German, Hindi, and Navajo have been alleged to admit constructions which appear to violate it.[31] And even in English, the facts are not exactly as the RRC predicts. Thus, Postal (1974, 92n) cites Witten (1972, IV-93) as the source for the examples in (71):

(71) a.   I have wanted to know exactly what happened to Rosa
            Luxemburg for many years.
      b.   I have wanted to know for many years exactly what
            happened to Rosa Luxemburg.

Example (71b) is clearly grammatical and equally clearly in violation of the RRC. Consider also the following examples, suggested to me by Janet Fodor:

(72) a.   I had hoped that it was true that Rosa Luxemburg had
            actually defected to Iceland for many years.
      b.   I had hoped that it was true for many years that Rosa
            Luxemburg had actually defected to Iceland.

(73) a.   I have wanted to meet the man who spent so much money
            planning the assassination of Kennedy for many years.
      b.   I have wanted to meet for many years the man who spent
            so much money planning the assassination of Kennedy.

Again, (72b) and (73b) are clear violations of the RRC. In fact, as Andrews (1975, 112) points out, all the starred sentences that Ross originally used to motivate the RRC were, in any case, excluded by the Sentential Subject Constraint. Andrews goes on to show that when the Sentential Subject Constraint does not interfere, the resulting RRC-violating strings are much more acceptable than those that Ross originally listed.[32]

In the light of these observations, I want to suggest, following Grosu (1972), that the RRC is not part of the grammar at all and instead that the facts it purports to explain are to be better explained in terms of performance considerations, in particular parsing strategies. Frazier (1979) and Frazier and Fodor(1978) have recently argued at length for a model of the natural language parser which attaches incoming material as low as it possibly can on the parse tree. This theory offers a natural explanation for the fact that the preferred reading of (74a) is (74b) rather than (74c):

(74) a. The woman believed that the man was ill who was here.
      b. The woman believed that the man who was here was ill.
      c. The woman who was here believed that the man was ill.

It also explains why Perlmutter's example (75a) (from Grosu (1971, 423)) is interpreted as being synonymous with (75b) rather than (75c):

(75) a. A woman hit a girl who was pregnant.
      b. A woman hit a pregnant girl.
      c. A pregnant woman hit a girl.

If the boundedness of rightward dependencies is a by-product of parser operation, then it need not be built into the syntactic rules which permit such dependencies. Accordingly, we may propose the following very general schema for rightward displacement,[33]

(76) $\langle 9, [_\alpha \alpha / \beta\ \beta], \ \lambda h_\beta [(\alpha / \beta)'](\beta') \rangle$

where α ranges over clausal categories and β can be any phrasal or clausal category. This schema will then give us extraposed relatives and will, for example, assign the following surface structure to (74a):

(77)

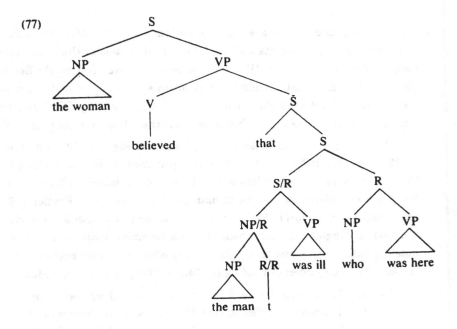

Extraposition of relative clauses *cannot* in general be the result of a movement or deletion rule, as the following examples (based on Perlmutter and Ross (1970)) clearly demonstrate:

(78) a.   A man just came in and a woman went out who were similar in all kinds of ways.

b.   A man just came in and a woman went out who hate each other like poison and always have.

These sentences show that extraposed relatives must be generated in situ, exactly as (76) proposes.

Extraposed relatives are not all that (76) will account for. Most interestingly, it interacts with the coordination schema given in (9) to achieve all the effects of the Right Node Raising (RNR) transformation without the need for additional machinery. This is a remarkable result for, as Jackendoff has pointed out, there are "no remotely coherent formalizations of RNR" (1977, 193). But we have an entirely coherent formalization that makes RNR otiose. The following tree makes it clear how this comes about:

(79)

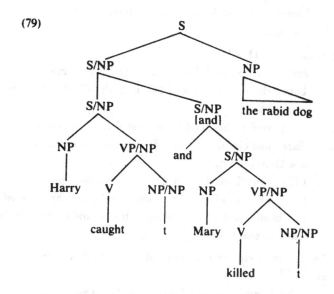

RNR is not bound by the RRC. This fact is puzzling when the former is a rightward movement rule and the latter a constraint on rightward movement rules. However, far from being puzzling, it is actually predicted by the present analysis. The Frazier-Fodor parser requires incoming material to be attached in the clause being parsed *when possible*. But the effect of the RNR construction is to make it impossible to attach the material following the hole in the clause which precedes the hole. For example, consider tree (79) above. When the parser has attached *caught* to the first VP, it is looking for the NP that *catch* subcategorizes for: but the incoming material (*and, and Mary, and Mary killed.* . . .) cannot be this NP. So, of necessity, the parser closes the VP and begins the analysis of a new clause.

RNR is often used as a test for constituenthood. Schema (76) predicts that only constituents can appear in the rightmost β position. Thus, the following strings cannot be generated.[34]

(80) a.   *I find it easy to believe--but Joan finds it hard to believe--
          Tom to be dishonest.

  b.   *John offered, and Harry gave, Sally a Cadillac.

  c.   *John told, and Harry showed, Seymour that Sally was
        a virgin.

But all the sentences in (81) will be:[35]

(81) a.   Jack may be t and Tony certainly is t a werewolf.

  b.   Tom said he would t and Bill actually did t eat a raw
        eggplant.

  c.   Tony used to be t and George still is t very suspicious.

  d.   Harry has claimed t but I do not believe t that Melvin
        is a Communist.

  e.   I like t but Tom doesn't like t to visit new places.

  f.   I can tell you when t, but I can't tell you why t, he left me.

  g.   I've been wondering whether t, but wouldn't positively
        want to state that t, your theory is correct.

RNR cannot be a movement or deletion rule, as the following examples
clearly demonstrate:[36]

(82) a.   John hummed t, and Mary sang t, the same tune.

  b.   John hummed t, and Mary sang t, at equal volumes.

  c.   John gave Mary t, and Joan presented t to Fred, books
        which looked remarkably similar.

  d.   The Red Sox beat t, and the Giants were beaten by t,
        different teams.

These examples require no extra syntactic apparatus or special devices.
On the present approach, they are as straightforward as the examples in
(81). But they pose an insuperable problem for conventional analyses.

5. Conclusion

This article has made five main proposals:

  I.   A single, very general, schema for constituent coordination.

  II.   A single, very general, schema allowing unbounded dependencies.

  III. A generalization of Ross's Left Branch Constraint.

IV.   A tensed VP analysis of apparent subject dependencies.

V.   A single, very general, schema allowing rightward dependencies.

Each proposal has been independently motivated. However, a wide variety of facts follow as theorems from the interaction of the various proposals. Thus, the distribution of complementizer *that* follows from II, III. and IV; the "complementizer conjoined *wh-* phrase" facts and the coordinate structure constraint facts follow from I and II; the across-the-board facts follow from I, II, III, and IV; and the "Right Node Raising" facts follow from I, II and V. These facts are explained in a grammatical framework that does not employ any rules of NP Movement, *Wh* Movement, or Coordination Reduction. Indeed, the explanations given are incompatible with the existence of such rules. Thus, the assumption made at the beginning to the effect that there are no transformations turns out to be not just *tenable*, but in fact *necessary*, if we are to achieve an explanatory, rather than merely stipulative, account of the data discussed in this article.

Footnotes

I am indebted, for comments, conversation, and criticism, to Emmon Bach, Lee Baker, Anne Cutler, Elisabet Engdahl, Janet Fodor, Paloma Garcia-Bellido, Paul Hirschbühler, Dick Hudson, Aravind Joshi, Ewan Klein, Robert May, Jim McCloskey, Barbara Partee, Stan Peters, Geoff Pullum, Andrew Radford, Ivan Sag, Lisa Selkirk, Neil Smith, Jean-Roger Vergnaud, Edwin Williams, and two anonymous L1 referees. This research was supported by grant HR 5767 from the SSRC (UK).

[1]See, for example, Marslen-Wilson (1973).

[2]This assumption commits us to what Bach (1976, 2) has called the *rule-to-rule* hypothesis concerning the semantic translation relation. Nothing to be said below hinges on our adopting this hypothesis, and the syntax given is entirely compatible with a less constrained view of the syntax-semantics relation, for example one in which the syntax simply admits structures, and a set of completely unrelated semantic rules interprets those structures.

[3]We can allow β in (10) also to range over the comparative complementizers *as* and *than*, but I shall not pursue this possibility here (see Gazdar (1980b) for discussion). Given schema (10), we can provide a phrase structure rule for the idiomatic *go and VP, come and VP* construction:

(i)   [$_{\text{VP}}$ V (PP) $\underset{[\text{and}]}{\text{VP}}$]

Following Ross (1967, 94) and Schachter (1977, 100), I am assuming that this construction does not involve genuine coordinate structure. But, pace Bever, Carroll, and Hurtig (1976, 170-173), I do assume that the construction should be characterized by the grammar of English.

[4]Harman (1963) deserves the credit for first seeing the potential of PS grammars incorporating a complex symbol system. The idea of employing grammar to induce the grammar is due originally to Van Wijngaarden (1969). For some discussion of the properties of systems which exploit a grammar to generate a grammar, see Langendoen (1976) and Gazdar (1982).

[5]Cf. Baker (1978, 113), Hellan (1977, 128).

[6]Definitions (14) and (15) allow only one hole to be "carried down"

through any node in the tree. This is desirable for English, which, by and large, does not allow multiple dependencies. However, (14) and (15) would need to be generalized to handle, for example, Scandinavian languages. See Engdahl (1980), Gazdar (1982), Maling and Zaenen (1982) for discussion of some of the issues involved.

[7]The question of how we formalize universal constraints is, of course, distinct from the question of how we motivate them. The discussion here addresses only the question of formalization, a question that is rarely taken up in the literature.

[8]A constraint like Subjacency cannot be reconstructed this way. However, if one wanted to impose it, then one could recast it as a tree filter and throw out all trees that involved a violation. Use of tree filters of this type would not allow the overall theory to generate any non-CF languages. This can be proved straightforwardly by defining a tree automaton of the appropriate kind, but I will not pursue this here. See Thatcher (1973) and Levy (1982) for discussion of tree automata.

[9]The GLBC is claimed to capture a fact about English, rather than a linguistic universal. Following the arguments in Klein (1980), we take *how many* to be an AP in the following sentence (which I owe to Emmon Bach and Barbara Partee):

(i)   How many did you buy of those pies at the fair?

Compare the following French sentence (due to Jean-Roger Vergnaud):

(ii)   Combien   as-tu   donné de ces   livres   à   ces   gens?
        how many have you given of these books to these people

[10]Rules are given for the various comparative constructions in Gazdar (1980b), and for topicalization and free relatives in Gazdar (1982). Gazdar, Pullum, and Sag (1980) gives a rule for VP fronting.

[11]The R and Q features can be motivated by the difference between relative and interrogative pronouns found in many languages (e.g. Albanian, German, Hindi).

[12]In view of the arguments in Andrews (1975), I have assumed an NP-S syntax in (24), but nothing in the present framework prevents one from adopting a NOM-S syntax: one would just replace (24) with [NOM NOM R] and change the semantics in appropriate ways. Likewise, the rule given

allows relatives to stack (pace Jackendoff (1977, 185-190)), but this is also an entirely incidental aspect of the analysis.

[13]We assume that the R feature, introduced originally by Andrews (1975, 16), is carried down onto the head of the relative clause in virtue of the Head Feature Convention discussed by Gazdar, Pullum, and Sag (1980) and Klein (1980). We also assume that the features mentioned in (27) and (28) can trickle through NP and PP onto embedded NPs to give us such relative heads as *in which, for whom, whose book, in whose book*, etc.

[14]The semantic rule for (25) when the NP is missing is as given except that NP′ is replaced by $\lambda PP(n)$.

[15]Metarule-like operations are proposed in Vergnaud (1973) and Roeper and Siegel (1978). For full discussion of the properties of metarules, see Gazdar (1982). The metarule given in (32) oversimplifies matters in a number of respects that are tangential to the main themes of this article. In particular, we need to distinguish the category which immediately dominates the subject-auxiliary construction from the one that dominates root constituent questions. See Gazdar, Pullum, and Sag (1980) for a more satisfactory metarule theory of Subject-Auxiliary Inversion.

[16]Semantically, we must substitute $(VP'(h_{NP}))$ for $(\Sigma/NP)'$ in the translation of the original rule.

[17]This makes sense from a language processing point of view: when the parser encounters a constituent that looks like a tensed VP, it can decide then and there that that is what it is, without needing to allow for the possibility of subsequently having to reanalyze it as a sentence with a missing subject.

[18]As Geoff Pullum has pointed out to me, most current theories commit their proponents to the claim that all sentences like (i) are structurally, though not semantically, ambiguous between the structures shown approximately in (ii) and (iii):

    (i)   Kim loves Sandy.

    (ii)   [$_{S[NP}$ Kim] [$_{VP}$ loves Sandy]]

    (iii) [$_{S[NP}$ Kim] [$_{S[NP}$ t] [$_{VP}$ loves Sandy]]

The present analysis only allows such sentences to have structure (ii), since the GLBC eliminates structure (iii).

[19]The use of the familiar " $\overline{S}$ " is slightly misleading here, since we are using the symbol to abbrieviate [±C, -R, -Q] and it is only [+C, -R, -Q] which expands as *that*-S. In this connection, notice that (39) will not apply to derived rules which introduce [+C, -R, -Q]/NP. Consequently, verbs like *regret* which require a [+C, -R, -Q] complement *cannot* be followed by a tensed VP, in contrast to verbs like *think* which take [±C, -R, -Q]. Thus, our analysis predicts the following contrasts:

(i) a. Who do you think (that) you saw?

   b. Who do you think (*that) saw you?

(ii) a. Who do you regret *(that) you saw?

   b. *Who do you regret (that) saw you?

[20]For the classic discussion of this configuration, see Bresnan (1977, 170-183).

[21]I am grateful to Geoff Pullum for drawing to my attention the fact that configuration (48) is blocked by the GLBC, and that consequently facts motivating Ross's (1967) Sentential Subject Constraint follow from the GLBC without modification. He also points out that (48) is not restricted to subjects, thus explaining the anomaly of (i), which is outside the scope of Ross's constraint.

(i) *What do you believe that iron is t to be a fact well known to virtually everybody?

[22]There is evidence to suggest that (52a) is the correct structure for matrix subject relatives in French also. I owe the following examples to Lisa Selkirk:

(i) a. L'homme qui est parti. . .

   the man who has left

   b. L'homme qu' est parti. . .

   the man who has left

She notes that one would expect (ib) to be ungrammatical if a trace intervened between the relative pronoun and the copula. On the VP analysis, there is no trace there to block the contraction. And Elisabet Engdahl reports that in Swedish relatives the matrix subject can never be realized as a resumptive pronoun, although resumptive pronouns can occur in other relativized NP positions. Again, this would be predicted by a VP analysis.

[23]Questions (i) adults: Read, Kraak, and Boves (1980) on Dutch; (ii) children: Stewart and Sinclair (1975), Tyack and Ingram (1977). Relative clauses (i) adults: Fodor, Bever, and Garrett (1974, 364), Sheldon (1976; 1977), Wanner and Maratsos (1978), Holmes (1979), Mills (1979) on German, Frauenfelder, Segui, and Mehler (1979) on French; (ii) children: Brown (1971), Smith (1974), Ferreiro et al. (1976), and de Villiers et al. (1979). I am grateful to Anne Cutler and Paloma Garcia-Bellido for drawing my attention to some of this literature.

[24]As Tom Wasow and one of my referees have reminded me, there are apparent exceptions to this claim such as *slowly and with great care* and *longwinded and a bully*. Such expressions are permitted to appear in some slot in a sentence only when either conjunct could appear alone in that slot. Thus, we find (ia-c) but not (ii) or (iii):

(i)   a.   He was longwinded.

       b.   He was a bully.

       c.   He was longwinded and a bully.

(ii)   *The [longwinded and a bully] man entered.

(iii)   *[Longwinded and a bully] entered.

Beyond this observation, I have nothing to say about such examples.

[25]Schachter (1977) almost draws the relevant inference but ends up explaining some CSC violations syntactically, others semantically.

[26]Paloma Garcia-Bellido informs me that the counterpart of (60c) is grammatical in Spanish. This would be predictable if, as is arguably the case, the GLBC does not apply in Spanish: (60c) could than have the structure S/NP & S/NP.

[27]This observation is due to Paul Hirschbuhler and Andrew Radford.

[28]I am indebted to Geoff Pullum for the examples in (70).

[29]Edwin Williams has suggested to me that the difference in acceptability between (70b) and (68a) may result from the fact that relatives require the complement clause to characterize a unique individual whereas interrogatives do not. If conjoined indefinite NPs like *who and whose friends* are necessarily disjoint in reference, then this would explain why they do not

show up as relative heads.

[30]Cf. Ross (1967, chapter 30, Fiengo (1977, 48-49).

[31]Circassian: Colarusso   (1976);   German: Kohrt   (1975):   Hindi:
Satyanarayana and Subbarao (1973); Navajo: Kaufman (1974), Perkins
(1975).

[32]Andrews exhibits the following "rather massive RRC violations" (1975,
234):

    (i)   a.   People are said to do crazier things at higher speeds there
                  by Dorothy than they are by other people.

            b.   People are said to do such crazy things at such high speeds
                  there by Dorothy that I am getting skeptical.

As Andrews remarks, these examples "strengthen the suspicion ... that the
RRC should be retired" (1975, 234).

[33]As Emmon Bach has pointed out to me, the semantic rule in (76) is too
simplistic to handle the examples in (78) and (82), below, correctly. However, in the absence of any serious proposals for the semantics of sym-
metric predicates, it is not obvious what to replace it with.

[34]Example (80a) is from Postal (1974, 128), and (80b,c) are due to Hankamer (1971, 76, cited by Abbott (1976, 639)). The problematic case for the
present analysis, as with every known alternative analysis of RNR, is
Abbott's (1976, 639) example:

    (i)   Smith loaned, and his widow later donated, a valuable collection
          of manuscripts to the library.

[35]Examples (81a-e) are from Postal (1974, 126-128) and (81f-g) are from
Bresnan (1974, 618).

[36]Example (82a) is from Jackendoff (1977, 192) and (82c) is due to Abbott
(1976, 642).

References

Abbott, B. (1976) "Right Node Raising as a Test for Constituenthood," *Linguistic Inquiry* 7, 639-642.

Andrews, A.D. (1975) *Studies in the Syntax of Relative and Comparative Clauses*, Doctoral dissertation, MIT, Cambridge, Massachusetts.

Bach, E. (1976), "An Extension of Classical Transformational Grammar," mimeo, University of Massachusetts at Amherst.

Bach, E. and R. Cooper (1978) "The NP-S Analysis of Relative Clauses and Compositional Semantics," *Linguistics and Philosophy* 2, 145-150.

Baker, C.L. (1978) *Introduction to Generative-Transformational Syntax*, Prentice-Hall, Englewood Cliffs, New Jersey.

Bever, T.G., J.M. Carroll, and R. Hurtig (1976) "Analogy or Ungrammatical Sequences That Are Utterable and Comprehensible Are the Origins of New Grammars in Language Acquisition and Linguistic Evolution," in T.G. Bever, J.J. Katz, and D.T. Langendoen., eds., *An Integrated Theory of Linguistic Ability*, Thomas Cromwell, New York, 149-182.

Bresnan, J.W. (1974) "The Position of Certain Clause-Particles in Phrase Structure," *Linguistic Inquiry* 5, 614-619.

Bresnan, J.W. (1976) "Evidence for a Theory of Unbounded Transformations," *Linguistic Analysis* 2, 353-393.

Bresnan, J.W. (1977) "Variables in the Theory of Transformations," in P.W. Culicover, T. Wasow, and A. Akmajian, eds., *Formal Syntax*, Academic Press, New York, 157-196.

Brown, H.D. (1971) "Children's Comprehension of Relativized English Sentences," *Child Development* 42, 1923-1936.

Colarusso, J. (1976) "An Instance of Unbounded Rightward Movement: Wh-Movement in Circassian," unpublished paper, University of Vienna.

Cooper, R. (1975) *Montague's Semantic Theory and Transformational Syntax*, Doctoral dissertation, University of Massachusetts, Amherst, Massachusetts.

Cooper, R. (forthcoming) *Formal Semantics and Transformational Grammar*, Reidel, Dordrecht.

Dougherty, R.C. (1970) "A Grammar of Coordinate Structures I," *Language* 46, 850-898.

Earley, J. (1970) "An Efficient Context-free Parsing Algorithm," *Communications of the ACM* 13, 94-102.

Engdahl, E. (1980) *The Syntax and Semantics of Questions in Swedish*, Doctoral dissertation, University of Massachusetts at Amherst.

Ferreiro, E., C. Othenin-Girard, H. Chipman, and H. Sinclair (1976) "How Do Children Handle Relative Clauses?" *Archives de Psychologie* 45, 229-266.

Fiengo, R. (1977) "On Trace Theory," *Linguistic Inquiry* 8, 35-61.

Fodor, J.A., T.G. Bever, and M. Garrett (1974) *The Psychology of Language: An Introduction to Psycholinguistics and Generative Grammar*, McGraw-Hill, New York.

Frauenfelder, U., J. Segui, and J. Mehler (1979) "Monitoring around the Relative Clause," unpublished paper.

Frazier, L. (1979) "On Comprehending Sentences: Syntactic Parsing Strategies," mimeo, Indiana University Linguistics Club, Bloomington, Indiana.

Frazier, L. and J.D. Fodor (1978) "The Sausage Machine: A New Two-Stage Parsing Model," *Cognition* 6, 291-325.

Gazdar, G.J.M. (1980a) "A Cross-categorial Semantics for Coordination," *Linguistics and Philosophy* 3, 407-409.

Gazdar G.J.M. (1980b) "A Phrase Structure Syntax for Comparative Clauses," in T. Hoekstra, H. v.d. Hulst, and M. Moortgat eds., *Lexical Grammar*, Foris Publications, Dordrecht, 165-179.

Gazdar, G.J.M. (1982) "Phrase Structure Grammar," In P. Jacobson and G.K. Pullum, eds., *The Nature of Syntactic Representation*, Reidel,

Boston, 131-186.

Gazdar, G.J.M., G.K. Pullum, and I. Sag (1980) "A Phrase Structure Grammar of the English Auxiliary System," in I. Sag, ed., *Stanford Working Papers in Grammatical Theory*, Volume I, Stanford Cognitive Science Group, 1-124.

Grimshaw, J. (1978) "On the Syntax of Conjoined *wh* Words in English," in R.M. Saenz, ed., *University of Massachusetts Occasional Papers in Linguistics* Volume 3, Graduate Linguistic Student Association, University of Massachusetts at Amherst, 1-10.

Grosu, A. (1971) "On Perceptual and Grammatical Constraints," in D. Adams et al., eds., *Papers from the Seventh Regional Meeting of the Chicago Linguistic Society*, University of Chicago, Chicago, Illinois, 416-427.

Grosu, A. (1972) "The Strategic Content of Island Constraints," *Ohio State University Working Papers in Linguistics* 13.

Hankamer, J. (1971) *Constraints on Delection in Syntax*, Doctoral dissertation, Yale University, New Haven, Connecticut.

Harman, G.H. (1963) "Generative Grammars without Transformation Rules: A Defense of Phrase Structure," *Language* 39, 597-616.

Hellan, L. (1977) "$\overline{\text{X}}$-syntax, Categorial Syntax and Logical Form," in T. Fretheim and L. Hellan, eds., *Papers from the Trondheim Syntax Symposium*, Trondheim, 83-135.

Holmes, V.M. (1979) "Some Hypotheses about Syntactic Processing in Sentence Comprehension," in W.E. Cooper and E. Walker, eds., *Sentence Processing Studies Presented to Merrill Garrett*, Erlbaum, Hillsdale, New Jersey.

Horn, G.M. (1974) *The NP Constraint*, Doctoral dissertation, University of Massachusetts at Amherst. Also distributed by the Indiana University Linguistics Club, Bloomington, Indiana.

Jackendoff, R. (1977) $\overline{X}$ *Syntax: A Study of Phrase Structure* Linguistic Inquiry Monograph 2, MIT Press, Cambridge, Massachusetts.

Karttunen, L. (1977) "Syntax and Semantics of Questions," *Linguistics and Philosophy* 1,3-44.

Kaufman, E.S. (1974) "Navajo Spatial Enclitics: A Case for Unbounded Rightward Movement," *Linguistic Inquiry* 5, 507-533.

Keenan, E.L. and B. Comrie (1977) "Noun Phrase Accessibility and Universal Grammar," *Linguistic Inquiry* 8, 63-99.

Keenan, E.L. and L. Faltz (1978) "Logical Types for Natural Language," *UCLA Occasional Papers in Linguistics 3*.

Klein, E.H. (1980) "Determiners and the Category Q," unpublished paper, University of Sussex.

Kohrt, M. (1975) "A Note on Bounding," *Linguistic Inquiry* 6, 167-171.

Langendoen, D.T. (1976) "On the Weak Generative Capacity of Infinite Grammars," *CUNY Forum* 1,13-24.

Levy, L.S. (forthcoming) "Automata on Trees: A Tutorial Survey," to appear in *Egyptian Computer Journal*.

Maling, J. and A. Zaenen (1982) "A Base-generated Account of `Extraction Phenomena´ in Scandinavian Languages," In P. Jacobson and G.K. Pullum, eds., *The Nature of Syntactic Representation*, Reidel, Boston, 229-282.

Marslen-Wilson, W.D. (1973) *Speech Shadowing and Speech Perception*, Doctoral dissertation, MIT, Cambridge, Massachusetts.

McCawley, J.D. (1968) "Concerning the Base Component of a Transformational Grammar," *Foundations of Language* 4, 243-269. Reprinted in *Grammar and Meaning*, Academic Press, New York, 35-58.

McCloskey, J. (1978) "Questions and Relative Clauses in Modern Irish," *Texas Linguistic Forum* 12.

McCloskey, J. (1979) *Transformational Syntax and Model Theoretic Semantics*, Reidel, Dordrecht.

Mills, A.E. (1979) "Surface Structure Order and Comprehension of Ambiguous Clauses," paper presented to the Spring meeting of the Linguistics Association of Great Britain, Hull.

Perkins, E. (1975) "Extraposition of Relative Clauses in Navajo," *The Navajo Language Review* 2.2 [cited by Andrews (1975, 114)].

Perlmutter, D.M. and J.R. Ross (1970) "A Nonsource for Comparatives," *Linguistic Inquiry* 1, 127-128.

Postal, P.M. (1974) *On Raising*, MIT Press, Cambridge, Massachusetts.

Postal, P.M. and G.K. Pullum (1978) "Traces and the Description of English Complementizer Contraction," *Linguistic Inquiry* 9, 1-29.

Read, C., A. Kraak, and L. Boves (1980) "The Interpretation of Ambiguous *Who*-Questions in Dutch: The Effect of Intonation," in W. Zonnefeld, ed., *Linguistics in the Netherlands, 1977-1979*, Foris Publications, Dordrecht.

Roeper, T. and M.E.A. Siegel (1978) "A Lexical Transformation for Verbal Compounds," *Linguistic Inquiry* 9, 199-260.

Ross, J.R. (1967) *Constraints on Variables in Syntax*, Doctoral dissertation, MIT, Cambridge, Massachusetts. Also distributed by the Indiana University Linguistics Club, Bloomington, Indiana.

Satyanarayana, P. and K.V. Subbarao (1973) "Are Rightward Movement Rules Upward Bounded?" *Studies in the Linguistic Sciences* 3, 182-192.

Schachter, P. (1976) "A Nontransformational Account of Gerundive Nominals in English," *Linguistic Inquiry* 7, 205-241.

Schachter, P. (1977) "Constraints on Coordination," *Language* 53, 86-103.

Sheldon, A. (1976) "Speakers' Intuitions about the Complexity of Relative Clauses in Japanese and English," in S. Mufwene, C. Walker, and S. Steever, eds., *Papers from the Twelfth Regional Meeting of the Chicago Linguistic Society*, University of Chicago, Chicago, Illinois, 558-567.

Sheldon, A. (1977) "On Strategies for Processing Relative Clauses: A Comparison of Children and Adults," *Journal of Psycholinguistic Research* 6, 305-318.

Shir, N.E. (1977) "On the Nature of Island Constraints," mimeo, Indiana University Linguistics Club, Bloomington, Indiana.

Smith, M. (1974) "Relative Clause Formation between 29-36 Months: A Preliminary Report," *Papers and Reports on Child Language Development* 8, 104-110.

Stewart, J. and H. Sinclair (1975) "Comprehension of Questions by Children between 5 and 9," *International Journal of Psycholinguistics* 3, 17-26.

Stump, G.T. (1978) "Interpretive Gapping in Montague Grammar," in D. Farkas, W.M. Jacobsen, and K.W. Todrys, eds., *Papers from the Fourteenth Regional Meeting of the Chicago Linguistic Society*, University of Chicago, Chicago, Illinois, 472-481.

Thatcher, J.W. (1973) "Tree Automata: An Informal Survey," in A.V. Aho, ed., *Currents in the Theory of Computing*, Prentice-Hall, Englewood Cliffs, New Jersey.

Tyack, D. and D. Ingram (1977) "Children's Production and Comprehension of Questions," *Journal of Child Language* 4, 211-224.

de Villiers, J.G., H.B. Tager Flusberg, K. Hakuta, and M. Cohen (1979) "Children's Comprehension of Relative Clauses," *Journal of Psycholinguistic Research* 8, 499-518.

Vergnaud, J.R. (1973) "Formal Properties of Lexical Derivations," *Quarterly Progress Report of the Research Laboratory in Electronics* No. 108, MIT, 280-287.

Wanner, E. and M. Maratsos (1978) "An ATN Approach to Comprehension," in M. Halle, J. Bresnan, and G.A. Miller, eds., *Linguistic Theory and Psychological Reality*, MIT Press, Cambridge, Massachusetts.

Wijngaarden, A. van (1969) "Report on the Algorithmic Language ALGOL 68," *Numerische Mathematik* 14, 79-218.

Williams, E.S. (1977) "Across-the-Board Application of Rules," *Linguistic Inquiry* 8, 419-423.

Williams, E.S. (1978) "Across-the-Board Rule Application," *Linguistic Inquiry* 9, 31-43.

Witten, E. (1972) "Centrality," in *Report No. NSF-28 to The National Science Foundation,* The Computation Laboratory of Harvard University, Cambridge, Massachusetts.

Younger, D.H. (1967) "Recognition and Parsing of Context-free Languages in Time n^3," *Information and Control* 10, 189-208.

Hans Uszkoreit and Stanley Peters

ON SOME FORMAL PROPERTIES OF METARULES*

1. Introduction

Grammars contain rules for generating sentences. Metarules are statements about these rules. They are metagrammatical devices that can be used to generate rules of the grammar or to encode certain relations among them, such as redundancies in their form.

The linguistic framework of Generalized Phrase Structure Grammar (GPSG) (Gazdar 1982; Gazdar, Pullum, and Sag 1981; Gazdar and Pullum 1982) utilizes metarules in describing natural languages. The rules of a GPSG are context-free (CF) phrase-structure rules. A metarule is an ordered pair of rule templates $<A, B>$ (often written $A \Rightarrow B$) that is to be interpreted as follows: if the grammar contains a rule of the form A, it also contains a corresponding rule of the form B. As this interpretation suggests, the set of grammar rules is closed under application of the metarules. It is therefore possible to give an inductive definition of the grammar by listing just a subset of the rules—called the basic rules—together with the list of metarules; the full set of rules is derived by applying the metarules to the basic rules and then, recursively, to the output of all such applications.

In GPSG, metarules are used to describe many of the linguistic phenomena for which transformations have previously been employed. Gazdar and other proponents of GPSG claim that GPSGs are powerful enough to capture all the generalizations about natural languages that were expressed by transformations and, at the same time, sufficiently constrained to generate only context-free languages. The design of the frame-

Linguistics and Philosophy, Vol. 9, No. 4, 1986, 477-494.
© 1986 by D. Reidel Publishing Company.

W. J. Savitch et al. (eds.), The Formal Complexity of Natural Language, 227–250.

work is built on the conjecture that all natural languages are CF.

We neither aim to discuss the theory of GPSG in its entirety nor to restrict our attention to this individual framework. We do not concern ourselves here with most of the mechanisms used by GPSG: derived categories, feature cooccurrence restrictions, ID/LP notation, subcategorization by rule, etc. Instead we are interested in certain formal properties of all grammars that use metarules of the form and in the way described above to close a set of CF grammar rules.[1] Since our definitions are abstract enough to make our results applicable to several such theories, we term the grammars studied in this paper Metarule Phrase Structure or MPS grammars (see the Appendix for definitions).

Our results mainly concern the weak generative capacity of MPS grammars. We show that the power of the formalism is greater than was previously assumed. Unconstrained MPS grammars have Turing machine power, i.e., they are capable of generating the full family of recursively enumerable string sets. Some constrained versions of the MPS grammar formalism still exhibit a certain degree of incommensurate excessive generative power. Finding a strong enough constraint that is both linguistically motivated and descriptively adequate will be a difficult task.

2. The Role of Variables and Phantom Symbols

What provides such a degree of generative power to a formalism that enumerates CF phrase structure rules? Clearly, a finite list of (basic) CF phrase-structure rules will generate only a CF language. How can metarules that merely add more CF rules alter the picture? To find an answer to this question, we begin by taking a closer look at metarules.

We have not yet said anything about the form of the rule templates that occur in metarules. A simple template might look exactly like a CF rule. It then matches just that one rule.[2] Most metarules proposed so far for grammars of natural language fragments are more general, in that they use templates that match a larger set of rules. This is achieved by employing variables in metarules. It is helpful to classify the variables that have been used into two categories. The first consists of abbreviatory, or inessential, variables, which range over finite sets of admissible values.

Such variables may be useful in permitting the expression of linguistically important generalizations. However, abbreviatory variables can always be eliminated from a grammar, since each metarule containing them can be replaced by the finitely many metarules obtained when these variables are instantiated in all admissible ways. Thus, inessential variables do not affect either the set of strings that can be generated or the sets of tree structures that can be assigned to generated strings by MPS grammars.

The second kind of variables are nonabbreviatory, or essential, variables, which range over all strings of terminal and nonterminal symbols. Rule (1) is an example of a metarule that contains both abbreviatory and essential variables. Here X and Y are essential variables and A is an abbreviatory variable with the range $\{NP, PP\}$ and α is an abbreviatory variable ranging over agreement feature specifications. The rule is supposed to generate VP rules with subject-controlled reflexivized constituents; the variable α over agreement features also determines the appropriate reflexive pronoun.[3]

$$(1)\ VP \rightarrow X\ A\ Y \Rightarrow VP \rightarrow X\ A\ Y$$
$$[\alpha] \qquad\qquad [\alpha] \qquad\quad [\alpha]$$
$$[self]$$

Clearly, the use of essential variables can not only create infinite rule sets, but, as has been noted, can also yield grammars that generate non-CF languages (Gazdar 1982; Thompson 1982). The designers of GPSG—intending to constrain their framework's potential for unwarranted power—have been concerned about this. But the formal properties of languages that can be generated with the aid of essential variables have not been known. Nor has it been clear how these properties are affected by the number of essential variables employed.

We understand that Aravind Joshi has made the following conjecture: using just one essential variable does not increase generative power beyond CF languages—even if infinitely many rules are derived. This conjecture was apparently accepted in GPSG as an established fact (Gazdar 1982, footnote 28). A single essential variable came to be considered 'safe'. In this paper, we take a closer look at the impact of essential variables on

MPS grammars and demonstrate that Joshi's conjecture is false. (We term MPS grammars with just one essential variable MPS/1 grammars.)

We shall see further that there is an interesting interaction between essential variables and the kind of nonterminals called 'useless symbols' in formal language theory. These are the symbols α for which no derivation $S \stackrel{*}{\mapsto} \phi\alpha\psi \stackrel{*}{\mapsto} w$ exists in a grammar for any strings ϕ, ψ and w, with $w \in V_T^*$. The theorem that every nonempty CF language is generated by a CF grammar with no such symbols explains their name (Hopcroft and Ullman, 1979, pp. 88-90). The term 'useless symbol' is misleading when applied to MPS grammars, however, for such symbols are not eliminable in this type of grammar.

To see why this is so, consider any rule-derivation of the form $R_1 \stackrel{*}{\Rightarrow} R_2 \stackrel{*}{\Rightarrow} R_3$ where R_1 is a basic rule, R_2 a rule containing a 'useless symbol' α, and R_3 a rule with no 'useless symbols'. Obviously it is conceivable that α may actually not be useless in this case, as it plays a role in the derivation of a useful rule. Indeed, R_3 may be derivable only through intermediate steps which, like R_2, contain a 'useless symbol'.

Within the framework of Generalized Phrase Structure Grammar, symbols of this kind have been utilized in grammars for natural-language fragments under the name 'phantom categories'. The first phantom category proposed was TVP, for transitive verb phrase. Gazdar and Sag (1980) offer the following basic rule for introducing verbs like *tell* in *She told him that it would rain.*

$$(2) \quad TVP \rightarrow V\overline{S}$$

The category TVP is not mentioned on the right-hand side of any rule. Therefore, the nonterminal cannot be used in the derivation of any string. Rule (2) contributes to the grammar by serving as the input to metarules. One of these metarules is (3), which derives active VP rules from TVP rules. The same set of TVP rules also matches the input template of a metarule that generates passive VP rules.

$$(3) \quad TVP \rightarrow V\ X \ \Rightarrow\ VP \rightarrow V\ NP\ X$$

Thus 'useless symbols' are not necessarily useless; nor do they have to be nonterminals, as the term 'phantom category' suggests. From now on we shall simply call them 'phantom symbols' and hope that this will be a reasonable compromise between accuracy and mnemonic value. We shall see that these symbols are indeed not always eliminable from MPS grammars (v. Theorem 5).

3. The Weak Generative Capacity of MPS Grammars

Before formulating and proving some theorems about MPS grammars, we briefly summarize our findings. They reveal that:

(i)   MPS/1 grammars generate all recursively enumerable (r.e.) languages.

Since MPS grammars generate only r.e. languages, it follows that MPS/1 grammars generate exactly the class of r.e. languages.

(ii)   MPS grammars without phantom symbols generate languages that, if infinite, are 'arithmetically dense'.

(iii)   MPS/1 grammars without phantom symbols generate some nonrecursive languages.

Since many context-sensitive languages, indeed many indexed languages are not 'arithmetically dense', MPS grammars without phantom symbols generate a class of languages that is incomparable with both the class of context-sensitive languages and the class of recursive languages. Of course,

(iv)   MPS/1 grammars without phantom symbols generate all context-free languages.

The most elegant counterexample we know to Joshi's conjecture is due to Chris Culy (1982). Because of its simplicity we present this grammar instead of our earlier example. Consider the following MPS/1 grammar, which consists of one basic rule and three metarules:

Basic rule:

$$S \to abc$$

Metarules:

$$S \to aX \;\Rightarrow\; S \to Xaa$$
$$S \to bX \;\Rightarrow\; S \to Xbb$$
$$S \to cX \;\Rightarrow\; S \to Xcc$$

X is the only essential variable. The sentences of the language are exactly the right-hand sides of the rules in the grammar. Recursive application of the metarules yields the language

$$\{abc,\; bcaa,\; caabb,\; aabbcc,\; abbccaa,\; bbccaaaa,\; bccaaaabb, ...\}.$$

The fact that this language is not CF can easily be verified by intersecting it with the regular set $a^*b^*c^*$. The class of CF languages is closed under intersection with regular sets. The result of this intersection, however, is

$$\{a^{2n}b^{2n}c^{2n} \mid n \geqslant 0\},$$

which, like any other infinite subset of $\{a^n b^n c^n \mid n \geqslant 0\}$, is not CF.

The classic example, $a^n b^n c^n$ itself, can also be generated by an MPS/1 grammar. Here is one that does the job:

Basic rule:

$$S \to AabcA$$

Metarules:

$$S \to AaaX \;\Rightarrow\; S \to AaXa$$
$$S \to AabX \;\Rightarrow\; S \to AbXaa$$
$$S \to AbbX \;\Rightarrow\; S \to AbXb$$
$$S \to AbcX \;\Rightarrow\; S \to AcXbb$$
$$S \to AccX \;\Rightarrow\; S \to AcXc$$
$$S \to AcAX \;\Rightarrow\; S \to AXccA$$
$$S \to AXA \;\Rightarrow\; S \to X$$

This time two nonterminals are used. Since one of them, A, never occurs on the left-hand side of any rule, it is therefore a phantom symbol. The question whether there is an MPS/1 grammar without phantom symbols that generates the same language is currently open.

Before we show that MPS/1 grammars generate all r.e. languages, we should mention the fact that they cannot generate anything outside the class of r.e. sets. (See the Appendix for definitions of terms pertaining to these grammars.)

Remark 1. Every language generated by an MPS grammar is an r.e. set of strings.

Proof: It is easy to show how the set $\underset{G}{\rightarrow}$ of all rules of G is recursively enumerated, starting from the finite set of basic rules and then iteratively applying the finitely many metarules of G. Since $\underset{G}{\rightarrow}$ is a r.e. relation, it can easily be demonstrated that $\underset{G}{\twoheadrightarrow}$ is likewise. But then $\underset{G}{\overset{*}{\vdash}}$ is also r.e., since r.e. relations are closed under the operation of taking ancestrals. But then $\{\phi \mid S \underset{G}{\overset{*}{\vdash}} \phi\}$ is an r.e. set of strings, since it is definable by existential quantification from an r.e. relation (viz., $\exists \psi\, [\, \psi = S \wedge \psi \underset{G}{\overset{*}{\vdash}} \phi])$. Hence $L(G) = V_T^* \cap \{\phi \mid S \underset{G}{\overset{*}{\twoheadrightarrow}} \phi\}$ is r.e., since V_T^* is and the class of r.e. sets is closed under intersection. ∎

The following theorem is the main step in proving that every r.e. set is generated by an MPS/1 grammar. It states that, for every r.e. language L over an alphabet Σ, there exists an MPS/1 grammar such that L is the intersection of Σ^* and the set of all strings generable from S by rules of the MPS/1 grammar. The proof is based on a procedure that converts any unrestricted rewriting system G', generating a language L over Σ into an MPS/1 grammar, that generates the union of L with a subset of the complement of Σ^*.

Theorem 2. There is a regular language R $(= \Sigma^*)$ such that, for any recursively enumerable language $L \subseteq \Sigma^*$, there is an MPS/1 grammar $G = \langle V_T, V_N, S, \rightarrow, V_V, \Rightarrow \rangle$ such that $L = R \cap \{\omega \mid S \underset{G}{\overset{*}{\twoheadrightarrow}} \omega\}$.

Proof: Given Σ and an r.e. language $L \subseteq \Sigma^*$, let $G' = \langle V_T', V_N', S', \rightarrow' \rangle$ be an unrestricted rewriting system such that $V_T' = \Sigma$ and $L =$

$\{x \in (V'_T)^* \mid S' \xrightarrow{*}_{G'} x\}$. Construct G as follows. Let S and A be two new symbols not in $V'_T \cup V'_N$. Give G the single basic rule $S \xrightarrow{G} AS'A$ and the following finite set of metarules, which make use of the single string variable X (where $V_V = \{X\}$).

(i) $S \to A\phi X \Rightarrow S \to A\psi X$ whenever $\phi \to' \psi$ is a rule of G'

(ii) $S \to A\alpha X \Rightarrow S \to AX\alpha$ whenever $\alpha \in V'_T \cup V'_N \cup \{A\}$

(iii) $S \to AXA \Rightarrow S \to X$

Note that S is the only symbol of G appearing on the left-hand side of any basic or derived rule. Furthermore, S does not appear on the right-hand side of any rule. Therefore, for any string ω other than S itself, $S \vdash^{*}_{G} \omega$ iff $S \to \omega$ is a rule of G. To establish that $L = \Sigma^* \cap \{\omega \mid S \xrightarrow{*}_{G} \omega\}$, it suffices to show that, for any $x \in \Sigma^*$, $S \xrightarrow{G} x$ is a rule of G if and only if $S' \vdash^{*}_{G'} x$. To this end, we now prove a more general statement from which this one follows directly, viz.: $S \xrightarrow{G} A\omega A$ is a rule of G if and only if $S' \vdash^{*}_{G'} \omega$ for any $\omega \in (V'_T \cup V'_N)^*$. (The final metarule of G and the fact that all other metarules preserve the property, possessed by G's basic rule, of there being exactly two As on the right-hand side establishes the required connection between this statement and the preceding one.)

If direction: Suppose $S' \vdash^{*}_{G'} \omega$. Let $\chi_1, \chi'_1, \ldots, \chi_n, \chi'_n \phi_1$, $\psi_1, \ldots, \phi_n, \psi_n$ be such that $S' = \chi_1 \phi_1 \chi'_1 \vdash_{G'} \chi_1 \psi_1 \chi'_1 = \chi_2 \phi_2 \chi'_2 \xrightarrow{G'} \cdots \chi_n \psi_n \chi'_n = \omega$.

Because a rule $S \xrightarrow{G} A\sigma\tau$ is derivable from the rule $S \xrightarrow{G} A\tau\sigma$ in G whenever $\sigma, \tau \in (V'_T \cup V'_N \cup \{A\})^*$, $S \xrightarrow{G} AS'A = S \xrightarrow{G} A\chi_1\phi_1\chi'_1 A \overset{*}{\Rightarrow}$ $S \xrightarrow{G} A\phi_1\chi'_1 A\chi_1 \Rightarrow S \xrightarrow{G} A\psi_1\chi'_1 A\chi_1 \overset{*}{\Rightarrow} S \xrightarrow{G} A\chi_1\psi_1\chi'_1 A = S \xrightarrow{G} A\chi_2\phi_2\chi'_2 A \overset{*}{\Rightarrow} S \xrightarrow{G} A\phi_2\chi'_2 A\chi_2 \Rightarrow \cdots S \xrightarrow{G} A\psi_n\chi'_n A\chi_n \overset{*}{\Rightarrow}$ $S \xrightarrow{G} A\chi_n\psi_n\chi'_n A = S \xrightarrow{G} A\omega A$ is a derivation via the metarules in G of the rule $S \underset{G}{\rightarrow} A \omega A$ from the basic rule $S \underset{G}{\rightarrow} AS'A$.

Only-if direction: Suppose $S \underset{G}{\rightarrow} A \omega A$ is a rule of G, and let

$$S \underset{G}{\rightarrow} AS'A \overset{*}{\Rightarrow} S \underset{G}{\rightarrow} \omega_1 \Rightarrow S \underset{G}{\rightarrow} \omega_2 \overset{*}{\Rightarrow} S \underset{G}{\rightarrow} \omega_3 \Rightarrow \cdots S \underset{G}{\rightarrow} \omega_{2n} \overset{*}{\Rightarrow} S \underset{G}{\rightarrow} A \omega A$$

be a derivation of this rule in G such that the metarule applied at each step $S \underset{G}{\rightarrow} \omega_{2i+1} \Rightarrow S \underset{G}{\rightarrow} \omega_{2(i+1)}$ is $S \rightarrow A\phi X \Rightarrow S \rightarrow A\psi X$ for some rule $\phi \rightarrow' \psi$ of G', and, in addition, where the only metarules needed to generate the relations $S \underset{G}{\rightarrow} \omega_{2i} \overset{*}{\Rightarrow} S \underset{G}{\rightarrow} \omega_{2i+1}$ (including $S \underset{G}{\rightarrow} AS'A \overset{*}{\Rightarrow} S \underset{G}{\rightarrow} \omega_1$ and $S \underset{G}{\rightarrow} \omega_{2n} \overset{*}{\Rightarrow} S \underset{G}{\rightarrow} A\omega A$) are of the form $S \rightarrow A\alpha X \Rightarrow S \rightarrow AX\alpha$, for $\alpha \in V'_T \cup V'_N \cup \{A\}$. Each ω_j must have A as its first symbol and contain exactly one other occurrence of A (no metarule adds or deletes A, since it is not a symbol of G'). Now let $\chi_0, \chi'_0, \ldots, \chi_{n-1}, \chi'_{n-1}, \phi_0, \psi_0, \ldots, \phi_{n-1}, \psi_{n-1}$ be such that $\omega_{2i+1} = A\phi_i \chi'_i A \chi_i$, $\omega_{2(i+1)} = A\psi_i \chi'_i A \chi_i$ and $\phi_i \rightarrow' \psi_i$ is a rule of G'. Clearly, $\chi_0 \phi_0 \chi'_0 \underset{G'}{\vdash} \chi_0 \psi_0 \chi'_0 = \chi_1 \phi_1 \chi'_1 \underset{G'}{\vdash} \cdots \chi_{n-1} \psi_{n-1} \chi'_{n-1}$ is a derivation in G'. Note that $\chi_0 \phi_0 \chi'_0 = S'$ and $\chi_{n-1} \psi_{n-1} \chi'_{n-1} = \omega$ and therefore $S' \underset{G'}{\vdash^*} \omega$. ∎

We obtain two corollaries by specifying in appropriate ways both the terminal and nonterminal vocabularies V_T and V_N of the grammar we have been constructing.

Corollary 3. Every r.e. set is generated by an MPS/1 grammar with at most one phantom symbol.

Proof: The MPS grammar constructed in the proof of Theorem 2 generates the r.e. set L if we choose its terminal vocabulary V_T to be Σ ($= V'_T$) and its nonterminal vocabulary V_N to be $\{S, A\} \cup V'_N$. In the grammar, all members of $\{A\} \cup V'_N$ are phantom symbols, as are those members of V'_T that do not occur in any string in L. To complete the proof, we need only show how to encode this grammar so that it uses just one phantom symbol.

One way to do this is as follows. Let $V_T \subseteq V'_T$ be the smallest set such that $L \subseteq V^*_T$. Now number the symbols of $\{A\} \cup V'_N \cup (V'_T - V_T)$ consecutively as $\alpha_0, \ldots, \alpha_n$. Choose some $c \in V_T$. Let $f\colon \{S,A\} \cup V'_N \cup V'_T \to \{S\} \cup V_T$ be defined by $f(\beta) = \beta$ if $\beta \in \{S\} \cup V_T$ and $f(\beta) = Ac^iA$ if β is the ith symbol in $\{A\} \cup V'_N \cup (V'_T - V_T)$. Extend f to $(\{S,A\} \cup V'_N \cup V'_T)^*$ by putting $f(\gamma\delta) = f(\gamma) f(\delta)$ for all strings γ and δ over the vocabulary. Now f is the encoding we need because it is one-to-one, i.e., if $f(\gamma) = f(\delta)$ then $\gamma = \delta$. Thus, the grammar we desire has the basic rule $f(S) \to f(AS'A)$ and the following metarules:

(i) $f(S) \to f(A\phi)X \Rightarrow f(S) \to f(A\psi)X$ whenever $\phi \to' \psi$ is a rule of G'

(ii) $f(S) \to f(A\alpha)X \Rightarrow f(S) \to f(A)Xf(\alpha)$ whenever $\alpha \in V_T \cup V'_N \cup \{A\}$

(iii) $f(S) \to f(A)Xf(A) \Rightarrow f(S) \to X$

The rule derivations of our new grammar are precisely the encoding of rule derivations in our old grammar.   ∎

Corollary 4. Some nonrecursive language is generated by an MPS/1 grammar without phantom symbols.

Proof: Let L be an r.e. but not recursive language, and let $G = \langle V_T, V_N, S, \to, V_V, \Rightarrow \rangle$ be the MPS/1 grammar whose basic rule $\to$ and metarules $\Rightarrow$ are constructed as in the proof of Theorem 2 and where $V_T = \Sigma \cup V'_N \cup \{A\}$, $V_N = \{S\}$ and $V_V = \{X\}$. Then $L = L(G) \cap \Sigma^*$, whence it follows that L is not recursive ─as Σ^* is, L is not, and the recursive sets are closed under intersection.   ∎

We now proceed to show that not all r.e. languages are generated by MPS/1 grammars without phantom symbols. Theorem 5 states that all languages generated by MPS grammars without phantom symbols, however many essential variables they employ, have the property of being arithmetically dense.[4] Thus, these languages constitute a proper subset of the class of r.e. languages. In fact, they omit some indexed, and therefore context-sensitive and *a fortiori* recursively decidable, languages such as $\{a^{n^2} \mid n \geqslant 0\}$. It is useful in formulating and proving the theorem to employ the following notation.

For any string ϕ, we let $|\phi|$ denote the length of ϕ, $[\phi]_\alpha$ denote the number of occurrences of the symbol α in ϕ, and $[\phi]_G$ denote the total number of occurrences in ϕ of all symbols other than nonterminals that cannot be rewritten in G to a nonempty terminal string. That is, when N $= \{A \in V_N \mid$ there is no $y \in V_T^+$ such that $A \overset{*}{\underset{G}{\vdash}} y\}$, *then* $[\phi]_G = \Sigma_{\alpha \in V_T \cup V_N - N}[\phi]_\alpha$. When context makes clear what grammar G is intended, we suppress the subscript and write $[\phi]$ instead of $[\phi]_G$.

Theorem 5. If G is an MPS grammar with no phantom symbols and if $L(G)$ is infinite, then there exists a constant c such that to any natural number n corresponds some $x_n \in L(G)$ satisfying $cn \leqslant |x_n| < c(n+1)$.

Proof. Let $G = \langle V_T, V_N, S, \rightarrow, V_V, \Rightarrow \rangle$ satisfy the hypotheses of the theorem. Our proof divides into two cases according to whether or not there is a bound on $[\phi]$ for all derived rules $A \rightarrow \phi$ of G. More precisely, we consider whether or not a number l exists such that every rule derivation $A_1 \rightarrow \phi_1 \Rightarrow A_2 \rightarrow \phi_2 \Rightarrow \cdots A_j \rightarrow \phi_j$ has $[\phi_j] \leqslant l$ if $A_1 \rightarrow \phi_1$ is a basic rule of G. Our strategy is to show that if such a bound exists, then $L(G)$ is a context-free language and thus has the desired density, whereas if there are derived rules $A_j \rightarrow \phi_j$ with arbitrarily large $[\phi_j]$, we can use these rules to generate an infinite, dense sublanguage of $L(G)$, whence $L(G)$ itself must be dense.

For the first case, we proceed by the following lemma, which does not exploit the lack of phantom symbols.

Lemma 6. If G is an MPS grammar for which there is a number l such that $[\phi] \leqslant l$ for every derived rule $A \rightarrow \phi$ of G, then $L(G)$ is a context-free language.

Proof. Let $G = \langle V_T, V_N, S, \rightarrow, V_V, \Rightarrow \rangle$ satisfy the hypotheses of the lemma, and let $N = \{A \in V_N \mid \forall\, y \in V_T^* \ (y = \epsilon$ if $A \overset{*}{\underset{G}{\vdash}} y)\}$. To obtain a finite set of context-free rules generating $L(G)$, we simply delete from the right-hand side of every basic and derived rule of G each occurrence of all nonterminals belonging to N. Let $\to'$ be the set of rules obtained in this way, and set $G' = \langle V_T, V_N, S, \to' \rangle$. We show that $L(G') = L(G)$ and that G' is a context-free grammar, viz., $\to'$ is finite.

To see that $L(G') \supseteq L(G)$, note that to each derivation from S to a terminal string x in G there corresponds a derivation from S to x in G', which differs only in that nonterminals A belonging to N are never introduced and, therefore, the steps in which they are rewritten, ultimately to ϵ, are omitted. For the other direction of inclusion, when given a derivation from S to a terminal string x in G', we can construct a derivation from S to x in G by stepwise (a) applying the same rule at the same place as applied in the given derivation, if that rule belongs to G as well as to G', or (b), if such is not the case, applying a rule of G that reduces to the rule of G' upon deletion of all occurrences of all $A \in N$, and then following this by steps that rewrite to ϵ each of the nonterminals $A \in N$, just introduced. Thus $L(G') = L(G)$.

To see that $\to'$ is a finite set, we observe that there is an upper bound on the length of the right-hand side of any rule in $\to'$. Finiteness follows because each rule is a string of bounded length in the finite vocabulary $V_T \cup (V_N - N)$—aired with a string of length 1 in the finite vocabulary V_N. The desired upper bound is simply the smallest l such that $|\phi| \leqslant l$ for every derived rule $A \to \phi$ of G; this number must exist by the hypotheses of the lemma. ∎

Returning to the proof of Theorem 5, recall that we were considering the case of any MPS grammar G that satisfies the hypotheses both of the theorem and of Lemma 6. In this case the conclusion of the theorem follows by virtue of the standard 'pumping lemma' for context-free languages. As $L(G)$ is a context-free language, there is a number p such that to every $z \in L(G)$ with $|z| > p$ there correspond u, v, w, x and y such that $|v| + |x| > 0$ and moreover, for all $j \geqslant 0$, $uv^j w x^j y$ belongs to $L(G)$. (We could have concluded the theorem with this stronger 'intercalation' statement as far as the present case is concerned, but in our second case our argument yields only the weaker conclusion we are about to deduce.) Since by hypothesis, $L(G)$ is infinite, we can certainly find a $z_1 \in L(G)$ such that $|z_1| > p$. Put $c = |z_1|$ and, letting u_1, v_1, w_1, x_1 and y_1 be the strings associated with z_1, put $z_j = u_1 v_1^j w_1 x_1^j y_1$ for each $j \geqslant 0$. Since $|z_j| = j(|v_1| + |x_1|) + (|u_1| + |w_1| + |y_1|)$ and both $|v_1| \neq |x_1|$ and $|u_1| + |w_1| + |y_1|$ are at most c, the different strings z_j occur with ample density to assure that at least one will have length lying between cn and $c(n + 1)$ for any natural number n that may be given. Thus, $L(G)$ is dense and the theorem is proved in the first case.

Turning now to the second case, we assume our given MPS grammar satisfies the hypotheses of the theorem and furthermore that for any number l there is a derivation $A_1 \to \phi_1 \Rightarrow A_2 \to \phi_2 \Rightarrow \cdots A_j \to \phi_j$ from a basic rule by metarules of G such that $[\phi_j] > l$.

We choose, for each $A \in V_N$, terminal strings x_A, y_A, and z_A so that $S \overset{*}{\underset{G}{\vdash}} x_A A z_A$ and $A \overset{*}{\underset{G}{\vdash}} y_A$, where $y_A \neq \epsilon$ if possible. The absence of phantom symbols in G guarantees that we can find such terminal strings. We also adopt the notation $\overline{\phi}$ for the terminal string which results from replacing all occurrences of every $A \in V_N$ in ϕ by y_A, where ϕ is any string in $(V_T \cup V_N)^*$.

To construct an infinite sequence $w_0, w_1, w_2, \ldots$ of strings in $L(G)$ and a constant c so that $cn \leqslant |w_n| < c(n + 1)$ for every $n \geqslant 0$, we proceed as follows. Choose w_0 to be y_S. We will take c to be $|y_S|$ + some positive number, assuring $|w_0| < c$. Now suppose $w_0, w_1, \ldots, w_m$ to be given, satisfying $cn \leqslant |w_n| < c(n + 1)$ for every $n = 0, \ldots, m$ and for the constant c that we will construct. To obtain w_{m+1} meeting the condition $c(m + 1) \leqslant |w_{m+1}| < c(m + 2)$, note that there is a derivation $A_1 \to \phi_1 \Rightarrow A_2 \to \phi_2 \Rightarrow \cdots A_j \to \phi_j$ from a basic rule by metarules of G such that $[\phi_j] \geqslant c(m + 1)$. We choose w_{m+1} from among the members $u_1, u_2, \ldots, u_j$ of $L(G)$, where $u_i = x_{A_i} \overline{\phi}_i z_{A_i}$, to be the one with the smallest subscript i' such that $|u_{i'}| \geqslant c(m + 1)$. This is possible since $|u_j| = |x_{A_j}| + |\overline{\phi}_j| + |z_{A_j}| \geqslant [\phi_j] \geqslant c(m + 1)$; each u_i is in $L(G)$ because $S \overset{*}{\underset{G}{\vdash}} x_{A_i} A_i z_{A_i}, A_i \to \phi_i$ is a rule of G and $\phi_i \overset{*}{\underset{G}{\vdash}} \overline{\phi}_i$. To show that $|w_{m+1}| < c(m + 2)$, as required, we observe that $|u_{i'-1}| < c(m + 1)$ by the choice of i' and will prove that $|u_{i'}| \leqslant |u_{i'-1}| + c$ for our constant c. (We guarantee that $i' > 1$ by choosing c greater than $[\phi]$ for any of G's finitely many basic rules $A \to \phi$.)

Note now that, because of the way $\overline{\phi}_{i'}$ and $\overline{\phi}_{i'-1}$ are constructed, $|u_{i'}| - |u_{i'-1}| = |x_{A_{i'}}| + |z_{A_{i'}}| - (|x_{A_{i'-1}}| + |z_{A_{i'-1}}|) + \Sigma_{\alpha \in V_T \cup V_N} y_\alpha | ([\phi_{i'}]_\alpha - [\phi_{i'-1}]_\alpha)$, if we take $y_\alpha = \alpha$ when $\alpha \in V_T$. Putting $k_0 = \max_{A \in V_N}(|x_A| + |z_A|)$, we see that $|x_{A_{i'}}| + |z_{A_{i'}}| - (|x_{A_{i'-1}}| + |z_{A_{i'-1}}|) \leqslant k_0$. Now let $k_1 = \max_{\alpha \in V_T \cup V_N}|y_\alpha|$ and $k_2 = $ the maximum size of any of G's finitely many metarules. We will show that $[\phi_{i'}]_\alpha - [\phi_{i'-1}]_\alpha) \leqslant k_2$ for every $\alpha \in V_T \cup V_N$, whence it follows that $|y_\alpha|([\phi_{i'}]_\alpha - [\phi_{i'-1}]_\alpha) \leqslant k_1 k_2$. Putting $k_3 = |V_T \cup V_N|$ then gives $\Sigma_{\alpha \in V_T \cup V_N}|y_\alpha|([\phi_{i'}]_\alpha - [\phi_{i'-1}]_\alpha) \leqslant k_1 k_2 k_3$, guaranteeing that $|u_{i'}| - |u_{i'-1}| \leqslant k_0 + k_1 k_2 k_3$. Our desired constant c can thus be chosen as $1 + \max(|y_S|, k_4, k_0 + k_1 k_2 k_3)$, where k_4 is the maximum of $[\phi]$ for any basic rule $A \to \phi$. To see that $[\phi_{i'}]_\alpha - [\phi_{i'-1}]_\alpha \leqslant k_2$ for each $\alpha \in V_T \cup V_N$, observe that the rule $A_{i'} \to \phi_{i'}$ is directly derived from $A_{i'-1} \to \phi_{i'-1}$ by application of a metarule of G. So there are a number p, a permutation $q_1, \ldots, q_p$ of the numbers $1, \ldots, p$, variables $\xi_1, \ldots, \xi_p \in V_V$ and strings $\sigma_1, \ldots, \sigma_{p+1}$, $\tau_1, \ldots, \tau_{p+1}, \omega_1, \ldots, \omega_p \in (V_T \cup V_N)^*$ such that G has the metarule $A_{i'-1} \to \sigma_1 \xi_1 \cdots \sigma_p \xi_p \sigma_{p+1} \Rightarrow A_{i'} \to \tau_1 \xi_{q_1} \cdots \tau_p \xi_{q_p} \tau_{p+1}$, and moreover $\phi_{i'-1} = \sigma_1 \omega_1 \cdots \sigma_p \omega_p \sigma_{p+1}$ and $\phi_{i'} = \tau_1 \omega_{q_1} \cdots \tau_p \omega_{q_p} \tau_{p+1}$. Thus for each symbol α, $[\phi_{i'}]_\alpha - [\phi_{i'-1}]_\alpha = t_1 + t_2$ where $t_1 = ([\tau_1]_\alpha + \cdots + [\tau_{p+1}]_\alpha) - ([\sigma_1]_\alpha + \cdots + [\sigma_{p+1}]_\alpha)$ and $t_2 = ([\omega_{q_1}]_\alpha + \cdots + [\omega_{q_p}]_\alpha) - ([\omega_1]_\alpha + \cdots + [\omega_p]_\alpha)$. But $t_2 = 0$ since $\omega_{q_1}, \ldots, \omega_{q_p}$ is a permutation of $\omega_1, \ldots, \omega_p$. And $t_1 \leqslant k_2$; indeed we might as well choose the maximum value of t_1 for any of G's metarules as k_2. So $[\phi_{i'}]_\alpha - [\phi_{i'-1}]_\alpha \leqslant k_2$ for each α, as was to be shown.

Clearly our constant c depends only on G and the fixed string y_S, not otherwise on a string w_n chosen at any stage. Thus repeating the procedure indefinitely yields the sequence $w_0, w_1, w_2, \ldots$ desired. ∎

The density theorem states one property exhibited by all languages generated by MPS grammars without phantom symbols. We conjecture that this density property is not a sufficient condition for an r.e. language to be generated by an MPS grammar without phantom symbols. Another open question is whether the commutative image [Parikh 1966] of any language generated by an MPS grammar without phantom symbols is a semi-linear set.

4. Discussion and Conclusion

The diagram below shows how MPS languages without phantom symbols fit into the schema known in formal language theory as the Chomsky hierarchy.

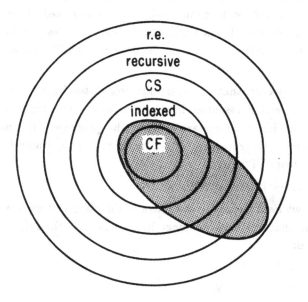

Our results strongly suggest that a grammatical framework for the description of natural language should not use metarules in the way they are defined here for MPS grammars. With or without phantom categories, MPS grammars are able to generate nonrecursive languages. And no linguist who takes into appropriate account the admittedly little knowledge we have about parsability and learnability constraints would want a theory of that power.

Of course, rather than abandon metarules, one can look for alternative ways of defining them. Two alternatives to the way we have defined metarules for MPS grammars have been proposed within GPSG. The first one, suggested by Gazdar (1982), redefines the form of metarules. Although Gazdar considered metarules with just one essential variable 'safe' with respect to the class of languages generated, he wanted nevertheless to rule out infinite rule sets. His remedy was to sacrifice essential variables. All his variables, string variables included, are supposed to be abbreviatory (although he does not specify the sets they range over).

Note, however, that the generalization stated by a metarule is weakened by converting essential into abbreviatory variables. Consider, for instance, the following metarule, which he proposed for providing VSO languages with the category VP. The metarule generates flat VSO sentence rules from VP rules:

(4) $VP \rightarrow V\ U \Rightarrow S \rightarrow V\ NP\ U$

Now we need to specify the range of the abbreviatory variable U. Let us imagine that the VSO language in question has the following small set of VP rules:

(5) $VP \rightarrow V$

$VP \rightarrow V\ NP$

$VP \rightarrow V\ \overline{S}$

$VP \rightarrow V\ \overline{VP}$

$VP \rightarrow V\ NP\ \overline{VP}$

The range of U has to be $\{\epsilon, NP, \overline{S}, \overline{VP}, NP\,\overline{VP}\}$. Since the VP rules under (5) are the only rules that satisfy the left-hand side of (4), therefore (4) generates exactly the same rules as a corresponding rule would in which U had been replaced with an essential variable. But now let us imagine that our language acquired a new subcategorization frame for verbs, e.g. has added a verb that takes an NP and an $\overline{S}$ as complements. We have to add this VP rule:

(6) $\quad VP \rightarrow V\ NP\ \overline{S}$

Our metarule (4) would predict that VPs headed by this verb do not have a corresponding flat SVO sentence rule. However, this situation is very unlikely to occur. The range of the abbreviatory variable U would have to be changed to extend the range of the metarule. It does not have to be a change in the basic rules that necessitates a change in the range of a variable; it could also be a change in a metarule that, either directly or indirectly, feeds the metarule containing the variable in question. The difference in meaning between a metarule with abbreviatory variables and the corresponding metarule with essential variables can be viewed as an extension—intension contrast. Metarule (4) in our example is supposed to express the fact (among others) that all VPs can occur in SVO sentences as discontinuous constituents. If U is an abbreviatory variable, the phrase 'all VPs' refers only to a specific list of VPs known to the grammar writer at the time the grammar is written. If U is an essential variable, the metarule encodes a stronger statement—i.e., that actually all VPs in the language, independently of our knowledge or the present coverage of the grammar, participate in the syntactic phenomenon.

A second strategy for constraining metarules is to leave their form as we have defined them but modify their role within the grammar. Thompson (1982), following a suggestion by Martin Kay, devised an alternative to simply closing the PS rules of the grammar under the metarules. Under his proposal the rules of the grammar are in the 'Finite Closure' of the metarules.

According to the definition of Finite Closure, a metarule $M = A \Rightarrow B$ generates a rule of the kind B from any rule that matches the template A and either is itself a base rule or is derived from a base rule without any application of M in its derivational history. Obviously, no infinite rule sets can be generated. The Finite Closure solution has now been generally adopted for GPSG.

Although the Finite Closure concept makes metarules 'safe', it is not a linguistically grounded solution. Many other stipulations would keep the rule set finite. As an example, let us consider a fictitious proposal to put a small upper bound on the length of the strings that essential variables can range over. This stipulation would be as ad hoc as the Finite Closure solution, but would not require a redefinition of metarule functioning; moreover, it would simplify the computation of the PS rules from the set of basic rules. Nevertheless, rescue measures such as the adoption of Finite Closure might constitute an appropriate research strategy as an intermediate step.

However, what is really needed is a linguistically motivated, well-defined concept of metarules. So far it is not even clear which classes of phenomena should be handled by metarules. Within GPSG, opinions regarding this question have been in flux. Two examples might illustrate this fluctuation. Word order phenomena, which at one point were handled by metarules, (Stucky, 1981) are now done with the ID/LP format, a mechanism that separates immediate dominance and linear precedence from each other in the grammar (Gazdar and Pullum, 1981). At first, long-distance dependencies were treated with the so-called slash categories and a special schema for deriving rules that contain them (Gazdar, 1981). Later metarules were used to derive the rules that eliminate and percolate gaps (Sag, 1981). In the newest version of the theory, metarules are less involved in gap handling; 'feature instantiation principles' have taken over most the task of gap percolation (Gazdar and Pullum, 1982).

A lack of consensus about the class of phenomena to be handled by metarules is not the only hurdle on the way to a sensible redefinition of metarules. If one considers the interaction between metarules and all the recently introduced mechanisms in GPSG, the task of redefining metarules becomes even more complicated. We have shown that the interaction of metarules and phantom symbols has an influence on the generative power of the framework. Uszkoreit (1982) has noted a similar interaction between metarules and the ID/LP format.   Assessing the influence of metarules on the generative power of an MPS grammar framework that also employs other formalisms can lead to unexpected results.

Any attempt at constraining or redefining metarules within a given grammatical framework has to be based on a thorough survey of the full variety of metarules that have been proposed, on a decision about the class of phenomena that should be captured by them, and on a detailed study of the interaction between metarules and other formalisms of the theory.[5]

Footnotes

[*]This research was supported by the National Science Foundation Grant IST-8103550. A preliminary report on some of the results contained in this paper was presented at the 1982 LSA meeting in San Diego (Peters and Uszkoreit, 1982). We are grateful to William Marsh, Jane Robinson and Stuart Shieber for comments on an earlier draft of the paper. Due to the extended period of time during which the paper was in preparation, several relevant recent publications are not referred to. Among those is Gazdar et al. (1985) where an extensive account of a new version of GPSG is presented.

[1]For an investigation of the use of metarules in the framework of Annotated Phrase Structure Grammar, see Konolige (1981).

[2]If the rules that serve as the input for metarules contain complex symbols, and if the symbols of the metarule template are allowed to underspecify these complex symbols by leaving out syntactic features, there might then be several rules that match a simple template.

[3]A similar rule, equipped with the appropriate semantic translation schema, was proposed by Gazdar and Sag (1980).

[4]This is identical with the constant-growth property, which is discussed in connection with Tree Adjoining Grammars in Joshi (1983).

[5]Since we finished the research for this paper, Shieber et al. (1983) have discussed a number of possible constraints on metarules (including several that have been actually proposed) and have arrived at largely negative conclusions as to their usefulness.

References

Culy, C. 'On the Generative Power of Metarules', unpublished manuscript, Stanford University, 1982.

Gazdar, G. 'Phrase Structure Grammar', in P. Jacobson and G.K. Pullum (eds.), *The Nature of Syntactic Representation*, Reidel, Dordrecht, 1982.

Gazdar, G. 'Unbounded Dependencies and Coordinate Structure', *Linguistic Inquiry* 12, 155-184, 1981.

Gazdar, G. and G.K. Pullum. 'Subcategorization, Constituent Order and the Notion "Head"', in M. Moortgat, H. v.d.Hulst and T. Hoekstra, eds., *The Scope of Lexical Rules*, 107-123, Foris, Dordrecht, 1981.

Gazdar, G. and G.K. Pullum. 'Generalized Phrase Structure Grammar: A Theoretical Synopsis', Indiana University Linguistics Club, Bloomington, Indiana, 1982.

Gazdar, G., G.K. Pullum, and I.A. Sag. 'Auxiliaries and related phenomena in a restrictive theory of grammar', *Language* 58, 591-638, 1981.

Gazdar, G. and I.A. Sag. 'Passives and Reflexives in Phrase Structure Grammar', in J. Groenendijk, T. Janssen, and M. Stokhof (eds.) *Formal Methods in the Study of Language, Proceedings of the Third Amsterdam Colloquium*, Mathematical Centre Tracts 135, Amsterdam, 1980.

Gazdar, G., E. Klein, G. Pullum, and I. Sag, *Generalized Phrase Structure Grammar*, Harvard University Press, Cambridge, Mass, 1985.

Hopcroft, J. and J. Ullman, *Introduction to Automata Theory, Languages, and Computation*, Addison-Wesley, Reading, Mass, 1979.

Joshi, A.K. 'How Much Context-Sensitivity Is Required to Provide Reasonable Structural Descriptions: Tree Adjoining Grammars', to appear in D. Dowty, L. Karttunen, and A. Zwicky, *Natural Language Processing: Psycholinguistic, Computational, and Theoretical Perspectives*, Cambridge University Press, Cambridge, 1983.

Konolige, K. 'Capturing Linguistic Generalizations with Metarules in an Annotated Phrase-Structure Grammar', in *Proceedings of the 18th Annual Meeting of the Association for Computational Linguistics*, Philadelphia, Pennsylvania, 1980.

Parikh, R., 'On Context-Free Languages,' *Journal of the Association for Computing Machinery*, **13**, 570-581, 1966.

Peters, S. and H. Uszkoreit. 'Essential Variables in Metarules', paper presented at the 1982 Annual Meeting of the Linguistic Society of America , San Diego, California, 1982.

Sag, I., 'Coordination, Extraction, and Generalized Phrase Structure Grammar,' *Linguistics Inquiry*, **13**, 329-336, 1982.

Shieber, S.M., S.U. Stucky, H. Uszkoreit, J.J. Robinson. 'Formal Constraints on Metarules', in *Proceedings of the 21st Annual Meeting of the Association for Computational Linguistics*, Cambridge, Mass, 1983.

Stucky, S. 'Word Order Variation in Makua', unpublished Ph.D. dissertation, University of Illinois, Urbana-Champaign, 1981.

Thompson, H. 'Handling Metarules in a Parser for GPSG', *Edinburgh DAI Research Paper No. 175*, J. Horecky, ed., *Proceedings of the Ninth International Conference on Computational Linguistics*, North Holland, Dordrecht, 1982.

Uszkoreit, H. 'German Word Order in GPSG', in D. Flickinger, M. Macken, and N. Wiegand (eds.), *Proceedings of the First West Coast Conference on Formal Linguistics*, Stanford University, Stanford, California, 1982.

Appendix: Definition of MPS Grammars

Definition 7. MPS grammars:

An MPS grammar is a sextuple $\langle\, V_T, V_N, S, \rightarrow, V_V, \Rightarrow \,\rangle$ such that V_T and V_N are finite, disjoint sets of terminal and nonterminal symbols respectively, $S \in V_N$, V_V is a finite set of essential variables disjoint from $V_T \cup V_V$, $\rightarrow$ is a finite subset of $V_N \times (V_T \cup V_N)^*$, and $\Rightarrow$ is a finite subset of

$$(V_N \times (V_T \cup V_N \cup V_V)^*) \times (V_N \times (V_T \cup V_N \cup V_V)^*) \text{ such that, if}$$

$\langle\langle A, \phi\rangle, \langle B, \psi\rangle\rangle \in \Rightarrow$, then each member of V_V occurs an equal number of times in ϕ and ψ and has at most one occurrence in each.

Let $G = \langle V_T, V_N, S, \rightarrow, V_V, \Rightarrow\rangle$ be an MPS grammar.

Definition 8. directly yields:

A pair $\langle A, \phi\rangle$ directly yields a pair $\langle B, \psi\rangle$ by a metarule of G (in symbols $\langle A, \phi\rangle \Rightarrow \langle B, \psi\rangle$) if, for some pair $\langle\langle A, \chi\rangle, \langle B, \omega\rangle\rangle \in \Rightarrow$, there are a positive integer n and strings $\alpha_1, ..., \alpha_n, \beta_1, ..., \beta_{n-1}, \gamma_1, ..., \gamma_n, \delta_1, ... \delta_{n-1} \in (V_T \cup V_n)^*$ and symbols $\varsigma_1, ..., \varsigma_{n-1}, \eta_1, ..., \eta_{n-1} \in V_V$ such that

(i) $\beta_i = \delta_j$ when $\varsigma_i = \eta_j$ $(1 \leqslant i, j < n)$

(ii) $\chi = \alpha_1 \varsigma_1 ... \alpha_{n-1} \varsigma_{n-1} \alpha_n$

(iii) $\phi = \alpha_1 \beta_1 ... \alpha_{n-1} \beta_{n-1} \alpha_n$

(iv) $\omega = \gamma_1 \eta_1 ... \gamma_{n-1} \eta_{n-1} \gamma_n$

(v) $\psi = \gamma_1 \delta_1 ... \gamma_{n-1} \delta_{n-1} \gamma_n.$

Definition 9. rule of G:

A pair $\langle A, \phi\rangle$ is a rule of G if there is a sequence $\langle B_1, \psi_1\rangle, \ldots, \langle B_n, \psi_n\rangle$ of pairs such that $\langle B_1, \psi_1\rangle \in \rightarrow$, $\langle B_n, \phi_n\rangle = \langle A, \phi\rangle$, and $\langle B_i, \psi_i\rangle$ directly yields $\langle B_{i+1}, \psi_{i+1}\rangle$ by a metarule of G for $1 \leqslant i < n$, i.e., $\langle A, \phi\rangle$ is a rule of G if there is a basic rule $\langle B, \psi\rangle$ of G such that $\langle B, \psi\rangle \stackrel{*}{\Rightarrow} \langle A, \phi\rangle$. We let $\underset{G}{\rightarrow}$ denote the set of all rules of G.

Definition 10. directly derives:

The relation $\underset{G}{\vdash}$ on $(V_T \cup V_N)^*$ holds of a pair $\langle \phi, \psi \rangle$ if and only if there are α, β, $\omega \in (V_T \cup V_N)^*$ and $A \in V_N$ such that $\phi = \alpha \, A \, \beta$, $\psi = \alpha \, \omega \, \beta$, and $\langle A, \omega \rangle \in \underset{G}{\to}$.

Definition 11. derives:

The relation $\underset{G}{\overset{*}{\vdash}}$ is the ancestral (reflexive, transitive closure) of $\underset{G}{\vdash}$.

Definition 12. language generated by G:

The language generated by G is $\{x \in V_T^* \mid S \underset{G}{\overset{*}{\vdash}} x\}$.

Definition 13. MPS/1 grammars:

An MPS/1 grammar is an MPS grammar $\langle V_T, V_N, S, \to, V_V, \Rightarrow \rangle$ with a singleton V_V.

Emmon Bach

SOME GENERALIZATIONS OF
CATEGORIAL GRAMMARS

0. Introduction

The last decade of work in syntax has seen a marked demotion in the importance of transformations in the classical sense. We see this not only in the various explicit proposals to do away with transformations altogether but also in recent developments in transformational theories themselves. With the reduction of the transformational component to the single rule "move alpha" almost all of the work of generating "all and only" the syntactic structures of a language must be borne by other devices and principles.

In this context, with a marked rise of interest in non-transformational models, it seems reasonable to re-consider theories which are based on categorial systems of the sort first proposed by Ajdukiewicz (1935), and indeed a number of writers have recently suggested various elaborations and extensions of categorial grammars.[1] In this paper, I wish to sketch one such set of elaborations that I have been pursuing and then consider a few challenging problems that arise in trying to describe the syntax and semantics of natural languages within an extended categorial framework.

1. Background

A fundamental property of categorial systems is that they encode at one and the same time an assignment of expressions to syntactic *and* semantic categories (Adjukiewicz called his categories "semantic categories"). Moreover, they adopt as basic the idea that linguistic expressions are organised into successively more elaborate/function-argument structures.[2] In these two ways they differ from phrase-structure systems, a fact which

F. Landman and F. Veltman (Eds), *Varieties of Formal Semantics: proceedings of the fourth Amsterdam Colloquium 1982*, 1-23, © 1984 Foris Publications, Dordrecht, Holland.

W. J. Savitch et al. (eds.), The Formal Complexity of Natural Language, 251–279.

should be borne in mind when making comparisons. Thus, although it is possible to mechanically map a categorial grammar (of the simplest form) into a corresponding phrase structure grammar, there is a loss of information:

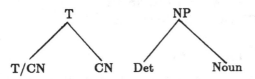

The significance of this fact is that it requires the grammarian to think about the semantics *and* the syntax of an expression when trying to motivate an analysis. Moreover, the basic function/argument relationships have a built-in asymmetry which becomes important in attempts to reconstruct notions like *head* or relationships like those given by configurational ideas like c-command for various purposes.

Let's now look, in a partly historical way, at some simple versions of categorial grammar. I will use as a framework or metalanguage to talk about various types of categorial systems and their extensions the general theory of Montague's Universal Grammar (UG: paper 6 in Montague, 1974). As linguists, we are faced with the task of delimiting the least set of categories and syntactic/morphological operations that is sufficient to describe and predict the limits of variation given to us by actual natural languages (Partee, 1979). Part of the important data that we must concern ourselves with is given by the rich typological literature represented by early works such as Finck, Schmidt, and more recently in the work of Joseph Greenberg (e.g. 1963), and much work inspired by him.

I. Ajdukiewicz's categories looked like this:

(i) primitive categories: s, n ϵ CAT (*sentence, noun*)

(ii) derived: for a, b in CAT, $(\frac{a}{b})$ ϵ CAT.

These categories were bidirectional. In UG terms, this means that all of the *rules* of the grammar must come in pairs, distinguished only by the two operations RCON and LCON:

$$RCON(x,y) = LCON(y,x) = \overset{\frown}{x\ y}$$

I have called languages generable by such grammars "mobile-languages" (Bach, 1975). Formally, they are a proper subset of the context-free languages.[3]

II. Bar-Hillel (1953) and Lambek (1961) introduced the possibility of restricting the directionality of the functor, that is, there can be rules with just RCON or LCON alone in a grammar. We adopt the notations a/b and b\a for this distinction, retaining ($\frac{a}{b}$) as above. We now obtain the full set of CF languages.

This notation already embodies a certain claim: the type of syntactic operation in a construction is determined by the functor expression and cannot be determined by the argument expression. This is interesting and may be wrong. (It is a rather weak claim; see Flynn, 1983 for an interesting study which starts from the position of wanting to strengthen the claim.) Note that the system allows the possibility that particular functor expressions corresponding to the same semantic type may have different order characteristics:

naar de stad	*de stad naar	PP/T
*vandaan Leiden	Leiden vandaan	T\PP
in de tuin	de tuin in (?)	$\frac{PP}{T}$

(The ? is intended to express my doubts that the two *in*'s are identical.) However, it doesn't allow a language like "Dutch" in which adpositions follow common nouns and precede neuter nouns. (A quite different issue arises with "long and heavy constraints" (Behaghel's Gesetz) and pronouns/clitics vs. full NP's, etc.)

Strictly speaking, then, we are departing from the setup of UG. Formally, we still start from a set Δ of syntactic categories and a family Γ of sets of n-place operations for $n = 1,2, ..., k$ for some k (here $k = 2$). We then redefine CAT as the least set such that

(i) $a_1, a_2, ..., a_m \in CAT$

(ii)   If a ϵ CAT and b ϵ CAT and γ (a two-placed operation) ϵ Γ, then the ordered triple <b, a,γ> ϵ CAT.

The general schema for function-argument (f/a) application rules is then this:

R1.   If $\beta \epsilon P_b$ and $\alpha \epsilon P_{<b, a, \gamma>}$, then $\gamma(\alpha,\beta) \epsilon P_a$.

The general claim about the relation between syntax and semantics in such systems is this: there is basically one semantic operation: function-argument application.[4] It's pretty obvious that this isn't enough: we need at least function composition as well (cf. Geach, 1972, for early suggestions, also Lambek, 1961, who has studied the general formal characteristics of such systems, also H. Levin, 1976). An easy example of this occurs in items like French *au* and German *zum*, what I've called "short-circuits" elsewhere, which are compositions of PP/T and T/CN to PP/CN. Most Montague-type grammars (in addition) make use of variable binding (by lambda's). Addition of function composition as a possibility adds significantly to the formal power of the systems. (For example, in unpublished work, Mark Steedman has shown how to give a grammar for the Dutch complement structures to be discussed below within a categorial grammar using function composition.)

III.   A recent paper by Ades and Steedman (1982) makes fundamental use of function composition in an interest way to deal with certain types of "long-distance" dependencies, (I'll draw on this work below and also on recent work in progress by Steedman). In an Ades-Steedman grammar (as in UG), categorial assignment is freed from any reference to order characteristics. A grammar is to be thought of as containing two components, one a list of basic vocabulary and a lexical function assigning lexical elements to (sets of) categories, the other a set of combination rules chosen from exactly the following four types:

1.   Forward combination(FC):

$\dfrac{a}{b}$ b $\Rightarrow$ a

2.   Backward combination(BC):

b $\dfrac{a}{b}$ $\Rightarrow$ a

Semantics

$\left(\dfrac{a}{b}\right)' (b')$

3.   Forward partial combination(FP):

$$\frac{a}{b} \ \frac{b}{c} \Rightarrow \frac{a}{c}$$

$$\left.\begin{array}{c} \\ \\ \\ \\ \\ \\ \end{array}\right\} \ (\frac{a}{b})' \circ (\frac{b}{c})'$$

4.   Backward partial combination(BP):

$$\frac{b}{c} \ \frac{a}{b} \Rightarrow \frac{a}{c}$$

(I hope this shorthand is clear: I'm oversimplifying; Ades and Steedman use variables over strings of categories and slashes and formulate a more general composition ("partial combination") rule.)

All of the systems I've mentioned so far embody an important claim: you can always say all that you need to say about the syntax and semantics of languages by considering elements that are right next to each other. Ades and Steedman call this the Adjacency Collary. A number of the problems I'll take up below constitute challenges to this hypothesis. Some have been successfully dealt with (by Ades and Steedman, for example); some remain. One quite remarkable fact has emerged from recent work, as well as from the parallel work in Generalized Phrase Structure Grammars (GPSG) (e.g. Gazdar, 1982, and the literature cited there): a lot of facts in natural languages that had been thought to motivate the addition of the relatively powerful notion of a structure-dependent transformation can in fact and contrary to claims in the literature be elegantly dealt with within the much more restricted frameworks of GPSG and related systems (see Gazdar, 1982, Pullum and Gazdar, 1983). It is an open question whether all facts can be dealt with, but I agree with Gazdar in his justification of the research strategy of taking such limited systems as a base and letting in just a little extra power as it becomes evident that it is needed (and we obviously haven't been thinking hard enough about really demonstrating that it is needed).

2. Extensions: Features

In three recent papers (Bach 1983 a, b, c), I have explored the consequences and possibilities of adding a restricted system of features to a basically categorial framework. For details, I refer the reader especially to the second paper. Here I will just give an informal sketch of my assumptions, which amount to little more than an attempt to incorporate and make precise a number of quite familiar ideas, both from the generative tradition and from the broader traditions of structuralist and traditional grammarians.

The basic idea is this: features are functions from expressions to sets of values. For each primitive syntactic category we have a family of mutually disjoint sets of values. For example, the category T (NP) in some language might have the sets that we call case, number, gender. We call such features *morphosyntactic features*. So for example the value of CASE for *him* is ACCUSATIVE. These latter values can themselves be interpreted as functions, or components of functions, the morphological *operations*. Features for functor expressions are built up as ordered pairs of the feature values defined for their argument category and those defined for their resultant category, possibly including some additional inherent features. If a functor expression, say a transitive verb or a preposition, requires a certain form for its argument we say that the functor *governs* that feature value. So, for example, German *zu* governs DATIVE, while almost all tensed verb phrases govern the nominative (in German) on their subjects. If a functor expression varies its form according to the nature of the argument we say that the functor *agrees* with its argument in that feature. Thus, in English tensed verb phrases agree with their subjects in number and person. Paradigms are a device for displaying the effects of morphological operations, the general form of which is to specify a function in which we first list all of the irregular cases (conventionally given in lexical entries) and end, where possible, with a general morphophonemic operation, definable solely on the phonological form of a word or other element (this represents the *regular* inflection or other operations associated with the morphological operation). For example, the operation PLURAL in English starts with functions like PLURAL*(man)=men* (I use orthography for convenience) and ends with the morphophonemic operation -IZ that gives us such forms as *stops, watches,* and *hens (s,* -\{z,z)$; -IZ is a suboperation that is also called in the definition of other morphological syntactic operations. (I follow Partee, 1979, in requiring that such morphosyntactic features entail *some* phonetic difference. Thus, for example, we might have NOM and ACC for English, but not OBLIQUE $\neq$ ACC).

There are two ways to interpret such features. One is suggested by work in Generalized Phrase Structure Grammar: they are essentially abbreviatory devices for capturing generalizations across lots of categories. As Gazdar and others have shown, this interpretation has a consequence that so long as there is only a finite number of feature values, the basic mathematical properties of the system are those of the "parent" system. If you start with a CF grammar, add a million features and a billion feature values you still have a context-free grammar. The same thing obviously goes through with a categorial system of some sort. The other way, and this is the way that I want to pursue in a little more detail here, is to think of the features as giving partial specifications of the interpretations of linguistic expression, in this case phonetic interpretations. The basic idea that I want to pursue in more depth in the syntactic/semantic end of our enterprise here is one that first became clear to me in working on phonology from a categorial perspective (cf. Bach and Wheeler, 1981; Wheeler, 1981): Language is not completely compositional: the interpretations of the pieces that you put together cannot be fully determined without taking context into account[5]. The moral that I believe we can draw from this is not to give up compositionality but to think of it not so much as a constitutive absolute principle, but rather as a heuristic or as part of an evaluation measure (here I believe I am in agreement with my colleague, Barbara Partee, cf. Partee, 1979, this volume). More particularly, it seems that we can adopt, with nice consequences, two principles of maxims:

1. Invariance: you cannot change interpretations, only make them more specific.

2. Locality: specify interpretations as locally as possible, consistent with invariance.

In phonology, these two principles lead, among other things, to the use of incompletely specified segments and entail many principles and analyses that have been proposed or stipulated as independent hypotheses in other theories (Kiparsky's elsewhere condition, strict-cyclicity, etc.).

Part of what we need to do in dealing with features is to spell out principles of "percolation" and "matching". The categorial framework provides a rather nice way to do this in a completely general way (see Bach, 1983 a,b,c).

3. Problems

Let's now turn our attention to some difficulties that appear to stand in our way if we adopt the relatively constrained system of categorial grammar just outlined. Consider first the problems offered by long-distance dependencies of the sort handled under the rubric "wh-movement". There are two general approaches to these problems. One proceeds by elaborating the syntax/semantics by addition of special categories or rules. For example, Ades and Steedman (1982) have shown how the ingenious use of function-compositions enables a categorial grammar to deal with a large number of such dependencies. The other approach is modeled on that of Gazdar: it is in effect to let functor categories act as if they already had the appropriate arguments (which they get in the semantics by acquiring variables of the right type for the functions) and then at the appropriate point to bind the variable to make a function out of the expression.

3.1 *Discontinuous constituents*

There is a tradition within Montague grammar which attributes the differences between verbs like *persuade* and *promise* to a difference in their argument structures (Thomason, 1976; Partee, 1973; Bach, 1979, and others): *persuade* is interpreted as denoting a function from properties to a function from terms to sets, *promise* as denoting a function from terms to a function (like *try*) from properties to sets. Now the fact is that in English syntax, the two come out, in most sentences, in identical environments:

1. I persuaded David to do the dishes

2. I promised Joel to do the dishes

(Although, as noted in Bach, 1979, there are some curious syntactic differences between the two in other respects.) I am going to assume that this is right, for now, and ask what we are to do about it. There are a number of ways of saving the theory and accommodating the facts (see Bach, 1981, for example). I want here to return to my original suggestion, which is to extend the power of the syntax beyond the meagre means of concatenation, by adopting a limited set of syntactic operations that go beyond simple concatenation (Yngve, 1961, should be given credit for first suggesting that simple CF grammars should be supplemented by this way of treating local discontinuities). I will discuss and refine somewhat the notion of an operation I called "right-wrap" and then defend the idea that this is a natural operation in human syntax and morphology. I want to suggest that various ways of getting around the use of such operations are simply artificial ways of dealing with a fundamental fact of human language. (Such operations were present in the earliest versions of transformational grammar.) One instance of the operation is illustrated in this simplified analysis tree:

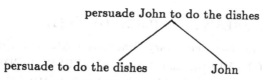

persuade John to do the dishes

persuade to do the dishes   John

The functions and operations I will define use a "LISP-y" system as a metalanguage. This language has quite different properties from the usual metalanguage of TG, and I think we ought to be catholic in thinking about alternative formalisms. Some things are easy in this formalism that are impossible or hard in TG language, and the reverse is also true.

First, let me say something about what I take to be the basic representational system of the language: it is to be a kind of bracketing of expressions, very much like a LIST structure.[6] I take these bracketings, not to be some artifice that must be gotten rid of to give us English, but rather as playing a definite role in determining phonetic interpretations. In particular, the bracketings will correspond in a way that I will not pursue further here, to the structures posited in hierarchical versions of phonology, such as those being developed by Selkirk, Prince, Kiparsky, Vergnaud, and many others, who are building on insights that go back to

Fischer-Joergensen, Pike, Fudge, Kuryłowicz, Firth, and many others. (I am following here the lead of Susan Schmerling, in her provocative paper: "The proper treatment of phonology in Montague's grammar" (1980).) (In the following I will omit innermost brackets, using spaces between words as an obvious notation.)

Assume that we have four one-place analytic operations on such structures: FIRST, LAST, RREST, LREST returning the first, last, right-remainder, and left-remainder of a structure, respectively.

That is, suppose we have $x = ((x_1) (x_2) \ldots (x_n))$, then

$$
\begin{aligned}
\text{FIRST}(x) &= (x_1) \\
\text{RREST}(x) &= (x_2) \cdots (x_n) \\
\text{LAST}(x) &= (x_n) \\
\text{LREST}(x) &= (x_1) \cdots (x_{n-1})
\end{aligned}
$$

Thus, for any structure x,

$$x = (\text{FIRST}(x) \ \text{RREST}(x)) = (\text{LREST}(x) \ \text{LAST}(x))$$

(LISPers: two of these are the elementary functions CAR and almost CDR, the other CAR of REVERSE and almost REVERSE of CDR of REVERSE). The "almost" is because lacking outerbrackets RREST and LREST don't deliver proper lists). Assuming now a standard function-argument order in stating rules we can define these operations:

$$
\begin{aligned}
\text{RWRAP}(x,y) &= \text{LINFIX}(y,x) = (\text{FIRST}(x) \ y \ \text{RREST}(x)) \\
\text{LWRAP}(x,y) &= \text{RINFIX}(y,x) = (\text{LREST}(x) \ y \ \text{LAST}(x)).
\end{aligned}
$$

So we have

RWRAP ((persuade to go), John) = (persuade John to go)

RWRAP ((see), Mary) = (see Mary)

In this last example, *Mary* is followed by the RREST of (*see*), namely, nothing.

Cases like these can be eliminated in a straightforward way by use of lambda's (Bach, 1981). That is, we can make up a translation for *persuade* that preserves the f/a difference in the semantics:

$\lambda \mathcal{P} \lambda P$ [persuade' (P) ($\mathcal{P}$)]. So in this case, it's clear that we have not added to the power of the system at all. But if this is so, then one conclusion might be that we ought to freely allow such operations as those just defined. Trying to keep everything strictly CF or pure-categorial has something of the dubious pleasure of dryfly fishing. You may eventually catch a trout but sometimes wet flies or worms work better. I now turn to a somewhat more complex case, Dutch complement structures, which has been the subject of considerable discussion in the last few years.[7]

Here is a simple example (from Zaenen, 1979):

1.   (Ik weet) dat Jan Piet met Marie in de tuin liet spelen

   '(I know) that Jan had Piet play with Marie in the garden'

(I'll just deal with the embedded structure for now.) We want to assign to this clause something like the syntactic/semantic structure indicated by the following analysis tree:

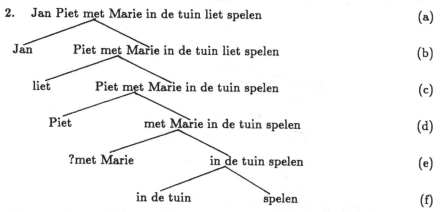

2.   Jan Piet met Marie in de tuin liet spelen   (a)

Jan   Piet met Marie in de tuin liet spelen   (b)

   liet   Piet met Marie in de tuin spelen   (c)

      Piet   met Marie in de tuin spelen   (d)

      ?met Marie   in de tuin spelen   (e)

            in de tuin   spelen   (f)

(The question mark at step (e) is meant to indicate that I'm not at all sure about whether the second phrase at (d) should be split up in this way.) Of particular interest here is the step from (c) to (b), where it looks at first as if we can get the desired effect by appealing to our right-infixing operation. There are two things to notice: in contrast to the *persuade* case, we are infixing the functor expression rather than the argument. The second thing to notice is that we somehow need to make the infixed verb form part of a unit with the last verb of the "embedded" sentence, since the construction can iterate indefinitely:[8]

3.   (Ik weet) dat Henk Jan Piet met Marie in de tuin zag laten spelen

'(I know) that Henk saw Jan have Piet play with Marie in the garden'

If we don't incorporate *laten spelen* into a unit of some kind, then we would generate the verbs in the order *...laten zag spelen*, which, I take it, is wrong.

Fortunately, there is independent evidence that we need to make the verbal groups at the ends of such sentences into constituents (see Evers, 1975; Bresnan et al., 1982); among other things in order to get the stress right. In transformational analyses which start from deep structures like (4) this is accomplished by having the operation of verb-raising Chomsky-adjoin the raised verb-form to the right of the higher verb, thus producing right-branching structures like that in (5):

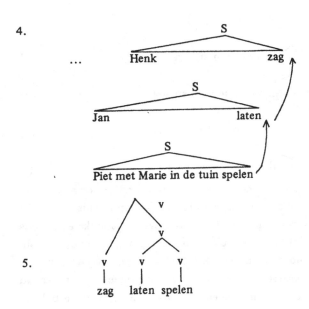

4.

5.

So the operation must be compounded with another, to give this result:

$f_1((\text{laten}),(\text{Piet met Marie in de tuin spelen})) =$
(Piet met Marie in de tuin (laten spelen))

(I omit irrelevant bracketings in most examples, the second argument of this operation should have at least this much structure: (Piet (met Marie) (in (de tuin)) spelen).) So it seems that, if we pursue this line, we need to allow our operations to do a little bit of analysis of structure but also a little bit of structure-building. Again, we can formulate these new operations straightforwardly in our formal system.

Are we using transformations? Well yes, in some very general and sloppy sense. But there's no way to formulate the operation LINFIX or RINFIX as a transformation in the technical sense, for two reasons: one, transformations cannot make use of predicates or functions like FIRST, which has built into it the non-Boolean idea of "first immediate constituent"; two, transformations cannot use structural descriptions that don't make mention of particular syntactic categories (some limited exceptions to this in X-bar theories). It's interesting to note that there are some classical problem cases - e.g. rightnode raising - or the definition of "second position" (see below) that seem to want to be able to make use of label-less structural conditions. Notice that the functions FIRST and LAST have built into them a sort of "X-over-Y" constraint. This is a particularly clear instance of the difference between our formal metalanguage and that of TG. Here it's hard to get down inside constituents, in TG formalism it's hard not to (various constraints must be invoked: A-over-A, subjacency, etc.). Notice one thing: as in LISP we can build any *finite* complex structure condition up out of FIRST, LAST etc. (that's bad, perhaps), but we cannot (unlike in LISP) build predicates like "FIRST*" (meaning FIRST (FIRST. . . (FIRST. . .)) with unbounded ". . ." i.e. "the deepest first constituent") (that's good, I think).

The kind of analysis of Dutch complement structures implicit in the above account (and I'm far from being in a position to deal with the whole range of complex facts that are omitted in that implied account) predicts that the order of elements in the complex clauses that we get will match that of the simpler sentences out of which they are built. This seems to be right, if we confine ourselves to full noun-phrases as in the example given sofar, omitting clitics.

Everything we need to know about the interpretation of complex sentences like (1) and (3) comes out "easily" from the analysis implied. Gazdar and Sag (1981) have shown how to recapitulate the analysis of English transitive verb-phrase sketched above in a GPSG involving metarules: that is rules that derive new rules from old rules. Their analysis involves introducing a "phantom category" TVP, which is then available for the formation of passive VP's and active VP's via a meta-rule which mimics my "right-wrap" operation. The rule looks like this.

$$[\quad V\ X] \rightarrow [\quad V\ NP\ X];$$
$$\text{TVP} \qquad\quad \text{VP}$$

and the semantic rule is simple function/argument application. The reason that this is so easy is also the same reason that it was easy to eliminate RWRAP from the grammar by giving a special translation to *persuade*: we are dealing with a very local and noniterable discontinuity. As far as I can see, no such simple solution is available for the Dutch case.

In a recently published paper, Gazdar and Pullum (1982) review the published arguments for the non-CF-hood of natural language. Among the cases considered are the Dutch complementation structures (pp. 485-490). After showing how, contrary to various claims in the literature, it *is* possible to give a CF characterization of the *strings* of terminal elements involved in such structure, they note: "the trees we have drawn are quite unsuitable for compositional semantic interpretation: semantic rules for assigning correct interpretations to Dutch sentences, constituent by constituent from the bottom up, cannot (as far as we can see) be provided on a rule-by-rule basis for the grammars given above." (p. 489) Footnote 13 (p. 501) contains some speculations about a possible solution which in effect generates the structures by a (lexical?) rule that derives complex verbs like *laten spelen, zien laten spelen,* etc. (In recent unpublished work, Mark Steedman has shown how the function composition rules of an Ades/Steedman grammar can be used to do just this, with a very nice prediction about the order of arguments.) I would now like to discuss a general problem that seems to arise in such approaches; we'll see more instances of it below.

Consider the interpretation of the complex verb *laten spelen*. It is perfectly straightforward to specify the meaning of this composite function as far as the argument structure of the second component is concerned. What we have in such instances is an instantiation of the scheme a/b b/c → a/c (for the time being let me use slashes in Ades and Steedman's way with no implications of directionality). Suppose *spelen* is in a category S/T and *laten* in the category (S/T)/S. Then *laten spelen* can be put into the derived category (S/T)/SoS/T(=(S/T)/T) and we can say what its meaning is. If *laten* takes a proposition p and creates a predicate that holds of x if and only if x brings about the truth of p and if *spelen* is a function which takes an argument y and yields the True just in case y plays, then *laten spelen* is that function from individuals y to properties P such that P holds of x just in case x brings it about that y plays. Now as we can see from the example of (1) this may not be good enough. What we want to be able to say about (1) is not just that Jan has Piet play but that he had him play with Marie *in the garden*, and we want at least to have available the interpretation in which the scope of *laten* is as indicated in the analysis tree (2), and maybe only that interpretation. (Note that we can easily make up examples with verbs like *willen* and creatures like *unicorns* to show that the scope can be quite crucial.)

Now, I know there are a number of technical tricks we could play at this point that would satisfy the requirements of dry-fly enthusiasts. One is the *store* mechanism. Another is to make up some fancy higher-order interpretations that would allow us to stuff the meanings of the modifiers down inside the meanings we've got, by adding appropriate variables (over *places in which, persons with whom, manners* and the like). I don't want to do either of these things now. I would rather face the problem squarely, we might call it the "optional modifier" problem, and note that we have a fairly straightforward trade-off between complications in the syntactic apparatus and complications in the compositional semantics. In my opinion, many of the tricks we can play are simply reflections of a basic fact about language: it just isn't quite left-to-right surface-compositional.

Note this: an analysis like mine *predicts* the correct scope facts.[9]

I promised that I would convince you that operations like my infixing operations are natural in natural language. Let me try to do that now by giving a few examples to illustrate my point.

3.2 In defense of the number 2nd (honore Wackernagel)

The second position figures over and over again in description of various syntactic (and morphological) structures: "Wackernagel's law" is the traditional name in Indo-European studies for the observation that certain characteristically unstressed or cliticized elements occurred/occur in the second position of clauses. Here are some modern examples:

1. John, *however*, tore his hair in rage

2. Ich, *aber*, bin ein Idiot

3. Henk *heeft* het niet gezien

Susan Steele has drawn attention to this special position in quite unrelated languages as typical for auxiliary-like elements: pronominal subject forms, mood markers, tense markers, and so on. The languages that show this phenomenon include such typologically and genetically diverse languages as Kwakiutl (British Columbia), Warlpiri (Australia). In this connection, we would think of the verb-second constraints on Modern Germanic languages like German, Dutch, Icelandic, and vestigially in English.

Cliticize onto the first X. Here X is sometimes to be read constituent, sometimes word (I suspect these positions are ultimately definable on the basis of a hierarchical organization in phonological terms which only indirectly reflect the syntactic organization of structures). Latin *que* is a familiar example. Let me show you a couple of less familiar ones.

Amharic definite markers. The (Semitic) language Amharic of Ethiopia marks definite noun-phrases with the suffixes -*u*/-*wa* (masc., fem.) (with an attached -*n* in the objective form). This element is suffixed to the first word of the CN phrase. Thus if there is a bare noun, the element is suffixed to it, but if there is an adjective the adjective gets the suffix:

bet '(a) house' betu 'the house' k'eyy bet '(a) red house'
k'eyyu bet 'the red house'

(with relative clauses, which normally precede their heads, the definiteness
is expressed as a suffix on the verb-form at the end of the clause.)

Xa'isla cats. In Xa'isla (the language of Kitamaat, B.C.) as in other
Kwakiutlan languages, there is an invariable second-position law with
respect to pronominal subjects. However, this law makes reference to
words, and even extends to subordinating conjunctions:

mayas	'cat'
mayas*in*	'I am a cat'
duqwel*in* mayas	'I see a cat'
mayas*in* duqwel	'It's a cat that I see'
kitatl*in* sakac	'I'm gonna shoot a grizzly' (non-specific)
sakac*in* kitatl	'It's a grizzly I'm gonna shoot'
q'al*in* qen*in* kitatl sakac	'I know that I'm gonna shoot a grizzly'

(Xa'isla is a VSO language).

These examples share with the Dutch examples a common property:
the infixed element is combined into a phonological unit with the first
(last) element of the structure in which it occurs. Wackernagel's law similarly is taken to reflect a phonological cliticization process.

Warlpiri wildness (from a handout by Ken Hale).

Kurdu-ngku *ka* maliki wajilipinyi
(child-ERG AUX dog chase)
the child is chasing the dog

maliki *ka* kurdu-ngku wajilipinyi
  etc. (any order, AUX second)

Kurdu-jarra-rlu *ka-pala* maliki wajilipinyi wita-jarra-rlu

(child-DUAL-ERG AUX   dog chase   small-DUAL-ERG)
the two small kids are chasing the dog

wita-jarra-rlu *kapala* maliki wajilipinyi kurdu-jarra-rlu
  etc.   (any order,AUX second)

3.3 *Variations in word order*

The last example naturally brings up the question of how we are to deal
with different possible orders. Familiar examples are German and Dutch,
with different order in root sentences and explicitly subordinated clauses:
German and Dutch are verb-second "upstairs" and verb-final "downstairs"
differing in the sorts of structures we looked at before in the final verb-
groups, which are (a few details aside) in a mirror-image relationship. A
theory of natural language syntax must accommodate this fact. Compare
the following versions of a sentence in English, Dutch, and German:

  Hank has seen Ann make the children feed the hippos
  Henk heeft Anneke de kinderen de nijlpaarden zien laten voeren
  Hans hat Aennchen die kinder die Nilpferde füttern lassen sehen

Subordination leaves the English string intact, in German and Dutch the
finite auxiliary appears at the beginning of the verb-group.

Facts like these have led transformational grammarians to posit one
or another of the two orders (or even another order) as basic and to derive
the other(s) transformationally (I may be the only linguist who has
defended all three hypotheses, thus ensuring that I will have been right all
along, no matter what!) I believe that within the framework of assumptions of transformational grammar the evidence is overwhelming that the
verb-final order originally argued for in Bach, 1962, and Bierwisch, 1963,
must be counted as basic.[10]

Within the present framework, however, there is no necessity to take
either as basic, they are simply two different kinds of syntactic objects.
Viewed abstractly (cf. G. Carlson, forthcoming) different orders of this sort
are "governed" in much the same way that different case forms of nominal

elements are governed. To put it another way, the order and organization of elements is every bit as much a part of the (phonological/phonetic) interpretation of the abstract entities that make up a language as are particular modulations of the airstream or conducting medium. We need to keep the two kinds of sentences or clauses separate, either by assigning them to separate categories or by giving them different values for some such feature as "matrix" or "independent" or whatever.

Differences in resultant categories in our framework are determined by different categorial (or featural) assignments to the functor categories. Assuming that tensed verb-phrases are functions on NP's, then we need to assign tensed verbs and auxiliaries to two (or three, cf. Bach, 1983 a) categories. Let's look at a simple example

4. Hij heeft de paarden al gevoerd

Here, we may analyse *heeft* as a functor taking verb-phrases to make a functor that takes NP's to make (matrix) S's. It governs the verbal inflection GE (and selects (perfect) VP's that take *hebben* rather than *zijn*) and makes a functor that governs the nominative on its subject. Thus, we might represent its category as:

$$(T\backslash S)/VP$$

$$\begin{bmatrix} NOM \\ 3RD \end{bmatrix} \quad \begin{bmatrix} GE \\ HEB \end{bmatrix}$$

(I will use S′ for subordinate clauses, S for matrix clauses.) In a sentence like (5) on the other hand we must give *heeft* another categorization

5. (dat) hij de paarden al gevoerd heeft
   (dat) hij de paarden al heeft gevoerd

In this case, *heeft* is of a category that takes (again) the same kind of VP only this time the resultant function takes a term-phrase to make an S′. As the two sentences indicate, *heeft* can be simply concatenated to its argument (the only possibility for the corresponding German auxiliary *hat*), or it can be infixed.

Now how can we account for other ordering possibilities, for example (6)?

6. De paarden heeft hij al gevoerd

One way is to have a derived category rule. $(T\backslash S)/VP \to (S/VP)/T$

If we look at the syntactic operations we have introduced so far, we can see that they allow us to specify the following linear relationships among arguments (A) and functors (F) (letting m and m′ stand for morphological functions):

I.   Immediately contiguous:
    (a) m(F) m′(A):   see him
    (b) m(A) m′(F):   he walks

II. Overlapping:
    (a) infixed to left:
        (i) m(L(A) m′(F) L′(A)): ich, aber, bin ein Idiot
        (ii) m(L(F) m′(A) L′(F)): persuade him to go (=rightwrap)
    (b) infixed to right:
        (i) m(R′(A) m′(F) R(A)):? . . .dat ik hem heb gezien
        (ii) m(R′(F) m′(A) R(F)):?
    (c) incorporating to left or right

This summary suggests that we might want to fill out this scheme by looking for expressions in natural language which exhibit the third logical possibility: that is, examples where functors and arguments are neither immediately contiguous nor 'overlapping'

III. Distant:
    (a) m(F). . .m′(A)
    (b) m(A). . .m′(F)

Let's allow for this possibility by adding to the list of possible 2-place operations the elements FR ('far-right' or //) and FL ('far left' or \\). We want to interpret these somehow as syntactic operations, although strictly speaking it doesn't seem as if they can be. One way of doing this involves a rather drastic extension of the categorial system, but one which seems rather natural.

In this new system, we generalize from categories that represent single coherent expressions to categories that represent sequences of expressions, and we split up the combination rules into two steps: (1) free combinations of expressions; (2) reduction of the sequence of categories associated with sequences of expressions according to the 'operational' character of the functors. Before giving a characterization of this system, let me give a simple example from Japanese. In Japanese, verbs must appear to the right of their arguments, period (more or less). So we have:

(1)   Nao-ga neko-o miru   Nao sees a cat
        PN-subj cat-obj sees

(2)   neko-o Nao-ga miru   Nao sees a cat

Suppose we want to say that *miru* is a functor that takes a term-phrase marked with *o* somewhere to its left to 'make' a functor that takes a term-phase marked with 'somewhere to its left' to make a sentence. So we assign *miru* the category $T\backslash\backslash(T\backslash\backslash S)$. For (1) this is straightforward since 'somewhere' includes 'right next to':

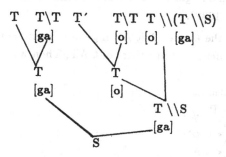

For (2) it is not so straightforward. However, if we allow the entire phrase to be indexed by a sequence of categories we can reduce the sequence by these steps:

$$<T, \quad T, \quad T\backslash\backslash \ (T\backslash\backslash S)>$$
$$[o] \quad [ga] \quad [o] \quad [ga]$$

$$<T, \quad T\backslash\backslash S>$$
$$[ga] \quad [ga]$$

$$<S>$$

Thus the entire phrase is an S-expression. We can derive this result if we separate the representation of the sentence as a sequence of categories from the representation of the sentence itself as a sequence of phrases. A Montague type analysis tree for one possible derivation of this sentence is this:

We could of course use one of our infixing operations to achieve this result also, but I'm interested here in the more general case presented by, for example, Warlpiri (for one way of getting the case government to come out right see Bach, 1983b, and for an interesting discussion of facts of Japanese 'free' word-order in categorial framework similar to the one under discussion here, see Miyara, 1982).

Here's how we can do the above: Let A range over members of CAT and ψ over possibly null sequences of members of CAT, Then we have:

R1. Free combination:
    If $\alpha \in P_A$, $\beta \in P_{<\psi>}$ then
      (i) $\alpha\beta \in P_{<A,\psi>}$
      (ii) $\beta\alpha \in P_{<\psi,A>}$

R2. Reduction schemata:

(i) $\quad$ < a/b,b >
$\quad\quad$ < b,b\a >
$\quad\quad$ < $\frac{a}{b}$,b >
$\quad\quad$ < b,$\frac{a}{b}$ >
$\left.\rule{0pt}{55pt}\right\}$ $\Rightarrow$ $\quad$ <a>

(ii) $\quad$ < a//b,ψ,b >
$\quad\quad$ < $\frac{a}{b}$,ψ,b >
$\left.\rule{0pt}{30pt}\right\}$ $\Rightarrow$ $\quad$ < a,ψ > for a $\neq$ b

(iii) < b,ψ,b\\a >
$\quad\quad$ < b,ψ,$\frac{b}{a}$ >
$\left.\rule{0pt}{30pt}\right\}$ $\Rightarrow$ $\quad$ < ψ,a >

(iv) $\quad$ < a//a,ψ,a > $\quad\quad$ $\Rightarrow$ $\quad$ < ψ,a >

(v) $\quad$ < a,ψ, a\\a > $\quad\quad$ $\Rightarrow$ $\quad$ < a,ψ >

(Our semantic rules must now be correspondingly modified to work on sequences of meanings.)

Note that we have extended the weak generative capacity of our systems, since we now have the possibility of describing the "scrambles" of various languages. Excercise: write a grammar for the scramble of the language (abc)*, i.e. the language consisting of all and only the strings consisting of equal numbers of *a*'s, *b*'s, and *c*'s. No natural languages are like this. So we want to impose restrictions on such systems. One natural restriction is to impose a minimum distance principle (cf. Wilkins, 1977; de Haan, 1981) by requiring that in the schemata (ii), (iii) and (iv) ψ contains no instance of *b*. If in addition we require that R2 apply everywhere as soon as possible we will rule out many possible languages, by keeping the free word order limited to very local domains.

Let's now look back at the Dutch complement structures to see if we can accommodate them in this new scheme. Suppose we make these assignments:

(dat) Hans Marie Piet de parden zag   laten   voeren

$\overline{S}/S'$ $<T,$ $T,$ $T,$ $T,$ $(T\backslash\backslash S')/S,(T\backslash\backslash S)/S,T\backslash\backslash(T\backslash\backslash S)>$

Then we have only one possible way of reducing the sequence.

Note that this analysis puts things together in exactly the right way. A single change in the categorial assignments will handle the corresponding German clause:

(dass) Hans Marie Peter die Pferde füttern   lassen   sah

      T   T   T   T $T\backslash(T\backslash S)$ $S\backslash(T\backslash S)$ $S\backslash(T\backslash S')$

You can check out this example and also note that there is no need for double slash operators for German. In both languages, of course, we are dealing with a highly restricted set of items that display many of the characteristics of lexical rules, idiosyncracies, requirement for *te* in Dutch, unpredictable semantics in part (blijven zitten = to stay behind in a class, kennen lernen = become acquainted with, etc.).[11]

Footnotes

[1] See Bach 1983a,b); Flynn (1983); Ades and Steedman (1982).

[2] It would be an interesting exercise to try to trace the history of the function/argument idea in linguistics. In recent times, Ed Keenan has probably done the most to emphasize the importance of the idea and to explore its consequences.

[3] The reason that they are a proper subset of the CFL is that sister constituents are necessarily pairwise permutable saving grammaticality. So for example the language $a^n b^n$ has no Ajdukiewicz grammar, as Stan Peters pointed out to me.

[4] In PTQ, functional application rules are interpreted semantically as applications of the interpretation of the functor to the *intension* of the interpretation of the argument.

[5] Theo Janssen (1983) objects to this way of talking. For extensive discussion of the question see Partee, this volume.

[6] I find it rather intriguing to think about phonology as just the relation R (the 'ambiguating relation') of Montague's UG.

[7] Evers (1975) was to my knowledge the first extensive study in the generative tradition to point out the importance of the 'Verb-raising' structures of Dutch and German for linguistic theory.

[8] Examples of this sort are quite unacceptable to many speakers of Dutch, posing the typical and difficult problem of trying to decide whether their deviance is to be attributed to the grammar or to difficulties in the production and processing system. I am currently engaged in some experimental work with colleagues at the Max Planck Institute for Psycholinguistics in Nijmegen aimed at trying to get a better idea of just what is going on in such structures (and the corresponding patterns in German). Note that if there is a strict bound in the grammar on the complexity of such verb-cluster sentences, then the argument of Bresnan et al. (see below) falls by the wayside.

[9] The optional modifier problem is noted in Hoeksema, 1981. Since writing this paper I have come to realize that the problem might be an artifact of a false theory of adverbial modification. McConnell-Ginet (1982) argues convincingly that the 'standard' Montague theory of adverbial

modification is insufficient to deal with such contrasts as *Mary rudely answered* vs. *Mary answered rudely*. She develops a theory of Ad-Verbs as playing the role of adding new argument positions to verbs. If this sort of analysis can be shown to be correct for cases like the ones discussed here, the problem disappears and we can stick with straightforward function composition.

[10]See Koster (1975), for a classic defense of the SOV-hood of Dutch. It is interesting to notice that recent theories, e.g. Evers (1982), in a sense incorporate all three theories as stages in a derivation (or allowable configurations in non-derivational frameworks): SOV → VSO → XVY, which modulo changes in frameworks etc. is the analysis of Bach (1962).

[11]The research reported on here was supported in part by the Max Planck Institute for Psycholinguistics, Nijmegen.

References

Ades, Anthony E. and Mark J. Steedman, 1982, On the order of words, *Linguistics and Philosophy* 4, 517-588.

Ajdukiewicz, Kazimierz, 1935, Die syntaktische Konnexität, *Studia Philosophica* 1, 1-27 (Appears in English translation in Storrs McCall, ed., *Polish Logic* (Oxford, University Press, 1967)).

Bach, Emmon, 1962, 'The order of elements in a transformational grammar of German', *Language* 38, 263-269.

Bach, Emmon, 1975, Order in base structure, In Charles N. Li, ed., *Word Order and Word Order Change* (Austin and London, U. Texas Press).

Bach, Emmon, 1979, Control in Montague Grammar, *Linguistic Inquiry*, 4, 515-531.

Bach, Emmon, 1981, Discontinuous constituents in generalized categorial grammar, NELS XI, 1-12.

Bach, Emmon, 1983a, Generalized categorial Grammars and the English Auxiliary, Papers presented at 4th Groningen Roundtable, 1980 *Auxiliaries and Related Puzzles* (Dordrecht, Reidel) II: 101-120, cf. I: 69-98. In F. Heny and B. Richards, eds., *Linguistic Categories*.

Bach, Emmon, 1983b, On the relationship between word-grammar and phrase-grammar, *Natural Language and Linguistic Theory* 1, 65-89.

Bach, Emmon, 1983c, Semi-compositionaliteit, GLOT G: 113-130.

Bach, Emmon and Deirdre Wheeler, 1981, Montague phonology: a first approximation, *University of Massachusetts Working Papers 7.*

Bar-Hillel, Yehoshua, 1953, A quasi-arithmetical notation of syntactic description, *Language* 29, 47-58.

Bierwisch, Manfred, 1963, 'Grammatik des deutschen Verbs', Berlin, (*Studia grammatica* II).

Bresnan, Joan, Ronald M. Kaplan, Stanley Peters and Annie Zaenen, 1982, Cross-serial dependencies in Dutch, *Linguistic Inquiry* 13, 613-636.

Carlson, Greg, Forthcoming, Marking constituents. Frank Henry and Barry Richards, eds., *Linguistic Categories*.

Evers, A., 1975, *The transformational cycle in Dutch and German,* Proefschrift: University of Utrecht.

Evers, Arnold, 1982, Twee functionele principes voor de regel "verschuif het werkwoord". GLOT 5, 11-30.

Flynn, Michael, 1983, A categorial theory of structure building, In Gerald Gazdar, Ewan Klein and Geoffrey K. Pullum, eds., *Order, Concord, and Constituency,* Dordrecht, Foris, 139-174.

Gazdar, Gerald, 1982, Phrase structure grammar, In P. Jacobson and G. K. Pullum, eds., *The Nature of Syntactic Representation* (Dordrecht, Reidel), 35-37.

Gazdar, Gerald and Ivan A. Sag, 1980, Passive and reflexive in phrase structure grammar, In J.A.G. Groenendijk, T.M.V. Janssen and M.J.B. Stokhof, eds., *Formal Methods in the Study of Language* (Amsterdam, Mathematisch Centrum), 131-152.

Geach, Peter, 1972, A program for syntax, In D. Davidson and G. Harman, *Semantics of Natural Language* (Dordrecht, Reidel), pp. 483-497.

Greenberg, Joseph H., 1963, '*Some universals of grammar with particular reference to the order to meaningful elements.*' Cambridge, Mass.

Haan, Germen Jan de, 1979, *Conditions on Rules,* Dordrecht, Foris.

Hoeksema, Jack, 1981, Verbale verstrengeling ontstrengeld, *Spektator* 10, 221-249.

Janssen, Theo M. V., 1983, *Foundations and Applications of Montague Grammar,* Amsterdam, Mathematisch Centrum.

Koster, Jan, 1975, Dutch as an SOV-language, *Linguistic Analysis* 1, 111-136.

Lambek, Joachim, 1961, On the calculus of syntactic types. In R. Jakobson, ed., *Structure of Language and its Mathematical Aspects* (= Proc. of Symposia in Applied Mathematics, XII, Providence, R.I.).

Levin, Harold D., 1976, *First Order Logic as a Formal Language: an Investigation of Categorial Grammar,* M.I.T., diss.

McConell-Ginet, Sally, 1982, Adverbs and logical form: a linguistically realistic theory, *Language* 58, 144-184.

Miyara, Shinsho, 1982, Reordering in Japanese, *Linguistic Analysis* 9, 307-340.

Montague, Richard, 1974, *Formal Philosophy*, Ed. by Richmond Thomason, New Haven.

Partee, Barbara H., 1976, (1973), Some transformational extensions of Montague grammar, In B.H. Partee, ed., *Montague grammar* (New York, Academic Press), First appeared in *Journal of Philosophical Logic*, 2, 509-534.

Partee, Barbara H., 1979, Constraining transformational Montague grammar: a framework and a fragment, In Steven Davis and Marianne Mithun, eds., *Linguistics, Philosophy, and Montague Grammar* (Austin, University of Texas Press), pp. 51-101.

Pullum, Geoffrey K. and Gerald Gazdar, 1982, Natural languages and context-free languages, *Linguistics and Philosophy*, 4, 471-504.

Schmerling, Susan, 1980, On the proper treatment of phonology in Montague grammar. Paper presented to the annual meting of the LSA.

Thomason, Richmond H., 1976, Some extensions of Montague grammar, In B.H. Partee, ed., *Montague grammar* (New York, Academic Press).

Wheeler, Deirdre, 1981, *Aspects of a Categorial Theory of Phonology*, Unpublished doctoral dissertation, University of Massachusetts, Amherst.

Wilkins, Wendy K., 1977, *The variable interpretation convention: a condition on variables in syntactic transformations*. Unpublished doctoral dissertation, University of California, Los Angeles.

Yngve, V.H., 1960, A model and a hypothesis for language structure, *Proceedings of the American Philosophical Society* 104, 444-466.

Zaenen, Annie, 1979, Infinitival complements in Dutch, CLS 15, 378-389.

Part III.

More than Context-Free and Less than Transformational Grammar

III. MORE THAN CONTEXT-FREE AND LESS THAN TRANSFORMATIONAL GRAMMAR

Introduction

The first four papers in this section present recent arguments against the context-freeness of natural language. The paper by Bresnan, Kaplan, Peters and Zaenen argues that a certain cross serial dependency construct in Dutch cannot be described by a context-free parse trees, and so, Dutch sentence structure is not representable by a context-free grammar. The usual way of phrasing this is to say that Dutch is not *strongly context-free.* The particular Dutch construction can be generated by a context-free grammar that produces the correct sentences as strings of symbols. The problem is that the parse trees produced by such a grammar violate the intuition of speakers about the phrase structure of these Dutch sentences. In other words Dutch appears to be weakly context-free but not strongly context-free. The paper by Sheiber describes a similar situation for Swiss-German, but in the case of Swiss-German the agreement constraints are more severe and so Sheiber is able to show that Swiss-German is not even weakly context-free. The paper by Higginbotham purports to show that English is not weakly context-free. The data is a bit subtle. It consists of certain uses of the "such that" construct in English. A possible weakness in the argument is the fact that nobody would ever say even short instances of the data sentences used, presumably due to processing constraints. However, they do appear to be part of English grammar, provide that you accept the logicians use of "such that" as part of English. The paper by Culy gives an argument against context-freeness based on the morphology of words in Bambara, an African language of the Mande family. Culy argues that the set of words in Bambara, as contrasted with the set of sentences, is not a context-free string set.

These first four papers appear to provide a definitive negative answer to the question "Is natural language context-free?" They do demonstrate that to maintain that absolutely all of natural language syntax can be done by a context-free grammar is an untenable position. However, it is

283

W. J. Savitch et al. (eds.), The Formal Complexity of Natural Language, 283–285.

still consistent with known results to maintain that the overwhelming bulk of natural language syntax is context-free. In English for example, the only proofs of noncontext-freeness are based on very marginal constructs such as "respectively" and uses of "such that" that are more like formal logic than conversational English. The Swiss-German data is more mainstream, but even in that case it is only one small part of the grammar. To put things in perspective, we should observe that mathematically correct proofs can be given to show that almost all common programming languages are not weakly context-free. Moreover, the proofs are based on critically important constructs used in virtually every program written in these languages. Two common but noncontext-free programming language constraints are requiring that variables be declared and requiring that statement labels be unique. (The relevant proofs can be found in Harrison (1978). Despite these proofs of noncontext-freeness, compilers are routinely written for these languages using context-free grammars and computer scientists generally find context-free grammar a "good" model for programming language syntax. Given what we know today, natural language appears to be more context-free than programming language and programming language syntax is routinely modeled by context-free grammars in both theoretical studies and production design projects. The complete answer to the question of the context-freeness of natural language has not yet been given.

Given that there are at least minor short-comings of the context-free grammar model and given that the transformational grammar model is more powerful than would be ideal, it makes sense to consider models intermediate in power. There are many: context-sensitive grammar, primitive recursive programs, polynomially time bounded programs to name a few. The problem is that few of these are linguistically well motivated. The context-sensitive grammar model most often comes to mind as a plausible model. Yet nobody ever seems to use it. This situation is easy to explain, but the explanation does not seem to have been archived and so we have include a short note by Savitch which presents the argument. It states that the context-sensitive languages, in an intuitive sense, contain all the recursively enumerable languages in a thin disguise. The paper by

Marsh and Partee discusses indexed languages, one class of grammars that is intermediate in power between context-free grammars and general recursively enumerable grammars, and that moreover does have some serious linguistic motivation. One model that is conspicuously absent from this anthology is lexical functional grammar. One reason to omit it is that its generative power has not yet been completely determined. A better reason is that material is already easily accessible in Bresnan (1982).

References

Bresnan, Joan, (ed), *The Mental Representation of Grammatical Relations*, 1982, The MIT Press, Cambridge, Mass.

Harrison, Michael A., *Introduction to Formal Language Theory*, 1978, Addison-Wesley, Reading, Mass.

Joan Bresnan, Ronald M. Kaplan, Stanley Peters, Annie Zaenen

CROSS-SERIAL DEPENDENCIES IN DUTCH

1. Are Natural Languages Context Free?

Chomsky's argument that natural languages are not finite state languages puts a lower bound on the weak generative capacity of grammars for natural languages (Chomsky (1956)). Arguments based on weak generative capacity are useful in excluding classes of formal devices as characterizations of natural language, but they are not the only formal considerations by which this can be done. Generative grammars may also be excluded because they cannot assign the correct structural descriptions to the terminal strings of a language; in this case, the grammars are excluded on grounds of strong generative capacity. Thus, the deterministic subclasses of context-free grammars (Knuth (1965)) can be rejected because they cannot assign alternative phrase structures to represent natural language ambiguities.

A question of some interest is whether natural languages can be characterized by utilizing the full class of context-free grammars. Despite the early rejection of such grammars by transformational grammarians (Chomsky (1957), Postal (1964a)), recent work has shown that context-free grammars are powerful devices that can describe many complex properties of natural languages in a formally restricted but linguistically general way (Gazdar (1981; 1982)). A convincing demonstration that natural language string sets are not context-free languages would indicate that these grammars are too restrictive to be capable in principle of even weakly characterizing natural language. Several attempts to establish this result have been offered in the literature (see Postal (1964b), Langendoen (1977), Huybregts (1976), and other references cited in Pullum and Gazdar (1982)). However, Pullum and Gazdar (1982) argue that all of these

Linguistic Inquiry, Volume 13, Number 4, Fall 1982, 613-635.
© 1982 by The Massachusetts Institute of Technology.

W. J. Savitch et al. (eds.), *The Formal Complexity of Natural Language, 286–319.*

attempts suffer from either formal or empirical deficiencies. Thus, it remains possible that natural languages considered as string sets are in fact weakly generable by context-free grammars.

There is another, arguably more interesting sense in which a natural language can be context free--namely, if there is a context-free grammar that assigns syntactically and semantically motivated structural descriptions to the strings of the language. If this is the case, we will say that the language is *strongly context free*. A language which is weakly context free need not be strongly context free. Even if the string set of the language is weakly generable by some context-free grammar, there may be no context-free grammar which assigns the correct set of structural descriptions to the language. We will show in this article that Dutch is just such a language, and thus, that natural languages in general are not strongly context free. This does not imply, however, that adequate natural language descriptions require the full power of transformational grammar: we also show that the troublesome Dutch constructions are strongly generated by a lexical-functional grammar (Kaplan and Bresnan (1982)).

2. An Invalid Lower Bound Argument Based on Dutch

Huybregts (1976) has argued that Dutch cannot be a (weakly) context-free language because it contains an infinite set of grammatical sentences which have cross-serial dependencies of the form given in (1)-(3).

(1)   ...dat Jan de kinderen zag   zwemmen
      that Jan the children see-past swim-inf

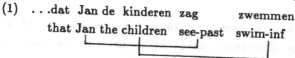

'...that Jan saw the children swim'

(2)   ... dat Jan Piet de kinderen zag   helpen   zwemmen
      that Jan Piet the children see-past help-inf swim-inf

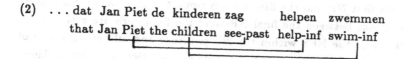

'...that Jan saw Piet help the children swim'

(3)

...dat Jan Piet Marie de kinderen zag   helpen laten   zwemmen

that Jan Piet Marie the children see-past help-inf make-inf swim-inf

'...that Jan saw Piet help Marie make the children swim'

Arbitrarily many of these sentences can be formed simply by inserting into the string a noun phrase and a verb that is subcategorized for both a noun phrase and an infinitival complement without the complementizer *te*. The verb in first position is formally distinguished by its marking for tense and its person and number agreement with the first NP. The verb in last position is distinguished from the others by its subcategorization restrictions. Although there are only a finite number of insertable verbs, they can be repeated, as in (4).

(4)

...dat de leraar   Jan Marie de kinderen leerde   laten   leren

   that the teacher Jan Marie the children teach-past make-inf teach-inf

zwemmen

swim-inf

'...that the teacher taught Jan to make Marie teach the children to swim'.

While it is true that the formal language $\{\omega\omega \mid \omega \in V^*\}$, whose strings exhibit arbitrarily deep cross-serial dependencies, is not context free if V contains at least two elements, the set of Dutch examples differs crucially from this language. For provided that the number of verbs matches the number of noun phrases, and provided that the agreement constraint between the first NP and the first verb is respected and the subcategorization restrictions between the final NPs and the final verb are satisfied, all permutations of the NPS within the NP sequence and all permutations of the verbs within the verb sequence produce grammatical sentences. These restrictions can be expressed by a context-free grammar, because even though the restrictions impose cross-serial dependencies, there are only finitely many of them (namely, two) to be encoded in the grammar. Thus, examples like the following are all grammatical.

(5)   . . .dat Jan Marie Piet de kinderen zag helpen laten zwemmen
      '. . .that Jan saw Marie help Piet make the children swim'

(6)   . . .dat Jan Marie de kinderen Piet zag helpen laten zwemmen
      '. . .that Jan saw Marie help the children make Piet swim'

(7)   . . .dat Jan Marie de kinderen Piet zag laten helpen zwemmen
      '. . .that Jan saw Marie make the children help Piet swim'

There are indeed infintely many cross-serial associations between the NP arguments and their corresponding predicates, but these are not formally encoded in the string set of Dutch in any way.

As a result of these considerations, we can see that the following context-free grammar suffices to generate the string set of this class of Dutch examples.

(8)a. $\text{S} \quad \rightarrow \quad \text{NP} \quad\quad \text{S}' \quad\quad \text{V}$

$$\text{S} \rightarrow \text{NP} \begin{bmatrix} \alpha \text{ pl} \\ \beta \text{ pers} \end{bmatrix} \text{S}' \begin{bmatrix} \alpha \text{ pl} \\ \beta \text{ pers} \\ +\text{n} \end{bmatrix} \text{V}\ [+\text{n}]$$

b. $\text{S}' \quad \rightarrow \quad \text{NP} \quad\quad \text{S}' \quad\quad \text{V}$

$$\text{S}' \begin{bmatrix} \alpha \text{ pl} \\ \beta \text{ pers} \\ +\text{n} \end{bmatrix} \rightarrow \text{NP} \ \text{S}' \begin{bmatrix} \alpha \text{ pl} \\ \beta \text{ pers} \\ +\text{n} \end{bmatrix} \text{V}$$

c.   S′   →   NP   S″   V

$$\begin{bmatrix} \alpha \text{ pl} \\ \beta \text{ pers} \\ +n \end{bmatrix} \qquad \begin{bmatrix} \alpha \text{ pl} \\ \beta \text{ pers} \\ +n \end{bmatrix}$$

d.   S″   →   NP^n V

$$\begin{bmatrix} \alpha \text{ pl} \\ \beta \text{ pers} \\ +n \end{bmatrix} \qquad \begin{bmatrix} \alpha \text{ pl} \\ \beta \text{ pers} \end{bmatrix}$$

In (8), α, β, and n are abbreviatory devices that provide schemata for a finite set of context-free rules. α ranges over $+$ and $-$; β ranges over 1,2,3; and $1 \leqslant n \leqslant u$, where u is the (finite) upper bound on the number of NPs that any Dutch verb can be subcategorized for.[1] For example, (8) generates example (2) in the way shown in (9). This grammar generates an artificially restricted (but infinite) proper subset of the relevant Dutch examples; see Pullum and Gazdar (1982) for discussion of how wider classes of examples can be described.

(9)

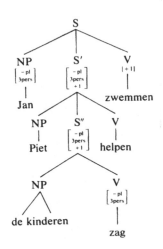

3. Evidence for the Correct Tree Structures

While the grammar of (8) weakly generates the cross-serial examples of Dutch, the constituent structures that it assigns are linguistically incorrect. Linguists have argued that the cross-serial constructions have the surface phrasal structure shown in (10)(Evers (1975)).

(10)

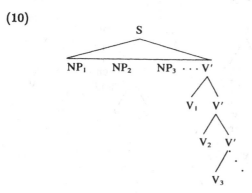

Working within a transformational framework, Evers (1975) proposed that structures like (10) are derived from structures like (11) by verb-raising and tree-pruning operations.

(11)

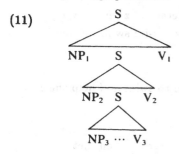

Specifically, the right-branching verbal group in (10) is produced by cyclically adjoining each verb or verb group to the higher verb on its right and then extraposing the former around the latter. The flat NP structure in (10) is produced by pruning the S nodes of the embedded clauses as their verbs are raised out of them.

There is good evidence for the right-branching verbal structure shown in (10). It is possible to conjoin single constituents in Dutch, but not in general nonconstituent sequences of categories. Hence, if the verbal group in cross-serial constructions has the constituent structure shown in (12a), the conjunction shown in (12b) should be well formed, whereas the one in (12c) should not.

(12)   a.

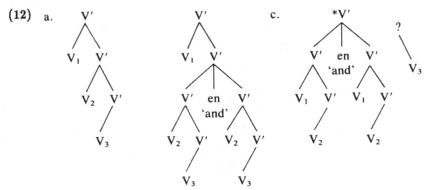

This accounts for the contrast between (13) and (14).

(13)

> ...dat Jan Marie de kinderen zag   leren   zwemmen en
>   that Jan Marie the children see-past teach-inf swim-inf   and
> helpen   lopen
> help-inf   run-inf
> '...that Jan saw Marie teach the children to swim and help the children to run'

(14)

> *?...dat Jan Marie de kinderen zag   leren   en liet
>   that Jan Marie the children see-past teach-inf and make-past
> helpen   zwemmen
> help-inf swim-inf
> '...that Jan saw Marie teach the children to swim and made her help the children to swim'

Example (14) is marginally acceptable with comma intonation setting off *en liet helpen;* this probably arises from the marginal applicability of the Right Node Raising rule, which differs from ordinary conjunction in requiring special intonation and in allowing only a single node to the right of the conjoined elements. Further evidence for the right-branching verb cluster is given by Evers (1975).

In contrast, the flat NP structure proposed by Evers and illustrated in (10) does not seem to be correct. There is evidence that the sequence of NPs has more constituent structure than the diagram in (10) shows. In general, PPs can occur in any order with respect to their sister constituents in Dutch. Accordingly, given the structure in (15), the examples in (16) are predicted.

(15)

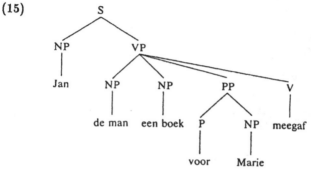

(16)a.   . . . dat Jan de man een boek voor Marie meegaf
    that Jan the man a book for Marie give-with-past
  '. . .that Jan gave a book to the man (to take with him) for Marie'

 b. . . . dat Jan de man voor Marie een boek meegaf

 c. . . . dat Jan voor Marie de man een boek meegaf

 d. *. . .dat voor Marie Jan de man een boek meegaf

The following examples indicate that in sentences exhibiting cross-serial dependencies only the last NP is a sister of the PP.

(17)a.   ...dat Jan Piet een boek op de   tafel zag   neerleggen
         that Jan Piet a   book on the table see-past-put-down
         '...that Jan saw Piet put a book down on the table'

   b.   dat Jan Piet op de tafel een boek zag neerleggen

   c.   *...dat Jan op de rafel Piet een boek zag neerleggen

   d.   *...dat op de tafel Jan Piet een boek zag neerleggen

This can be explained under the assumption that the tree in (18), not the
one in (10), is the correct form of constituent structure for cross-serial sentences.[2]

(18)

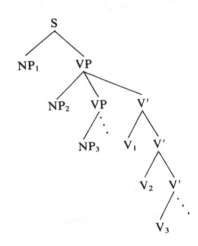

The type of constituent structure shown in (18) also explains a contrast in
the cojoinability of material before the verb sequence:

(19)

      ...dat Jan de kinderen een treintje   aan Piet en   een   pop aan
        that Jan the children a   toy train to Piet and a   doll to
   Henk zag   geven   voor Marie
   Henk see-past give-inf for   Marie
   '...that Jan saw the children give a toy train to Piet and a doll
   to Henk for Marie'

(20)

> ??...dat Jan de meisjes een treintje aan Piet en de jongens
> that Jan the girls a toy train to Piet and the boys
> een pop aan Henk zag geven voor Marie
> a doll to Henk see-past give-inf for Marie
> '...that Jan saw the boys give a toy train to Piet and the girls give
> a doll to Henk for Marie'.

As shown in (21), the sequence NP_2 PP_1 forms a constituent (VP_1), while the sequence NP_1 NP_2 PP_1 = NP_1 VP_1 does not form a constituent.

(21)

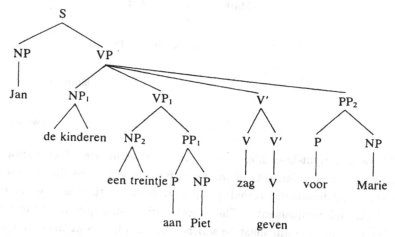

Hence, it should be possible to conjoin two NP_2 PP_1 sequences, as in (19), but not two NP_1 NP_2 PP_1 sequences, as in (20). The PP_2 has been included in these examples to exclude the possibility of deriving (20) by Right Node Raising of the V sequence, which must be final in the VP for that rule to apply.

In summary, the correct structural descriptions of these Dutch sentences can be characterized as follows. ((22) provides an example for reference.)

(22)

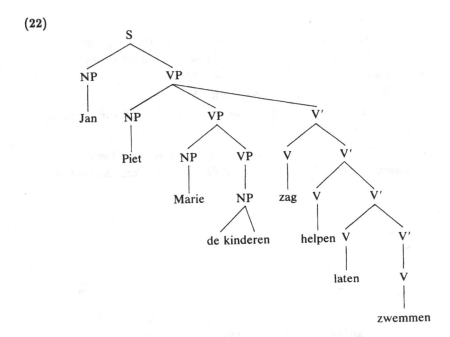

There is a right-branching complement VP structure which contains the objects and complements of the verbs but not the verbs themselves, and a sister right-branching verbal group that contains the verbs without their objects and complements. The subcategorization requirements of a particular verb on the right must be satisfied by the phrases at the corresponding level of embedding in the structure on the left. Failure to observe this restriction leads to ungrammatical examples like the following:

(23)
    *. . .dat Jan de leraar de kinderen zag   helpen laten
          that Jan the teacher the children see-past help-inf make-inf
    leren   zwemmen
    teach-inf swim-inf

(24)

   *...dat Jan Piet Marie de leraar   de kinderen zag   leren
      that Jan Piet Marie the teacher the children see-past teach-inf
  zwemmen
  swim-inf

These restrictions hold for Dutch examples of arbitrary depth.

Given this characterization of the correct tree structures and given the uncontroversial assumption that subcategorization restrictions are syntactic (on which see Grimshaw (1982a)), the question arises of how the subcategorization restrictions between the verbs and their complements are to be stated within a context-free grammar. One might think that some set of context-free feature propagation devices could do the job, but it turns out that this is not possible: as we show in the next section, there is no context-free grammar that can generate all and only the syntactically well-formed trees for Dutch sentences of this type.

4. Dutch is Not Strongly Context Free

If Dutch cross-serial constructions are correctly described by trees of the form characterized in the preceding section, then there is no context-free grammar that can assign the correct structural descriptions to Dutch sentences. To establish this result, we will argue for a slightly stronger conclusion, namely, that the structural descriptions of Dutch do not constitute a set of trees recognizable by a finite state tree automaton. The fact that Dutch is not strongly generable by any context-free grammar then immediately follows by virtue of the theorem that the derivation trees of any context-free grammar constitute a recognizable set (Thatcher (1967)).

We use a pumping lemma on recognizable sets of trees to demonstrate that no such set can have the formal property isolated at the end of the last section, namely, that the trees contain two right-branching subrees of matching heights. For every recognizable set of trees, there is a constant n such that any tree in the set having height greater than n can be partitioned into three parts t_1, t_2, t_3 where the height of the subtree t_2 t_3 is less than n (see figure 1) and any tree formed by iterating the middle part

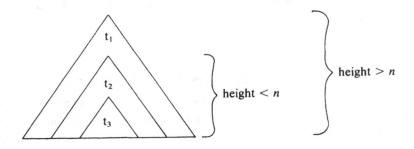

Figure 1

t_2 as in figure 2 also belongs to the recognizable set (Thatcher (1973)).

Now let us assume that the trees of Dutch constitute a recognizable set, and let n be the appropriate constant for this set. Consider a tree of the form in (18) whose height is greater than n. If we partition it into the parts t_1, t_2, t_3, part t_2 must either be in the VP branch of the tree, as shown in figure 3, or else it must be in the V′ branch, as shown in figure 4. In either case, iterating t_2 produces a tree in which the VP and V′ subtrees are not of corresponding heights. In general, such trees are not well-formed structural descriptions of Dutch, as the ungrammaticality of examples (23) and (24) illustrates. This contradicts the assumption that Dutch structural descriptions form a recognizable set of trees.

We have shown that there is no context-free grammar than can generate all and only the correct structural descriptions for Dutch. Thus, this natural language lies beyond the strong generative capacity of context-free

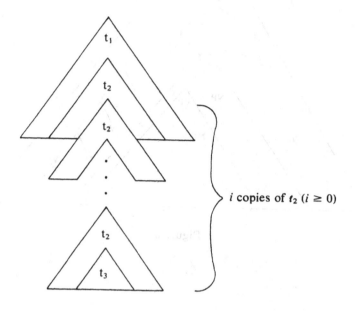

Figure 2

grammars. From this we can also conclude that Dutch cannot be strongly generated by a categorial grammar, because the structures that such grammars generate are included in the structures generated by context-free grammars (Bar-Hillel, Gaifman, and Shamir (1960)). This result also extends to Bach's (1979; 1980; 1981) generalization of categorial grammars if his right-wrap operation is sufficiently constrained.[3]

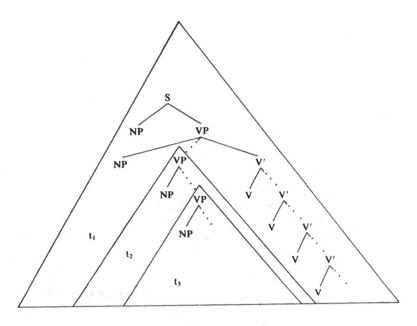

Figure 3

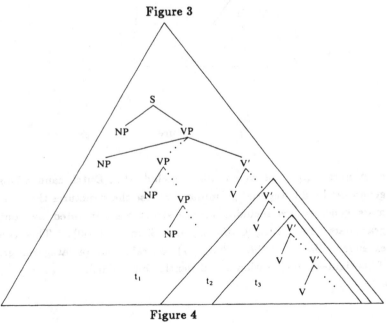

Figure 4

5. A Lexical-Functional Grammar Generates the Set of Correct Tree Structures

Whether or not context-free grammars can weakly generate the string sets of natural languages, they are not in general sufficient for generating the correct structural descriptions of natural language. This, however, is not an argument that transformational devices are necessary. In fact, we can show that the correct descriptions can be assigned to the class of Dutch cross-serial constructions by a more restrictive system than transformational grammars, the lexical-functional grammars (LFGs) of Kaplan and Bresnan (1982). We will limit our attention to the class of examples discussed in section 2, for these are sufficient to illustrate the essential formal properties of the LFG solution.

A lexical-functional grammar includes a set of context-free rules for generating the constituent structures ("c-structures") of sentences. These rules are annotated with functional schemata that combine with similar lexical schemata to determine the functional structure ("f-structures") corresponding to those c-structures. F-structures are hierarchical structures that formally represent the grammatical relations of sentences in terms of such universal functions as SUBJ(ect), OBJ(ect), and COMP(lement), abstracting away from language-particular differences in surface form. For a string to be grammatical, it must be assigned not only a well-formed c-structure according to the standard interpretation of context-free rules, but also an f-structure that satisfies the general well-formedness conditions of Uniqueness, Completeness, and Coherence (Kaplan and Bresnan (1982)). The Uniqueness Condition asserts that every grammatical function or feature must be assigned a single value. The Completeness and Coherence Conditions require that all and only the grammatical functions mentioned by a lexical predicate are local to that predicate in the f-structure. Together they guarantee that the subcategorization requirements of lexical entries are satisfied. Because of these three functional well-formedness conditions, the functional component of a lexical-functional grammar serves as a filter on the output of the c-structure rules, marking as ungrammatical strings that have otherwise valid c-structures.

The linguistically motivated c-structures for sentences with cross-serial dependencies have two parallel right-branching structures, as illustrated in (22). Trees of this sort can be generated by the following simple context-free grammar:

(25)   S → NP VP
     VP → (NP) (VP) (V′)
     V′ → V (V′)

It is obvious that this grammar generates far more than just the set of correct Dutch trees, since the grammar does not express the dependency between the depth of the branching structures on the left and right. However, when the appropriate functional schemata are added to these rules, they determine for each c-structure a corresponding f-structure which does represent the dependency. The general well-formedness conditions on f-structures will eliminate those trees in which the depth of branching on the left and right is mismatched.

The f-structure for sentence (26), whose c-structure is shown in (27), is given in (28).

(26) . . .dat Jan Piet Marie zag   helpen zwemmen
     that Jan Piet Marie see-past help-inf swim-inf
     '. . .that Jan saw Piet help Marie swim'

(27)

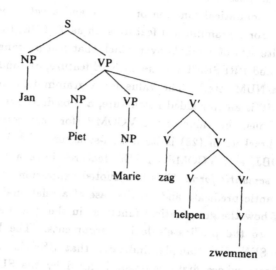

(28)

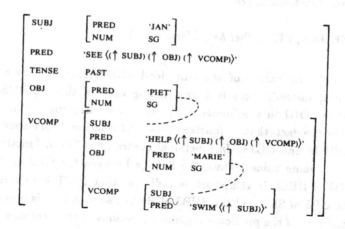

As (28) shows, an f-structure is a set of ordered pairs, each consisting of the name of a grammatical function or feature and a *value* for that function or feature. For a grammatical feature such as TENSE, the values are drawn from finite sets of symbols over which that feature ranges (e.g. the symbols PAST and PRESENT for the TENSE feature, SG and PL for the number feature NUM, etc.). The value for a grammatical function like SUBJ or VCOMP is an embedded f-structure, a subsidiary set of functions and features. Thus, the value of the VCOMP (for verb complement) in the outermost brackets in (28) is itself an f-structure with internal functions SUBJ, OBJ, and VCOMP. PRED features have a third type of value, called a *semantic form*. This is a quoted expression containing the name of a semantic predicate and, in the case of a relational predicate, a specification of how the grammatical functions in the local f-structure are to be assigned to the predicate's logical arguments. The list in angle brackets after SEE, for example, indicates that SEE is a three-place semantic predicate whose first argument is filled by the SUBJ ('JAN'), whose second argument is the OBJ ('PIET'), and whose third argument is the hierarchical VCOMP. Thus, the predicate argument relations for the outermost clause of sentence (26) may be read directly from the outermost PRED and functions in (28):

(29) SEE(JAN, PIET, *Piet help Marie swim*)

In (28) the values of the embedded SUBJ functions are not fully spelled out; instead, there is a line linking each of those SUBJS to the value of the OBJ in the immediately enclosing f-structure. This linkage represents the fact that a *functional control* relation holds between the linked SUBJS and OBJS. In functional control, the linked functions have exactly the same value. Thus, the linkage between the OBJ of SEE and the SUBJ of HELP in this example indicates that PIET is understood as both the OBJ of SEE and the SUBJ of HELP, so that (30) is a more complete rendition of the predicate argument relations of this sentence:

(30) SEE(JAN, PIET, HELP(PIET, MARIE, SWIM(MARIE)))

Because of the identities represented by control linkages such as these, f-structures technically are acyclic directed graphs, not just simple hierarchies.[4]

F-structures are assigned to subconstituents of the c-structure by virtue of functional annotations associated with the context-free rules and lexical entries of a lexical-functional grammar; the f-structure that the grammar assigns to a sentence as a whole is taken to be the one assigned to its root S node. These annotations specify a node's f-structure in terms of its own lexical or grammatical features and its daughter's f-structures.[5] An illustration of the notation in which these functional specifications are expressed is given in (31), a partial lexical entry for the proper noun *Jan*:

(31) *Jan*: N($\uparrow$ PRED) = 'JAN'
            ($\uparrow$ NUM) = SG

This entry lists N as the c-structure category of *Jan* and provides a set of equations that define feature values of the f-structures corresponding to any nodes headed by this word. A parenthetic expression of the form $(f\ \alpha)$ refers to the value of the α function or feature in the f-structure designed by f. Thus, the first equation in (31) asserts that the value of the PRED feature in the f-structure designated by $\uparrow$ is the semantic form 'JAN', and the second equation defines the value of the NUM feature of that f-structure to be SG. Note that these equations would both be true if the f-structure designated by $\uparrow$ were the value of the outermost SUBJ in (28), and thus that f-structure is a "solution" to this pair of equations. In general, the LFG machinery produces such equations from functional annotations throughout the c-structure, and the f-structure for a sentence is the solution to that set of simultaneous equations.

The rule in (32) is an annotated version of the context-free S rule in (25).

(32) S$\rightarrow$ NP   VP
              ($\uparrow$ SUBJ) = $\downarrow$ $\uparrow$ = $\downarrow$

The equation under the NP category, $(\uparrow \text{SUBJ}) = \downarrow$, asserts that the value of the SUBJ function of the f-structure designated by $\uparrow$ is the f-structure designated by the symbol $\downarrow$. When this rule is used to expand a node, $\uparrow$ and $\downarrow$ are taken to designate the f-structure associated with the S and NP nodes, respectively. Thus, in equations that are produced in expanding the NP, $\uparrow$ must also refer to the same f-structure that is referred to by $\downarrow$ in the SUBJ equation in the S rule. (33) associates these functional annotations with the nodes of the tree and shows an assignment of f-structures to the $\uparrow$ and $\downarrow$ symbols such that all of the equations are simultaneously satisfied.

(33)

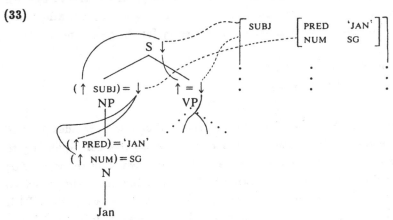

In the example, the solid curves connect symbols which must designate the same f-structure by virtue of the tree relations of the nodes with which they are associated. The broken curves indicate the f-structure assigned to those related sets of $\downarrow$ and $\uparrow$ symbols. An additional $\downarrow$ appears at the root of the tree to stand for the f-structure assigned to the sentence as a whole. The equation $\uparrow = \downarrow$ indicates that the S and VP nodes have the same f-structure. Because of this, the equations will be satisfied only by an f-structure in which the functions and features of the VP's f-structure are merged with the functions and features of the S's, thus expressing the fact that the verb phrase is the head of the sentence.

The information represented graphically by the curves in (33) is expressed symbolically by means of the *instantiation procedure* described in Kaplan and Bresnan (1982). The equations on the tree in (34) are derived from those in (33) by replacing codesignating ↑ s and ↓ s with common indices f_1, f_2, etc. Kaplan and Bresnan (1982) show that it is decidable whether or not there exists an f-structure satisfying an instantiated set of equations (called a *functional description* or "f-description") and present an algorithm for actually synthesizing the f-structure that an f-description describes. The present discussion, however, depends only on the procedure for verifying that a given candidate f-structure is in fact a solution for a particular f-description.

(34)

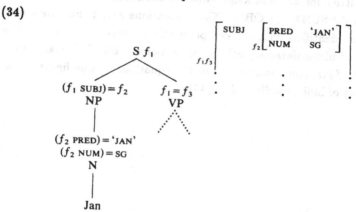

The additional rules and lexical entries necessary to generate sentence (26) are given in (35) and (36).

(35)　VP　→　$\left(\begin{array}{c} \text{NP} \\ (\uparrow \text{OBJ}){=}\downarrow \end{array}\right)\left(\begin{array}{c} \text{VP} \\ (\uparrow \text{VCOMP}){=}\downarrow \end{array}\right)\left(\begin{array}{c} \text{V}' \\ \uparrow{=}\downarrow \end{array}\right)$

　　　V′　→　V　$\left(\begin{array}{c} \text{V}' \\ (\uparrow \text{VCOMP}){=}\downarrow \end{array}\right)$

　　　NP　→　N

(36)

zag:　　V　　$(\uparrow \text{PRED}){=}$'SEE$<(\uparrow \text{SUBJ})(\uparrow \text{OBJ})(\uparrow \text{VCOMP})>$'
　　　　　　　　$(\uparrow \text{TENSE}){=}$PAST
　　　　　　　　$(\uparrow \text{SUBJ NUM}){=}$SG
　　　　　　　　$(\uparrow \text{VCOMP SUBJ}){=}(\uparrow \text{OBJ})$

helpen:	V	($\uparrow$ PRED)='HELP<($\uparrow$ SUBJ)($\uparrow$ OBJ)($\uparrow$ VCOMP)>'
		($\uparrow$ VCOMP SUBJ)=($\uparrow$ OBJ)
zwemmen:	V	($\uparrow$ PRED)='SWIM<($\uparrow$ SUBJ)>'
Piet:	N	($\uparrow$ PRED)='PIET'
		($\uparrow$ NUM)=SG
Marie:	N	($\uparrow$ PRED)='MARIE'
		($\uparrow$ NUM)=SG

The lexical entries for *zag* and *helpen* include the functional control equations ($\uparrow$ VCOMP SUBJ)=($\uparrow$ OBJ). These equations assert that the object of the verb is identified with its complement's subject. (37) shows the complete set of instantiated equations for sentence (26). The reader may verify that the f-structure satisfies all of the equations in this figure under the assignment of indices indicated in (38).

(37)

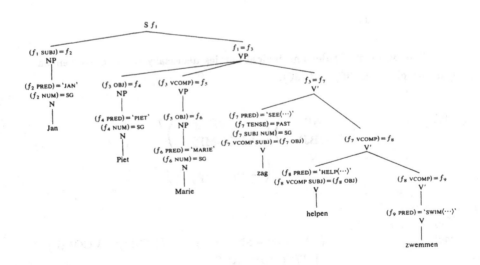

(38)

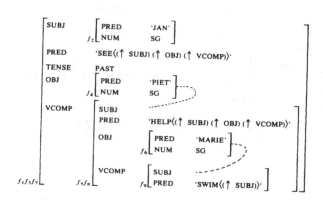

In (37) the specifications just on the left branches of the VP subtree characterize an f-structure containing only one embedded VCOMP with an OBJ but no PRED, as shown in (39).

(39)

$$
f_3 \begin{bmatrix} \text{OBJ} & f_4 \begin{bmatrix} \text{PRED} & \text{'PIET'} \\ \text{NUM} & \text{SG} \end{bmatrix} \\ \text{VCOMP} & f_5 \begin{bmatrix} \text{OBJ} & f_6 \begin{bmatrix} \text{PRED} & \text{'MARIE'} \\ \text{NUM} & \text{SG} \end{bmatrix} \end{bmatrix} \end{bmatrix}
$$

In contrast, specifications on the V′ subtree characterize a VCOMP hierarchy with PREDS and functional control relations between SUBJS and OBJS (40), but the internal features of these functions are not specified on that branch.

(40)

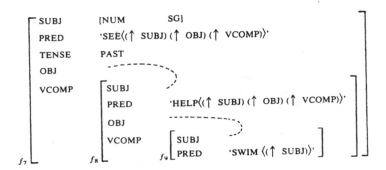

However, because the identity ↑ = ↓ on the topmost V′ node is instantiated as $f_3 = f_7$, the only f-structure that satisfies together all of the equations under the highest VP is one in which the information specified on the two branches is hierarchically merged, as shown in (41). The "merger" of the discontinuous functional specifications of (39) and (40) is a formal consequence of the Uniqueness Condition.

(41)

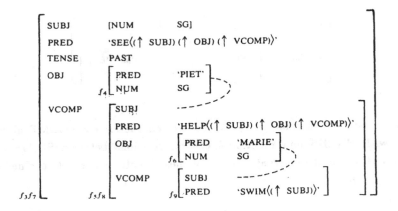

The requirement that subject-verb agreement hold between the first NP and the finite verb also follows from the Uniqueness Condition. A finite form of the verb such as *zag* specifies a value for the NUM feature of its SUBJ. This feature of the verb is propagated to the f-structure of the sentence by virtue of the fact that the verb is the head of the VP and the VP is the head of the sentence, as indicated by the ↑ = ↓ identity annotated to the VP in rule (32). The Uniqueness Condition holds if the specifications defined on the verb and the specification derived from lexical material within the SUBJ NP both assign the same value, as is the case for sentence (26). However, example (42) is ungrammatical because the lexical entry for *zagen* specifies a plural number for its SUBJ, by means of the alternative equation (↑ SUBJ NUM)=PL.

(42) *...dat Jan Piet Marie zagen helpen zwemmen

This is inconsistent with the SG specification contributed by the lexical entry for *Jan.*

We have seen how the grammar fragment and lexical entries above do in fact assign the f-structure (28) to sentence (26). This f-structure also satisfies the Completeness and Coherence Conditions: the functions subcategorized by each verb are in one-to-one correspondence with the functions found in its local f-structure. Now consider how these rules and annotations would apply for the string (43), which has an additional verb but not an additional NP.

(43) *...dat Jan Piet Marie zag   helpen laten   zwemmen
     that Jan Piet Marie see-past help-inf make-inf swim-inf

As (44) shows, the V′ branch in the c-structure for this string contains an extra level, and the f-description associated with that branch specifies an extra VCOMP level with the PRED feature for *laten.* A corresponding level does not exist in the VP structure, so there are no specifications for the OBJ of that VCOMP.

(44)

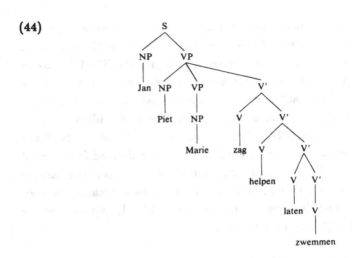

In the resulting f-structure (45), the MAKE and SWIM PREDS refer to grammatical functions (OBJ and SUBJ) for which no values are specified; the string is ungrammatical because its f-structure violates the Completeness Condition.

(45)

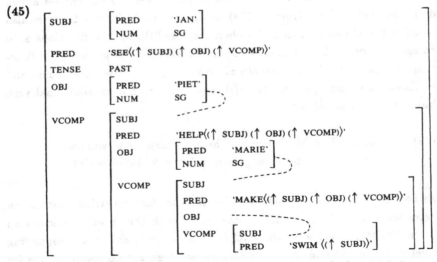

The tree in (47) is the c-structure for the string (46), which has an additional NP but not an additional verb.

(46) *...dat   Jan Piet Marie Hans zag   helpeu zwemmen
        that   Jan Piet Marie Hans see-past help-inf swim-inf

(47)

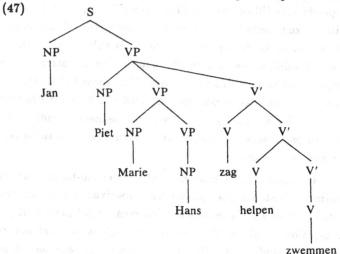

An extra VCOMP level containing an OBJ function is specified on
the VP branch of this c-structure. As shown in (48), this becomes
the OBJ for the SWIM PRED. Because the SWIM semantic form
does not subcategorize for OBJ, this f-structure violates the Coherence Condition. Again the sentence is rejected.

(48)

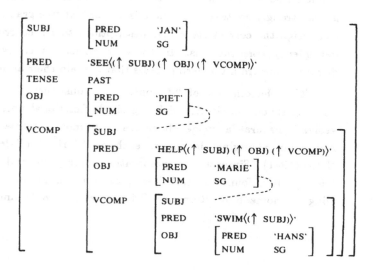

Note that because of the optional expansions of V´ under both VP and V´, these rules generate grammatical sentences with nested dependencies (illustrated in (11)) as well as grammatical sentences with mixed nested and crossed dependencies. Generation of the same verb in both positions, however, is ruled out by the Uniqueness Condition, because of the unique instantiation of semantic forms (Kaplan and Bresnan (1982), Grimshaw (1982b)); and omission of a verb in both positions is ruled out by the Coherence Condition. Thus, the general well-formedness conditions on f-structures explain why these two structures appear to be related by a movement of the verb.

In summary, we have presented a lexical-functional grammar fragment that assigns syntactically motivated c-structures to an infinite set of Dutch sentences with cross-serial argument-predicate associations. Given the general conditions on f-structure well-formedness and the functional annotations that are needed independently to assign grammatical relations appropriate for subcategorization (Grimshaw (1982a)) and semantic interpretation (Halvorsen (1981)), this grammar generates no examples where the numbers of subcategorized objects and predicates are not properly matched.

6. Conclusion

While Dutch may or may not be context free in the weak sense, it is not strongly context free: there is no context-free grammar that can assign the correct structural descriptions to Dutch cross-serial dependency constructions. In these constructions the verbs are discontinuous from the verb phrases that contain their arguments.

The phenomenon of "discontinuous constituents" --that is, noncontiguous constituents defining single functional units--is pervasive in natural language. It occurs in its most extreme forms in Australian aboriginal languages such as Warlpiri (Hale (1979), Nash (1981), Simpson (in preparation), Simpson and Bresnan (1982)). It is found in much less extreme forms in the clitic doubling phenomena of Romance (Montalbetti (1981)) and in the verb-agreement phenomena of Athapaskan (Roberts (1981)). The transformational solution to the Dutch case does not generalize to these kinds of cases, but the LFG solution does. This in itself is remarkable in view of the greater restrictiveness of lexical-functional grammars.

Acknowledgements

We are indebted to Oliver Gajek, Geoff Pullum, and Koos van der Wilt for commenting on earlier drafts of this article. This study is based on work supported in part by the National Science Foundation under Grant Nos. BNS-80-14730 to the Massachusetts Institute of Technology and BNS-76-20307 to the University of Texas at Austin, in part by the Cognitive and Instructional Sciences Group of the Xerox Palo Alto Research Center, and in part by the Center for Advanced Study in the Behavioral Sciences.

Footnotes

[1] For an exposition of such abbreviatory notations for context-free grammars, see Gazdar (in press).

[2] This explanation was suggested by Ewan Klein (personal communication). Evers (1975) gives several arguments for flat NP structure, based on extraposition, clitic placement, quantifier hopping, and clause negation in Dutch, but all of his evidence is consistent with the weaker hypothesis that the NP sequence in cross-serial examples lacks S structure, as in (18).

[3] One constraint that suffices, for example, is that whenever A is right-wrapped around B, the position where B is inserted in A's leftmost branch is a bounded distance from the bottom or top of that branch.

[4] Halvorsen (1981) shows that this representation supports a model-theoretic semantic interpretation for control and quantification phenomena.

[5] As described by Kaplan and Bresnan (1982), f-structure specifications also come from more remote nodes in cases of long-distance dependencies (called *constituent control*). Specifications from these remote sources are not relevant to the current discussion.

References

Bach E. (1979) "Control in Montague Grammar", *Linguistic Inquiry 10, 515-531.*

Bach, E. (1980) "In Defense of Passive," *Linguistics and Philosophy* 3, 297-341.

Bach, E. (1981) "Discontinuous Constituents in Generalized Categorial Grammars," in V. Burke and J. Pustejovsky, eds. *Proceedings of the Eleventh Annual Meeting of the Northeastern Linguistic Society,* Graduate Linguistics Student Association, University of Massachusetts at Amherst.

Bar-Hillel, Y., C. Gaifman, E. Shamir (1960) "On Categorial and Phrase-Structure Grammars," *Bulletin of the Research Council of Israel,* 9F.

Chomsky, N. (1956) "Three Models for the Description of Language," *IRE Transactions on Information Theory IT-2,* 113-134.

Chomsky, N. (1957) *Syntactic Structures,* Mouton, The Hague.

Evers, A. (1975) *The Transformational Cycle in Dutch and German,* Doctoral dissertation, Rijks-universiteit, Utrecht, Holland.

Gazdar, G. (1981) "Unbounded Dependencies and Coordinate Structure," *Linguistic Inquiry* 12, 155-184.

Gazdar, G. (1982) "Phrase Structure Grammar," in P. Jacobson and G.K. Pullum, eds., *The Nature of Syntactic Representation,* Reidel, Dordrecht.

Grimshaw, J. (1982a) "Theories of Subcategorization," paper presented at the First West Coast Conference on Formal Linguistics, Stanford University, January 1982.

Grimshaw, J. (1982b) "On the Lexical Representation of Romance Reflexive Clitics," in J. Bresnan, ed., *The Mental Representation of Grammatical Relations*, MIT Press, Cambridge, Mass.

Hale, K. (1979) "On the Position of Walbiri in a Typology of the Base," available from the Indiana University Linguistics Club, Bloomington, Indiana.

Halvorsen, P.K. (1981) "An Interpretation Procedure for Functional Structures," unpublished manuscript, MIT, Cambridge, Mass.

Huybregts, M.A.C. (1976) "Overlapping Dependencies in Dutch," *Utrecht Working Papers in Linguistics* 1, 24-65.

Kaplan, R.M. and J. Bresnan (1982) "Lexical-Functional Grammar: A Formal System for Grammatical Representation," in J. Bresnan, ed., *The Mental Representation of Grammatical Relations*, MIT Press, Cambridge, Mass.

Knuth, D. (1965) "On the Translation of Languages from Left to Right," *Information and Control* 8, 607-639.

Langendoen, D.T. (1977) "On the Inadequacy of Type-3 and Type-2 Grammars for Human Languages," in P.J. Hopper, ed., *Studies in Descriptive and Historical Linguistics: Festschrift for Winfred P. Lehmann*, John Benjamin, Amsterdam, 159-171.

Montalbetti, M. (1981) "Consistency and Clitics," unpublished manuscript, Dept. of Linguistics and Philosophy, MIT, Cambridge, Mass.

Nash, D. (1981) *Topics in Walbiri Grammar*, Doctoral dissertation, MIT, Cambridge, Mass.

Postal, P. (1964a) *Constituent Structure*, Indiana University Research Center in Anthropology, Folklore, and Linguistics, Publication 30, Indiana University, Bloomington, Indiana.

Postal, P. (1964b) "Limitations of Phrase Structure Grammars," in J. Fodor and J. Katz, eds., *The Structure of Language*, Prentice-Hall, Englewood Cliffs, NJ, 137-151.

Pullum, G.K. and G. Gazdar (1982) "Natural Languages and Context-free Languages," *Linguistics and Philosophy* 4, 471-504.

Roberts, J. (1981) "Towards a Unified Analysis of the Passive in Navajo," unpublished manuscript, Department of Linguistics and Philosophy, MIT, Cambridge, Mass.

Simpson, J. (1983) *Aspects of Walpiri Morphology and Syntax*, Doctoral dissertation, MIT, Cambridge, Mass.

Simpson, J. and J. Bresnan (1982) "Control and Obviation in Warlpiri," paper presented at the First West Coast Conference on Formal Linguistics, Stanford University, January 1982.

Thatcher, J.W. (1967) "Characterizing Derivation Trees of Context-Free Grammars through a Generalization of Finite Automata Theory," *Journal of Computer and System Science* 1, 317-322.

Thatcher, J.W. (1973) "Tree Automata: An Informal Survey," in A.V. Aho, ed., *Currents in the Theory of Computing*, Prentice-Hall, Englewood Cliffs, NJ, 143-172.

Stuart M. Shieber*

EVIDENCE AGAINST THE CONTEXT-FREENESS
OF NATURAL LANGUAGE**

1. Introduction

In searching for universal constraints on the class of natural languages, linguists have investigated a number of formal properties, including that of context-freeness. Soon after Chomsky's categorization of languages into his well-known hierarchy (Chomsky, 1963), the common conception of the context-free class of languages as a tool for describing natural languages was that it was too restrictive a class - interpreted *strongly* (as a way of characterizing structure sets) and even *weakly* (as a way of characterizing string sets).

The issue was brought back to the attention of linguists a few years ago, however, by Gerald Gazdar's arguments for a context-free phrase-structure theory of syntax (Gazdar, 1982). Subsequently, Gazdar and Goeffrey K. Pullum (1982) chronicled common thinking on the issue, and argued compellingly against all previous published arguments maintaining the weak non-context-freeness of natural language. Since then, to the author's knowledge, no published proof of the weak non-context-freeness of natural language has been forthcoming.[1]

However, one of the arguments discussed by Gazdar and Pullum - that concerning the Dutch cross-serial clause construction (Bresnan *et al.*, 1982) - came quite close. The class of structures propounded on linguistic grounds for grammatical subordinate clauses with the cross-serial construction was demonstrated to be non-context-free. That is, although the string set of Dutch was not (and could not be) shown to be ungenerable by a context-free grammar, the constituent structure set nevertheless was - if Bresnan et al. are right about the linguistic motivation for those

Linguistics and Philosophy 8 (1985) 333-343.
© 1985 *by D. Reidel Publishing Company*

W. J. Savitch et al. (eds.), The Formal Complexity of Natural Language, 320–334.

structures. Of course, their demonstration relied greatly upon linguistic arguments as well as formal language theory and, in fact, several authors have presented alternative analyses (Culy, 1983; Joshi, 1983; Thompson, 1983). Although all these linguistically motivated analyses have been strongly non-context-free, one in particular (Culy, 1983) maintained weak context-freeness.[2]

This paper offers evidence for the *weak* non-context-freeness of natural language. Using data collected from native Swiss-German speakers, we will provide a formal proof of the weak non-context-freeness of Swiss German. In doing so, we will make as few (and as uncontroversial) linguistic assumptions as possible - in particular, we make no assumptions about the structure or semantics of Swiss German. We also present a few putative counterarguments and show that they are not seriously detrimental to our claim.

2. Some Swiss-German Data

Two facts about Swiss-German grammar are crucial to our argument. First, Swiss German uses case-marking (dative and accusative) on objects, just as standard German does; different verbs subcategorize for objects of different case. Second, Swiss German, like Dutch, allows cross-serial order for the structure of subordinate clauses.[3] Of critical importance is the fact that Swiss German requires appropriate case-marking to hold even within the cross-serial construction.

These linguistic claims are, however, stronger than the assumptions we need to show non-context-freeness. We will present some pertinent data below, later pinpointing exactly what claims we require for the proof. The sample subordinate clauses given here should be envisaged as preceded by the string " Jan säit das" ("Jan says that") or a similar precedent so as to form a complete sentence.

(1)   mer em Hans   es huus   hälfed aastriiche
        we Hans-DAT   the house-ACC helped paint
        'we helped Hans paint the house.'

Example (1) displays the cross-serial semantic dependencies found also in Dutch: *em Hans* is the objected of hälfed, *es huus*, the object of *aastriiche*. Furthermore, correlated with this semantic dependency, there is a syntactic dependency between the pairs of constituents, namely, case-marking. The verb hälfed requires its NP object to be marked with dative case. A verb like lönd, which requires accusative case could appear in clauses like:

(2)   mer de hans   es huus   lönd aastriiche
        we Hans-ACC the house-ACC let   paint
        'we let Hans paint the house'

but not in

(3)   *mer em Hans   es huus   lönd aastriiche
        we   Hans-DAT the house-ACC let   paint
        'we   let Hans paint the house'

Informants uniformly find this example ungrammatical and identify the case marking on *Hans* as the culprit. Similarly, since *aastriiche* requires an accusative object, the clause

(4)   *mer de Hans   em huus   lönd aastriiche
        we   Hans-ACC the house-DAT let   paint
        'we let Hans paint the house'

is also found to be ungrammatical.

This phenomenon of case marking across cross-serial verb constructions is quite robust, holding in quite complex clauses. For example, the following triply embedded cross-serial clause is perceived as grammatical if and only if the case marking is correct.

(5)   mer d'chind   em Hans es huus
        we the children-ACC Hans-DAT the house-ACC
        lönd hälfe aastriiche
        let   help paint
        'we let the children help Hans paint the house.'

(6)   *mer d'chind   de Hans   es   huus
        we   the children-ACC Hans-ACC the house-ACC
        lönd hälfe aastriiche
        let   help paint
        'we let the children help Hans paint the house.'

As further evidence of the robustness of the phenomenon, additional so-called raising verbs can occur between the string of NPs and the string of Vs, e.g.:

(7)   mer em Hans   es   huus   haend wele   hälfe
        we Hans-DAT the house-ACC have   wanted help
        aastriiche
        paint
        'we have wanted to help Hans paint the house.'

(8)   mer d'chind   em Hans   es   huus   haend
        we the children-ACC Hans-DAT the house-ACC have
        wele   laa hälfe aastriiche
        wanted let help paint
        'we have wanted to let the children help Hans paint the house.'

3. A Non-Context-Freeness Argument

An argument for the weak non-context-freeness of Swiss German can be built from the foregoing data. On that basis we make the following minimal set of claims about the string set of Swiss German. Note that these claims are weaker than the analysis presented in the previous section.

Claim 1:   Swiss-German subordinate clauses can have a structure in which all the Vs follow all the NPs.

In particular, some sentences of the following schema are grammatical: *Jan säit das mer NP* es huus haend wele V* aastriiche* where the NPs are either *d'chind* or *em Hans* and the Vs are either *laa* or *hälfe*. See sentences (7) and (8) for instances supporting this claim.

Claim 2:   Among such sentences, those with all dative NPs preceding all accusative NPs, and all dative-subcategorizing Vs preceding all accusative-subcategorizing Vs are acceptable.

In particular, some sentences of the following schema are grammatical *Jan säit das mer (d'chind)* (em Hans)* es huus haend wele laa* hälfe* aastriiche*. Again, see sentences (7) and (8) for instances supporting this claim.

Claim 3:   The number of Vs requiring dative objects (e.g., *hälfe*) must equal the number of dative NPs (e.g., *em Hans*) and similarly for accusatives (*laa* and *d'chind*); note that this holds even if all the Vs follow all the NPs.[4]

See sentences (6), and (12) through (22) for instances supporting this claim.

Claim 4:   An arbitrary number of Vs can occur in a subordinate clause of this type (subject, of course, to performance constraints).

Now, given any language L that satisfies these claims, we can take its image under the homomorphism f, where

$$
\begin{aligned}
f(\text{``d'chind''}) &= a \\
f(\text{``em Hans''}) &= b \\
f(\text{``laa''}) &= c \\
f(\text{``hälfe''}) &= d
\end{aligned}
$$

$$f(\text{``Jan säit das mer''}) \quad = \quad w$$
$$f(\text{``es huus haend wele''}) \quad = \quad x$$
$$f(\text{``aastriiche''}) \quad = \quad y$$
$$f(s) \quad = \quad z \text{ otherwise,}$$

and then intersect the language $f(L)$ with the regular language $r = wa^*b^*xc^*d^*y$. According to the claims above, $f(L) \cap r = wa^mb^nxc^md^ny$, which is weakly non-context-free.[5] But since context-free languages are closed under homomorphisms and under intersection with regular languages (Hopcroft and Ullman, 1979, pp. 130-135), the original language L, whatever it is, must also be weakly non-context-free. Now since our claims hold for Swiss German, the argument holds as well, and Swiss German is thus shown to be weakly non-context-free.[6]

As a trivial corollary, Swiss German is not strongly context-free either, regardless of one's view as to the appropriate structures for the language. Thus, we have an argument for the strong non-context-freeness of natural language that is not subject to the same frailty as the Dutch argument, i.e., its reliance on a linguistic motivation for its analysis of Dutch clause structure. Unlike the Dutch argument, ours does not mention, let alone hinge on, the constituent structure of the sentences in question or their semantics.

4. Possible Counterarguments

The premises of the argument are quite explicit, namely the four claims presented above; counterarguments could be directed against any of them. We discuss several possibilities.

4.1 *"The Data Are Wrong"*

An argument can always be made that the grammaticality judgments expressed by our sample sentences are just wrong - that is, that the informants were mistaken about their own judgments or the transcriber simply misconstrued those judgments. This situation is, of course, hardly unique to this research, but pervades the linguistic method in general; it is especially problematic in the light of psychological research such as that of

Rosenthal (1966). It is the counterargument used against the "comparatives" argument (Gazdar and Pullum,1982).

There being no adequate response to this objection, we will merely present details of our method in collecting the pertinent data and leave it to the reader to form an individual opinion. Four native Swiss-German speakers were interviewed separately, eliciting their grammaticality judgments on 62 Swiss-German clauses with varying word orders (disjoint, nested, cross-serial), depth of embedment, and lexical items. In an attempt to eliminate at least the most extreme of priming effects, the data were presented in a shuffled order. All four speakers were of the Zürich dialect of Swiss German, though one speaker claimed to have some Bernese traits in his dialect. (The Bernese dialect is freer than the Zürich in its constituent order.) The vast majority of examples (including all those presented in this paper except for (11)) showed unanimity of judgment among the speakers, and the phenomena came across as being surprisingly robust. It must be admitted, however, that the conclusions presented herein are not based on a controlled experiment. Such is usually and, for the most part, unavoidably the case in this area of linguistic research.

4.2 "Other Constituent Orders are Possible"

Claims 1 and 2 require that clauses allow a particular order in which all verbs follow all NPs and NPs and Vs are "sorted" by case. Although we have noted that cross-serial orders may occur in Swiss-German subordinate clauses, other orders of constituents may also be permitted. Now, the mere fact that a certain subset of a language is non-context-free does not imply that the whole language is as well. This counterargument was effective against Postal's Mohawk argument, for instance, and the argument based on "respectively" constructions (Gazdar and Pullum, 1982).

Indeed, Swiss German does allow other constituent orders in relative clauses. For instance, the following examples are found to be grammatical:

(9)   mer em Hans   hälfed es huus   aastriiche
        we Hans-DAT helped the house-ACC paint

'we helped Hans paint the house'

(10)   mer em Hans es huus   aastriiche hälfed
        we Hans-DAT the house-ACC paint   helped
        'we helped Hans paint the house'

and, depending on the particular dialect and context, even

(11)   em Hans mer es huus   hälfed aastriiche
        hans   we the house helped paint
        'we helped Hans paint the house.'

Similar examples can be found for the triply embedded examples.

However, the proof presented does not depend on the exclusion of orders other than the cross-serial. In fact, through intersection with the appropriate regular expression *r*, all sentences with other constituent orders or lexical items were removed from consideration. The proof is thus independent of the part of the language thereby abstracted. It is similarly immaterial whether or not the semantics of the construction is cross-serial, as the proof rests completely on the form of the sentences viewed as strings. (In fact, in Examples (9) through (11) above, the semantics are not strictly cross-serial.) Finally, the argument does not hinge on any aspect of the *constituent structure* of the sentences whatsoever, since it is a purely formal stringset argument.

All that is critical is that no orders be allowed in which the case requirements of the verbs do not match the cases of the noun phrases (cf. Claim 3), but such clauses are found to be clearly ungrammatical whether cross-serial or not, e.g.,

(12)   *mer de Hans   hälfed es huus   aastriiche
        we   Hans-ACC helped the house-ACC paint
        'we helped Hans paint the house'

(13)   *mer em Hans   hälfed em huus   aastriiche
        we   Hans-DAT helped the house-DAT paint
        'we helped Hans paint the house'

(14)   *mer em Hans   lönd es   huus   aastriiche
      we   Hans-DAT let   the   house-ACC   paint
      'we let Hans paint the house'

(15)   *mer de Hans   lönd em   huus   aastriiche
      we   Hans-ACC let   the   house-DAT   paint
      'we let Hans paint the house'

(16)   *mer de Hans   es huus   aastriiche hälfed
      we   Hans-ACC the house-ACC paint   helped
      'we helped Hans paint the house'

(17)   *mer em Hans   em huus   aastriiche   hälfed
      we   Hans-DAT the   house-DAT   paint   helped
      'we helped Hans paint the house'

(18)   *mer em Hans   es huus   aastriiche lönd
      we   Hans-DAT the house-ACC   paint   let
      'we let Hans paint the house'

(19)   *mer de Hans   em huus   aastriiche lönd
      we   Hans-ACC the   house-DAT   paint   let
      'we let Hans paint the house'

(20)   *mer de Hans   haend wele   hälfe es   huus
      we   Hans-ACC have   wanted help   the   house-ACC
      aastriiche
      paint
      'we have wanted to help Hans paint the house'

(21)   *mer d'chind   lönd de Hans   hälfe
      we   the children-ACC   let   Hans-ACC   help
      es   huus   aastriiche
      the   house-ACC paint
      'we let the children help Hans paint the house'

(22)   *mer d'chind   de Hans   es   huus   lönd
      we   the children-ACC Hans-ACC the house-ACC   let
      hälfe aastriiche
      help   paint
      'we let the children help Hans paint the house.'

Thus, additional permitted orders of constituents do not provide a counterargument to our first two claims, or our conclusion.

4.3. *"Case Is Not Syntactic"*

An argument could be put forth that Claim 3 is in error. Case agreement, one might argue, need *not* hold for these sentences to be *syntactically* correct; case agreement, one would then hold, is actually extrasyntactic, perhaps even semantic. This type of argument was used against both the "respectively" non-context-freeness argument and the argument based on the digits of π (Gazdar and Pullum, 1982).

Clearly, the burden of proof is on the proponent of this straw man to furnish some evidence for the radical claim that case marking in Swiss German is a purely extrasyntactic or semantic notion. It would need to be demonstrated that the case requirements of verbs are completely predictable from their meanings. In particular, it is not sufficient to note that the case marking on NPs provides information as to the semantic role played by the NP in a clause.

Certainly, the native informants did not find the starred clauses above semantically anomalous, but ungrammatical. No consistent semantic distinction between raising verbs requiring a dative object and those taking an object in the accusative case seems forthcoming, nor do clear distinctions between the meanings of dative versus accusative NPs independent of context. Finally, in related languages, e.g., German and Dutch, case is widely considered a purely syntactic phenomenon.

4.4 *"Clauses are Bounded in Size"*

Finally, Claim 4 could be rejected. Much beyond triple embedding of clauses, judgments get weaker (though it should be noted that the judgments on Clause (5) and the even more deeply embedded Clause (8) did not seem to be on the margin of performance bounds). One could argue that the phenomenon of cross-serial clause structure is bounded by, say, five embeddings or, to be more generous, one hundred. In either case, the language with bounded cross-seriality would be context-free, regardless of case-marking properties.

Down this path lies tyranny. Acceptance of this argument opens the way to proofs of natural languages as regular, nay, finite. The linguist proposing this counterargument to salvage the context-freeness of natural language may have won the battle, but has certainly lost the war.

5. Conclusion

Using a particular construction of Swiss German, the cross-serial subordinate clause, we have presented an argument providing evidence that natural languages can indeed cross the context-free barrier. The linguistic assumptions on which our proof rests are small in number and quite weak; most of the proof is purely formal. In fact, the argument would still hold even if Swiss German were significantly different from the way it actually is, i.e., allowing many more constituent orders, cases and constructions, and even if the meanings of the sentences were completely different.

What has *not* been shown by this argument is equally important to keep in mind. By proving the non-context-freeness of the language of the Swiss-German competence grammar, we have still not demonstrated that natural languages are impossible, or even difficult, to parse. Both the Dutch and Swiss-German constructions are linear-parsable, and, were they not so in theory, performance constraints might well make them so. We have not demonstrated that powerful grammar formalisms with context-sensitive or even the weaker indexed power are essential for describing natural language. Indeed, the difficulty of finding evidence for the non-context-freeness of natural language remains a challenge and mystery.

In a more speculative vein, we believe that, though the search for tight formal constraints on grammars and restrictive mathematical properties of natural languages (in the spirit of the context-free hypothesis) is a worthy goal, the present research may be a clue leading in a slightly different methodological direction. It raises the possibility that the most revealing account of a natural language may be one in which the formalism describing the competence grammar is powerful, well beyond context-free power, but where the learning, parsing, and/or generation mechanisms provide the constraints that mutually allow learnability, parsability, and generability. The search for formalism restrictions should therefore be accompanied by research on precise models of language mechanisms, which may one day lead to a resolution of the Swiss-German paradox and challenge - to find theories that are powerful enough to yield revealing accounts of complex data, yet restrictive enough to be explanatory in form.

Footnotes

*The author would like to thank Beat Buchmann, Mark Domenig, Hans Huonker and Patrick Shann for their patience in providing the Swiss-German data, and the researchers at the Dalle Molle Institut pour les Etudes Semantiques et Cognitives for providing the impetus and opportunity to pursue this study. Special thanks go to Thomas Wasow for his extensive and continued support of this research.

**The research reported in this paper has been made possible in part by a gift from the System Development Foundation, and was also supported by the National Science Foundation grant number IST-83-07893 and by the Defense Advanced Research Projects Agency under Contract N00039-80-C-0575 with the Naval Electronic Systems Command. The views and conclusions contained in this document are those of the author and should not be interpreted as representative of the official policies, either expressed or implied, of the Defense Advanced Research Projects Agency, or the United States government.

[1] Several new arguments have been proposed recently. Those of Higginbotham (1984) and of Postal and Langendoen (1985) have been convincingly refuted by Pullum (1985). However, simultaneous, independent evidence based on the vocabulary of Bambara has been uncovered by Chris Culy (1985).

[2] Gazdar and Pullum (1982) provide a context-free grammar for the string set of Dutch, thus demonstrating its weak context-freeness, but they make no claim as to the linguistic motivation of the grammar.

[3] Though other orders are allowed as well, our argument is independent of such orders. See section 4.2.

[4] This claim holds, of course, only for those sentences in which the number of NPs equals the number of Vs, as in all of the sample clauses presented here. Only sentences of this form are critical in the proof below, so that this weaker claim is still sufficient. Thus optionality of objects does not affect the proof and is not an issue here.

[5] This can be seen clearly by taking another image to remove the w, x, and y, thereby yielding the standard example of a non-context-free language $a^m b^n c^m d^n$ (Hopcroft and Ullman, 1979, p. 128).

[6] A similar argument showing the non-context-freeness of a fictitious language Dutch' has been presented by Culy (1983).

References

Bresnan, J., R. M. Kaplan, S. Peters, and A. Zaenen: 1982, 'Cross-Serial Dependencies in Dutch', *Linguistic Inquiry* **13**, 613-635.

Chomsky, N.: 1963, 'Formal Properties of Grammars', in R. D. Luce, R. R. Bush, and E. Galanter (eds.), *Handbook of Mathematical Psychology*, Volume II, John Wiley, New York, pp. 323-418.

Culy, C. D.: 1983, 'An Extension of Phrase Structure Rules and its Application to Natural Language', Master's thesis, Stanford University, Stanford, California (May).

Culy, C. D.: 1985, 'The Complexity of the Vocabulary of Bambara', *Linguistics and Philosophy 8*, pp. 345-351.

Gazdar, G.: 1982, 'Phrase Structure Grammar', in P. Jacobson and G. K. Pullum (eds.), *The Nature of Syntactic Representation*, D. Reidel, Dordrecht.

Gazdar, G. J. M. and G. K. Pullum: 1982, 'Natural Languages and Context-Free Languages', *Linguistics and Philosophy* **4**, 469-470.

Higginbotham, J.: 1984, 'English is not a Context-Free Language', *Linguistic Inquiry* **15**, 119-126.

Hopcroft, J. E. and J. D. Ullman: 1979, *Introduction to Automata Theory, Languages, and Computation*, Addison-Wesley, Reading, Massachusetts.

Joshi, A. K.: 1983, 'How Much Context-Sensitivity is Required to Provide Reasonable Structural Descriptions: Tree Adjoining Grammars', to appear in D. Dowty, L. Karttunen, and A. Zwicky (eds.), *Natural Language Processing: Psycholinguistic, Computational, and Theoretical Perspectives*, Cambridge University Press, Cambridge, England.

Postal, P. and T. Langendoen: 1985, 'English and the Class of Context-Free Languages', *Computational Linguistics* **10**, 177-181.

Pullum, G. K.: 1985, 'On Two Recent Attempts to Show that English is Not a CFL', *Computational Linguistics* **10**, 182-186.

Rosenthal, R.: 1966, *Experimenter Effects in Behavioral Research*, Appelton-Century-Crofts, New York.

Thompson, H.: 1983, 'Cross Serial Dependencies: A Low-Power Parseable Extension to GPSG', *Proceedings of the 21st Annual Meeting of the Association for Computational Linguistics*, Massachusetts Institute of Technology, Cambridge, Massachusetts (15-17 June).

James Higginbotham

ENGLISH IS NOT A CONTEXT-FREE LANGUAGE

The question whether English is a context-free language has for some time been regarded as an open one. In this article, I argue that the answer is negative. I exhibit a *regular set L* (a set that can be generated by a finite-state grammar or accepted by a finite automaton), whose intersection with English is not a context-free language. Since context-free languages are closed under intersection with regular sets, that $L \cap$ English is not a context-free language proves that English is not a context-free language either.

The argument has two parts, one empirical and the other mathematical. Section 1 gives an overview of the argument, whose empirical premises are defended in section 2. Section 3 sketches in elementary terms the considerations behind the mathematical part of the argument; proofs are deferred to the appendix. Section 4 contains some concluding remarks.

1. The Argument

Let us define

$L =$ the woman such that (the man such that)* she (gave (this $\cup$ him) to (this $\cup$ him))* left is here

where '*' is Kleene-star and '$\cup$' expresses union. L is a regular set. Further, let us introduce some abbreviations by setting:

$X =$ 'the woman such that'
$Y =$ 'the man such that'
$Z_1 =$ 'gave him to him'
$Z_2 =$ 'gave him to this'
$Z_3 =$ 'gave this to him'
$Z_4 =$ 'gave this to this'

Linguistic Inquiry Vol. 15, No. 2, Spring 1984 225-234
© 1984 by *The Massachusetts Institute of Technology.*

W. J. Savitch et al. (eds.), The Formal Complexity of Natural Language, 335–348.

$W =$ 'left is here'

$$Z = \{Z_1\} \cup \{Z_2\} \cup \{Z_3\} \cup \{Z_4\}$$

'Z' thus abbreviates any expression among Z_1, Z_2, Z_3, Z_4.

The members of L are expressions beginning with an occurrence of X, followed by 0 or more occurrences of Y, followed by 'she', followed by 0 or more occurrences of Z, followed by W.

First, we assert (1):

(1) $L \cap$ English $= \{\ XY^n$ she $Z^n\ W$: n $\geqslant$ 0, and, reading from left to right, the number of occurrences of 'this' never exceeds by more than 1 the number of occurrences of 'him'$\}$

Let A be the abstract indicated on the right-hand side of (1). We can show (2):

(2) A is not a context-free language.

It follows from (1) and (2) together that English is not a context-free language.

2. That $L \cap$ English $= A$

Consider the shortest expression in the regular set L, namely (3);

(3) the woman such that she left is here

(3) is an English sentence, with subject NP, 'the woman such that she left' and predicate 'is here'. (3) belongs to A, being

$X\ Y^0$ she $Z^0\ W$

and so vacuously satisfying the condition on occurrences of 'this' and 'him'. The following expression also belongs to both A and L:

(4) the woman such that the man such that the man such that she gave this to him gave him to this left is here

(4) may be seen to be an English sentence from the phrase structure shown in figure 1. More transparently, perhaps, one can paraphrase (4) in a standard logical notation as (5), suppressing the predicates 'man' and 'woman' and using Russell's inverted iota for the definite article,

(5) $F(\imath x)\ (G(\imath y)\ (H(\imath z)(Jxz)\ y))$

with 'F ①' for '① is here', 'G ①' for '① left', 'H ① ②' for '①
gave ② to this', and 'J ① ②' for '① gave this to ②'. In this paraphrase, the pronouns are to be understood as bound variables, a point
to which we shall return.

Consider now the result of deleting or adding an occurrence of Y
or Z in (4). The result will be ungrammatical: the expressions of L
that belong to English all must be taken as having 0 or more center-
embedded 'such that'-relatives, so that any deletions or additions of Y
or Z will unbalance the parity of occurrences of heads and sentences,
resulting un ungrammaticality. Therefore, we conclude (6):

(6) If $X \, Y^i$ she $Z^j \, W$ belongs to English, then $i=j$.

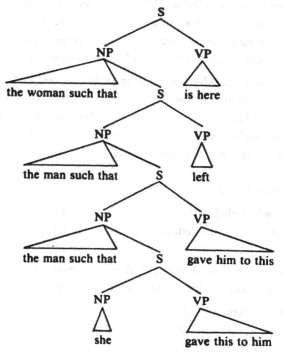

Figure 1

Besides parity of the number of occurrences of Y and Z, there is a
further condition on membership in A, as given in (1). We now argue:
first, that elements of A that meet this condition belong to English; and

second, that elements of L that have equal numbers of occurrences of Y and Z and belong to English also belong to A. This will complete the argument for (1).

An element of A has the property that within the part Z^n (which is always uniquely recoverable, and to which all occurences of 'this' and 'him' are confined, as we see by inspection of the definition of L) no initial segment Z^k of Z^n has more occurrences of 'this' than it does of 'him'. Counting each occurrence of Y or Z as one unit of length, this means that we can assign occurrences of 'him' to occurrences of 'the man such that' in a one-to-one fashion, such that no occurrence of 'him' is assigned to an occurrence of 'the man such that' that is less far from the center 'she' of the expression than the 'him' is. This condition is met, for instance, in (4). It is possible for it to be met in many different ways; this multiplicity of possible assignments occurs just when there is an initial segment of Z^n that contains more occurrences of 'him' than it does of 'this'.

We shall want another observation, this time about English. In general, if z is an ordinary English declarative sentence that contains an occurrence of a third-person pronoun that does not have to be taken as having its antecedent within z, then, where N is any noun that agrees properly with the pronoun in number and gender, the expression

the N such that z

is a well-formed English NP. Crucially, the occurrence of the pronoun may be arbitrarily deeply embedded, as in (7) where it is four clauses down:

(7)   the man such that [I thought that [the book that [you put on the shelf that [I bought for *him*]]] was interesting]

Where an expression as in (a)

(a) XY^i she $Z^{i-1} Z_q W$

belongs to A, $i \neq 0$, and $q = 1,2,3$ or 4, the expression (b),

(b) XY^{i-1} she $Z^{i-1} W$

got by removing the last Z and some Y, belongs to A also; for if (b) violated the condition on occurrences of 'this' and 'him', then (a) would violate it as well. Now, given that (b) is an English sentence, it follows that (c),

(c) Y^{i-1} she $Z^{i-1} Z_q$

got by adding Z_q to the right of (d),

(d) Y^{i-1} she Z^{i-1}

the center factor of (b), will also be an English sentence; the reason is that (d) will be an NP, and of course all of the Z's are Verb Phrases. The condition on A requires that, unless there are more occurrences of 'him' than there are of 'this' in Z^{i-1}, there be at least one occurrence of 'him' in Z_q; that is, that $q \neq 4$. Hence, in either case there are at least as many occurrences of 'him' as of 'this' in (c), and so at least one more occurrence of 'him' in (c) than there are of Y. (c) is an English sentence, then, that satisfies the condition that there is an occurrence of 'him' within it that does not have to be taken as bound within (c). Consequently, the generalization about English relatives with 'such that' implies that (e),

(e) Y^i she $Z^{i-1} Z_q$

the center factor of (a), is a well-formed English NP. Hence, (f)

(f) Y^i she $Z^{i-1} Z_q$ left

is an English sentence. (f) contains an occurrence of 'she' that need not (in fact, cannot) be taken as bound within (c). Hence, (g)

(g) the woman such that Y^i she $Z^{i-1} Z_q$ left
     is again an English NP, and (h)

(h) the woman such that Y^i she $Z^{i-1} Z_q$ left is here

is an English sentence. But (h) = (a). It follows that, if our generalization about English relatives with 'such that' is correct, every member of A is an English sentence.

It remains to argue for the converse inclusion, that every member of $L \cap$ English belongs to A. To derive this conclusion, we use the fact that English, unlike, say, quantification theory, does not allow anything like *vacuous quantification*. In particular, it does not allow relatives constructed with the *wh*-expressions or with 'such that' to occur without eligible positions to be related to in the clauses with which they are in construction. The prohibition against vacuity has been noted in the literature in connection with examples like (8) and (9):

(8)   *every book such that it rains

(9)   *the main such that I saw Mary[1]

Every expression in $L \cap$ English will have some number n of occurrences of Y, and each of these must be eligible to be related to some occurrence of 'him' somewhere among the n occurrences of Z. However, no occurrence of 'him' can be used twice for this purpose (that is, linked to two difference occurrences of Y). If that could happen, we would expect NPs such as (10) or (11):

(10)   *the man such that the man such that she gave this to him gave this to this

(11)   *the man such that I saw the man such that you saw him

It follows that any expression in $L \cap$ English must have not only just as many occurrences of Y as of Z, but also at least as many occurrences of 'him' as of Y. However, more is true. Since the only way of construing the expressions of $L \cap$ English as English sentences is as illustrated in figure 1, it is required in addition that for each initial segment Z^k of the Z's, there be at least k occurrences of 'him'. An expression that satisfies the weaker condition but not the stronger one is (12):

(12)   *the woman such that the man such that the man such that she gave this to this gave him to him left is here

(12) fails to be English, because the condition on vacuity is violated in the segment 'the man such that she gave this to this'. The expressions of $L \cap$ English all satisfy the stronger condition; but then they all belong to A. This completes the argument that $L \cap$ English $= A$.

3. That A is not a Context-Free Language

The reason A is not a context-free language is that context-free grammars cannot "keep track" of the type of multiple dependencies shown in (1). Context-free grammars can easily express single dependencies such as the one exhibited in the following language B, the canonical example of a language that is context-free but not a regular set.

$$\{a^n b^n : n \geqslant 1\}$$

A context-free grammar for B is given by means of the two rules:

$S \to a S b$
$S \to a b$

The following language C, however, is not a context-free language:

$$\{a^n b^n a^j : 1 \leqslant j \leqslant n\}$$

C has multiple dependencies, in the sense that the words in C must both have equal numbers of a's and b's in one part, with all the a's preceding all the b's as in the case of B, but also on the right a sequence of a's that does not overbalance the sequence of a's on the left.

The language A shows multiple dependencies of the same sort as the hypothetical B. For expository purposes, let us regard the expressions whose abbreviations are given in section 1 as if they were single, distinct letters; and let us further abbreviate 'she' by 'Q'. With these conventions, the regular set L is:

$$X\, Y^* Q(Z_1 \cup Z_2 \cup Z_3 \cup Z_4)^* W$$

and the members of A must all be of the form

$$X\, Y^n\, Q(Z_1 \cup Z_2 \cup Z_3 \cup Z_4)^n W$$

with the further condition that in no initial segment does the number of occurrences of Z_4 ever exceed the number of occurrences of Z_1. This further condition, expressing a second dependency on numbers of occurrences of expressions, takes A out of the class of context-free languages.

The standard device for proving that languages like C or A are not context-free is Ogden's Lemma of 1968, cited in the Appendix to this article in a form taken from Harrison (1978).[2] The more familiar "pumping lemma" for context free languages, for which the reader may refer to any textbook on formal languages and automata, is a special case of Ogden's Lemma. The latter, however, is more powerful; and indeed it would appear that the pumping lemma is by itself insufficient to prove that languages like C or A are not context-free. Besides Harrison (1978), Aho and Ullman (1972) contains a clear statement of the more powerful lemma.

The second dependency, responsible for A's not being a context-free language, has shown up on the empirical side as a condition prohibiting vacuous quantification. This condition appears to be universal among natural languages. Its imposition upon formalized languages will normally result in their not being context-free as well. By methods similar to those of this article, for instance, it can be shown that the set of formulas of quantificational logic that contain no vacuous quantifiers is not context-free. Harrison (1978) gives similar results for certain computer languages.

4. In Conclusion

Two further technical points may be noted. First, it does not appear possible to carry out a construction such as that given above for the case where, instead of 'such that' - relatives, true relative pronouns are used, the possible positions of binding being indicated in this event by gaps. The reason is that a position bound to a relative pronoun cannot be too deeply embedded, so that (13), for instance, is already ungrammatical:

(13)   *the woman who the man whom _____ gave this to _____
        left is here.

Second, the construction presented above uses center-embeddings, which are notoriously difficult to understand. It has not occurred to me how to reproduce it with unidirectional branching constructions; but it may well be possible to do so, and I should welcome any communication in this regard.

Not everybody who speaks English uses the 'such that' construction in relatives, although many do. Thus, strictly speaking, the most that can have been shown here is that the language of the author (and, I believe, of many of his readers) is not context-free. Such limitations, however, are inevitable in any inquiry of this kind.

The above argument cannot be taken at once as showing that some language having a *core grammar* in the sense of Chomsky (1981) is not context-free. However, give the ease with which the 'such that' construction may be grasped, the variety of human languages that indicate bound positions in relative clauses by pronouns, and the ubiquity of the prohibition against vacuous quantification in natural languages, I doubt very much that this further conclusion should not be drawn. In any event, once our attention turns to core grammar as the primary object of linguistic study, questions such as the one that I have tried to answer here are of secondary importance.

Appendix

We here carry through a direct demonstration that A is not a context-free language, applying Ogden's Lemma for the purpose. In executing the proof, we represent the spaces between words by terminals, inserting '#' to the right of every word.

The abbreviations of section 1 remain unchanged, except that we are now to consider '#' inserted according to the convention just adopted. Thus, for example, we now have

$Z_4 = $ 'gave#this#to#this#'

and the like.

Ogden's Lemma is the following assertion (I):

(I) Let G be a context-free grammar (V, Σ, S, P), where V is the set of variables, Σ the set of terminals, S the start symbol, and P the set of productions of G. Then there exists a number n depending on G such that, if K is any set of positions in any word z of the language $L(G)$ of G, and the cardinality of K exceeds n, there is a factorization

$$\phi = (u_1, u, w, v, v_1)$$

of z such that:

(i) w contains a position in K;

(ii)   either both u and u_1, or else both v and v_1, contain positions in K;

(iii)   the concatenation $u\ w\ v$ of the second through fourth factors of ϕ contains at most n positions in K;

(iv) $u_1\ u^i\ w\ v^i\ v_1$ belongs to $L(G)$, for every i $\geqslant$ 0.

Suppose now that G is a context-free grammar (V, Σ, S, P) such that $L(G) = A$, where $\Sigma =$ the English alphabet augmented by '#'. Choose n as in Ogden's Lemma (I), and let z be an expression

$$X\ Y^{2k}\ she\ \#\ Z_1^k\ Z_4^k\ W$$

with $k > n$. Let the set K of distinguished positions consist of the positions in the occurrences of Z_4 in z. Now, z belongs to A. So, let z be factored as follows,

$$\phi = (u_1,\ u,\ w,\ v,\ v_1)$$

satisfying (i)-(iv) of (I). We will show that, however the factors of ϕ are assigned compatibly with (i)-(iv), some expression that is an *iterate* of z, of the following form,

$$u_1\ u^i\ w\ v^i\ v_1$$

does not belong to A. This will complete the proof.

Let us factor z as

$$\psi = (X,\ Y^{2k},\ she\#,\ Z_1^k,\ Z_4^k,\ W)$$

We shall say that a factor of ψ *overlaps* a factor of ϕ if they have some positions in common, and that a factor of ψ is *confined* to a factor ϕ_j, $1 \leqslant j \leqslant 5$, of ϕ if every position in it is also in ϕ_j.

By (i) of (I) we have (a):

(a) $\psi_5 = Z_4^k$ overlaps $\phi_3 = w$

Suppose that ψ_5 overlaps ϕ_1 and ϕ_2. In this case, the first four factors of ψ are confined to ϕ_1. Hence,

$$u = xZ_4^j\, y$$

for some x and y, and some $j \geqslant 0$. Suppose that u contains some occurrence of 'this#'. Then the iterate

$$u_1 u^2 w v^2 v_1$$

of z will contain exactly $2k$ occurrences of 'him#', but at least $2k + 1$ occurrences of 'this#', and so will fail to belong to A. Therefore, u does not contain an occurrence of 'this#'. By the same reasoning, u cannot contain an occurrence of either of the letters 'g' or 'l': not 'g', because the number of occurrences of 'g' in an expression belonging to A must be exactly the same as the number of occurrences of Y; and not 'l', because each expression belonging to A has exactly one 'l' in it. We must, then, have $j = 0$, and $u = x\, y$ a nonempty substring of (i)

(i)   ave#this#to#this#

that does not reach so far as to contain an occurrence of 'this#'. Evidently, iterations u^i for any choice of u will produce substrings that do not occur in the members of A. Therefore, ψ_5 does not overlap ϕ_2, and by (ii) of (I) we conclude:

(b) ψ_5 overlaps $\phi_4 = v$, and also overlaps $\phi_5 = v_1$

Next, observe that every member of A contains exactly one occurrence of 'she#', which by (a) and (b) together must overlap either ϕ_1 or ϕ_2 or ϕ_3. Suppose it overlaps $\phi_1 = u_1$. Then $\psi_2 = Y^{2k}$ is confined to u_1, and every iterate of z contains exactly $2k$ occurrences of Y. Then, by reasoning quite like that leading to (b), v can contain no occurrences of 'g' or of '1' and must be a nonempty substring of (i), so that the iterates of z again fail to belong to A. Hence, $\psi_3 = $ 'she#' does not overlap u_1.

ψ_3 cannot be confined to u, since in that case the iterates of z will contain more than one occurrence of 'she#'. Hence, ψ_3 overlaps $\phi_3 = w$. Thus,

(c) $\psi_4 = Z_1^k$ is confined to ϕ_3.

From (a) and (b) it follows that the positions in the iterating fourth factor v of ϕ are all positions in $\psi_5 = Z_4^k$. But from (c) it follows that all occurrences of 'him#' in any iterate of z are confined to the center factor w; that is, no iterate of z contains more than $2k$ occurrences of 'him#'. Then, if the iterates of z are to belong to A, the iterating factor $v = \phi_4$ can contain no occurrences of 'this#'. As mentioned earlier, v cannot contain occurrences of '1'. Therefore, v must be a nonempty substring of (ii)

(ii)   gave#this#to#this#gave#this#to#this

that contains no occurrences of 'this#'. The iterates v^i of v will then contain substrings that are not substrings of any member of A. Then all possibilities lead to a contradiction, and $L(G) \neq A$. Note that (iii) of (I) was not needed in the proof.

This argument is complicated by our having to take into account the fact that the intuitively operative pieces of the members of A--namely, the words and phrases X, Y, etc.--are not single letters, but are instead composed of letters. Of course, our use of the written Roman alphabet is inessential; the argument can be reproduced for expressions given in phonetic transcription, ignoring the idiosyncrasies of English orthography.

Footnotes

[1]My premise, therefore, is that (8) and (9) are ungrammatical, and not merely hard, or even impossible, to interpret cogently. Likewise, relatively acceptable examples such as (i) and (ii) I take to be not English NPs, although they are interpretable as ellipses:

(i)   every triangle such that two sides are equal

(ii)   the number system such that 2 and 3 make 5

An alternative explanation for (8)-(9) and (i)-(ii) might be suggested; specifically, it may be proposed that all of these examples are grammatical NPs, although (8) and (9) are not interpretable in any natural way, perhaps owing to the irrelevance of the sentence following 'such that' to the content of the head noun.

For discussion of the alternative, I am indebted to a colloquium audience at the University of Massachusetts, and especially to Emmon Bach, Barbara Partee, Mats Rooth, and Edwin Williams. It does not seem to me likely to be correct, for the following reasons. First, the sentence following 'such that', even in cases like (i) and (ii), is in fact *never* interpreted as closed; rather, it is interpreted, where possible, as elliptical for a sentence that is not merely relevant to the content of the head noun, but further supplies a place into which binding is possible. Thus, (i) and (ii) are intuitively taken as elliptical for (iii) and (iv), respectively:

(iii)   every triangle such that two sides *of it* are equal

(iv)   the number system such that 2 and 3 make 5 *therein*

Their mode of interpretation, then, not only is consistent with, but further supports, the premise employed in this article. Second, notice that there is nothing semantically odd about sentences that use NPs of the sort shown in (8) or (9); for instance, (v), whose subject is (8), would, if grammatical, be logically equivalent to (vi):

(v)   every book such that it rains is on the table

(vi)   either every book is on the table, or it does not rain

Hence, the elliptical character of (i) and (ii), and similar examples, is a fact of grammar, for which the alternative suggestion provides no explanation.

[2]Harrison (1978, 186-187). Harrison refers to Ogden's Lemma as "the iteration theorem."

Acknowledgment

I am grateful to George Boolos for his careful scrutiny of an earlier draft. Any errors, of course, belong to me.

References

Aho, A.V. and J.D. Ullman (1972) *The Theory of Parsing, Translation, and Compiling*, Prentice-Hall, Englewood Cliffs, New Jersey.

Chomsky, N. (1981) *Lectures on Government and Binding*, Foris, Doredrecht.

Harrison, M. (1978) *Introduction to Formal Language Theory*, Addison-Wesley, Reading, Massachusetts.

Christopher Culy

THE COMPLEXITY OF THE VOCABULARY
OF BAMBARA

In this paper I look at the possibility of considering the vocabulary of a
natural language as a sort of language itself. In particular, I study the
weak generative capacity of the vocabulary of Bambara, and show that the
vocabulary is not context free. This result has important ramifications for
the theory of syntax of natural language.

A language can be defined, from the point of view of formal language
theory, as being "a set of strings of symbols from some one alphabet"
(Hopcroft and Ullman, 1979, p. 2), where a string is "a finite sequence of
symbols juxtaposed" (Hopcroft and Ullman, 1979, p. 1), and an alphabet
is "a finite set of symbols" (Hopcroft and Ullman, 1979, p. 2).[1] Given a
language, one can study its complexity in different ways. The weak generative capacity of a language is the complexity of the set of strings of the
language. The strong generative capacity of a language is the complexity
of the set of structures that are assigned to the strings of the language.

In terms of generative capacity, linguists usually think of the case
where the "alphabet" is the vocabulary of a natural language, and the
"strings of symbols" are strings of vocabulary items, i.e., sentences. There
has been a lot of controversy concerning the generative capacity, taken in
this way, of natural language. I will not go into details here, but see Pullum and Gazdar (1982) for a lengthy discussion, and Bresnan et al. (1982)
and Culy (1983) for more recent developments.

Returning to the definition of language, this time considering the
vocabulary of a natural language, we see that the vocabulary itself can be
thought of as a language in the above sense. In this case, the "alphabet"
is the set of morphemes of the natural language, and the "strings of

Linguistics and Philosophy 8 (1985) 345-351.

W. J. Savitch et al. (eds.), The Formal Complexity of Natural Language, 349–357.

symbols" are strings of morphemes. Given this observation that the vocabulary of a natural language is itself a language, we can study the weak and strong generative capacities of the vocabulary. For the rest of the paper, I consider the weak generative capacity of the vocabulary of Bambara, a Northwestern Mande language spoken in Mali and neighboring countries.

Bambara has a construction of the form Noun *o* Noun, where the two nouns have the same form. This construction translates as "whichever Noun" or "whatever Noun".[2]

(1)(a) wulu o wulu
  dog dog
  "whichever dog"

(b) malo   o malo
  uncooked rice rice
  "whatever uncooked rice"

(c) *wulu o malo[3]
    dog   rice

(d) *malo o wulu
    rice   dog.

This construction is very productive, with few, if any, restrictions on the choice of the noun.

There is evidence that the Noun *o* Noun construction belongs in the vocabulary rather than in the syntax. Bambara is a tone language, and as such it has two types of rules governing the interaction of tones: rules dealing with the interaction of adjacent lexical items, and rules dealing with the interaction of components of a compound, be it nominal, verbal, or whatever. Internally, the Noun *o* Noun construction does not follow the rules for adjacent lexical items, but rather has its own peculiar rule. (Cf. Bird et al., pp. 8-9, 166, for a description of the first sort of rules and for the Noun *o* Noun construction.) Thus, tonal evidence indicates that the Noun *o* Noun construction does indeed belong in the vocabulary rather than the syntax.

Bambara also has an agentive construction: Noun(N) + Transitive Verb(TV)+*la*, which translates as "one who TVs Ns".

(2)(a) wulu+nyini+la = wulunyinina[4]
    dog   search for
    "one who searches for dogs", i.e., "dog searcher"

(b) wulu+filè+la = wulufilèla
    dog   watch
    "one who watches dogs", i.e. "dog watcher"

(c) malo+nyini+la = malonyinina
    rice search for
    "one who searches for rice", i.e. "rice searcher"

(d) malo+filè+la = malofilèla
    rice watch
    "one who watches rice", i.e. "rice watcher".

This construction is also very productive, with interpretability being virtually the only restriction. In particular, the construction is recursive, that is, the noun in the construction can be of the same form.[5]

(3)(a) wulunyinina+nyini+la = wulunyininanyinina
    dog searcher search for
    "one who searches for dog searchers"

(b) wulunyinina+filè+la = wulunyininafilèla
    dog searcher watch
    "one who watches dog searchers"

(c) wulufilèla+ nyini+la = wulufilèlanyinina
    dog watcher search for
    "one who searches for dog watchers"

(d) wulufilèla+ filè+ la = wulufilèlafilèla
    dog watcher watch
    "one who watches dog watchers"

(e) malonyinina+ nyini+la = malonyininanyinina
    rice searcher search for
    "one who searches for rice searchers"

(f)   malonyinina+ filè+la = malonyininafilèla
rice searcher watch
"one who watches rice searchers"

(g)   malofilèla+ nyini+la = malofilèlanyinina
rice watcher search for
"one who searches for rice watchers"

(h)   malofilèla+ filè+la = malofilèlafilèla
rice watcher watch
"one who watches rice watchers".

These agentive nouns from the second construction can be used in the Noun *o* Noun construction.

(4)(a)wulunyinina o wulunyinina
dog searcher dog searcher
"whichever dog searcher"

(b)   wulufilèla o wulufilèla
dog watcher dog watcher
"whichever dog watcher"

(c)   wulunyininanyinina o wulunyininanyinina
one who searches for dog searchers
one who searches for dog searchers
"whoever searches for dog searchers"

(d)   wulunyininafilèla o wulunyininafilèla
one who watches dog searchers
one who watches dog searchers
"whoever watches dog searchers"

(e)   wulufilèlanyinina o wulufilèlanyinina
one who searches for dog watchers
one who searches for dog watchers
"whoever searches for dog watchers"

(f)   wulufilèlafilèla o wulufilèlafilèla
one who watches dog watchers
one who watches dog watchers
"whoever watches dog watchers"

(g) malonyinina o malonyinina
rice searcher rice searcher
"whichever rice searcher"

(h) malofilèla o malofilèla
rice watcher rice watcher
"whichever rice watcher"

(i) malonyininanyinina o malonyininanyinina
one who searches for rice searchers
             one who searches for rich searchers
"whoever searches for rice searchers"

(j) malonyininafilèla o malonyininafilèla
one who watches rice searchers
          one who watches rice searchers
"whoever who watches rice searchers"

(k) malofilèlanyinina o malofilèlanyinina
one who searches for rice watchers
            one who searches for rice watchers
"whoever searches for rice watchers"

(l) malofilèlafilèla o malofilèlafilèla
one who watches for rice watchers
         one who watches for rice watchers
"whoever watches rice watchers".

The two nouns still have to have the same form.

(5)(a)*wulunyinina o wulufilèla
dog searcher dog watcher

(b) *wulunyinina o malonyinina
dog searcher rice searcher

(c) *wulunyinina o malofilèla
dog searcher   rice watcher.

This very free process of redoubling causes the vocabulary of Bambara to be non-context-free[6,7] as I now show. Let B be the vocabulary of Bambara. Thus, B is a set of strings of morphemes. Let

$R = \{\text{wulu(filèla)}^{h}\text{(nyinina)}^{i} \quad o \quad \text{wulu(filèla)}^{j}\text{(nyinina)}^{k} \mid h,i,j,k \geqslant 1\}.$

The intersection of B and R is

$B \cap R = B' = \{\text{wulu(filèla)}^{m}\text{(nyinina)}^{n} \ o$

$\text{wulu(filèla)}^{m}\text{(nyinina)}^{n} \mid m,n \geqslant 1\}.$

B' is of the form $\{a^{m}b^{n}a^{m}b^{n} \mid m,n \geqslant 1\}$ (the o can be disregarded without loss of generality), and hence, it is easy to show that it is not context-free (cf. Hopcroft and Ullman, 1979, p. 136, Example 6.5). Since R is a regular language, and the intersection of a context-free language and a regular language is always a context-free language (cf. Hopcroft and Ullman, 1979, p. 135), if B were context-free, B' would also be context-free. But B' is not context-free, so neither is B. Thus, the vocabulary of Bambara is not context-free.

Note that the above argument does not determine how complex the vocabulary of Bambara is. It merely gives a lower bound for the weak generative capacity. Hence, one is led to the conclusion that the complexity of the vocabulary of a natural language can be more than context-free.

This argument raises several interesting points. The first point is, can one find a smallest upper bound for the complexity of the vocabulary of a natural language? One can also divide the vocabulary into subsets and consider the generative capacity of each subset. For example, in the above case of Bambara, B' was actually just a set of nouns. One could also consider verbs, adjectives, etc.

The other points have to do with syntax. For Bambara at least, and probably for many other languages (cf. Pullum and Gazdar, 1982; Langendoen, 1981; Carden, 1983) there are an infinite number of vocabulary items from which sentences can be formed. This is contrary to the definition of language given at the beginning since the "alphabet" is no longer finite. We can get around this point by saying that the syntax generates a language of strings of lexical categories (with all their features). The natural language is obtained by substituting items from the vocabulary for the lexical categories (which is how we tend to think of things, intuitively at least). That is, a natural language can be obtained by the composition of two other languages.

It turns out that once we allow the vocabulary of a language to be infinite, we have to have something like the substitution mentioned above if we want to keep the syntax in a reasonable state. Each symbol in the syntax must be introduced by some rule, so if we have an infinite number of vocabulary items to be introduced in the syntax, we have to have an infinite number of rules. This is a highly undesirable state of affairs from the point of view of the weak generative capacity of the syntax (cf. Culy, 1982; Peters and Uszkoreit, 1982). Thus, syntacticians studying weak generative capacity should consider the language to be strings of lexical categories rather than vocabulary items. Since the natural language is obtained by substitution, they do not have to worry about actual vocabulary items, just the lexical categories. That is to say, the study of the generative capacity of the syntax is independent of the study of the generative capacity of the vocabulary.

Acknowledgment

My sincere appreciation goes to Adama Koné and Saloum Soumaré and especially to the Center for the Study of Language and Information (CSLI), Stuart Shieber, and Thomas Wasow for their generous help in preparing this article. Of course, all deficiencies are the responsibility of the author.

Footnotes

[1] This is only one narrow point of view which ignores many aspects of language, including, among other things, the meanings associated with the symbols.

[2] The Bambara is transcribed in the official Malian orthography.

[3] I want to thank the two anonymous referees for pointing out the necessity of including the ungrammatical examples.

[4] Due to a very pervasive rule, /1/ becomes [n] after a syllable containing a nasal consonant or nasal vowel.

[5] These constructions soon become awkward, due to their length. However, my informants maintained the grammaticality of the examples.

[6] The Chomsky hierarchy is a means of classifying the complexity of languages. There are four successive levels, each level properly including the ones before it. The least complex level is that of regular languages, followed by context-free, context-sensitive, and finally recursively enumerable languages.

[7] This is in answer to Langendoen (1981), who states he knows of no language with a vocabulary more complex than a regular language.

References

Bailleul, C.: 1981, *Petit Dictionnaire Bambara-Français Français-Bambara*, Avebury Publishing Company, England.

Bird, C., J. Hutchison, and M. Kanté: 1977, *An Ka Bamanankan Kalan: Beginning Bambara*, Indiana University Linguistics Club, Bloomington, Indiana.

Bresnan, J., R. M. Kaplan, S. Peters, and A. Zaenen: 1982, 'Cross-serial Dependencies in Dutch', *Linguistic Inquiry* **13**, 613-635.

Carden, G.: 1983, 'The non-finiteness of the word formation component', *Linguistic Inquiry* **14**, 537-547.

Culy, C.: 1982, 'String Variables and Metarules', unpublished manuscript, Department of Linguistics, Stanford University, Stanford, California.

Culy, C.: 1983, *An Extension of Phrase Structure Rules and Its Application to Natural Language*, unpublished M.A. thesis, Stanford University, Stanford, California.

Hopcroft, J. E. and J. D. Ullman: 1979, *Introduction to Automata Theory, Languages, and Computation*, Addison-Wesley, Reading, Massachusetts.

Langendoen, T.: 1981, 'The Generative Capacity of Word-Formation Components', *Linguistic Inquiry* **12**, 320-322.

Peters, P. S., and H. Uszkoreit: 1982, 'Essential Variables in Meta-rules', paper presented at the annual meeting of the Linguistic Society of America, San Diego, December.

Pullum, G. K. and G. Gazdar: 1982, 'Natural Languages and Context-free Languages', *Linguistics and Philosophy* **4**, 471-504.

Walter J. Savitch

CONTEXT-SENSITIVE GRAMMAR
AND NATURAL LANGUAGE SYNTAX

Introduction

A theory of grammar, such as transformational grammar, context-free
grammar, categorial grammar, or any of the many descendants of these
grammatical formalisms, serves at least two functions. The formal model
should be rich enough to allow descriptions for the full range of data
observed for natural language syntax (or at least a good approximation to
the full range). Additionally, the formalism should embody a description
of the nature, and hence limits, of natural language syntax. The importance of the first function is obvious: if a theory is inconsistent with the
data it cannot be correct. The importance of the second function, or even
what it is, may not be as clear. Certainly, any theory must explain and
must ultimately aid understanding, but the meaning of these terms can be
illusive when applied to a formal model for natural language. This is especially true when the topic is weak generative capacity since that context
strips languages of all but their surface strings leaving them no structure
other than that of a mathematical set. In this context, the facts to be
explained are why natural languages produce the strings sets that they do,
and not some larger, or smaller, or incomparable collection of string sets.
The most obvious way that a theory can explain the phenomena of these
natural language string sets is to (weakly) generate exactly these sets. In
light of what we now know, it is trivial to produce a model that generates
"all possible" string sets, where "all possible string sets" means all recursively enumerable sets, or less formally all string sets that can be described
by any algorithmic process whatsoever. Hence, generating *exactly* the
string sets of natural languages becomes a problem of restricting power
rather than producing power.

Many grammar models, including most versions of transformational
grammar, are powerful enough to yield "all possible string sets" (i.e., all

358

W. J. Savitch et al. (eds.), The Formal Complexity of Natural Language, 358–368.
© *1987 by D. Reidel Publishing Company.*

recursively enumerable sets.) [See Bach and Marsh (1978), reproduced in this volume; Ginsburg and Partee (1969); Peters and Ritchie (1971); Salomaa (1971).] Such models are certainly adequate to describe any natural language string set. However, they do not meet the second function of a model. They do not tell us anything about which string sets are possible human languages. They do not tell us anything that can distinguish natural language syntax from any other classification task carried out by humans or other animals or machines. We may as well say that natural language syntax is described by Turing machines, Pascal programs, or idealized hand held calculators with no size limit on the integer arguments. Any of these models can generate all recursively enumerable sets and so presumably any natural language. All models that are this powerful witness no properties of human language other than the fact (or assumption) that it lends to some sort of algorithmic analysis. Hence, it makes sense to look for weaker models that more exactly capture the string sets produced by real and potential human languages.

An obvious candidate to consider in our quest for a characterization of weak generative capacity is the context-free grammar model. However, many researchers have a suspicion, or even a firm conviction, that the context-free grammar model is not capable of weakly generating all natural languages. [See for example, Shieber (1984), Higginbotham (1984), and Culy (1985) all reproduced in this volume.] On the other hand, the evidence available thus far indicates that there are very few features of human language that are beyond its capacity. [See for example Gazdar (1981), Pullum and Gazdar (1982), and Gazdar and Pullum (1985), all reproduced in this volume.] It thus makes sense to look for models that are somewhat more powerful than the context-free model but significantly less powerful than the most general transformational grammar models.

One class of grammars that lies between the context-free grammars and the grammars of unlimited power is the class of so called "context-sensitive grammars." These are the type 1 grammars of Chomsky (1959). In addition to lying strictly between the limited context-free model and the unlimited models, this model has at least one additional and desirable formal property that places it closer in character to context-free grammar than to the other extreme. Context-sensitive grammars generate only recursive sets; in other words, we can write a program to test whether a candidate string is or is not generated by a specified grammar. Thus, the adequacy of any particular grammar can be tested against any given data. This property is shared by context-free grammar and many other grammar models, but not by the powerful versions of transformational grammar. These formal properties make context-sensitive grammar sound like a plausible candidate for describing natural language syntax. Indeed, there seem to be no known proofs showing that any well known language structure is beyond the reach of context-sensitive grammar.

Context-Sensitive Grammar

Context-sensitive grammars are formally very similar to context-free grammars. Like context-free grammars they use rewrite rules to generate strings. However, they allow a wider class of rewrite rules. Rewrite rules for these grammars are of the form:

$\alpha\, A\, \beta \rightarrow \alpha\, \gamma\, \beta$, where α and β are arbitrary strings, A is a nonterminal symbol and γ is any nonempty string.

So one can think of such a rule as specifying that A may be rewritten as γ in the context of α on the left and β on the right.

Unfortunately, this class of grammars is not as interesting as the name "context-sensitive" might suggest. This is because the character of the class of languages generated is determined as much by the seldom emphasized restriction that γ be nonempty as it is by the fact that context may be used. If we omit the restriction that γ be nonempty, then the class of languages generated expands to the full class of recursively enumerable sets. A formal definition can append any name to any concept. However, it would be more appropriate and less misleading to call these grammars "nonerasing grammars" or "nonerasing context-sensitive grammars" rather than "context-sensitive grammars" and to use the unmodified term "context-sensitive grammar" for the unrestricted type 0 grammars of Chomsky, or perhaps to not use the name "context-sensitive grammar" as a technical term at all. But history dictates terminology and we will accept our lot and use the unfortunate, but accepted, terminology.

If we accept the standard definition of context-sensitive grammar, then, as shown by Kuroda (1964), the class of languages generated is exactly the class of languages generate by nondeterministic Turing machines with a linear bound on the amount of storage used. This class of languages is interesting because it is characterized by a specific bound on the amount of storage used. However, it does not appear to be particularly more interesting than any other class of languages characterized by a restriction on available storage. Indeed, most work on storage limited classes is either applicable to all such classes or is restricted to one of three different storage bounds (*log n*, polynomial in *log n*, and polynomial in *n*). Thus far there is no evidence to indicate that the storage bound associated with context-sensitive grammar is very special.

A Problem with Context-Sensitive Grammar

Perhaps a more telling reason to reject the class of context-sensitive grammars as a model for natural language is that the languages that they generate are in a sense just as structurally complex as those of the unrestricted (type 0) grammars. They do not generate all the recursively enumerable languages, but for each recursively enumerable language, they do generate a related language which intuitively is just as complex. The details are not very difficult to explain.

Suppose L is an arbitrary recursively enumerable language and that $ is some symbol that does not occur in any string of the language L. We will use $ to derive a related context-sensitive language that is intuitively just the language L with some extra markings added to the ends of sentences of L. To obtain the context-sensitive language we simply add a string of occurrences of $ to the end of each sentence in L. You can think of $ as being a kind of blank symbol. It serves no intuitive grammatical or semantic function whatsoever, but it is obligatory that a specified number of these be appended to the end of each sentence. Moreover, the number that is appended will differ from one sentence to another according to some, possibly very complex, rule. The formal statement of this result follows this paragraph. The notation $w\$^n$ used in the statement of the theorem means the string w followed by n occurrences of the symbol $.

We postpone a proof until after considering the consequences of this result.

Theorem: If L is any recursively enumerable set, then there is another language L' such that,

1.) L' is generated by a context-sensitive grammar, and
2.) for all candidate strings w:

  w is in L if and only if there is an n such that $w\$^{n}$ is in L', where $\$$ is some extra symbol (i.e., one that is not used in any string in L).

Although there is a very simple relationship between the language pairs L and L' mentioned in the theorem, the relationship is not as simple as a casual reading of the theorem might lead you to believe. There need not be any algorithm which, given a candidate string w, will calculate the number n mentioned in the theorem. Indeed, it can be proven that there are language pairs for which no such algorithm exits. Nonetheless, it is trivial to obtain the recursively enumerable language L given the context-sensitive language L'. All you need do is erase all the $\$$'s.

This theorem says that there is some clear sense in which all the recursively enumerable languages can be found among the context-sensitive languages. Thus, if the class of recursively enumerable languages is rejected because it is of unrestricted complexity, then the same argument can be convincingly applied to the class of context-sensitive languages and so to the corresponding class of grammars.

One can argue that this analysis is inappropriate for at least two reasons. First one can simply reject the idea of studying weak generative capacity at all. Other papers in this volume address that question. [See Peters (1987) and Wasow (1978).] We will not address the question in this paper, but will argue from the assumption that there is some point to studying weak generative capacity. The other argument is peculiar to this particular analysis. It can be claimed that the above theorem is not talking only about string sets but is in fact analyzing the structure of the language under discussion. Although this argument does at first glance seem reasonable, on closer inspection it proves to be empty. The above analysis of context-sensitive languages does not depend on or mention tree structure or any other type of structural description of the sentences. It only mentions string sets. No structural properties are attributed to the symbol $. It is just a symbol, nothing more. Moreover, if the context-sensitive languages in the theorem are treated as natural languages, then the symbol $ will appear in the surface sentence. If there were speakers of these languages, then they would say "$." Our discussion referred only to sets of surface strings of the languages and not to the sort of structures that are considered part of strong generative capacity.

It could also be argued that this result is a purely formal trick, almost a play on words. Embedding one language in another is often very simple, even if the task is to embed a very complex language in a very simple language. The set of all strings over a given alphabet is one of the simplest of all languages. It can certainly be generated by a context-free grammar. It is even a finite state language. Yet *every* language over the alphabet is a subset of it. Nonetheless, we would not argue that the set of all strings over an alphabet is too complex to be a natural language. On the contrary, we would argue that it is too simple. The fact that any set is a subset of it is not relevant. The plays of Shakespeare were contained in all the ink bottles of the world since before Shakespeare was born. However, we would not have found it easy to extract such plays given only a pen and a pot of ink. By contrast, it *is* very easy to get all the recursively enumerable languages if you are given all the context-sensitive languages. As our theorem indicates, all you need do is erase all the $'s. Those who require the name of a formal operation that is generally accepted as simple, can call it a "homomorphism." However, it is a particularly simple homomorphism. The phrase "erase the $'s" may be more appropriate for conveying just how simple the operation is.

Proof

The proof is not original here, but it is difficult to attribute it to any one source. It follows by what are now standard techniques and seems to be a by-product of the collective research of innumerable workers in complexity and formal language theory. A purely grammar-based proof can be built on the results in Savitch (1973). The proof we present here is based on the automata theoretic characterization of context-sensitive grammars proven in Kuroda (1964). The technique used has its roots in Ruby and Fischer (1965). Our proof will be informal and rather sketchy. It will be easy for the specialist in automata and formal language theory to formalize it, and the informality may make it more understandable to the nonspecialist.

As shown by Kuroda a language is generated by a context-sensitive grammar if and only if it is accepted by a nondeterministic linear bounded automaton. A linear bounded automaton is a restricted type of (single-tape) Turing machine. The restriction says that there is a bound on the amount of storage used by the machine. Specifically, there is a constant c (depending on the machine) such that for inputs (candidate sentences) of length n, the machine can use at most cn storage. By cn storage we mean that the machine can use at most that many squares on its tape. In less formal terms, this means that the machine can remember at most that many symbols. The fact that the machine can be nondeterministic is not important to the issue being discussed here. We will only use the weaker result that every language accepted by a deterministic (ordinary) linear bounded automaton is a context-sensitive language. We will show the following:

Lemma: If L is any recursively enumerable set, then there is another language L' such that,

1.) L' is accepted by a deterministic ("ordinary") linear bounded automaton.

2.) for all candidate strings w:

w is in L if and only if there is an n such that $w\$^n$ is in L' where $\$$ is some extra symbol (i.e., one that is not used in any string in L).

The Theorem follows directly from the lemma since any language accepted by a deterministic linear bounded automaton is a context-sensitive language. All that remains is to prove the lemma and so we embark on that task.

Let L be an arbitrary recursively enumerable language. It is well know that L is accepted by some (deterministic i.e., "ordinary") single tape Turing machine M. (In some theories this is just a definition; in other theories that use a different but equivalent definition of recursively enumerable languages it is one of the basic theorems.) Without loss of generality, we can assume that M has a one-way infinite tape with an infinite string of blanks to the right of the input, but that there is no tape to the left of the input. We can reprogram M to convert it into a linear bounded automaton M' that accepts a different language L' which has the properties in the lemma.

The reprogramming of M is as follows. We add an new input symbol $\$$. The reprogrammed machine M' first checks to see that the input is in the form $w\$^n$, where w does not contain the symbol $\$$. If it is not in this form, then it halts without accepting. That part is trivial and so we will only consider inputs that are of this form. Given an input that is of the form $w\$^n$, where the w does not contain any $\$$, M' computes just like the original M on input w, but it treats the symbol $\$$ as if it were the blank: If it reads a $\$$ it behaves as M would behave seeing a blank; whenever M would write the blank symbol, M' will instead write a $\$$. If M' ever gets beyond the string of $\$$'s and sees a true blank then it halts without accepting.

The only interesting cases are those with enough $\$$'s to allow the machine M' to compute without ever seeing a blank. We have programmed M' so that, in all other cases, it does not accept the input. Let us confine our attention to those cases in which there are sufficient $\$$'s to insure that M' never sees a true blank. Those cases are accounted for by (1) and (2) below:

(1)   accepts w.

This is trivially true since M' is mimicing M.

Conversely if the linear bounded automaton M accepts a string w, then it does so in a finite amount of time using a finite amount of tape. If we choose n to be larger than the amount of tape used then:

(2)   If M accepts w, then M' accepts $w\$^n$.

The lemma follows directly from (1) and (2). The theorem follows directly from the lemma.

Summary

We have seen that there is at least one intuitive sense in which the full class of recursively enumerable languages is embedded in the class of context-sensitive languages. Primarily for this reason, we contend that the class of context-sensitive languages is a poor choice for a formal model of natural language syntax.

Acknowledgment

This work was supported in part by NSF grant DCR86-04031.

References

Bach, E. and W. Marsh 1978, "An Elementary Proof of the Peters-Ritchie Theorem," NELS 8, Amherst, MA, November, 1983. (reproduced in this volume.)

Chomsky, N. 1956, "Three models for the Description of Language," *IRE Transactions on Information Theory* 2, 113-124.

Chomsky, N. 1959, "On Certain Formal Properties of Grammars," *Information and Control* 2, 137-167.

Gazdar, G. 1981, "Unbounded Dependency and Coordinate Structure," *Linguistic Inquiry* 12, 155-184. (reproduced in this volume.)

Gazdar, G. and G. K. Pullum, 1985, "Computationally Relevant Properties of Natural Languages and Their Grammars," *New Generation Computing*, 3, 273-306. (reproduced in this volume.)

Ginsburg, S. and B. Partee, 1969, "A Mathematical Model of Transformational Grammars," *Information and Control* 15, 297-334.

J. Higginbotham, 1984, "English is not a Context-Free Language," *Linguistic Inquiry* 15, 225-234. (reproduced in this volume.)

Hopcroft, J. and J. Ullman, 1979, *Introduction to Automata Theory, Languages and Computation*, Addison- Wesley, Reading, Mass.

Kuroda, S. Y., 1964, "Classes of Languages and Linear-Bounded Automata," *Information and Control* 7, 207-223.

S. Peters, 1987, "What is Mathematical Linguistics?," this volume.

Peters, S. and R. Ritchie, 1971, "On Restricting the Base Component of Transformational Grammars," *Information and Control* 18, 493-501.

G. K. Pullum and G. Gazdar, 1982, "Natural Language and Context-Free Language," *Linguistics and Philosophy*, 4, 471-504. . (reproduced in this volume.)

S. Ruby and P.C. Fischer, 1965, "Translational Methods and Computational Complexity," *Proc. Sixth Annual IEEE Symp. on Switching Circuit Theory and Logical Design*, 173-178.

Salomaa, A., 1971, "The Generative Capacity of Transformational Grammars of Ginsburg and Partee," *Information and Control* 18, 227-232.

Savitch, W.J., 1973, "How to Make Arbitrary Grammars Look Like Context-Free Grammars," *SIAM Journal on Computing* 2, 174-182.

T. Wasow, 1978, "On Constraining the Class of Transformational Languages," *Synthese* 39, 81-104. (reproduced in this volume.)

William Marsh and Barbara H. Partee

HOW NON-CONTEXT FREE IS VARIABLE BINDING?

0. Introduction

Within and across theoretical frameworks, linguists have debated whether various phenomena related to variable binding should be handled within syntax, as part of a syntax-to-semantics mapping, or possibly by one or more separate levels of rules or principles specifically dedicated to such phenomena. Relevant phenomena include the interpretation of pronouns and reflexives as bound variables and the binding of gaps or traces by WH-phrases or other operators. Given current interest in the generative capacity of alternative syntactic theories, it is important to note that whatever level of grammatical description deals with variable binding must involve some non-context-freeness if certain natural restrictions on well-formedness (spelled out below) are taken to belong to grammar at all. In this paper we investigate the formal properties of variable binding via an investigation of two restricted versions of predicate logic. We first review the familiar fact that the set L of *formulas* of first-order predicate logic (FOPL) (allowing free variables and vacuous quantifiers) is a context free (CF) language. We then consider two restricted sublanguages of L, the set S of *Sentences* of FOPL (formulas with no free variables), and the set U of formulas of FOPL with *no vacuous quantifiers*. Both S and U can be shown by established methods to be non-CF. We then describe the *indexed grammars* of Aho (1968); the class of indexed languages falls strictly between CF and context-sensitive languages. We show that indexed grammars can capture the no-free-variables constraint by exhibiting an indexed grammar for S. We then introduce and motivate our main conjecture, which is that indexed grammars cannot capture the no-vacuous-quantifiers constraint, i.e. that U is *not* an indexed language. In the last part of the paper, we discuss the linguistic relevance of our formal investigations.

369

W. J. Savitch et al. (eds.), The Formal Complexity of Natural Language, 369–386.

1. A CFG for a Fragment L of Formulas of FOPL.

For the issues that will concern us in this paper, we can restrict our attention to a very simple fragment of FOPL, with just one quantifier, one binary connective, and one binary relation. To assure an infinite supply of variables from a finite terminal vocabulary, we must "encode" variables as strings. This could be done in many ways, e.g. using "prime" ($'$) as a terminal symbol and generating x, x $'$, x $''$, x $'''$,..., or encoding subscripts as binary numbers and generating x0, x1, x10, x11,... We choose to generate x, xx, xxx,... as our variables; we will standardly abbreviate them as x, x^2, x^3,..., or equivalently as x_1, x_2, x_3,... (The former abbreviation accords with the usual conventions of formal language theory, while the latter makes our formulas look more like standard FOPL.) The choice of encodings of variables *can* matter, since e.g. the binary number choice would require "string-matching" power to check for identity or nonidentity of variables in some cases where our notation or the prime notation would require only "counting" power.

Our fragment L of formulas of FOPL is generated by the following CFG:

$$V_T = \{\&, =, \forall , x, (,)\}$$
$$V_N = \{S, V\}$$
$$S \to (S \ \& \ S) \qquad V \to Vx$$
$$S \to (V = V) \qquad V \to x$$
$$S \to \forall \ V \ S$$

2. "No Free Variables" is Not CF.

Let S be the set of *sentences* of L, i.e. the set of formulas of L with no free variables. It is known[1] that S is not CF.

Proof.

Let R be the set of all formulas of L of the form $\forall \ x^i(x^j = x^k)$.

R is a regular language.

$S \cap R$ is the set of all formulas of the form $\forall \ x^i(x^i = x^i)$.

$S \cap R$ is not CF. (Compare $a^n b^n c^n$.)

Since the intersection of a CF and a regular language is always CF, S itself is therefore not CF.

$$\text{Q.E.D.}$$

3. "No Vacuous Quantifiers" is Not CF.

Let U be the set of formulas of L with no vacuous quantifiers. That is, any occurrence of a quantifier $\forall\, x_i$ in a formula of U must be immediately followed by a formula in which x occurs free, so that the quantifier occurrence does actually bind at least one occurrence of a variable. U is not CF.

Proof

Let R$'$ be the set of all formulas of L of the form:
$$\forall\, x^i \,\forall\, x^j (x^k = x^m)$$
R' is a regular language.
$U \cap R'$ is the set of all formulas of the forms:
$$\forall\, x^i \,\forall\, x^j (x^i = x^j), \; i \neq j, \; \text{or}$$
$$\forall\, x^i \,\forall\, x^j (x^j = x^i), \; i \neq j.$$

(Note that if $i = j$ in either subcase, the first quantifier is vacuous and the formula is not in U; hence the condition $i \neq j$.) $U \cap R'$ is not CF. (Proof longer but straightforward.) Therefore U is not CF.

$$\text{Q.E.D.}$$

4. Indexed Grammars.

In his 1967 Princeton Ph.D. thesis, Alfred V. Aho defined indexed grammars, which characterize the class of indexed languages (the standard reference is Aho (1968), but a more readable introduction can be found in Hopcroft and Ullman (1979).) The indexed languages include all the CF languages and such non-CF ones as $a^n b^n c^n$ and $\alpha\alpha$ as well as S as we shall see below. The indexed languages are very properly contained in the class of context-sensitive languages.

Informally: an indexed grammar is like a CFG but with "index strings" attached to its non-terminals. The index strings work like pushdown stores: only the most recently added index is "visible", and "reading" an index removes it.

More formally, one kind of normal form for indexed grammars can be defined as follows:

1. The vocabulary consists of three finite disjoint sets, V_T (terminals), V_N (non-terminals), and V_I (indices).

2. Rules are of three sorts:

(i) <u>Index-introducing rules</u> are of the form A → B<i>, A,B ϵ V_N, i ϵ V_I.

(ii) <u>Index-removing rules</u> are of the form A<i> → B, A,B ϵ V_N, i ϵ V_I.

(iii) <u>CF rules</u> as in CFG's. In applying them, however, the index string (if any) on the mother node is copied onto all non-terminal daughters.

The next section includes an example of an indexed grammar and a derivation.

5. "No Free Variables" is an Indexed Language.

We show that indexed grammars can capture the "no free variables" restriction by exhibiting an indexed grammar for the language S defined in section 2 and showing some relevant derivations. In the grammar below, an index (sub) string $t^n s$ encodes the variable x^{n+1}; the heart of the bookkeeping lies in the configuration in Figure 1, which shows how each V node ("variable") comes to have an index string that includes encodings of all the quantifiers that c-command it and hence could bind it. Subsequent rules which expand V constrain it to expand as one of the encoded variables.

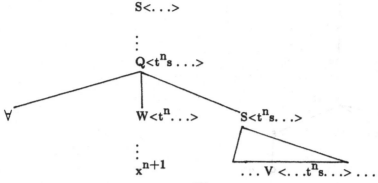

Figure 1

Here is an indexed grammar for S:

$$V_T = \{\&, =, \forall, x, (,)\}$$
$$V_N = \{S, V, Q, W, U, X, E\}$$
$$V_I = \{s, t\} \quad \text{"indices"}$$

$S \rightarrow (S \& S)$	$S \rightarrow Q<s>$	index-introducing rules
$S \rightarrow (V = V)$	$Q \rightarrow .Q<t>$	
$Q \rightarrow \forall\, WS$		
$V \rightarrow W$	$W<t> \rightarrow U$	
$V \rightarrow E$	$W<s> \rightarrow X$	index-removing rules
$U \rightarrow Wx$	$E<t> \rightarrow E$	
$X \rightarrow x$	$E<s> \rightarrow V$	

Figure 2 shows the beginning of a derivation, which the reader can use to check the operation of the index-introducing, index-removing, and CF (index-propagating) rules. Filling in the missing steps in the derivations from the three W nodes will show that a W must expand as the *first* variable encoded in its index string. The V nodes in figure 2 remain to be expanded.

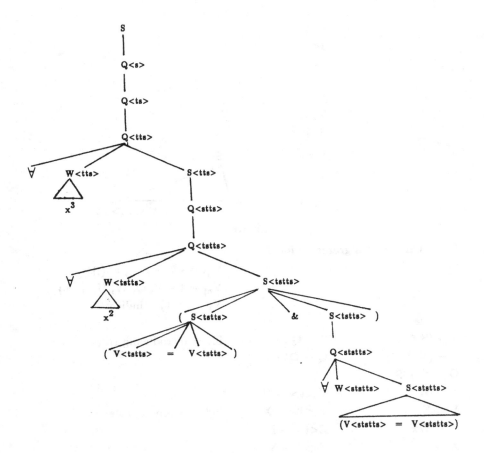

Figure 2

Now we want to show that each V node can be non-deterministically expanded into any of the variables encoded in its index string, but no others. We take V<tstts> as a representative and consider its possible expansion by cases in Figure 3.

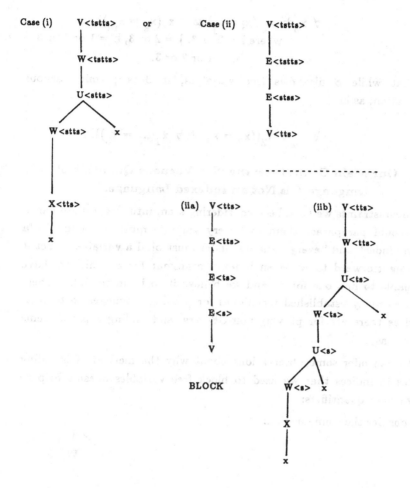

Figure 3

So V<tstts> can expand as either x_2 or x_3, and nothing else. Similarly V<ststts> can expand as x_1, x_2, or x_3. Sentences generated from the above tree are all sentences of the form

$$\forall \ x_3 \ \forall \ x_2((x_i = x_j) \ \& \ \forall \ x_1(x_k = x_m)),$$
where $i = 2$ or 3, $j = 2$ or 3, $k = 1$ or 2 or 3,
$m = 1$ or 2 or 3.

Note that while S disallows free variables, it does permit vacuous quantification, as in

$$\forall \ x_3 \ \forall \ x_2((x_3 = x_3) \ \& \ \forall \ x_1(x_3 = x_3)).$$

6. Our Main Conjecture: the "No Vacuous Quantifiers" Language U is Not an Indexed Language.

The two constraints we have been considering seem intuitively quite parallel; we could paraphrase them as "every variable must be bound by a variable-binder" and "every variable-binder must bind a variable." Yet it was straightforward to write an indexed grammar for S, while we have been unable to find one for U, and we believe it to be impossible. There are not as many established techniques for proving languages to be non-indexed as there are for proving non-CF-ness, and finding a proof seems not to be easy.

We can offer some observations about why the method of encoding variables in indices that we used to block free variables doesn't help to block vacuous quantifiers:

(i)   Consider the configuration:

For S, we encoded an x_3 in the index of the lower S and propagated it downward to signal that an x_3 *may* occur anywhere within that S. For U, an x_3 *must* occur somewhere within that S, and furthermore must occur free, i.e. with no more closely c-commanding occurrences of $\forall \ x_3$ above it.

(ii) In the grammar for S, each V node introduced by the rule S $\rightarrow$ (V = V) carried an index string encoding the indices of all the quantifiers that bound it, and we could non-deterministically choose any of those indices as we expanded the V. But if we wish to prevent vacuous quantifiers, the expansions of the V's can no longer be independent from one another: if there are two quantifiers $\forall \, x_2 \, \forall \, x_3$ c-commanding a formula with three variables, and the first two variables are expanded as x_3, then the third *must* be expanded as x_2. But there is no bound on how far down the "licensing" variable may be.

(iii) Suppose we began the indexing as we did for S; then a node S<tstts>, which we may abbreviate as $S<x_2 x_3>$ would "mean" "x_2 and x_3 *must* occur free below". Now consider the conjunction rule, S → (S & S). We don't want to produce

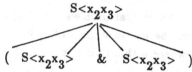

as we did before, since it's *not* required that x_2 and x_3 both occur free in each conjunct. Rather, we would have to find a way to produce all of the following:

S	&	$S<x_2 x_3>$
$S<x_2>$	&	$S<x_2 x_3>$
$S<x_3>$	&	$S<x_2 x_3>$
$S<x_2 x_3>$	&	$S<x_2 x_3>$
$S<x_2>$	&	$S<x_3>$
$S<x_2 x_3>$	&	$S<x_3>$
$S<x_3>$	&	$S<x_2>$
$S<x_2 x_3>$	&	$S<x_2>$
$S<x_2 x_3>$	&	S

We don't see how to do this with the permissible rules of index grammars.

<u>Note:</u> It's easy to imagine a natural bottom-up procedure which makes the free variables of the conjunction just the union of the free variables of the conjuncts; but we don't see any way to mimic such a procedure with an

indexed grammar, which (a) must be defined top-down, and (b) can't read´ an index symbol without erasing it.

(iv) Suppose we are expanding an S which has encoded on it that the variables x_1, x_3 and x_4 must occur free within it. Then we must not allow the expansion S → (V = V), since that can have at most two distinct variables. But again the problem is that we can't read indices without erasing them; we can't check that there are more than two variables without losing our record of what the first two were.

7. A Further Conjecture.

The restriction against vacuous quantifiers has two aspects, of which one can be partly handled.

(i) The central problem: For any occurrence of a quantifier $\forall\, x_i$, there must be an occurrence of x_i in the S which it c-commands (but no limit on where within that S it occurs.)

(ii) The secondary problem: A quantifier $\forall\, x_i$ may be vacuous even if it c-commands an x_i, if there is another "lower" occurrence of $\forall\, x_i$ binding that x_i. If we could prevent a quantifier from c-commanding another quantifier which uses the same variable, we would have only the central problem to worry about.

Consider formulas in prenex form:

$$\forall x^{n_1} \quad \forall x^{n_2}. \ldots \quad \forall x^{n_k}(\ldots) \text{ no quantifier in } (\ldots)$$

If all the n_i could be required to be distinct, then preventing vacuous quantification for such formulas would involve only the central problem. But can even that be done by an indexed grammar?

Let D be the set of all prenex prefixes´ of the form

$$ab^{n_1}\ ab^{n_2} \ldots ab^{n_k} \text{ such that if } i = j, \text{ then } n_i = n_j.$$

Conjecture 2: D is not an indexed language.

Observation: If we require $n_1 < n_2 < \ldots < n_k$, then D as so modified *is* an indexed language. A natural way of generating it changes the encoding of variables so that $Wt^{n_1}st^{n_2}s \ldots t^{n_k}s$ produces $x^{n_1+n_2+\cdots+n_k}$. A similar move could block nested identical quantifiers in non-prenex formulas. And 'expressive power' is unaffected by this restriction.

But even if the quantifiers can be regimented in this way, the central problem remains, and our main conjecture stands, even for the set of formulas in prenex form with quantifiers regimented as above.

8. Linguistic Issues.

Do these results or the outcome of our main conjecture affect the question of whether English or other natural languages are CF? Not necessarily. They don't even show that first-order predicate logic is non-CF, since there is no *a priori* reason to impose either constraint in the *syntax* of FOPL. It is not clear, moreover, that there is any reason to stipulate either restriction in the semantics of FOPL either. Vacuous quantifiers are benign but otiose: a formula with vacuous quantifiers receives the same interpretation as the same formula with the vacuous quantifiers omitted. The set of sentences (or closed formulas) *is* often accorded special status: it is customary to first give a recursive definition of the set of formulas, then define what it is for an occurrence of a variable to be *bound,* then define *free* as not bound, then define a sentence as a formula with no free occurrences of variables. It is really the semantic interpretation rules that give the notions *free* and *bound* their significance, but it is necessary to have syntactic definitions of them as well in order to give a sound proof theory. It is less clear that there is any essential need for the notion of *sentence;* it plays no role in the recursive definition of the set of formulas, since it is crucial for the expressive power of the language to do the syntactic and semantic recursion on formulas rather than sentences. One reason for interest in sentences is that they have a truth value independent of assignment of values to variables, but that semantic property also holds of some open formulas such as $x_3 = x_3$ and $(Px_1 \& {\sim}Px_1)$. Perhaps sentences are simply the largest natural syntactically definable subclass of formulas with a truth value independent of assignment. But even if the languages S and U are of no inherent syntactic importance, the notions of free and bound variables are, and we conjecture that close analogs of our formal results could be obtained for the problem of characterizing free variable occurrence´ and bound variable occurrence´ syntactically -- e.g. trying to generate a language in which an occurrence of x_i was preceded by a special symbol * if it was a free occurrence and by \$ if it was a bound occurrence. We conjecture that there is an indexed grammar but no CF grammar which generates a * in front of every free occurrence (and only bound variables after \$), but that no indexed grammar can generate a \$ in front of every bound occurrence (and only free variables after *.) If these conjectures are correct, we could say that the *distinction* between bound and free variables is beyond the power of CF grammars, and one direction of the distinction is beyond the power of indexed grammars.

For natural languages, the difficulty of assessing the relevance of these formal results is compounded by the existence of controversial open questions about the best division of linguistic labor among different components of the grammar or different sets of rules and principles. Certainly it would not be unreasonable for a theorist to argue that if English was CF except for variable-binding phenomena, then that should count as some evidence for the existence of a CF syntactic component and a separate component for handling variable-binding. Another theorist might reply, "But at least you've conceded that there has to be some non-CF power somewhere".[4] It seems that in order to pursue such arguments fruitfully, we need formal measures of the power of systems of syntax-cum-semantics, including syntactic generative capacity, the "expressive power" of the semantics, and the power of the systems for mapping from syntax to semantics.

As a case in point, Higginbotham (1984) argues that English is not CF on the basis of *such that* relative clauses. His argument depends on the claim that NP's like "every triangle such that two sides are equal", "a number system such that $2 + 2 = 5$," and "costumes such that you can't tell the good guys from the bad guys" are ungrammatical. In a footnote he addresses the contention that such NP's are grammatical, argues that insofar as they are acceptable they are interpreted as elliptical, and that their necessarily elliptical mode of interpretation supports his position. But in the absence of any theory of what it would mean for a whole grammar, including interpretation, to be CF or not, it does make a difference whether the NP's in question are judged *syntactically* ill-formed or not; if not, Higginbotham's arguments have no effect on the question of whether English syntax is CF or not.

Suppose we did regard as syntactically ill-formed those NP's containing *such that* clauses in which there was no pronoun available to be construed as bound by the *such that*. And suppose our conjecture that U is non-indexed is correct. It would then be interesting to ask whether Higginbotham's argument that English is not CF could be strengthened to an argument that English is not an indexed language. The constraint Higginbotham is focusing on is that *such that* cannot be a vacuous variable-binder, which is analogous to the constraint that makes U non-indexed. But Higginbotham does not put overt indices (subscripts on pronouns and operators) into the syntax; he considers rather the problem of trying to generate just those strings to which a consistent indexing *could* be applied in such a way that no *such that* would come out vacuous. The formal problem appears at first to boil down to the question of whether the following language, which Higginbotham demonstrates to be non-CF, is also non-indexed:

> $A = ab^n q(c_1 \cup c_2 \cup c_3 \cup c_4)^n d$, with the further condition that in no initial segment does the number of occurrences of c_4 ever exceed the number of occurrences of c_1.

This language *is* indexed; the following indexed grammar generates it.

$$V_T = \{a, b, c_1, c_2, c_3, c_4, d, q\} \quad V_N = \{S, T\} \quad V_I = \{i, k\}$$

$$S \rightarrow aT{<}k{>}d \qquad\qquad\qquad T{<}i{>} \rightarrow bTc_1$$
$$T \rightarrow bTc_2 \qquad\qquad\qquad\qquad T \rightarrow T{<}i{>}$$
$$T \rightarrow bTc_3 \qquad\qquad\qquad\qquad T{<}k{>} \rightarrow q$$
$$T \rightarrow bT{<}i{>}c_4$$

However, Higginbotham used only a subset of *such that* constructions, sufficient to demonstrate non-CF-ness. A larger subset, in which there was no bound on the number of NP positions within each relative clause, might well form the basis for a proof that English is non-indexed if such constraints are put into the syntax. (This leads to another formal conjecture, which we leave open: consider a language L' like L but with only a single variable x, and consider the sublanguage U' consisting of all those formulas of L for which each occurrence of x *could* be assigned a subscript in such a way that the resulting formula contains no vacuous quantifiers. Is U' also non-indexed?)

Another important caveat that must be borne in mind in trying to apply the formal results to natural languages is that neither the no-free-variable constraint nor the no-vacuous-quantifier constraint would necessarily force a language beyond CF if there were additional constraints on where variables and variable-binders could occur. As the GPSG literature amply demonstrates, the association of WH-phrases with gaps in English can be handled by a CFG; threats to CF-ness have arisen from languages like Swedish (Engdahl 1980) with *fewer* constraints on WH-extraction than English. Locality constraints of various kinds, as well as constraints on multiple extractions and crossed dependencies, can all help serve to limit the variable-binding possibilities to ones describable by CFG's even with constraints against free variables or vacuous quantifiers. Reflexives, for instance, seem generally to be interpreted as bound variables; but in most languages there are tight locality constraints which keep their distribution within the capacity of a CFG to describe.

The fact that words like *every* and *some* occur as determiners rather than sentence-prefixes in English and perhaps all languages means that the no-vacuous-quantifier problem does not arise for them; syntactically, each determiner occurrence is locally paired with a common noun occurrence, and in the semantics, the interpretation of the noun phrase introduces a variable for the quantifier to bind whether or not there are any subsequent pronouns interpretable as further variables bound by the same quantifier. Also, (thanks to Janet Fodor for raising this issue), one cannot conclude from the fact that a syntax like May's including a rule of Q-movement at LF may be able to guarantee no vacuous quantifiers that that syntax generates a non-CF language; it might, but one cannot be sure without further investigation, since there are additional constraints imposed by the grammar (e.g. each quantifier originates in a deep structure NP position, and

Q-movement is subject to various constraints) which could in principle cut the language down to a CF subset of a non-indexed language.

English also contains "unselective quantifiers" (Lewis 1975) like *always, in many cases,* etc., but these typically do not require any overt syntactic element to bind; their semantics is notoriously flexible, but the question of what sort of power is required to describe their semantics is one which must await the development of formal measures of power in domains other than syntax.

One further point deserves mention. In order to generate the set of formulas of FOPL with CFG, we had to generate variables as phrases rather than as terminal symbols, so as to keep the terminal vocabulary finite. We don't know whether it's possible to interpret variables compositionality if the interpretation of x^{n+1} must be built up from the interpretation of x^n. If an adequate semantics for variable-binding phenomena requires an infinite stock of variables, one would want to know something about the formal properties of grammars with an infinite terminal vocabulary, which we do not. Such considerations might also weigh in favor of separating variable-binding from syntax proper in the division of labor among components.

To summarize this section, we have drawn no firm conclusions about the CF-ness of natural languages from our formal results, and have urged caution in any attempt to do so. If our conjecture is correct, some variable-binding languages are not only not CF, but non-indexed. This raises a host of interesting questions for further research, both on how natural languages manage (if they do) to keep these phenomena from forcing the syntax into non-CF-ness, and on how to characterize the formal properties of other components of a grammar so as to be able to pursue further the question of whether "there must be some non-CF-ness somewhere," and to define and explore potentially even more interesting questions about the formal properties of full grammars including syntax, semantics, and the mapping between them.

Acknowledgements

Our thanks to the gifted students in the 1982 and 1983 Hampshire College Summer Studies in Mathematics, and to the participants in the Fall 1983 seminar on Mathematical Linguistics taught by Marsh and Emmon Bach at UMass., to Emmon Bach especially for focusing attention on the need for formal studies of the power of combined systems of syntax and semantics and to Mats Rooth for helping to stimulate the genesis of our main conjecture. Marsh's work was partially supported by National Science Foundation grant #1ST 8314396.

Footnotes

1. This result and the corresponding result for the language defined in section 3 have been available in the "oral tradition" for some time, but we do not know of any standard written reference for them, perhaps because they are straightforward to prove when the question arises. The result for S may have first come to attention in the study of the syntax of ALGOL, a programming language which requires all variables to be declared before they are used; if this requirement is put into the syntax, the language is not CF, but otherwise it is CF -- it is a matter of choice whether to call programs which fail to satisfy the requirement syntactically ill-formed or well-formed but uninterpretable (Pullum 1983). For standard methods for filling in the details of the proofs in sections 2 and 3, see Hopcroft and Ullman (1979).

2. While the set of S of sentences of L does have some independent interest in logic and some programming languages, the set U does not, as far as we know.

3. We thank those colleagues who have tried and failed to prove or refute the conjecture in the six months since we came up with it. Should we thank them by name (they include some fine mathematicians who have worked with indexed grammars), or should we assume that they would prefer to stay off the record? Deep Throat thinks the conjecture is true.

4. The earliest reference we know of to the non-CF-ness of variable-binding phenomena and its relevance to the question of what component(s)

should handle variable-binding phenomena in natural language is Fodor (1970), which is marred by a non-proof of the non-CF-ness of "no vacuous quantifiers" but includes a very careful discussion of the difficulty of drawing any immediate linguistic conclusions from the formal results. Partee (1979a) and (1979b) contain some speculations about the inter-connections among unbounded syntactic rules, variable-binding semantic rules, and the non-CF-ness of the set of sentences of FOPL; some of these are too vague to evaluate precisely, but at least one claim made in Partee (1979a) seems to be false, namely that it is clearly the "unboundedness" of variable binding that is responsible [for the non-CF-ness of S].

References

Aho, Alfred V. (1968) "Indexed Grammars - An Extension of Context-Free Grammars", *JACM* 15, 647-671.

Engdahl, Elisabet (1980) *Questions in Swedish,* unpublished doctoral dissertation, University of Massachusetts, Amherst.

Fodor, Janet, (1970) "Formal linguistics and formal logic" in John Lyons, ed., *New Horizons in Linguistics,* Penguin Books Ltd., Middlesex, pp. 198-214.

Higginbotham, James (1984) "English is not a Context-Free Language", *Linguistic Inquiry,* 15, 225-234.

Hopcroft, J. E. and J. Ullman (1979) *Introduction to Automata Theory, Languages and Computation,* Addison Wesley.

Lewis, David (1975) "Adverbs of quantification", in E. L. Keenan, ed., *Formal Semantics of Natural Language,* Cambridge Univ. Press, Cambridge, (3-15).

Partee, Barbara (1979a) "Montague Grammar and the Well-Formedness Constraint", in F. Heny and H. Schnelle, eds., *Syntax and Semantics,* vol. 10 (275-313).

Partee, Barbara (1979b) "Constraining Montague grammar: a framework and a fragment", in S. Davis and M. Mithun (eds.) *Linguistics, Philosophy and Montague Grammar,* University of Texas Press, Austin (52-101).

Pullum, Geoffrey K. (1983) "Context-freeness and the computer processing of human languages", *Proceedings of the 21st Annual Meeting of the Association for Computational Linguistics,* pp. 1-6.

EPILOGUE

Gerald Gazdar and Geoffrey K. Pullum

COMPUTATIONALLY RELEVANT PROPERTIES OF NATURAL LANGUAGES AND THEIR GRAMMARS

Abstract

This paper surveys what is currently known about natural language morphology and syntax from the perspective of formal language theory. Firstly, the position of natural language word-sets and sentence-sets on the formal language hierarchy is discussed. Secondly, the contemporary use by linguists of a range of formal grammars (from finite state transducers to indexed grammars) in both word-syntax (i.e. morphology) and sentence-syntax is sketched. Finally, recent developments such as feature-theory, the use of extension and unification, default mechanisms, and metagrammatical techniques, are outlined.

1. Introduction *

Our starting assumption is that as computers continue to increase in complexity and functionality by orders of magnitude, it will in due course become not just desirable but actually necessary for them to have command of natural languages (henceforth NLs). They will need NL ability if they are to be used to their full capacity by human beings, whether expert or not. In this paper we review some crucial things that must be kept in mind as the necessary research and development is done to make it possible for computers to attain competence in NLs.

An article such as this cannot cover the entire extent of the field of natural language processing (NLP). We focus here on grammar: syntax, morphology, and lexicon. Omitted from our discussion for reasons of space

New Generation Computing 3 (1985), 273-306. Copyright © 1985 OHMSHA, LTD.

W. J. Savitch et al. (eds.), The Formal Complexity of Natural Language, 387–437.

are considerations having to do with the two endpoints of a linguistic system: meaning and sound. We have too little to say about computational implementation in semantics to merit a section here, but clearly this is a topic of fundamental importance that needs to be addressed at length. The same can be said for the crucially interrelated areas of pragmatics and multisentence discourse. Also omitted is any consideration of the recognition or synthesis of speech. What we do offer in this paper is a survey of recent results in the theory of NLs and their grammars, with an emphasis on issues and properties that appear to be of computational relevance.

There is a crucial connection between the theory of parsing and the formal theory of languages: *There can be no parsing without a grammar.* There are two senses in which this is true, we believe. To begin with, it is true trivially, in that a working parser for any language automatically instantiates a definition of its membership, and hence necessarily embodies a grammar. But there is a less trivial sense in which we must recognize that parsing implies the existence of a grammar. It is clear enough in the literature on the definition and parsing of programming languages, but it has often been denied in the context of the much larger and richer multipurpose languages spoken by humans. As we shall hope to show, for serious, theoretically-based reasons, engineering in a domain as complex as NL will have to be based on what linguists can determine about the structure of languages.

The definition of the language that a parser instantiates need not by any means be perspicuous one. Moreover, it will be an implementation-specific definition; and implementations--even implementations of a programming language that is thought to be well understood--can differ significantly and unexpectedly. It is for this reason that computer scientists have turned in recent years away from procedural definitions of the semantics for programming languages and toward denotational semantics (see e.g. Stoy.[152]). Rather similar considerations hold when we consider writing programs that process NL input: both syntactically and semantically, we need to have a secure definition of the NL (or approximation to a NL) that we are processing if we are to have any idea how the system should behave under a wide range of conditions. Parsability is thus connected to definability, and it is therefore essential for parser-designers to pay attention to the grammar for the language they are trying to parse.

In assessing whether some formal theory of grammar is an adequate theory for NLs, at least the following two criteria are relevant:

(1) Does it permit NLs, considered as sets of strings, to be defined?

(2) Does it permit significant generalizations about the defined NLs to be expressed?

In the second section of this paper, we look at the current state of knowledge in respect of the first of these questions. In the third section, we look at the use linguists have made of the grammatical tools made available by formal language theory, and make reference to the parsers that have been constructed with the help of these tools. In the fourth section, we look selectively at some recent syntactic developments that are addressed to the second question.

2. Language Types

NLs can be regarded under a useful idealization as sets of strings of symbols, and can thus be made amenable to mathematical analysis of a straightforward kind. In this section, we look first at NL lexicons (i.e. word sets) construed as sets of strings defined over a vocabulary of atomic morphological elements, and then, in the second subsection, at NLs themselves (i.e. sentence sets), which are standardly construed as sets of strings defined over the set of well-formed words. (Notice that in formal language theory, the term **word** denotes a string that is a member of a language, and linguists use the term **sentence** for this; when we speak of words in this paper, we always mean words in a dictionary sense, and in the syntax of a NL these correspond to the atomic symbols of the terminal vocabulary.) Occasionally, when it is relevant to do so, we will make a comment about the properties of the sets of structural representations or parses that are associated with the strings. However, our primary concern in this section is with sets of strings.

2.1 Words

If we regard a sentence of a NL as a string of words, then there is a fundamental difference between the formal nature of NLs and the usual formalizations of computer programming languages. Although there may be structure to the individual symbols such as names of constants and variables that are the terminal symbols in the grammar of a programming language, that structure is usually trivial. For example, a variable name may be simply any string of alphanumeric symbols that does not appear on the list of reserved words. Moreover, such structure as a terminal symbol has is simply a matter of concatenation of symbols, and has no contribution to make to the syntax.

Things are different with the set of words in a NL. Words are not trivial in their structural properties. In many cases they have a complex internal constituent structure and a set of idiosyncratic properties that are crucial for determining aspects of the syntactic structure of sentences. Consider one simple example from English. The verb *donate* has a stem *don* (also appearing in *donor*) and a verb-forming derivational suffix *-ate* (also appearing in *translate*); we can regard these as atomic symbols. The usual linguistic terminology for such word components is **morpheme**. *Donate* also has the property (shared with the synonym *give*) of syntactically demanding cooccurrence with a noun phrase and a prepositional phrase with *to* (as in *donate this money to the church*); it has the property (not shared by *give*) of not co-occurring with two following NP's (we do not find **donate the church some money* [the prefixed asterisk being used here to indicate a string disallowed by the grammar]); it has the property of not allowing intransitive use (contrasting with *translate*: compare *How does this translate into Japanese?* with the ungrammatical **When did this money donate to the church?*; it forms a related noun ending in the morpheme *-ion* denoting the act or result of donating (unlike, say, *berate*; donating something constitutes a donation, but berating someone does not constitute a **beration*); and so on.

Many items in many languages have much more complicated lexical properties than this; for example, all of the inflectional morphology of *donate* is predictable (*donate, donates, donated, donating*), whereas this is not at all true of the verb *be* (cf. *am, are, is was, were been, being*). Defining the complete sets of lexical items in a NL with all their internal structure and associated properties is a nontrivial language-definition task. The following subsections deal with various logical possibilities concerning the character of such languages.

[1] Finite languages

Do all languages have a finite lexicon? The common sense answer is "yes"; after all, dictionaries contain all the words in a language, and, while dictionaries may be very long (the *Oxford English Dictionary* runs to 12 very large volumes), they are not infinitely long. But the common sense answer is incorrect: there are few if any languages whose dictionaries contain all the words of the language. No Finnish dictionary contains all the possible forms of Finnish verbs - each one has around 10,000 inflected forms. In languages (such as certain American Indian languages, e.g. Tuscarora) that allow a noun stem to be incorporated into a verb stem, the number of distinct inflected forms for each verb goes into the millions.

However, this example only shows the premise on which the common sense answer is based to be false. It does not cast doubt on the answer itself. But we do not have to look far to find the evidence we need. Most languages employ word-formation processes that can apply iteratively to each other's output, and, in so doing, trivially induce an infinite language: Some lexical items are made up by compounding stems from a technical vocabulary (e.g. *deoxyribonucleic*) or by compounding out of whole words (*CPU-cycle-consumptive*) or by reduplicating affixes or stems (*anti-anti-missile-missile-missile*). Noting this, Langendoen[94] posed the question of what the power of the word-formation component of the grammar had to be. Since, as we have just seen, NL lexicons are typically not finite, that grammar cannot simply be a list. In the following subsections we explore the alternatives to a list.

[2] Finite state languages

Langendoen[94] raises in a short note the issue of whether infinite word-sets in NLs are always regular sets like, e.g., the set (*great-*)*-

grandparent in English (a great-great-grandparent is the parent of a great-grandparent). He notes an incorrect claim to the contrary by Bar-Hillel and Shamir,[6] and characterizes some unattested but imaginable situations which, if found in the morphology of a NL would render the word-sets non-finite-state. He notes that actual word-sets encountered in NLs up to that time had apparently always been finite-state, though there was no reason in principle why they should be.

[3] Context-free languages

Langendoen[94] also points out that certain patterns of prefixation and suffixation could in principle lead to a non-context-free (non-CF) word-set, yet (a fortiori, given the claim of the previous subsection) no language yet known appeared to have a non-CF word-set. He observed that if certain prefixes demanded the presence of certain suffixes, non-finite-state word-sets of (e.g.) the type $\{a^m c b^n \mid m = n+1\}$ could result. He also notes that if substrings of arbitrary length could be reduplicated (doubled), word-sets that were not even CF could be derived.

Of both the finite-stateness property and the CF-ness property, Langendoen asks whether the absence of NL word-sets lacking them is accidental, or whether it is "a consequence of some yet-to-be formulated principles of word-formation" (p. 321).

[4] Beyond the context-free languages

Facts recently reported by Culy[24] suggest that Langendoen's question can now be answered. Bambara, an African language of the Mande family, seems to have a set of words that is not a CFL. Culy notes that Bambara forms from noun stems compound words of the form "Noun-o-Noun" with the meaning "whatever N". Thus, given that *wulu* means "dog", *wulu-o-wulu* means "whatever dog." But Bambara also forms compound noun stems of arbitrary length; *wulu-filela* means "dog-watcher," *wulu-nyinila* means "dog-hunter," *wulu-filela-nyinila* means "dog-watcher-hunter," and so on. From this it is clear that arbitrarily long words like *wulu-filela-nyinila-o-wulu-filela-nyinila* "whatever dog-watcher-hunter" will be in the language. This is a realization of one of the hypothetical situations imagined by Langendoen,[94] in which reduplication applies to a class of stems whose members have no upper length bound. Culy provides a formal demonstration that this phenomenon renders the entire word-set of Bambara non-CF.

Alexis Manaster-Ramer has observed in unpublished lectures that other languages offer similar phenomena; he finds reduplication constructions that appear to have no length bound in Polish, Turkish, and a number of other languages.

This discovery raises a very interesting question: how hard can the recognition problem be for words in the (typically infinite) vocabulary of a NL? In fact, we believe that no significant problem arises for known non-CF cases, all of which involve simple string reduplication. This is fairly easy to show, as pointed out to us by Carl Pollard (personal communication). Determining whether the first half of a substring is identical to its second half takes time proportional to the length of the string. A standard algorithm for parsing CFLs, such as the CKY algorithm, could therefore be modified to included an operation of this sort as well as the usual operation of comparison against right hand sides of rules. For example, if a string x is analyzable as a noun, i.e. if $N \Rightarrow {}^{+}x$, then a string $x\text{-}o\text{-}y$ could be allowed also to be analyzed as a noun provided $x = y$. The CKY algorithm runs in cubic time, so the modified algorithm will too, the string-comparison adding only a linear element to the total time taken. Hence recognition of strings in a language that fails to be CF solely in virtue of the occurrence of reduplication has a time complexity no worse than the general problem of CFL recognition.

We do not know whether there exists an independent characterization of the class of languages that includes the regular sets and languages derivable from them through reduplication, or what the time complexity of that class might be, but it currently looks as if this class might be relevant to the characterization of NL word-sets.

2.2 Sentences

In this section we take NLs to be sets of sentences, and sentences to be strings of words in the linguist's sense. As in the case of NL lexicons discussed above, the question we are addressing is: what is the smallest known natural class of formal languages that can reasonably be taken to include all the NLs?

[1] Finite languages

This section will be brief since it is so obvious that NLs are not finite languages. Indeed, as far as is known, no NL is a finite language. The range of constructions that make a language infinite is typically rather large. Coordination, for example, always permits an unbounded number of conjuncts (whether this happens by iteration or by nesting is irrelevant). And, in English, for example, adjectives can be iterated indefinitely (*a nice, large, cheerful,..., well-lit room*), as can relative clauses, which can contain verb phrases which can contain noun phrases which can contain relative clauses which...

[2] Finite state languages

Chomsky's[19] claim that NLs are not in general finite-state was correct, although his own argument for the non-regular character of English was not given in anything like a valid form, as has often been remarked (cf. Daly[25] for a thorough critique). However, the following argument, patterned after a suggestion by Brandt Corstius (see Levelt,[98] pp. 25-26), is valid. The set (1):

$$\{\text{A white male (whom a white male)}^n \text{ (hired)}^n \text{ hired another white male.} \mid n > 0\} \tag{1}$$

is the intersection of English with the regular set (2):

$$\text{A white male (whom a white male)}^* \text{ hired}^* \text{ another white male.} \tag{2}$$

(In ordinary grammatical terms, this is because each occurrence of the phrase *a white male* is a noun phrase which needs a verb such as *hired* to complete the clause of which it is the subject.) But (1) is not regular; and the regular sets are closed under intersection; hence English is not regular. *Q.E.D.*

It is perfectly possible that some NLs happen not to present the inherently self-embedding configurations that are likely to make a language non-regular. Languages in which parataxis is used much more than hypotaxis (i.e. languages in which separate clauses are strung out linearly rather than embedded) are common. However, we would expect non-regular configurations to be at least as common in the languages of the world. There are a number of languages that furnish better arguments for a non-regular character than English does; for example, according to Hagège,[48] center-embedding phenomena in grammar seem to be commoner and more acceptable in several Central Sudanic languages than they are in English.

The fact that NLs are not regular sets is both surprising and disappointing from the standpoint of parsability. It is surprising because there is no simpler way to obtain infinite languages than to admit the operations of concatenation, union, and Kleene closure on finite vocabularies, and there is no obvious a priori reason why humans could not have been well served by regular languages. And it is disappointing because if NLs were regular sets, we know we could recognize them in deterministic linear time using the fastest and simplest abstract computing device of all, the finite state machine. Of course, given any limitation to finite memory in a given machine, we are in fact doing just that, but it is not theoretically revealing to use this as the basis for an understanding of the task.

[3] Deterministic context-free languages

The finite state languages, luckily, are not the only languages that can be efficiently recognized: there are much larger classes of languages that have linear-time recognition. One such class is the deterministic CFLs (DCFLs), i.e. those CFLs that are accepted by some deterministic pushdown stack automaton. It would be reasonable, therefore, to raise the question of whether at least some NLs were DCFLs. To the best of our knowledge, this question has never previously been considered, much less answered, in the literature of linguistics or computer science. Rich[123] is not atypical in dismissing the entire literature on DCFLs, LR parsing, and related topics without a glance on the basis of an invalid argument (from subject-verb agreement) which is supposed to show that English is not even a CFL, hence a fortiori not a DCFL.

English cannot be shown to be a non-DCFL on the grounds that it is ambiguous. Ambiguity must be carefully distinguished from inherent ambiguity. An inherently ambiguous language is one such that all of the grammars that weakly generate it are ambiguous. LR grammars are never ambiguous; but the LR grammars characterize exactly the set of DCFLs, hence no inherently ambiguous language is a DCFL. But it has never been argued, as far as we know, that English or any other NL is inherently ambiguous. Rather, it has been argued that a descriptively adequate grammar for it should, to account for semantic intuitions, be ambiguous. But obviously, a DCFL can have an ambiguous grammar; **all** languages have ambiguous grammars.

The relevance of this becomes clear when we observe that in NLP applications it is often taken to be desirable that a parser or translator should yield just a single analysis of an input sentence. One can imagine an implemented NL system in which the language accepted is properly described by an ambiguous CF-PSG but is nonetheless (weakly) a DCFL.

The idea of a deterministic parser with an ambiguous grammar, which arises directly out of what has been done for programming languages in, for example, the **yacc** system (Johnson[67]), is explored for natural languages in work by Fernando Pereira and Stuart Shieber. Shieber[144] describes an implementation of a parser which uses an ambiguous grammar but parses deterministically. The parses uses shift-reduce scheduling in the manner proposed by Pereira,[111] and uses rules for resolving conflicts between parsing actions that are virtually the same as the ones given for **yacc** by Johnson.[67]

We believe that techniques such as LR parsing which come straight out of programming language and compiler design (and which have much greater formal interest and variety than has often been recognized; see Bermudez[10] for some theoretical explorations) may be of considerable interest in the context of NLP applications. For example, Tomita[160] uses pseudo-parallelism to extend the LR technique to encompass multiple parses in NLP, and Shieber goes so far as to suggest psycholinguistic implications. Interestingly, human beings are prone to fail almost as badly as Shieber's parser on certain types of sentence that linguists would regard as grammatical (basically, sentences that lack the prefix property -- that is, they have an initial proper substring which is a sentence).

[4] Context-free languages

The belief that CF-PSGs cannot cope with the structure of NLs, and hence that NLs are not CFLs, is well entrenched. Introductory linguistics textbooks and other pedagogically oriented works have falsely stated that such phenomena as subject-verb agreement show English to be non-CF (see Pullum and Gazdar[120] for references). This is not so. Even finite state languages can exhibit dependencies between symbols arbitrarily far apart. To take an artificial example, suppose the last word in every sentence had to bear some special marking that was determined by what the first morpheme in the sentence was; a finite automaton to accept the language could simply encode in its state the information about what the sentence-initial morpheme was, and check the last word's marking against the state before accepting.

Expository works in the field of generative grammar have generally offered nothing that could be taken seriously as an argument that NLs are not CFLs. Worse, even the technical literature exhibits a quarter-century of mistaken efforts to show that not all NLs are CFLs. This history is carefully reviewed by Pullum and Gazdar.[120] In addition to the fallacies concerning agreement just mentioned, they deal with arguments based on

(1)   *respectively* constructions (Bar-Hillel and Shamir[6] ; Langendoen[93])

(2)   English comparative clauses (Chomsky[20])

(3)   Mohawk noun-stem incorporation (Postal[117])

(4) Dutch infinitival verb phrases (Huybregts[58])

(5) assertions involving numerical expressions (Elster[28]).

Such mistaken efforts have continued:

(6) English *such that* clauses (Higginbotham[50])

(7) English "sluicing" clauses (Langendoen & Postal[97])

Both these arguments are based on false claims about what is grammatical in English (see Pullum[119]).

However, recently at least one apparently valid instance of a natural language with a weakly non-CF syntax has been found. Shieber[146] argues that the dialects of German spoken around Zurich, Switzerland, show evidence of a pattern of word order in certain subordinate infinitival clauses that is very similar to that observed in Dutch: an arbitrary number of noun phrases (NP's) may be followed by a finite verb and a specific number of nonfinite verbs, the number of NP's being a function of the lexical properties of the verbs, and the semantic relations between verbs and NP's exhibiting a crossed serial pattern: verbs further to the right in the string of verbs take as their objects NP's further to the right in the string of NP's. The crucial substrings have the form $NP^m V^n$. In a simple case, where $m = n = 5$, such a substring might have a meaning like

Alf watched Bob let Cal help Don make Ed work   (3)

but with a word order corresponding to

Alf	Bob	Cal	Don	Ed	watched	let	help	make	work
NP_1	NP_2	NP_3	NP_4	NP_5	V_1	V_2	V_3	V_4	V_5

This construction does not render Dutch non-CF, as was shown in Pullum and Gazdar.[120] But in Swiss German, unlike Dutch, there is an additional property that makes this phenomenon relevant to stringset argumentation: certain verbs demand dative rather than accusative case on their objects, as a matter of pure syntax. This pattern will in general not be one that a CF-PSG can describe. For example, if we restrict the situation (by intersecting with an appropriate regular set) to clauses in which all accusative NP's (NP_a) precede all dative NP's (NP_d), then the grammatical clauses will be just those where the accusative-demanding verbs (V_a) precede the dative-demanding verbs (V_d) and the numbers match up; schematically:

$$NP_a{}^m NP_d{}^n V_a{}^m V_d{}^n \qquad\qquad (5)$$

But this schema has the form of a language like $\{a^m b^n c^m d^n \mid n > 0\}$, which is non-CF. Shieber presents a rigorously formulated argument along similar lines to show that the language does indeed fail to be a CFL because of this construction.

It is possible that other languages will also turn out to be non-CF, though the necessary configurations of properties seem at present to be very rare. Certain properties of Swedish have given rise to suggestions in this direction, though no careful argument has been published; Carlson[17] notes a possibly non-CF reduplication construction in the syntax of Engenni, an African language, though he does not regard the case as clear; Alexis Manaster-Ramer (personal communication) suggests that the English idiomatic construction exemplified by *RS-232 or no RS-232, this terminal isn't working* (where the pattern *X or no X* is essential to acceptability, and *X* can take infinitely many values) also illustrates this possibility; and there may well prove to be properties of other languages that are worth investigating further.

[5] Indexed languages

The indexed languages (ILs, Aho[2]) are a natural class of formal languages which form a proper superset of the CFLs and a proper subset of the context-sensitive languages. The class includes some NP-complete languages (Rounds[132]). They are of interest in the present context because no phenomena are known which would lead one to believe that the NLs fell outside their purview. In particular, it is clear that indexed grammars are available for the Swiss German facts and for most other sets of facts that have been even conjectured to hold problems for CF description (but cf. Marsh & Partee[101] for a possibly harder problem, relating more to semantics than syntax).

The indexed languages thus provide us, at least for the moment, with a kind of upper bound for syntactic phenomena. We can no longer be surprised by non-CFL patterns (though their rarity is a matter of some interest), but we should be very surprised at, and duly suspicious of, putatively non-IL phenomena.

[6] Beyond the indexed languages

As we have just indicated, we do not believe that any currently known facts give one reason to believe that the NLs fall outside the ILs, and in the absence of such facts, the conservative conclusion to draw is that the NLs fall within the ILs. Chomsky[21] has speculated in rather vague terms that NLs may not even be recursively enumerable sets, but this speculation amounts to a rejection of the idealisation that makes generative grammar a possible enterprise, and, as such, it is not a speculation that we can see any grounds for embracing or any point in considering.

Unlike Chomsky, Hintikka[51] has actually argued that English is not recursively enumerable, since a decision as to grammaticality for some of its sentences depends, in his view, on an undecidable question of logical equivalence. His argument (which, incidentally, Chomsky[21] rejects) is based on a controversial claim concerning the grammaticality of sentences containing the word *any*, and is closely tied to a controversial proposal for game-theoretic treatments of the semantics for natural languages. As such, the claim is highly theory-dependent and we will not consider it further here.

Langendoen and Postal[96] also argue that English is not recursively enumerable (and nor is any other natural language), on the grounds that the simplest and most general idealization of natural languages is one that allows them to have sentences of infinite length. Of this, we note simply that if it is accepted, the questions discussed above can be rephrased as questions about the finite-length-string subsets of the natural languages. It is only these subsets that are of computational interest anyway.

3. Grammar Types and their Parsers

The theoretical linguist's primary criterion in evaluating a type of grammar has always been its ability to capture significant generalizations within the grammar of a language and across the grammars of different languages. However, capturing significant generalizations is largely a matter of notation, and classes of grammars, taken as sets of mathematical objects, have properties which are theirs independently of the notations that might be used to define them. Thus they determine a certain set of string sets, they determine a certain set of tree sets, they stand in particular equivalence relations, and so on. Unfortunately, theoretical linguists have consistently confused grammar formalisms, with grammars. This tendency reaches its apogee in the "Government Binding" framework associated with N. Chomsky and his students where the formalism employed entirely lacks a mathematical underpinning in terms of a class of admissible grammars.

Thanks to the confusion just noted, argumentation purporting to show that some class of grammars will necessarily miss significant generalizations about some NL phenomenon has been woefully inadequate. Typically it has consisted simply of providing or alluding to some member of the class which obviously misses the generalization in question. But, clearly, nothing whatever follows from such an exhibition. Any framework capable of handling some phenomenon at all will typically make available indefinitely many ugly analyses of the phenomenon. But this fact is neither surprising nor interesting. What is surprising, and rather disturbing, is that arguments of this kind (beginning, classically, in chapter 5 of Chomsky[19]) were taken so seriously for so long.

In this section we are concerned, not with the formalisms that have been employed in recent grammatical and morphological work, but rather with the underlying formal grammars that have been assumed, and with the parsers that have been used with these grammars.

3.1 Words

Linguists use the term "morphology" to refer to that branch of their subject that deals with the internal syntax of words. The subject was much studied in the 1940's and 1950's but was then largely neglected for two decades. The following subsections briefly examine some recent developments.

[1] Finite state transducers

The idea of using finite state transducers (FSTs) to determine the mapping between syntactic and morphological/phonological structures originates in Johnson,[66] but current interest in the topic was provoked by unpublished work of Kaplan and Kay.[73] Their proposal involved the use of a cascade of two-tape FSTs to mediate between a phonemic representation of a word and a more abstract lexical representation. It is in principle possible to convert any such cascade of FSTs into a single (large) FST. Subsequent work by Koskenniemi[89] showed that a serial arrangement of FSTs could be replaced by a parallel arrangement. It is quite feasible to reduce the latter to a single FST, although implementation is also possible without any reduction. A lot of further work has been done, both of a computational character (Karttunen,[74] Gajek et al.,[39] Khan et al.[84]),and on various languages including English(Karttunen and Wittenberg[76]), Japanese (Alam[4]), Rumanian (Khan[83]), French (Lun[99]), and Finnish (Koskenniemi[88]). The basic Koskenniemi two-tape model can handle infixation and (finite) reduplication but not, it seems, in an elegant or perspicuous manner. The most recent work by Kay[80] has explored the use of n-tape FSTs (for n greater than 2) in order to handle such phenomena as the vowel harmony and discontinuous roots found in Semitic languages.

[2] Context-free phrase structure grammars

The classical structuralist model of morphology, dubbed "Item and Arrangement" by Hockett,[54] which was prevalent in the 1940's and 1950's, was essentially a CF-PSG model although, of course, it predated the mathematical theory of CF-PSGs. This model of lexical structure was radically inconsistent with the transformationalist view of sentence syntax that became dominant in the 1960's. The latter claimed, in effect, that there was no distinction to be made between the syntax of words and the syntax of sentences; they were to be handled with the same machinery and that machinery was not CF-PSG.

But recent influential work has seen a return to an Item and Arrangement position, though not *eo nomine*, most notably in that of Selkirk[143] who argues that "English word structure can be properly characterized solely in terms of a context-free grammar". In fact, Selkirk then goes on to employ context-sensitive rules to handle the subcategorization requirements of affixes although there is no need for her to do so. Interestingly from our perspective, Selkirk appears to regard the CF-PSG hypothesis that she espouses as the most conservative hypothesis that could be espoused. She never considers the possibility of using finite state machinery, and yet none of the phenomena she deals with show any trace of strict context-freeness when viewed language-theoretically. It may be true, however, that the structure of words cannot be adequately handled in terms of finite-state grammars; Carden[16] briefly argues that this is so. We discuss Selkirk's work further in Section 3.3[1], below.

[3] Context-sensitive phrase structure grammars

In an influential 1979 thesis on Semitic word structure, McCarthy[104] claimed that "morphological rules must be context-sensitive rewrite rules, and no richer rule type is permitted in the morphology" (p. 201). Like Selkirk, McCarthy is really reacting here to the totally unconstrained views of morphology that linguists had previously found acceptable. He points out that Chomsky's[18] morphological transformations could "perform their arbitrary operations on only the prime or factor-of-twelve numbered segments in the word with no further enrichment of the formalism" (p. 201). Seen in that context, his proposal is a restrictive one, but seen in the language-theoretic context assumed here, his proposal is, of course, radically unconstrained. None of the phenomena that he deals with involve even strict context-freeness, much less strict context-sensitivity. Indeed, as noted above, Kay[80] has been able to develop finite state analyses of

McCarthy's data using multi-tape transducers.

3.2 Sentences

In the following subsections we look at the application of formal grammars in recent work on the syntax of sentences by linguists and computational linguists.

[1] Finite state grammars

The fact that natural languages are not regular does not necessarily mean that techniques for parsing regular languages are irrelevant to natural language parsing. Such writers as Langendoen,[92] Church,[22] Ejerhed and Church,[27] and Langendoen and Langsam[95] have, in rather different ways, proposed that hearers process sentences as if they were finite automata (or as if they were pushdown automata with a finite stack depth limit, which is weakly equivalent) rather than showing the behavior that would be characteristic of a more powerful device. To the extent that progress along these lines casts light on NL parsing, the theory of regular grammars and finite automata will continue to be important in the study of natural languages even though they are not regular sets.

[2] Categorial grammars

Categorial grammars, which were developed by Bar-Hillel and others in the 1950's, have always had a somewhat marginal status in linguistics. There has always been someone ready to champion them, but never enough people actually using them to turn them into a paradigm. The currency they have today is due in large measure to Montague[105] who based his semantic work on a modified categorial grammar.

The elegance and unprecedented explicitness of Montague's grammars provoked a good deal of work in computational linguistics, for example, that of Bronnenberg et al.,[14] Friedman,[34,35] Friedman, Moran & Warren,[36] Friedman & Warren,[37] Fuchi,[38] Hobbs & Rosenschein,[53] Indurkhya,[60] Ishimoto,[61] Janssen,[62,63,65] Landsbergen,[90,91] Matsumoto,[102,103] Nishida et al.,[110] Nishida & Doshita,[108,109] Root,[127] Saheki,[136]

Sawamura,[139] Sondheimer & Gunji,[150] Warren,[164] and Warren and Friedman,[165]

Montague's own generalizations of categorial grammar were not exactly principled and most of the work just cited is more concerned with semantic issues than it is with the niceties of the underlying syntactic theory. Pure categorial grammar is really a variant of CF-PSG and has exactly the same weak generative capacity. Recently some fairly principled attempts have been made, notably by Ades and Steedman[1] and Bach,[5] to preserve the spirit of categorial grammar (which Montague, arguably, did not) whilst extending it to non-CF constructions such as that found in Swiss German (cf. Steedman[151] on the analogous Dutch construction).

[3] Context-free phrase structure grammars

Since 1978, following suggestions by Stanley Peters, Aravind Joshi, and others, there has been a strong resurgence in the linguistics literature of the idea that phrase structure grammars could be used for the description of natural languages. PSGs had been all but abandoned in linguistics during the period from 1957 to 1978 because arguments given by the proponents of transformational grammar had convinced essentially all linguists interested in writing formal grammars that no phrase structure account of the grammar of a natural language could be adequate.

One of the motivations suggested for continuing to take an interest in PSGs, in particular CF-PSGs, was the existence of already known high-efficiency algorithms (recognition in deterministic time proportional to the cube of the string length) for recognizing and parsing CFLs. Indeed, as Perrault[113] reminds us, "it is useful to remember that no known CFL requires more than linear time, nor is there even a nonconstructive proof of the existence of such a language". Context-free parsing is such a basic tool of computer science, including NLP, that there have even been proposals for implementing CF-PSG parsers in special-purpose NLP hardware (Dubinsky and Sanamrad[26] ; Schnelle[140]).

But parsability has not been the central motivation for the interest that significant numbers of linguists began to show in CF-PSGs from early

1979. Linguists were mainly interested in achieving elegant solutions to purely linguistic problems, and work by linguists such as Borsley,[12] Cann,[15] Flickinger,[32] Gunji,[42-45] Horrocks,[56,57] Ikeya,[59] Kameshima,[71] Maling and Zaenen,[100] Nerbonne,[107] Sag,[134,135] Saito,[137] Stucky,[153,155] Udo,[161] Uszkoreit,[162] and Zwicky[168] is directed toward this end.

The idea of returning to CF-PSG as a theory of NLs may have appeared highly retrogressive to some linguists in 1979; but, as we have seen, the published arguments that had led linguists to consign CF-PSGs to the scrap-heap of history were all quite unsatisfactory. In view of that, the development of theories of the structure of English and other languages in terms that guaranteed context-freeness of the analyzed language became eminently sensible.

The CF-PSGs enjoy a wealth of literature providing them with numerous distinct but equivalent mathematical characterizations which illuminate their many computationally relevant properties. They are relatively simple to write and to modify. They are associated with a successful tradition of work in computation that has provided us with a thorough understanding of how to parse, translate, and compile them (Aho and Ullman[3]). Much work was done in the period 1979-1984 to establish a basis for handling the syntax and semantics of NLs as effectively and precisely as the structures of programming languages or the artificial languages of logicians.

What attitude should NLP research and development work take toward the pieces of evidence that indicate that NLs are not all CFLs? We believe the fundamental thing that should be kept in mind is this: *The overwhelming majority of the structure of any NL can be elegantly and efficiently parsed using context-free parsing techniques.* That is, we think it is essential to keep a sense of proportion. Too often the most sweeping conclusions about the uselessness of context-free parsing for NLs have been made even on the basis of transparently fallacious arguments. The truth is that nearly all constructions in nearly all languages can be parsed using techniques that limit the system to the analysis of CFLs. It has taken linguists nearly thirty years (since 1956, when Chomsky raised the question of whether NLs were CFLs and whether CF-PSGs could be used to describe them) to correctly identify even one construction in a NL that lends non-CFL status to the whole language.

Unsurprisingly, the new linguistic work on CF-PSG has been accompanied by a whole genre of parallel work in computational linguistics by such researchers as Bear & Karttunen,[8] Evans & Gazdar,[31] Evans,[30] Gunji, et al.,[47] Hirakawa,[52] Joshi,[68] Joshi & Levy,[70] Karttunen,[75] Kay,[78] Keller,[81,82] Kilbury,[85] Konolige,[87] Phillips & Thompson,[114] Pulman,[121,122] Robinson,[125,126] Rosenschein & Shieber,[129] Ross,[130,131] Sampson,[138] Schubert,[141] Schubert & Pelletier,[142] Shieber,[144,145] Shirai,[148] Thompson,[156-158] Thompson & Phillips,[159] and Uszkoreit.[163] CF-PSGs have been used as the syntactic basis for sophisticated NL front-ends to databases (see the work reported initially by Gawron et al.,[40] and subsequently developed as outlined by Pollard & Creary,[116] Flickinger, Pollard & Wasow,[33] and Proudian & Pollard[118]) and highly effective machine translation systems (Slocum et al.[149]).

[4] Head grammars

Pollard[115] presents several generalizations of context-free grammar, the most restrictive of which he refers to as head grammar (HG). The extension Pollard makes in CF-PSG to obtain the HGs is in essence fairly simple. First, he treats the notion "head" as a primitive. The strings of terminals his syntactic rules define are headed strings, which means they are associated with an indication of a designated element to be known as the head. Second, he adds "wrapping" operations to the standard concatenation operation on strings that a CF-PSG can define. This permits a limited amount of interleaving of sister constituents, as opposed to the straightforward concatenation of sisters to which CF-PSG is restricted; a string x can be combined with a string yhz, where h is the head, not only to yield $xyhz$ or $yhzx$ but also by an operation that yields $yhxz$ or $yxhz$. The intuitive element of context-freeness that a grammar of this sort retains lies in the fact that constituents are defined independently of other constituents: where two headed strings are to be combined to form a new string A, no context outside of A can be relevant to the operation.

Using just concatenation and head wrapping, Pollard[115] shows how an analysis of the special subordinate verb phrase constructions of Dutch or Swiss German can readily be obtained. The discontinuities between syntactically associated constituents that is made available by head wrapping is just enough to associate the right verbs with the right noun phrases in Dutch or Swiss German subordinate VP's, without introducing the whole power of arbitrary context-sensitive grammars.

The HG framework is not just another notation for highly powerful arbitrarily augmented phrase structure grammars, and does not introduce exponential levels of difficulty into the recognition or parsing problems. HGs have a greater expressive power, in terms of weak and strong generative capacity, than the CF-PSGs, but only to a very limited extent. Pollard shows that an arbitrary HG language can be recognized, by means of a modified version of the CKY algorithm, in deterministic time proportional to the seventh power of the length of the string. Though worse than the worst-case result for CFLs, this is not a result that indicates intractability of the recognition problem for HG languages.

Roach[124] has proved that the languages generated by head grammars constitute a full abstract family of languages, showing all the significant closure properties that characterize the class of CFLs, and has observed a striking similarity to the properties found in the tree-adjunction grammars (TAGs) studied by Joshi and others (cf. Joshi[69]), which are defined in an intuitively very different way and were conceived quite independently. TAGs and HGs both offer the prospect of efficient recognition for what Joshi calls "mildly context-sensitive languages", and the convergence between these two lines of research is very encouraging.

[5] Indexed grammars

If nonterminal symbols are built up using sequences of indices affixed to members of a finite set of basic nonterminals, and rules are able to add or remove sequence-initial indices, then the expressive power achieved is that of the indexed grammars of Aho[2] and Hopcroft & Ullman.[55] Indexed grammars are similar to CF-PSGs which employ complex symbols, except that there is no finite limit on the number of distinct complex symbols that can be used. The indexed grammars have an automata-theoretic characterization in terms of a stack automaton that can build stacks inside other stacks but can only empty a stack after all the stacks within it have been emptied. The time complexity of the recognition problem is exponential.

No theoretical linguists have yet embraced indexed grammars, although it is clear that generalization of category valued features to allow n-tuples of categories as feature values (as envisaged by Maling & Zaenen,[100] and subsequently Pollard[115]) leads one directly to the indexed grammars unless the system is otherwise constrained. It is also clear that indexed grammars of a rather straightforward kind are available for the Swiss German/Dutch construction discussed in preceding sections, for reduplications, and for multiple wh-type dependencies in Scandinavian languages and the variable-binding issue that this gives rise to (see Engdahl[29] and Maling & Zaenen[100]). They can also handle the nesting of equative and comparative clauses discussed by Klein.[86] Thus, as noted in Section 2.2[5], above, indexed grammars provide us with an upper bound. There are no grammatical phenomena that we know of that they cannot handle, but the same is true, of course, of Turing machines.

[6] Beyond the indexed grammars

If nonterminal symbols have internal hierarchical structure and parsing operations are permitted to match hierarchical representations one with another globally to determine whether they unify (see Section 4.3, below), and if the number of parses for a given sentence is kept to a finite number by requiring that we do not have $A \Rightarrow^+ A$ for any A, then the expressive power seems to be weakly equivalent to the grammars that Bresnan and Kaplan have developed under the name lexical-functional grammar (LFG; see Bresnan, ed.[13]). The LFG languages include some non-indexed languages (Roach, unpublished work), and apparently have an NP-complete parsing problem.[9]

The LFG languages may not even be included in the context-sensitive languages. Kaplan and Bresnan[72] (260ff) state without proof that any language with an LFG grammar is accepted by some nondeterministic linear bounded automaton, provided each grammar observes a fixed numerical upper bound on the number of crossing dependencies permitted (a "crossing limit"). If limits of this sorter are embraced, comparisons of generative power across frameworks are of course undercut; the reduplication of noun stems in Bambara could be handled by even a finite state grammar if, for example, grammars observed a restriction to a finite upper bound on the number of times a given noun stem could occur in a sentence. Likewise, a CF-PSG could be given for the cross-serial verb-object dependencies in Dutch and Swiss German, assigning suitable constituent structure, provided a crossing limit was imposed. Thus it is unclear whether Kaplan and Bresnan see the imposition of crossing limits as a motivated part of their theory or simply as a sufficient condition to achieve context-sensitivity. Note that further numerical conditions would allow a proof of CF-ness or even finite-state-ness for LFGs.

3.3 The Word-Sentence Interface

In this section we consider the relation that obtains between the syntax of words and the syntax of sentences. At least three distinct positions can be distinguished and have been maintained at one time or another. One possible position says that there is no distinction to be made and that a single grammar unifies both. We will call this the holistic position. This was essentially the position maintained by transformational grammar in the 1960's and early 1970's. A second position, which we refer to as "the orthodox view" below, maintains that they are distinct autonomous systems, but that the syntax of words is properly embedded within the syntax of sentences. Where the latter ends, the former begins. And a third position, recently dubbed "autolexical syntax", claims that they are distinct but parallel systems that need not define compatible analyses of the entire morpheme string.

[1] The orthodox view

The orthodox view, as we have characterised it above, is essentially that of the American structuralist tradition of the 1940's and 1950's. It is classically embodied in the analytical technique known as immediate constituent analysis. The immediate constituents of sentences were phrases, the immediate constituents of phrases were words (or other phrases), and the immediate constituents of words were morphemes. Thus the syntax of words was properly nested within the syntax of phrases and sentences.

This position finds its modern expression in the work of Selkirk.[143] For her, sentential syntactic structures are phrase structure trees and the leaves of these trees are words. But these words each have their own self-contained structure and this too is represented as a phrase structure tree.

It is easy to see that Selkirk's position is only separated from the holistic position by a very thin line. If the sentence syntax is simply a PSG (though it is not, for Selkirk) and the word syntax is also, and if the latter is permitted to introduce nonterminal symbols that belong conceptually to the former (as various incorporation phenomena might lead one to want), then one simply ends up with one large PSG whose terminal symbols are morphemes.

[2] Autolexical syntax

In a radical break with the traditions just discussed, Sadock[133] has proposed that the sentence syntax and the word syntax are both CF-PSGs, but that strings of morphemes are to be regarded as grammatical just in case they receive both a sentence-syntactic structure and a word-syntactic structure. Crucially, these structures need not be isomorphic: words as defined by the morphology are not required to coincide with some syntactic constituent as they are in the orthodox view. Thus, for example, in English, the morpheme sequence *I'll* in *I'll go to bed* is a constituent in Sadock's word-syntax, but not, of course, in his sentential syntax.

Oversimplifying somewhat, Sadock's work suggests a parsing model in which two CF-PSG parsers, one corresponding to the sentence syntax and the other to the word syntax, run in series or in parallel, a string being grammatical just in case both parsers succeed. Such a dual CF-PSG parsing system would identify languages falling in the intersection of two CFLs. As is well known, the CFLs are not closed under intersection and thus, for example, such a system could recognize $a^n b^n c^n$ (cf. the cascaded RTNs of Woods[167]). However, the recognition time complexity is no worse than that of the CFLs, i.e. $O(n^3)$. Borgida[11] provides an excellent introduction to a range of dual grammar systems.

4. Recent Developments in Formal Linguistics

4.1 Grammars for Grammars

The idea of using one grammar to generate another originates in computer science with the work of van Wijngaarden[166] who used the technique to give a perspicuous syntax for ALGOL68. A good introduction to his work can be found in Cleaveland & Uzgalis.[23] Janssen[64] employs a van Wijngaarden-style two-level grammar to define a generalization of Montague's PTQ syntax.

The same idea emerges in recent linguistic work in the guise of the "lexical rule"[13] or metarule.[41] A metarule is a grammar characterization device (i.e. a clause in the definition of the grammar), one which enables one to define one set of rules in terms of another set, antecedently given. Generalizations which would be lost if the two sets of rules were merely listed are captured by the metarule.

For example, suppose that our grammar contains, inter alia, the following set of rules expanding VP:

$$VP \rightarrow V[0]$$
$$VP \rightarrow V[1]\ NP$$
$$VP \rightarrow V[2]\ NP\ NP$$
$$VP \rightarrow V[3]\ NP\ PP \qquad\qquad (6)$$
$$VP \rightarrow V[4]\ NP\ VP$$
$$VP \rightarrow V[5]\ NP\ S$$
$$VP \rightarrow V[6]\ NP\ NP\ S$$
$$VP \rightarrow V[7]\ S$$

Then we can augment the grammar by means of the following metarule:

$$VP \rightarrow V \ NP \ W \ \Rightarrow$$
$$VP[PAS] \rightarrow V \ W \ (PP[by]) \tag{7}$$

This says that for every rule in the grammar which expands VP as a verb followed by an NP possibly followed by arbitrary other material, there is also a rule expanding a passive VP as the verb followed by the other stuff (if there was any) followed optionally by an agentive PP. This metarule will thus add the following rules to our grammar:

$$VP[PAS] \rightarrow V[1] \ (PP[by])$$
$$VP[PAS] \rightarrow V[2] \ NP \ (PP[by])$$
$$VP[PAS] \rightarrow V[3] \ PP \ (PP[by])$$
$$VP[PAS] \rightarrow V[4] \ VP \ (PP[by])$$
$$VP[PAS] \rightarrow V[5] \ S \ (PP[by])$$
$$VP[PAS] \rightarrow V[6] \ NP \ S \ (PP[by]) \tag{8}$$

These rules will now allow the grammar to generate passive sentences directly. Another example is provided by Gunji,[45] who shows how metarules can capture reflexive pronoun generalizations in the definition of a CF-PSG for Japanese.

Recent work in computational linguistics that employs or explores the notion of metarule includes Gawron et al.,[40] Kay,[78] Konolige,[87] Robinson,[125] Schubert and Pelleitier,[142] Shieber, Stucky, Uszkoreit and Robinson,[147] Stucky,[154] and Thompson.[157]

4.2 Feature-Theoretic Syntax

Harman[49] was the first person to see the linguistic potential of PSGs incorporating complex symbols. The use of a finite set of complex symbols, in place of the traditional finite set of monadic symbols, leaves the mathematical properties of grammars unchanged. For example, every CF-PSG employing complex symbols generates a tree set that is isomorphic to the tree set generated by some CF-PSG not employing complex symbols.

Typically, syntactic categories are defined as sets of syntactic feature specifications. A feature specification is an ordered pair consisting of a feature (e.g. CASE) and a feature value. The latter may either be atomic (e.g. ACCUSATIVE) or it may be a syntactic category (i.e. features are allowed to take categories as their values). A syntactic category is then a partial function from features to their values. The internal make-up of categories is further constrained by feature cooccurrence restrictions which are simply Boolean conditions which restrict the permissible combinations of feature specifications.[41] Syntactic structures are thus phrase structure trees of the familiar kind whose nodes are labelled with syntactic categories as characterized above.

Principles of feature instantiation are then invoked to ensure the identity of certain features on adjacent or connected nodes. Most current work assumes a "Head Feature Convention" which is responsible for equating one class of feature specifications as they appear on the mother category and its head daughter(s). Thus, for example, a verb phrase inherits the tense of its verb. Other principles match agreement features between locally connected agreeing categories (e.g. between a subject noun phrase and its verb phrase sister), or deal with the copying of category valued features between mother and daughter categories.

Category-valued features allow many significant syntactic generalizations to be captured rather straightforwardly.[41] For example, they are able to capture those underlying the class of unbounded dependency constructions (e.g. relative clauses, wh-questions, topicalization, etc.). Here is a topicalization example, where the category-valued feature specification [NP] encodes the absence of the object in the final verb phrase.

```
              S
            /   \
          NP     S[NP]
         /  \    /   \
       Det   N  NP    VP[NP]
        |    |   |      |
      that problem Sandy V[7]    S[NP]                    (9)
                    |          /     \
                  thinks     NP      VP[NP]
                              |         |
                            Felix     V[1]
                                        |
                                     solved
```

4.3 Unification, Extension, and Generalization

The formal definitions of principles of feature instantiation, such as those mentioned above, crucially depend upon notions of extension and unification definable in a graph-theoretic or partial function theory of categories. These notions were introduced into linguistics by Kay[77] and have been profoundly influential, finding their way into essentially all current formal syntactic frameworks.

Assuming, for the sake of illustration, the partial function theory of categories sketched above, we can define extensions as follows.

A category C2 **is an extension of** of a category C1 if and only if

(1) every atom-valued feature specification in C1 is in C2, and

(2) for every category-valued feature specification in C1, the
value of the feature in C2 is an extension of the value in C1.

This recursive definition says first of all that any specification for an atom-valued (i.e. non-category valued) feature in a category is also in all extensions of that category. It also guarantees that if a category specifies a value v for some category-valued feature, then any extension of that category specifies a value for that same feature that is an extension of v. Note that an extension of a category C may contain a specification for a category-valued feature which is unspecified in C. The relation "is an extension of" is thus a generalization of the relation "is a superset of", one which takes proper account of category-valued features, and it defines a partial order on the set of categories.

An important operation on categories is that of unification. This notion is closely analogous to the operation of union on sets except that, as in the case of extension, the resulting set must be a function. Unification is undefined for categories containing features specifications that contradict each other.

> The **unification** of a set of categories K is the smallest category which is an extension of every member of K, if such a category exists; otherwise the unification of K is undefined.

As can be seen, this notion is equivalent to the standard notion of least upper bound in lattice theory. A second operation on categories is generalization, which provides the analogy to the operation of intersection on sets. It can be defined as follows.

> The **generalization** of a set K is the smallest category which contains (1) the intersection of the categories in K, and (2) the set of category-valued feature specifications each of whose values is the generalization of the set of values assigned to the feature by the categories in K.

Karttunen[75] provides a good introduction to the linguistic uses of generalization, and Pereira & Shieber[112] discuss the denotational semantics of unification-based linguistic formalisms.

In discussing these notions, we have restricted ourselves to the theory of features for the purposes of illustration. However, some current linguistic frameworks, notably Kay's[79] "Functional Unification Grammar", allow one to perform unification on structural descriptions, and even on grammars.

4.4 Default Mechanisms

In any feature-theoretic linguistic framework, certain feature values are the expected case, the values that ordinarily get assigned, other things being equal. Linguists call these expected values the "unmarked" or default values, and they can be handled by feature specification defaults which are

Boolean conditions analogous to feature cooccurrence restrictions, but employed differently. Feature cooccurrence restrictions are absolute conditions that have to be met, whereas feature specification defaults are conditions that a category must meet if it can, but need not meet if it cannot.[41] Thus, for example, the default value for CASE might be ACCUSATIVE, but a given noun phrase could appear in some other case if it was required to do so by a feature instantiation principle, say.

Feature instantiation principles themselves have typically imposed an absolute condition (identity or extension in one direction) on the relation between the feature sets found on adjacent or connected nodes in a tree. But this clearly does not need to be the case. An absolute condition could be replaced by a default inheritance mechanism, a technical device of considerable generality, and potentially wide application.

One, nonlinguistic, example of a default inheritance mechanism comes from the work on semantic networks in AI (see Barr and Feigenbaum[7] : pp. 180-189 for a survey). On the one hand one wishes to be able to say that all birds can fly (thus avoiding the need to stipulate that eagles can fly), but on the other hand one wishes to accord penguins the status of being a bird (even though they cannot fly). To take an example that is familiar from the AI literature, consider the network shown below.

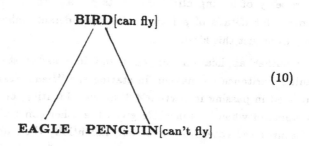

(10)

The arcs here represent the **ISA** relation, and the material in brackets stands for properties, so this network just records that eagles and penguins are birds, that birds can fly, and that penguins cannot. If properties are simply inherited from a dominating node, then we will derive a contradiction to the effect that penguins are both able to fly and unable to fly. But if properties are inherited by a default inheritance mechanism, then we will be able to derive the flight of eagles without contradicting ourselves over penguins.

One potential linguistic application for a default inheritance mechanism concerns irregularity in NL lexicons. On the one hand we wish to give general morphological rules to predict the form of, say, plurals. And, on the other hand, we want these rules to be over-ridden by the mere existence of irregular forms.

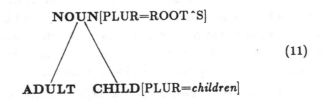

$$\textbf{NOUN}[\text{PLUR}=\text{ROOT}\string^\text{S}]$$

$$(11)$$

$$\textbf{ADULT} \quad \textbf{CHILD}[\text{PLUR}=children]$$

This says that **adult** and **child** are both nouns and that the plural form (PLUR) of a noun is formed by concatenating its stem (ROOT) with **s**. This property of nouns will be inherited by **adult** which thus has **adults** as its plural. In the case of **child** however, this property of nouns is not inherited since it is inconsistent with an existing property of **child**, namely the property of having **children** as its plural. See Flickinger, Pollard & Wasow[33] for details of a lexicon that uses default inheritance to handle examples of just this kind.

Another application can be found in Gazdar et al.[41] who use a default inheritance mechanism in stating the "Head Feature Convention" mentioned in passing in Section 4.2, above. Identity for a given feature is only imposed when it is possible given the other constraints that apply to the features and categories involved. Essentially their definition works by examining the space of possible instantiations of a rule that are permitted by feature cooccurrence restrictions, other feature principles, and so on. If this space contains an instantiation exhibiting the relevant identity, then the principle requires identity; if it does not, then identity is not required.

5. Conclusion

The arguments originally given at the start of the era of modern linguistics were correct in their conclusion that NLs cannot be treated as simply regular sets of strings, as some early information-theoretic models of language users would have had it. However, questions of whether NLs were CFLs were dismissed rather too hastily; English has never been shown to be outside the class of CFLs or even the DCFLs, and even for other languages the first apparently valid arguments for non-CFL status are only now being framed.

The two non-CF construction types that have been shown to exist in NLs are not indicative of profound difficulties standing in the way of the efficient processing of NLs by computers. They are well understood in linguistic terms, and efficient techniques for recognizing and parsing languages with these constructions are already known to exist, as we have noted. Thus, although future work on NLP may face major difficulties in areas like speech, semantics, and pragmatics, there is reason to think that difficulties in the area of morphology and syntax have often been exaggerated. The vast majority of the regularities of structure in the words and sentences of NLs can be captured in terms of the tractable and mathematically developed framework of CF-PSG. And in the cases where supra-CF devices are called for, there are numerous promising extensions or generalizations of CF-PSG that are clearly capable of doing the job and are already being explored by linguists and computational linguists.

The traditional attitude toward natural languages in computer science has probably not been very different from the traditional attitude among logicians. Rosenbloom[128] (p. 153), for example, asserts:

> As in all natural languages...the rules of word and sentence formation in English are so complicated and full of irregularities and exceptions that it is almost impossible to get a general view of the structure of the language, and to make generally valid statements about the language.

Modern work on morphology and syntax does not bear out this pessimestic view. On the contrary, our conclusion from this review of morphological and syntactic work on the computationally relevant properties of NLs and their grammars is, in short, that a cautious optimism is in order.

Footnotes

*Readers interested in pursuing the matters discussed in this paper in greater detail than space has allowed us are directed to Gunji[46] and Perrault[113] for excellent surveys of the relevant linguistics and mathematics, respectively. We are grateful to Takao Gunji, Lauri Karttunen, Jerrold Saddock, and Stuart Shieber for conversations and comments on topics covered by the present paper. The paper was prepared while the authors were visiting the Center for the Study of Language and Information (CSLI) at Stanford University, and whilst Gazdar was a fellow at the Center for Advanced Study in the Behavioral Sciences (CASBS), Stanford. Support was provided by a gift to CSLI from the System Development Foundation (Pullum), by grants from the Sloan Foundation and the System Development Foundation to CASBS (Gazdar), and by an ESRC personal research grant to Gazdar.

References

1) Ades, Anthony E. and Steedman, Mark J., "On the order of words," *Linguistics and Philosophy, 4.* pp. 517-588, 1982.

2) Aho, Alfred V., "Indexed grammars - an extension of context-free grammars," *Journal of the ACM, 15,* pp. 647-671, 1968.

3) Aho, Alfred V. and Ullman, Jeffrey D., *The Theory of Parsing, Tranlation, and Compiling,* Prentice-Hall, Englewood Cliffs, New Jersey, 1972.

4) Alam, Yukiko Sasaki, "A two-level morphological analysis of Japanese," in *Texas Linguistic Forum, 22*(Mary Dalrymple et al., eds.), University of Texas, Austin, Texas, pp. 229-252, 1983.

5) Bach, Emmon, "Discontinuous constituents in generalized categorial grammars," in *Proceedings of the 11th Annual Meeting of the North Eastern Linguistic Society,* (V.A. Burke and J. Pustejovsky, eds.), Department of Linguistics, University of Massachusetts at Amherst, Amherst, Massachusetts, pp. 1-12, 1981.

6) Bar-Hillel, Yehoshua and Shamir, E., "Finite state languages: formal representations and adequacy problems," 1960. As reprinted in *Language and Information* (Yehoshua Bar-Hillel, ed.), Addison-Wesley, Reading, Massachusetts, pp. 87-98, 1964.

7) Barr, Avron and Feigenbaum, Edward (eds.), *The Handbook of Artificial Intelligence, Volume I,* William Kaufman, Los Altos, California, 1981.

8) Bear, John and Karttunen, Lauri, "PSG: a simple phrase structure parser," *Texas Linguistic Forum, 15,* pp. 1-46, 1979.

9) Berwick, Robert C., "Computational complexity and lexical-functional grammar," *American Journal of Computational Linguistics, 8, 3-4,* pp. 97-109, 1982.

10) Bermudez, Manuel, "Regular Lookahead and Lookback in LR Parsers," *PhD thesis,* University of California, Santa Cruz, California, 1984.

11) Borgida, Alexander T., "Some formal results about stratificational grammars and their relevance to linguistics," *Mathematical Systems Theory, 16,* pp. 29-56, 1983.

12) Borsley, Robert, "On the nonexistence of VP's," in *Sentential Complementation,* (Willem de Geest and Yvan Putseys, eds.), Foris, Dordrecht, pp. 55-65, 1984.

13) Bresnan, Joan W. (ed.), *The Mental Representation of Grammatical Relations,* MIT Press, Cambridge, Massachusetts, 1982.

14) Bronnenberg, W.J.H.J., Bunt, H.C., Landsbergen, S.P.J., Scha, R.J.H., Schoenmakers, W. J. and van Utteren, E.P.C., "The question-answering system PHLIQA 1," in *Natural Language Question-Answering Systems* (L. Bolc, ed.), Carl Hanser Verlag, Munich, West Germany, pp. 217-305, 1980.

15) Cann, Ronald, "An approach to the Latin accusative and infinitive," in *Order, Concord and Constituency* (Gerald Gazdar, Ewan H. Klein and Geoffrey K. Pullum, eds.), Foris, Dordrecht, pp. 113-137, 1983.

16) Carden, Guy, "The non-finite-state-ness of the word formation component," *Linguistic Inquiry, 14,* pp. 537-541, 1983.

17) Carlson, Greg, "Marking constituents," in *Auxiliaries and Related Puzzles, Vol. 1.* (Frank Heny, ed.), D. Reidel, Dordrecht, Holland, pp. 69-98, 1983.

18) Chomsky, Noam, "Morphophonemics of Modern Hebrew," *MA thesis,* University of Pennsylvania, Philadelphia, Pennsylvania, 1951.

19) Chomsky, Noam, *Syntactic Structures,* Mouton, The Hague, Holland, 1957.

20) Chomsky, Noam, "Formal properties of grammars," in *Handbook of Mathematical Psychology, Volume II* (R. D. Luce, R. R. Bush and E. Galanter, eds.), Wiley, New York, pp. 323-418, 1963.

21) Chomsky, Noam, *Rules and Representations,* Blackwell, Oxford, England, 1980.

22) Church, Kenneth, "On Memory Limitations in Natural Language Processing," *M. Sc. thesis,* MIT, Cambridge, Massachusetts, 1980.

23) Cleaveland, J. and Uzgalis, R., *Grammars for programming languages: what every programmer should know about grammar*, Elsevier, New York, New York, 1975.

24) Culy, Christopher, "The complexity of the vocabulary of Bambara," *Linguistics and Philosophy, 8*, pp. 345-351, 1985.

25) Daly, R. T., *Applications of the Mathematical Theory of Linguistics*, Mouton, The Hague, Holland, 1974.

26) Dubinsky, Stanley and Sanamrad, Mohammad Ali, "A universal natural language processor suitable for the hardware realization of phrase structure grammars," unpublished paper, Kobe University, 1984.

27) Ejerhed, Eva and Church, Kenneth, "Recursion-free context-free grammar," paper presented at the *Workshop on Scandinavian Syntax and Theory of Grammar*, University of Trondheim, June 3-5, 1982.

28) Elster, J., *Logic and Society: Contradictions and Possible Worlds*, Wiley, New York, New York, 1978.

29) Engdahl, Elisabet, "The syntax and semantics of questions in Swedish," *PhD dissertation*, University of Massachusetts at Amherst, Amherst, Massachusetts, 1980.

30) Evans, Roger, "Program - A development tool for GPSG grammars," *Linguistics, 23*, pp. 213-243, 1985.

31) Evans, Roger and Gazdar, Gerald, "The ProGram Manual," *Cognitive Science Research Paper, 35 (CSRP 035)*, University of Sussex, Brighton, England, 1984.

32) Flickinger, Daniel, "Lexical heads and phrasal gaps," in *Proceedings of the Second West Coast Conference on Formal Linguistics* (Michael Barlow, Daniel Flickinger and Michael Wescoat, eds.), Stanford Linguistics Department, Stanford, pp. 89-101, 1983.

33) Flickinger, Daniel, Pollard, Carl and Wasow, Thomas, "Structure-sharing in lexical representation." *Proceedings of the 23rd Annual Meeting of the Association for Computational Linguistics*, Association for Computational Linguistics, Morristown, NJ, pp. 262-267, 1985.

34) Friedman, Joyce, "Computational and theoretical studies in Montague Grammar at the University of Michigan," *SISTM Quarterly, 1,* pp. 62-66, 1978.

35) Friedman, Joyce, "Expressing logical formulas in natural language," in *Formal Methods in the Study of Language* (Jeroen A. G. Groenendijk, Theo Janssen and Martin Stokhof, eds.), Mathematical Centre Tracts, Amsterdam, pp. 113-130, 1981.

36) Friedman, Joyce, Moran, D. and Warren, D., "An interpretation system for Montague Grammar," *American Journal of Computational Linguistics, microfiche, 74,* pp. 23-96, 1978.

37) Friedman, Joyce and Warren, David, "A parsing method for Montague Grammars, " *Linguistics and Philosophy, 2,* pp. 347-372, 1978.

38) Fuchi, Kazuhiro, "Natural language and its formal representation: a case study of translation in Montague style from a programmer's point of view," paper presented to the *First Colloquium on Montague Grammar and Related Topics,* Kyoto, February, 1981.

39) Gajek, Oliver, Beck, Hanno T., Elder, Diane and Whittemore, Greg, "KIMMO Lisp implementation," in *Texas Linguistic Forum, 22* (Mary Dalrymple et al., eds.), University of Texas, Austin, Texas, pp. 187-202, 1983.

40) Gawron, Jean Mark, King, Jonathan, Lamping, John, Loebner, Egon, Paulson, Anne, Pullum, Geoffrey K., Sag, Ivan A., and Wasow, Thomas, "The GPSG linguistics system," in *Proceedings of the 20th Annual Meeting of the Association for Computational Linguistics,* Association for Computational Linguistics, Menlo Park, California, pp. 74-81, 1982. Also distributed as *Hewlett Packard Computer Science Technical Note, CSL-82-5.*

41) Gazdar, Gerald, Klein, Ewan, Pullum, Geoffrey K. and Sag, Ivan A., *Generalized Phrase Structure Grammar,* Blackwell, Oxford, and Harvard University Press, Cambridge, Ma., 1985.

42) Gunji, Takao, "A phrase structural analysis of the Japanese language," *MA dissertation,* Ohio State University, 1981.

43) Gunji, Takao, "Apparent object control of reflexives in a restrictive theory of grammar," *Papers in Japanese Linguistics, 8*, pp. 63-78, 1982.

44) Gunji, Takao, "Control of gaps and reflexives in Japanese," in *Proceedings of the Second Japanese-Korean Joint Workshop on Formal Grammar*, Logico-Linguistic Society of Japan, pp. 151-186, 1983. [in Japanese]

45) Gunji, Takao, "Generalized phrase structure grammar and Japanese reflexivization," *Linguistics and Philosophy, 6*, pp. 115-156, 1983.

46) Gunji, Takao, *Introduction to Linguistics for Computer Scientists*, Information Technology Promotion Agency, Tokyo, 1983. [in Japanese]

47) Gunji, Takao, et al., "Some aspects of generalized phrase structure grammar," *ICOT Technical Memo, TM-0103*, Institute for New Generation Computer Technology, Tokyo, 1985.

48) Hagège, Claude, "Relative clause center-embedding and comprehensibility," *Linguistic Inquiry, 7*, pp. 198-201, 1976.

49) Harman, Gilbert, "Generative grammars without transformation rules: a defense of phrase structure," *Language, 39*, pp. 597-616, 1963.

50) Higginbotham, James, "English is not a context-free language," *Linguistic Inquiry, 15*, pp. 225-234, 1984.

51) Hintikka, Jaakko, "On the limitations of generative grammar," in *Proceedings of the Scandinavian Seminar on Philosophy of Language, Vol. 1 (Filosofiska Studier, Vol. 26)*, Philosophical Society and Department of Philosophy, Uppsala University, Uppsala, Sweden, pp. 1-92, 1975.

52) Hirakawa, Hideki, "Chart parsing in Concurrent Prolog," *ICOT Technical Report, TR-008*, Institute for New Generation Computer Technology, Tokyo, 1983.

53) Hobbs, Jerry and Rosenschein, Stanley, "Making computational sense of Montague's intensional logic," *Artificial Intelligence, 9*, pp. 287-306, 1978.

54) Hockett, Charles F., "Two models of grammatical description," *Word, 10*, pp. 210-233, 1954.

55) Hopcroft, John and Ullman, Jeffrey, *Introduction to automata theory, languages, and computation*, Addison-Wesley, Reading, Massachusetts, 1979.

56) Horrocks, Geoffrey, "The order of constituents in Modern Greek," in *Order, Concord and Constituency* (Gerald Gazdar, Ewan H. Klein and Geoffrey K. Pullum, eds.), Foris, Dordrecht, pp. 95-112, 1983.

57) Horrocks, Geoffrey, "The lexical head constraint, X'-theory and the 'pro-drop' parameter," in *Sentential Complementation* (Willem de Geest and Yvan Putseys, eds.), Foris, Dordrecht, pp. 117-125, 1984.

58) Huybregts, M. A. C., "Overlapping dependencies in Dutch," *Utrecht Working Papers in Linguistics, 1*, pp. 24-65, 1976.

59) Ikeya, Akira, "Japanese honorific systems in generalized phrase structure grammar," in *Proceedings of the ICOT Workshop on Non-Transformational Grammars*, Institute for New Generation Computer Technology, Tokyo, pp. 17-20, 1983.

60) Indurkhya, B., "Sentence analysis programs based on Montague grammar," *M.E.E. thesis*, Netherlands Universities Foundation for International Cooperation, 1981.

61) Ishimoto, I., "A Lesniewskian version of Montague grammar," in *COLING 82* (Jan Horecky, ed.), North-Holland, Amsterdam, pp. 139-144, 1982.

62) Janssen, Theo, "A computer program for Montague Grammar: theoretical aspects and proofs for the reduction rules," *Amsterdam Papers in Formal Grammar, I*, pp. 154-176, 1976.

63) Janssen, Theo, "Simulation of a Montague Grammar," *Annals of System Research, 6*, pp. 127-140, 1977.

64) Janssen, Theo, "On problems concerning the quantification rules in Montague grammar," in *Time, tense, and quantifiers* (C. Rohrer, ed.), Max Niemeyer, Tubingen, pp. 113-134, 1980.

65) Janssen, Theo, *Foundations and Applications of Montague Grammar*, Mathematisch Centrum, Amsterdam, 1983.

66) Johnson, C. Douglas, "On the formal properties of phonological rules," *POLA Report, 11*, University of California, Berkeley, 1970.

67) Johnson, S. C., "YACC - yet another compiler compiler," *CSTR, 32*, Bell Laboratories, Murray Hill, N.J., 1975.

68) Joshi, Aravind, "Factoring recursion and dependencies: an aspect of tree-adjoining grammars (TAG) and a comparison of some formal properties of TAGs, GPSGs, PLGs, and LFGs," in *Proceedings of the 21st Annual Meeting of the Association for Computational Linguistics*, pp. 7-15, 1983.

69) Joshi, Aravind, "Tree Adjoining Grammars: How much context-sensitivity is required to provide reasonable structural descriptions?" in *Natural Language Processing: Psycholinguistic, Computational, and Theoretic Perspectives* (David R. Dowty, Lauri Karttunen and Arnold M. Zwicky, eds.), Cambridge University Press, New York, New York, 1985.

70) Joshi, Aravind and Levy, Leon, "Phrase structure trees bear more fruit than you would have thought," *American Journal of Computational Linguistics, 8*, pp. 1-11, 1982.

71) Kameshima, Nanako, "CNPC Violations in Japanese; A GPSG Account," unpublished paper, University of Wisconsin-Madison, 1984.

72) Kaplan, Ronald M. and Bresnan, Joan, "Lexical-functional grammar: a formal system for grammatical representation," in (Bresnan, ed.), pp. 173-281, 1982.

73) Kaplan, Ronald M. and Kay, Martin, "Phonological rules and finite state transducers," *ACL/LSA paper*, New York, 1981.

74) Karttunen, Lauri, "KIMMO: A general morphological processor," in *Texas Linguistic Forum, 22* (Mary Dalrymple et al., eds.), University of Texas, Austin, Texas, pp. 165-186, 1983.

75) Karttunen, Lauri, "Features and values," in *Proceedings of Coling 84*, Association for Computational Linguistics, Menlo Park, pp. 28-33, 1984.

76) Karttunen, Lauri and Wittenburg, Kent, "A two-level morphological analysis of English," in *Texas Linguistic Forum, 22* (Mary Dalrymple et al., eds.), University of Texas, Austin, Texas, pp. 217-228, 1983.

77) Kay, Martin, "Functional grammar," in *Proceedings of the Fifth Annual Meeting of the Berkeley Linguistic Society* (Christina Chiarello et al., eds.), pp. 142-158, 1979.

78) Kay, Martin, "When meta-rules are not meta-rules," in *Automatic Natural Language Parsing* (Karen Sparck-Jones and Yorick Wilks, eds.), Ellis Horwood, Chichester, pp. 94-116, 1983. Also in *Developments in Generalized Phrase Structure Grammar: Stanford Working Papers in Grammatical Theory, Volume 2* (Michael Barlow, Daniel Flickinger, and Ivan A. Sag, eds.), Indiana University Linguistics Club, Bloomington, pp. 69-91, 1983.

79) Kay, Martin, "Functional unification grammar: a formalism for machine translation," in *Proceedings of Coling 84*, Association for Computational Linguistics, Menlo Park, pp. 75-78, 1984.

80) Kay, Martin, "Two-level morphology with tiers," presented to the *CSLI Workshop on Morphology*, July, 1985.

81) Keller, William R., "Generating logic from ProGram parse trees," *Cognitive Science Research Paper, 39 (CSRP 039)*, University of Sussex, Brighton, England, 1984.

82) Keller, William R., "A lexicon handler for the ProGram grammar development system," *Cognitive Science Research Paper, 40 (CSRP 040)*, University of Sussex, Brighton, England, 1984.

83) Khan, Robert, "A two-level morphological analysis of Rumanian," in *Texas Linguistic Forum, 22* (Mary Dalrymple et al., eds.), University of Texas, Austin, Texas, pp. 253-270, 1983.

84) Khan, Robert, Liu, Jocelyn S., Ito, Tatsuo and Shuldberg, Kelly, "KIMMO user's manual," in *Texas Linguistic Forum, 22* (Mary Dalrymple et al., eds.), University of Texas, Auston, Texas, pp. 203-215, 1983.

85) Kilbury, James, "GPSG-based parsing and generation," to appear in *Probleme des (Text-) Verstehens - Ansatze der Kunstlichen Intelligenz* (Claus-Rainer Rollinger, ed.), Max Niemeyer, Tubingen, 1984.

86) Klein, Ewan H., "The syntax and semantics of nominal comparatives," in *Atti de Seminario su Tempo e Verbale Strutture Quantificate in Forma Logica* (M. Moneglia, ed.), Presso l'Accademia della Crusca, Florence, pp. 223-253, 1981.

87) Konolige, Kurt, "Capturing linguistic generalizations with metarules in an annotated phrase-structure grammar," in *Proceedings of the 18th Annual Meeting of the Association for Computational Linguistics,* Association for Computational Linguistics, Menlo Park, California, pp. 43-48, 1980.

88) Kostenniemi, Kimmo, "Two-level Morphology: A General Computational Model for Word-Form Recognition and Production," *Publications, No. 11*, Department of General Linguistics, University of Helsinki, Helksinki, 1983.

89) Koskenniemi, Kimmo, "Two-level model for morphological analysis," *Proceedings of IJCAI-83*, pp. 683-685, 1983.

90) Landsbergen, Jan, "Adaptation of Montague grammar to the requirements of parsing," in *Formal Methods in the Study of Language* (Jeroen A. G. Groenendijk, Theo Janssen and Martin Stokhof, eds.), Mathematical Centre Tracts, Amsterdam, pp. 399-419, 1981.

91) Landsbergen, Jan, "Machine translation based on logically isomorphic Montague grammars," in *COLING 82* (Jan Horecky, ed.), North-Holland, Amsterdam, pp. 175-182, 1982.

92) Langendoen, D. Torence, "Finite-state parsing of the phrase-structure languages and the status of readjustment rules in grammar," *Linguistic Inquiry, 5*, pp. 533-554, 1975.

93) Langendoen, D. Terence, "On the inadequacy of type-2 and type-3 grammars for human languages," in *Studies in descriptive and historical linguistics* (P. J. Hopper, ed.), John Benjamin, Amsterdam, pp. 159-171, 1977.

94) Langendoen, D. Terence, "The generative capacity of word-formation components," *Linguistic Inquiry, 12*, pp. 320-322, 1981.

95) Langendoen, D. Terence and Langsam, Yedidyah, "The representation of constituent structures for finite-state parsing," in *Proceedings of Coling 84*, Association for Computational Linguistics, Menlo Park, pp. 24-27, 1984.

96) Langendoen, D. Terence and Postal, Paul M., *The Vastness of Natural Languages*, Blackwell, Oxford, 1984.

97) Langendoen, D. Terence and Postal, Paul M., "English and the class of context-free languages," *Computational Linguistics, 10*, pp. 177-181, 1985.

98) Levelt, W. J. M., *Formal Grammars in Linguistics and Psycholinguistics (Vol. II): Applications in Linguistic Theory*, Mouton, The Hague, Holland, 1974.

99) Lun, S., "A two-level morphological analysis of French," in *Texas Linguistic Forum, 22* (Mary Dalrymple et al., eds.), University of Texas, Austin, Texas, pp. 271-278, 1983.

100) Maling, Joan and Zaenen, Annie, "A phrase structure account of Scandinavian extraction phenomena," in *The Nature of Syntactic Representation* (Pauline Jacobson and Geoffrey K. Pullum, eds.), D. Reidel, Dordrecht, pp. 229-282, 1982.

101) Marsh, William E. and Partee, Barbara H., "How non-context-free is variable binding?," in *Proceedings of the Third West Coast Conference on Formal Linguistics* (Mark Cobler et al., eds.), Stanford Linguistics Association, Stanford, California, pp. 179-190, 1984.

102) Matsumoto, Yuji, "Software implementation of Montague grammar and related problems," in *Formal Approaches to Natural Language: Proceedings of the First Colloquium on Montague Grammar and Related Topics* (Shogo Iguchi, ed.), Kyoto Working Group of

Montague Grammar, Kyoto, pp. 148-158, 1981.

103) Matsumoto, Yuji, "A Montague grammar of Japanese with special regard to meaning adjustment," paper presented to the *Second Colloquium on Montague Grammar and Related Topics*, Kyoto, March, 1982.

104) McCarthy, John J., "Formal Problems in Semitic Phonology and Morphology," *PhD thesis*, MIT, 1979. Reproduced by the Indiana University Linguistics Club, Bloomington, Indiana, 1982.

105) Montague, Richard, *Formal Philosophy*, Yale University Press, New Haven, Connecticut, 1974.

106) Moran, Douglas B., "Dynamic partial models," *PhD dissertation*, University of Michigan, Ann Arbor, Michigan, 1980.

107) Nerbonne, John, "German temporal semantics: three dimensional tense logic and a GPSG fragment," *Working Papers in Linguistics*, *30*, Ohio State University, Columbus, Ohio, 1984.

108) Nishida, Toyo-aki and Doshita, Shuji, "An English-Japanese machine translation system based on formal semantics of natural language - a progress report," in *COLING 82* (Jan Horecky, ed.), North-Holland, Amsterdam, pp. 277-282, 1982.

109) Nishida, Toyo-aki and Doshita, Shuji, "An application of Montague Grammar to English-Japanese machine translation," in *Proceedings of the Conference on Applied Natural Language Processing* (Santa Monica, California), Association for Computational Linguistics, Menlo Park, California, February, 1983.

110) Nishida, Toyo-aki, Kiyono, Masaki and Doshita, Shuji, "An English-Japanese machine translation system based on formal semantics of natural language," in *Formal Approaches to Natural Language: Proceedings of the First Colloquium on Montague Grammar and Related Topics*, Kyoto Working Group of Montague Grammar, Kyoto, pp. 104-147, 1981.

111) Pereira, Fernando C. N., "A new characterization of attachment preferences," in *Natural Language Processing: Psycholinguistic, Computational and Theoretical Perspectives* (David R. Dowty, Lauri

Karttunen and Arnold M. Zwicky, eds.), Cambridge University Press, New York, New York, 1985.

112) Pereira, Fernando C. N. and Shieber, Stuart M., "The semantics of grammar formalisms seen as computer languages," in *Proceedings of Coling 84*, Association for Computational Linguistics, Menlo Park, pp. 123-129, 1984.

113) Perrault, C. Raymond, "On the mathematical properties of linguistic theories," *Computational Linguistics* (formerly *American Journal of Computational Linguistics*), 10, pp. 165-176, 1985.

114) Phillips, John D. and Thompson, Henry S., "GPSGP - A parser for generalized phrase structure grammars," *Linguistics, 23*, pp. 245-261, 1985.

115) Pollard, Carl J., "Generalized Phrase Structure Grammars, Head Grammars, and Natural Languages," *PhD thesis*, Stanford University, Stanford, California, 1984.

116) Pollard, Carl and Creary, Lewis, "A computational semantics for natural language," *Proceedings of the 23rd Annual Meeting of the Association for Computational Linguistics,* pp. 172-179, Association for Computational Linguistics, Morristown, NJ, 1985.

117) Postal, Paul, "Limitations of phrase structure grammars," in *The structure of language: readings in the philosophy of language* (J.A. Fodor and J. J. Katz, eds.), Prentice-Hall, Englewood Cliffs, New Jersey, pp. 137-151, 1964.

118) Proudian, Derek and Pollard, Carl, "Parsing head-driven phrase structure grammar," *Proceedings of the 23rd Annual Meeting of the Association for Computational Linguistics,* pp. 167-171, Association for Computational Linguistics, Morristown, NJ, 1985.

119) Pullum, Geoffrey K., "On two recent attempts to show that English is not a CFL," *Computational Linguistics* (formerly *American Journal of Computational Linguistics*), 10, pp. 182-186, 1985.

120) Pullum, Geoffrey K. and Gazdar, Gerald, "Natural languages and context-free languages," *Linguistics and Philosophy, 4*, pp. 471-504, 1982.

121) Pulman, Stephen, "Generalised phrase structure grammar, Earley's algorithm, and the minimisation of recursion," in *Automatic Natural Language Parsing* (Karen Sparck-Jones and Yorick Wilks, eds.), Ellis Horwood, Chichester, pp. 117-131, 1983.

122) Pulman, Stephen, "Limited domain systems for language teaching," in *Proceedings of Coling 84,* Association for Computational Linguistics, Menlo Park, pp. 84-87, 1984.

123) Rich, Elaine, *Artificial Intelligence,* McGraw-Hill, New York, New York, 1983.

124) Roach, Kelly, "Formal properties of head grammars," unpublished paper, Xerox Palo Alto Research Center, Palo Alto, California, 1984.

125) Robinson, Jane, "Computational aspects of the use of metarules in formal grammars," *Research Proposal No. ECU 80-126,* S.R.I. International, Menlo Park, California, 1980.

126) Robinson, Jane, "DIAGRAM: a grammar for dialogs," *Communications of the ACM, 25,* pp. 27-47, 1982.

127) Root, Rebecca, "SMX: a program for translating English into Montague's intensional logic," unpublished manuscript, University of Texas at Austin, Texas, 1981.

128) Rosenbloom, Paul, *The Elements of Mathematical Logic,* Dover, New York, New York, 1950.

129) Rosenschein, S. J. and Shieber, Stuart M., "Translating English into logical form," in *Proceedings of the 20th Annual Meeting of the Association for Computational Linguistics,* Association for Computational Linguistics, Menlo Park, California, pp. 1-8, 1982.

130) Ross, Kenneth, "Parsing English phrase structure," *PhD dissertation,* University of Massachusetts at Amherst, Amherst, Massachusetts, 1981.

131) Ross, Kenneth, "An improved left-corner parsing algorithm," in *COLING 82* (Jan Horecky, ed.), North-Holland, Amsterdam, pp. 333-338, 1982.

132) Rounds, William C., "Complexity of recognition in intermediate-level languages," *Proceedings of the IEEE Symposium on Switching and Automata Theory*, pp. 145-158, 1973.

133) Sadock, Jerrold M., "Autolexical syntax: A theory of noun incorporation and similar phenomena," *Natural Language and Linguistic Theory*, *3*, pp. 379-439, 1985.

134) Sag, Ivan A., "A semantic theory of 'NP-movement' dependencies," in *The Nature of Syntactic Representation* (Pauline Jacobson and Geoffrey K. Pullum, eds.), D. Reidel, Dordrecht, pp. 427-466, 1982.

135) Sag, Ivan A., "On parasitic gaps," *Linguistics and Philosophy*, *6*, pp. 35-45, 1983. Also in *Proceedings of the First West Coast Conference on Formal Linguistics* (Daniel Flickinger, Marlys Macken and Nancy Wiegand, eds.), Stanford Linguistics Department, Stanford, pp. 35-46, 1982.

136) Saheki, Motoji, "A software program for a language like natural language," paper presented to the *Second Colloquium on Montague Grammar and Related Topics*, Kyoto, March, 1982.

137) Saito, Mamoru, "An analysis of the *tough* construction in Japanese," *MA dissertation*, Stanford University, Stanford, California, 1980.

138) Sampson, Geoffrey, "Context-free parsing and the adequacy of context-free grammars," in *Parsing Natural Language* (Margaret King, ed.), Academic Press, London, pp. 151-170, 1983.

139) Sawamura, Hajime, "Intensional logic as a basis of algorithmic logic," paper presented to the *First Colloquium on Montague Grammar and Related Topics*, Kyoto, February, 1981.

140) Schnelle, Helmut, "Concurrent parsing in programmable logic array (PLA-) nets: problems and proposals," in *Proceedings of Coling 84*, Association for Computational Linguistics, Menlo Park, pp. 150-153, 1984.

141) Schubert, Lenhart, "An approach to the syntax and semantics of affixes in 'conventionalized' phrase structure grammar," in *Proceedings of the 4th Biennial Conference of the Canadian Society for Computational Studies of Intelligence*, pp. 189-195, 1982.

142) Schubert, Lenhart and Pelletier, Jeffry, "From English to logic: Context-free computation of 'conventional' logical translation," *American Journal of Computational Linguistics, 8*, pp. 27-44, 1982.

143) Selkirk, Elisabeth O., *The Syntax of Words*, MIT Press, Cambridge, Massachusetts, 1982.

144) Shieber, Stuart M., "Sentence disambiguation by a shift-reduce parsing technique," in *Proceedings of the 21st Annual Meeting of the Association for Computational Linguistics*, pp. 113-118, 1983.

145) Shieber, Stuart M., "Direct parsing of ID/LP grammars," *Linguistics and Philosophy, 7*, pp. 135-154, 1984.

146) Shieber, Stuart M., "Evidence against the context-freeness of natural language," *Linguistics and Philosophy, 8*, pp. 333-343, 1985.

147) Shieber, Stuart M., Stucky, Susan, Uszkoreit, Hans and Robinson, Jane, "Formal constraints on metarules," *Technical Note, 283*, SRI International, Menlo Park, California, 1983. Also in *Proceedings of the 21st Annual Meeting of the Association for Computational Linguistics*, pp. 22-27, 1983.

148) Shirai, Hidetoshi, "Deterministic parser," in *Proceedings of the ICOT Workshop on Non-Transformational Grammars*, Institute for New Generation Computer Technology, Tokyo, pp. 57-61, 1983.

149) Slocum, Jonathan, Bennett, Winfield S., Bear, John, Morgan, Martha and Root, Rebecca, "METAL: The LRC machine translation system," *Linguistics Research Center Working Paper LRC-84-2*, Austin, Texas, 1984.

150) Sondheimer, Norman and Gunji, Takao, "Applying model-theoretic semantics to natural language understanding: representation and question-answering," in *Proceedings of the Seventh International Conference on Computational Linguistics*, Bergen, Norway, 1978.

151) Steedman, Mark, "Dependency and coordination in the grammar of Dutch and English," *Language, 61*, pp. 523-568, 1985.

152) Stoy, Joseph E., *Denotational Semantics: The Scott-Stracchey Approach to the Semantics of Programming Languages*, MIT Press,

Cambridge, Massachusetts, 1977.

153) Stucky, Susan, "Word order variation in Makua: a phrase structure grammar analysis," *PhD dissertation*, University of Illinois at Urbana-Champaign, Urbana, Illinois, 1981.

154) Stucky, Susan, "Metarules as meta-node-admissibility conditions," *Technical Note, 304*, SRI International, Menlo Park, California, 1983.

155) Stucky, Susan, "Verb phrase constituency and linear order in Makua," in *Order, concord and Constituency* (Gerald Gazdar, Ewan H. Klein and Geoffrey K. Pullum, eds.), Foris, Dordrecht, pp. 75-94, 1983.

156) Thompson, Henry, "Chart parsing and rule schemata in PSG," in *Proceedings of the 19th Annual Meeting of the Association for Computational Linguistics*, Association for Computational Linguistics, Menlo Park, California, pp. 167-172, 1981.

157) Thompson, Henry, "Handling metarules in a parser for GPSG," *Edinburgh D.A.I. Research Paper, No. 175*, University of Edinburgh, U.K., 1982. Also in *Developments in Generalized Phrase Structure Grammar: Stanford Working Papers in Grammatical Theory, Volume 2* (Michael Barlow, Daniel Flickinger and Ivan A. Sag, eds.), Indiana University Linguistics Club, Bloomington, pp. 26-37. Also in *Proceedings of the 21st Annual Meeting of the Association for Computational Linguistics*, pp. 26-37.

158) Thompson, Henry, "Crossed serial dependencies: a low-power parseable extension to GPSG," in *Proceedings of the 21st Annual Meeting of the Association for Computational Linguistics*, pp. 16-21, 1983.

159) Thompson, Henry and Phillips, John, "An implementation of GPSG within the MCHART chart parsing framework," *Technical Report*, Department of Artificial Intelligence, University of Edinburgh, U.K., 1984.

160) Tomita, Masaru, "LR parsers for natural languages," in *Proceedings of Coling 84*, Association for Computational Linguistics, Menlo Park, pp. 354-357, 1984.

161) Udo, Mariko, "Syntax and morphology of the Japanese verb - a phrase structural approach," *MA thesis*, University College London, 1982.

162) Uszkoreit, Hans, "German word order in GPSG," in *Proceedings of the First West Coast Conference on Formal Linguistics* (Daniel Flickinger, Marlys Macken and Nancy Wiegand, eds.), Stanford Linguistics Department, Stanford, pp. 137-148, 1982.

163) Uszkoreit, Hans, "A framework for processing partially free word order," in *Proceedings of the 21st Annual Meeting of the Association for Computational Linguistics*, pp. 106-112, 1983.

164) Warren, David S., "Syntax and semantics in parsing: an application to Montague Grammar," *PhD dissertation*, University of Michigan, Ann Arbor, Michigan, 1979.

165) Warren, David S. and Friedman, J., "Using semantics in non-context-free parsing of Montague grammar," *American Journal of Computational Linguistics, 8*, pp. 123-138, 1982.

166) Wijngaarden, A. van, "Report on the algorithmic language ALGOL68," *Numerische Mathematik, 14*, pp. 79-218, 1969.

167) Woods, William A., "Cascaded ATN grammars," *American Journal of Computational Linguistics, 6*, pp. 1-12, 1980.

168) Zwicky, Arnold M., "German adjective agreement in GPSG," *Linguistics, 24*, 1986.

INDEX OF LANGUAGES

NAME INDEX

Abbott, B. 219
Ades, A. E. 254, 255, 258, 264, 275, 405
Aho, A. V. 139, 144, 342, 370-1, 399, 406, 408
Ajdukiewicz, K. 117-20, 128, 251, 295
Akmajian, A. 74, 140, 173
Alam, Y. S. 402
Allerton, D. J. 142
Andrews, A. D. 215-6, 219
Aristotle 15
Arnauld, A. 15

Bach, E. 17, 21, 41, 76, 81, 137, 141, 192, 214-5, 219, 253, 257-60, 262, 269, 272, 275-6, 299, 347, 359, 384, 405
Bach, M. 17
Baker, C. L. 214
Bar-Hillel, Y. 135, 148, 151, 253, 299, 397, 404
Barr, A. 417
Bear, J. 407
Beck, H. T. 402
Bennett, W. S. 407
Bermudez, M. 397
Bever, T. G. 1, 60, 214, 218
Bickford, A. xvi
Bierwisch, M. 268
Bonnenberg, W. J. H. J. 404